Christianity is a world religion not only because it is globally widespread but also because it is locally rooted. This book is a valuable addition to the growing literature detailing the many "Christianities" worldwide. Not only does it provide a reliable historical guide, but also its focus on Renewal movements elicits important transcultural theological observations and its dedication to Asia and Australia gives geographical coherence as well as context.

—Kirsteen Kim
Professor of Theology and World Christianity
Leeds Trinity University

Asia, only 11 percent Christian, can become a growth engine of global Christianity, if Pentecostals (half of Asian believers) live truthfully to their Spirit-empowered call. Thus, this book serves a unique role by helping Pentecostals to sharpen their identity, empoweredness, and missional call.

—Wonsuk Ma, PhD
Executive Director of David Yonggi Cho Research Tutor
of Global Christianity, Oxford Centre for Mission Studies,
Oxford, United Kingdom

Having attended the Empowered21 Global Congress in Jerusalem in 2015, I can truly appreciate this book. The contributors are world-class scholars and yet write with a wide appeal to the body of Christ. There is a balance of non-Western and Western authors, and women and men from various Christian traditions. This is indeed an enriching read for me as a Pentecostal, having the Word, Spirit, and testimonies all in one book. I can't wait for volume 2!

—Teresa Chai
John Bueno Chair of Intercultural Studies
Director of Global Missions Center, Asia Pacific Theological
Seminary, Baguio, Philippines.

This volume is a fascinating and interesting record and analysis of the growth and development of Spirit-empowered movements in

Asia and Oceania. The editors and contributors are honest, frank, and self-analytical without diminishing their affection for the movement to which most belong. The professionalism of writing and quality of research is intermingled with plenty of human interest and anecdotal information. I appreciated the focus on antipodean areas, which have been often overlooked in past Pentecostal historiography and thoroughly recommend this volume.

—Dr. Barry Chant
Author of *The Spirit of Pentecost: The Origins and Development of the Pentecostal Movement in Australia, 1870-1939*

I believe this volume, and the coming series of volumes on "Spirit-empowered movements," marks a new era of Pentecostal scholarship. In fact, what we see here may be a new genre of academic scholarship describing and analyzing Christian movements. In this first volume careful attention is paid—as a type of thick description—to local movements, but often in the same chapter larger statements are made that show a careful cultural or theological analysis. For the historian, theologian, sociologist, or even Christian anthropologist, this volume is a new window into Asian Christianity as well as to Spirit-empowered movements.

—Scott W. Sunquist
Author of *A History of the World Christian Movement*
Editor of *A Dictionary of Asian Christianity*

VOLUME ONE
ASIA AND OCEANIA

GLOBAL RENEWAL
Christianity

VINSON SYNAN, PhD
—and—
AMOS YONG, PhD

GENERAL EDITORS

CHARISMA
HOUSE

Most CHARISMA HOUSE BOOK GROUP products are available at special quantity discounts for bulk purchase for sales promotions, premiums, fund-raising, and educational needs. For details, write Charisma House Book Group, 600 Rinehart Road, Lake Mary, Florida 32746, or telephone (407) 333-0600.

GLOBAL RENEWAL CHRISTIANITY: SPIRIT-EMPOWERED MOVEMENTS
   PAST, PRESENT, AND FUTURE, VOLUME I: ASIA AND OCEANIA
   by Vinson Synan, PhD, and Amos Yong, PhD, General Editors
Published by Charisma House
Charisma Media/Charisma House Book Group
600 Rinehart Road
Lake Mary, Florida 32746
www.charismahouse.com

Cover design by Lisa Rae McClure
Design Director: Justin Evans

Visit the Empowered21 website at http://empowered21.com/.

Library of Congress Control Number: 2015939689
International Standard Book Number: 978-1-62998-688-3
E-book ISBN: 978-1-62998-689-0

First edition

16 17 18 19 20 — 987654321
Printed in Canada

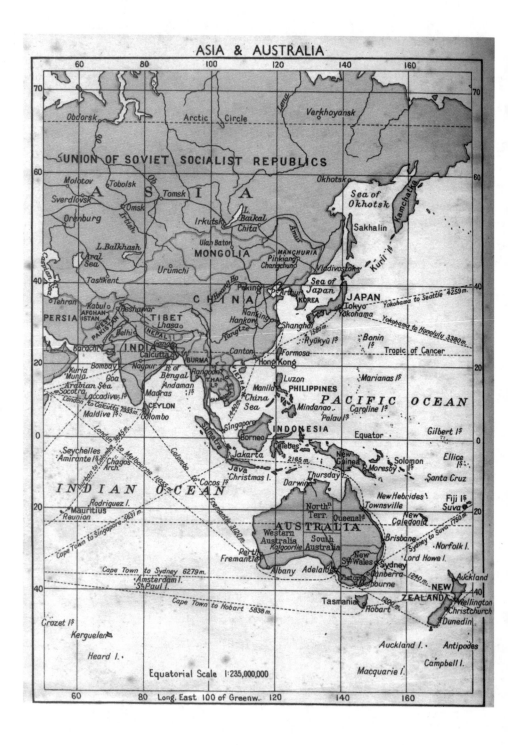

Contents

Part III: Southeast Asia

Part IV: Oceania

Part V: Roman Catholicism and Other Theological Themes

Foreword

THE WORK OF the Holy Spirit around the world in our lifetime is changing the face of global Christianity. The prayer movements from across Asia, to worship in Africa and Latin America, to church revitalization in Europe and North America and the masses being evangelized daily worldwide give evidence that a significant spiritual shift has taken place. At the heart of this shift are millions of Spirit-empowered believers. This volume of exceptional scholarly analysis, one of four on the global Spirit-empowered movement, helps bring definition, understanding, and depth to the dynamic work that God is doing today.

Spirit-empowered, or renewalist, Christianity continues to expand exponentially. As this growth takes place, the depth of the movement and a clear twenty-first century hermeneutic must also grow. Isaiah 54:2 provides prophetic encouragement for this increased depth by stating, "Enlarge the place of your tent, and let them stretch out the curtains of your habitations; spare not, lengthen your cords, and strengthen your stakes" (MEV).

As the tent of Spirit-empowered Christianity grows, the stakes of theological understanding must also deepen. This will allow the movement to withstand the twenty-first century storms that will rage against us while sheltering those believers in this ever-enlarging tent.

Empowered21 is committed to serving the broad spectrum of Spirit-empowered Christianity including Pentecostals, Charismatics, and every subsequent wave of Holy Spirit expression in the body of Christ. It is with deep gratitude to our editors, Dr. Vinson Synan and Dr. Amos Yong, that we publish this exciting volume of essays with the hope that God will use this work to indeed "deepen our stakes" for the exciting days ahead.

My prayer is that as you absorb this material, God's presence will overshadow you so you may personally experience the Holy Spirit, who is moving globally today.

Serving a movement, empowering a generation,

—DR. WILLIAM M. WILSON

PRESIDENT OF ORAL ROBERTS UNIVERSITY

GLOBAL COCHAIR OF EMPOWERED21

Foreword

IN HIS VISION, John the Revelator saw "a great multitude which no one could count, from all nations and tribes and peoples and tongues, standing before the throne and before the Lamb, clothed with white robes, with palm branches in their hands. They cried out with a loud voice: 'Salvation belongs to our God who sits on the throne, and to the Lamb!'" (Rev. 7:9–10, MEV).

What was for John a revelation of the end times is increasingly for us a picture of the present. No longer is it possible—if, in fact, it ever was!—for Western Christians to speak of the faith of Jesus Christ as a European and North American faith. Instead, we must speak of global Christianity, for the faith has gone out from Jerusalem to the ends of the earth (Acts 1:8).

In the last one hundred years, global Pentecostalism has been used by God to advance the good news of the kingdom of God within every nation, tribe, people, and language. The volume you are reading is proof of that. It is one of four volumes assaying the past, present, and future of global Pentecostalism.

I said that John's end-times vision is "increasingly" a picture of the present for us, but that adverb reminds us that there is still work to do. May God use this scholarly volume to inform and inspire a new generation of Spirit-empowered leaders to take the good news about His Son into every global nook and cranny, so that today's unreached may become tomorrow's white-robed, palm-waving praisers of Jesus Christ! Then, and only then, will John's vision be realized in full.

—DR. GEORGE O. WOOD
GENERAL SUPERINTENDENT OF THE ASSEMBLIES OF GOD (USA)
CHAIRMAN OF THE WORLD ASSEMBLIES OF GOD FELLOWSHIP
GLOBAL COCHAIR OF EMPOWERED21

Series Preface

THE EMPOWERED21 MOVEMENT had its origin in a vision given to Robert Fisher concerning a fitting celebration of the centennial of the Azusa Street revival that began in 1906. To plan for the event, Fisher organized the Center for Spiritual Renewal in 2000 in Cleveland, Tennessee. Unfortunately he passed away before the event took place, and his friend Billy Wilson was asked to complete the plans for the celebration and lead the conference. The celebration, which met in the Staples Center in Los Angeles in April of 2006, was a resounding success as more than fifty thousand persons attended the various events that were celebrated in several Los Angeles venues.

After the Azusa Street celebration in 2006, the Center began a connection with Oral Roberts University (ORU) when Wilson and his friend Mart Green were chosen to lead the Board of Trustees of the university. From this association came a vision for another meeting on the campus of ORU. Although the meeting was under the auspices of ORU, the Center for Spiritual Renewal was chosen to administer the event. Called the "Global Congress on Holy Spirit Empowerment," the Tulsa meeting drew ten thousand persons to the campus in April 2010.

In preparing for the Tulsa meeting, Mart Green and his associates conducted a broad ranging survey of the young people of the next generation to find out what term best described the Pentecostal/ Charismatic renewal in their minds. In the end the word *empowered* won out over the terms "Pentecostal," "Charismatic," or "full gospel." Also, since everyone wanted to look toward the future instead of the past, the numeral 21 was added, referring to the twenty-first century. Thus the term "Empowered21" (or E21) was born.

The vision statement of Empowered21 is powerful and pointed: "That every person on earth would have an authentic encounter with Jesus Christ through the Power and Presence of the Holy Spirit...by Pentecost 2033." Its mission statement proclaims that: "Empowered21 will help shape the future of the Global Spirit Empowered movement throughout the world by focusing on crucial issues facing the movement and connecting generations for intergenerational blessing and impartation." Thus the major focus is on what is called the "Nextgen" (next generation) in order to continue the "spiritual grace" of the Pentecostal/Charismatic renewal into future generations. Underlining all the efforts of this vision is a prayer for a "fresh outpouring of the Holy Spirit in the twenty-first century." These themes have permeated all the events and planning sessions of E21 from the beginning.

At the early years of the E21 movement Wilson led seventeen unique "conversations" with some five hundred church leaders and scholars from fifty-four nations and fifteen universities with the goal of answering the questions "What does it mean to be Spirit empowered in the twenty-first century?" and "What steps can be taken to engage new generations in the Spirit-filled experience?" Armed with the wealth of knowledge from these conversations, E21 conducted two major events on university campuses. The first was the aforementioned Global Congress on Holy Spirit Empowerment, which drew ten thousand persons to Oral Roberts University in April 2010 where 210 workshops produced a futuristic book edited by Vinson Synan titled *Spirit-Empowered Christianity in the 21st Century* (Charisma House, 2011). The second was a meeting at Regent University in 2012 in conjunction with the Society for

Pentecostal Studies, which emphasized the "convergence" of Spirit-empowered generations and movements. More than five hundred leaders registered for this event.

During this time the E21 movement was organized on an international scale with a global cabinet and eleven regional cabinets around the world. Included in these groups were leaders from most of the Pentecostal and Charismatic movements in the world. The first global gathering after the American events at ORU and Regent University was the E21 Asia Congress held in Jakarta, Indonesia, in October 2011, which drew some fifteen thousand persons.

Other plans for the future include worldwide celebrations on Pentecost Sunday each year to celebrate the birthday of the church and the outpouring of the Holy Spirit in the Upper Room (Acts 2). On Pentecost Sunday 2012 many thousands gathered in local celebrations around the world. Totally ecumenical, the vision is to see Pentecost Sunday rise to the level of Easter and Christmas as great days to make a common witness to the world.

An important part of the E21 vision has been to gather scholars from around the world to study the past, present, and future of the Empowered movements on every continent and from as many nations as possible. To accomplish this goal, three meetings convened before the final one in Jerusalem in 2015. One was held in Oxford, England, in 2012 under the leadership of Dr. Harold Hunter. Another took place in Sydney, Australia, in 2013, where the focus was on Asia. Vinson Synan and Amos Yong directed this latter consultation and those that followed. The third meeting was in Quito, Ecuador, in 2014, where the focus was on Latin America. The last meeting of scholars was in Jerusalem in 2015 in the culminating congress where thousands of people gathered for one of the largest Christian meetings held in the Holy Land in modern times.

Here the scholars read papers focusing on Africa, North America, and Europe.

In the end, four volumes of the papers read in these gatherings will be published and edited by Synan and Yong. They will be on Asia, Africa, Latin America, Europe, and North America, and will be published by Charisma House in Lake Mary, Florida. Many of the papers published in these volumes were initially presented in the above-mentioned conferences and consultations, but not all. Those who could not attend the conferences or consultations were invited to write specifically for the project. Most of the chapters across the volumes were intended thus to be read, although a few were written to be presented and heard and have retained their oral character (which will be easily identifiable as such in what follows). In all cases, scholars with a PhD or its equivalent and a recognized publication record were invited, although in a good number of cases our first choices were not able to participate because of other commitments or circumstances. In most cases, scholars are also personal participants in Pentecostal, Charismatic, or renewal movements, although again, not all. In any of the latter cases, of course, authors were invited because of their recognized capacity to present and discuss Pentecostal/Charismatic movements with sympathetic objectivity.

This mix of both confessional Pentecostal/Charismatic "insiders" and "outsiders" may result for some readers in a certain sense of unevenness as they move from chapter to chapter in each volume. Some writers write more from a first-person perspective, while others remain more distant. A few approached their task more pastorally, while many more academically, in overall orientation. Last but not least, many of the latter remain more descriptive in their approach while others are more normative with regard to the theology, practice, and mission of Spirit-empowered churches and communities. The editors hope that such a combination of voices, stances, and dispositions will introduce readers to the broad spectrum of Pentecostal/Charismatic scholarship. "Outsiders" might come to appreciate the animating concerns of Pentecostal/ Charismatic scholars who are in touch with pastoral and ecclesial realities and challenges, while readers who are lay and ecclesial leaders, pastors, and bureaucrats (used here descriptively rather than pejoratively) in the Spirit-empowered renewal movement worldwide may perhaps also glean something useful from their academic colleagues.

The editors are hopeful that these volumes will be of wide-ranging benefit to readers from both of these domains in part because of the conceptual layout for the project. The task presented to each of the invitees was to write about the history and theology of Pentecostal/Charismatic or renewal movements in a specified region or country. With this, some assessment of theological orientation and development was expected, as well as analyses of opportunities and challenges lying ahead of these movements, especially on the theological front. Most chapters in these volumes follow this general format, although not all.

The Empowered21 movement, under the able leadership of Billy Wilson and the many worldwide leadership groups that he has gathered, seems poised to bring more coordination to all the Spirit-filled Pentecostal and Charismatic movements in the world to a level that has not been seen heretofore. In the long run, it is hoped that this set of books produced by these scholars will be a permanent and important milestone in the history and theology of the Empowered21 movement from the vantage point of the middle of the second decade of the twenty-first century.

Acknowledgments

MANY FRIENDS CONTRIBUTED to making this book a reality. First, we thank the E21 leadership team whose vision brought this and the other books in the series into being. They include Billy Wilson, Mart Green, Ossie Mills, Assif Reid, Robin Cole, Gloria Smith, and their colleagues. Also, special thanks are due to Tessie DeVore and to Charisma House, publisher of the book; to Debbie Marrie and Adrienne Gaines for their editorial work; and to Mike Schatz for his help with the publication process.

This Asian volume owes much to the Alphacrucis College in Sydney, Australia, that hosted the scholars who gathered there in 2013. Special thanks go to (then) Academic Dean Jacqui Grey and Principal Stephen Fogarty, whose organizational oversight and hard work made the meeting possible, and to all Alphacrucis College faculty and staff who participated and whose hospitable welcome made the meeting a success. Also our deep gratitude belongs to Ryan Seow, Amos Yong's graduate assistant, for his help with finalizing the manuscript and work on the index. Above all, thanks to the authors of the following pages whose excellent research and writing made this important book such a great contribution to the study of current Spirit-empowered movements.

Contributors

Denise A. Austin (PhD, University of Queensland) is Director of Quality and Standards, Director of the Australian Pentecostal Studies Centre and Head of History at Alphacrucis College, Australia.

Simon Chan (PhD, University of Cambridge) is Earnest Lau Professor of Systematic Theology, Trinity Theological College, Singapore.

Shane Clifton (PhD, Australia Catholic University) is Dean of Theology, Alphacrucis College, Sydney, Australia.

Sarah Eßel is currently finishing her doctoral studies at the University of Heidelberg, Germany, and works as a research assistant in its Department of History of Religion and Intercultural Theology.

Jacqueline Grey (PhD, Charles Sturt University) is Associate Professor of Biblical Studies at Alphacrucis College, Sydney, Australia.

James Hosack (MA, Biola University) is Country Moderator for the Assemblies of God Missionary Fellowship Thailand, serving there since 1984.

Mark Hutchinson (PhD, University of NSW) is Dean, Humanities and Academic Projects, at The Scots College, Sydney, and core member, Religion and Society Research Centre, University of Western Sydney.

David Hymes (PhD, University of Wales, Bangor) is Academic Dean at Central Bible College, Tokyo, Japan.

Iap Sian-Chin is a PhD candidate at Taiwan's National Chengchi University, and an adjunct faculty member in the Assemblies of God School of Theology, Taichung, Taiwan.

Alan R. Johnson (PhD, University of Wales, Oxford Centre for Mission Studies) has served with Assemblies of God World Missions in Thailand since 1986.

Brett Knowles (PhD, University of Otago) is a retired Senior Lecturer in Church History, formerly of the University of Otago, Dunedin, New Zealand, and of Sydney College of Divinity, Sydney, Australia.

Vince Le is PhD candidate at Regent University School of Divinity, Virginia Beach, Virginia, and has been a member of the house church movement in Vietnam since 1999.

Sang Yun Lee (PhD, The University of Birmingham, United Kingdom) is lecturer of Pentecostal Studies at Hansei University and pastor of the Yoido Full Gospel Church, Seoul, South Korea.

Timothy Lim T. N. (PhD, Regent University School of Divinity) is adjunct professor at King's Evangelical Divinity School, London.

Giovanni Maltese (Dipl.-Theol., University of Heidelberg) is Wissenschaftlicher Mitarbeiter and teacher at the Department of History of Religion and Intercultural Theology at the University of Heidelberg, Germany.

Thomson K. Mathew (EdD, Oklahoma State University; DMin, Oral Roberts University) is Professor of Pastoral Care and Dean of the College of Theology and Ministry at Oral Roberts University, Tulsa, Oklahoma.

Robert Menzies (PhD, University of Aberdeen) is the Director of Synergy, an organization that seeks to enable rural village people in Southwest China to live productive and fruitful lives.

Finny Philip (PhD, University of Durham, United Kingdom) is Professor of New Testament and Principal at Filadelfia Bible College, Udaipur, Rajasthan, India.

G. P. V. Somaratna (PhD, University of London) is Research Professor of Colombo Theological Seminary, Sri Lanka.

Maurie Sween (PhD, University of Edinburgh) is a missionary who has lived in Taiwan for twenty-five years, working among the disabled and teaching in seminaries; at present he is writing a novel.

Vinson Synan (PhD, University of Georgia) is Professor Emeritus of Christian History at Regent University School of Divinity, Virginia Beach, Virginia.

Jonathan Y. Tan (PhD, The Catholic University of America) is the Archbishop Paul J. Hallinan Professor in Catholic Studies at Case Western Reserve University, Cleveland, Ohio.

Ekaputra Tupamahu is PhD candidate, Vanderbilt University, Nashville, Tennessee.

Yalin Xin (PhD, Asbury Theological Seminary) is an associate professor of Intercultural Studies at William Carey International University, Pasadena, California.

Amos Yong (PhD, Boston University) is Professor of Theology and Mission at Fuller Theological Seminary, Pasadena, California.

The Many Tongues of Asian and Oceanian Pentecostalisms: An Introduction and Some Theological Prognostications

Amos Yong

I T HAS BECOME fashionable in recent decades to talk about Pentecostalism not as if there were a single homogeneous movement but about Pentecostalism*s* in the plural.[1] Yet such fashionableness is not faddish when set against the backdrop of the wider realization that the diversity of Pentecostalisms is part and parcel of the heterogeneity of the worldwide Christian movement. In the present global context, "Christianity" is more often than not a shorthand or placeholder for what can be specifiable in multiple directions, albeit not always consistently or coherently in the same respect. Thus Christianity in North America is recognizably different from Christianity in Asia, even as we realize that there is a diversity of Christianities within both the North American and Asian contexts.[2]

This emphasis on diversity is arguably heightened when focused, as this volume is, not only on the Asian continent but also across the Oceanian region. And it is not just that we are extending our reach beyond the Asian horizon to include Oceania, but that the diversity of the latter is arguably parallel to the pluralism of the former. Not without reason, then, one of the more recent introductions to and overviews of Christian theological achievements across the Asian landscape needed eighteen hundred pages and three volumes (not just one), and this did not even attempt to discuss Oceania.[3]

As the pages in this volume will reveal, there are a variety of Asian Pentecostalisms, as much if not more than in other parts of the world. This introductory chapter will map such diversity across five registers: the ethnic/linguistic, the cultural/religious, the socio/political, the economic/transnational, and the ecclesial. Our discussion in each case will inevitably be succinct, although each ought to be understood as being interwoven with the others rather than existing as its own autonomous domain. Our goal is twofold: first, to whet the appetite for the feast to come in the rest of this book precisely by suggesting how the many tongues of the Day of Pentecost (Acts 2), from which the modern Pentecostal movement derives its name, can be seen as continuing to inspire the flourishing of Pentecostalisms in the Asian world, even as the complexity and cacophony of the latter was already present in the former event. Second, we aim to make some observations about how Asian and Oceanic Pentecostalisms can engage and inform wider Pentecostal theological conversations as we look ahead, precisely part of the goal of this book and the series of which it is a part.

ETHNIC AND LINGUISTIC DIVERSITY

Pentecostalisms within the Asian continent stretch across more than seventeen million square miles and upwards of forty-five countries.[4] The 4.164 billion plus inhabitants come from a dozen or so language-groups and speak upwards of forty official languages (not counting the various unofficial dialects). It is not uncommon across the immense spread to speak of six continental regions: West Asia (including the Middle Eastern region), North Asia (including Asian Russia and Mongolia), Central Asia (with the five former

Soviet Socialist Republics alongside Afghanistan), South Asia (including India, Pakistan, and the smaller neighboring countries), East Asia (China, Korea, and Japan), and Southeast Asia (divided into the mainland arenas from Myanmar through to the Malay peninsula and the maritime islands from Indonesia through to the Philippines). When Oceania is added into the mix, that includes the subregions of Melanesia, Micronesia, Polynesia, and Australasia (and that includes Australia, Papua New Guinea, and New Zealand, among other island groups).

Even the preceding regional overview masks more than it unveils. My characterization might be likened at least from a distance to the decision of the author of the Book of Acts to explicate the expansion of the gospel to the "ends of the earth" (Acts 1:8, MEV) by deploying his own shortened version of the available lists of seventy/seventy-two nations and paring that down to the eighteen categories he provides (Acts 2:9–11).[5] The point is that neither of us are attempting to be exhaustive in enumerating either "all nations [of] the whole earth" (cf. Acts 17:26, NRSV) or all the national, ethnic, or linguistic groups of the Asian-Oceanian hemisphere.[6] Instead, these representative adumbrations provide a window into the many tongues manifest at the original Day of Pentecost event even as they alert us to the exceedingly assorted ethnic and linguistic diversity across Asia and Oceania.

To be sure, Pentecostalisms are not equally dispersed across these continents. Pentecostal groups and churches are much less prevalent, although by no means completely absent, in Western and Northern Asia, and minimally present, as is Christianity in general, in Japan (even if this volume includes a chapter on Pentecostal movements in Japan).[7] On the other hand, there are vibrant Pentecostal churches and movements in China and South Korea—so we have more chapters on East Asian Pentecostalisms, comparatively speaking—even as there is a palpable Pentecostal presence across the Southeast Asian maritime and also coming out of Australasia. Taken as a whole, if at the end of the first decade of the third millennium Christians are estimated as constituting 8.5 percent of the Asian demographic, Pentecostal-types in all their diversity are thought to amount to a bit more than half of this, about 4.3 percent of the total population or around 179 million plus in Asia; we do not need to add to this the almost 5 million Pentecostals across Oceania to realize that there are more Pentecostals in Asia than in any other continent in the world.[8]

Regardless of the exact numbers, given the pluralism of Asian and Oceanian ethnic and linguistic groups, Pentecostal believers in these contexts speak different languages, worship variously, and express themselves in their own idioms and styles. One could argue that the manifestation and vernacularization of Asian Pentecostalisms in their many tongues is a logical and expected extension of the original *glossolalia* recorded on the biblical Day of Pentecost.

CULTURAL AND RELIGIOUS PLURALITY

Ethnic and linguistic diversity is of course informed also by cultural and religious plurality. Yet I am separating these out for discussion because the cultural-religious domain is potentially more charged, at least theologically, than the ethnic-linguistic register. For Pentecostals and their closest of kin, evangelical believers, there is at least current awareness that Christian faith comes expressed in cultural clothes, although there is perennial suspicion that cultural adaptation does not become cultural accommodation to the point of syncretism: when Christian identity is believed to be compromised by local cultural expressions and commitments.[9] Arguably, Pentecostal inclinations toward indigenization related to their

vernacularizing tendencies have nurtured a wider range of culturally diverse expressions as compared with their evangelical counterparts.[10] This applies certainly not only to Asian and Oceanian
Pentecostalisms as to the movement globally.

Yet the cultural and religious spheres, while distinctive in some
respects, are not ultimately disparate. If in the African context
Pentecostal growth opens up to questions regarding interfaces with
especially Islam and the various African indigenous traditions, in
the Asian and Oceanian domains there are not just one but multiple world religions even as there remain in play the various local
traditions and aboriginal spiritualities. Hence to talk about the cultural *and* religious dimensions of Pentecostalisms in these Asian
and Oceanian regions is to confront Pentecostal identity with questions far surpassing ethnic and linguistic considerations. The situation is complexified when we consider not only the great world
religions across the Asian geoscape—what we call Hinduism (in
India), Buddhism, and Confucianism (both of the latter throughout
Northern, Eastern, and Southeastern Asia), for instance, besides
the ever-present Islam in the largest Islamic nation in the world
(Indonesia) but also stretching from Pakistan and India through
the Malay straits to the Philippines—but also the fact that there
are popular forms and expressions of each of these traditions, so
that we ought more seriously to talk about Hinduisms, Buddhisms,
Confucianisms, and perhaps even Islams as well.[11]

Pentecostalisms across Asia and throughout Oceania exhibit
an additional level or layer of complication. Recognition that
Pentecostal spirituality resonates with indigenous traditions and
that this explains, at least in part, the movement's portability and
explosive growth in some majority world contexts,[12] has led scholars
like Walter Hollenweger to call for a "theologically responsible syncretism," one that is capable of exploiting the interfaces with oral

cultural commitments for Pentecostal and Christian gain but yet does so in a discerning manner.[13] The reason this is important should be obvious particularly in the Asian context where Pentecostal indigenization includes not only cultural but also (competing) global and local religiosities. As already indicated, Pentecostalism in any Asian context thus has to contend not only with the official versions of the great religions but also with their popularized forms. And since the lines between these are oftentimes blurred, it is then also difficult to clearly demarcate Pentecostal engagements with *the* religions (for instance, a Pentecostal-Confucian or Pentecostal-Buddhist dialogue) from Pentecostal interwovenness with popular religious cultures (for instance, a Pentecostal-Confucian-Buddhist-shamanist orientation).[14] Although few of the chapters to follow take up these questions in depth, they percolate underneath the discussion not only for developments in Asian Pentecostal discourse but also for global Pentecostal theology as well. Asian Pentecostals shaped by a deep experience of religious pluralism will begin to emerge as leading voices in furthering theological discussion on this important matter.[15]

SOCIAL AND POLITICAL VARIETY

Religious movements, Pentecostalisms not excepted, are also socially and politically inflected, if not thoroughly charged. To be sure, as will be mentioned along the way in the coming pages, there are forms of Asian and Oceanic Pentecostalisms that are intentionally apolitical; especially some of the older or more classical expressions of the movement are, consistent with the tendencies of those churches and denominations coming out of the early twentieth-century Azusa Street revival in Southern California, focused on traditional activities of mission and evangelism and little concerned with, if not even entirely opposed to, explicit political engagement and improvement of this-worldly affairs. Yet a new generation of Pentecostal believers is emerging, one much more ecumenically informed, perhaps in part through cross-fertilization with Charismatic renewal movements throughout the historic Protestant denominations and even Roman Catholicism, that is also more sensitive to the importance of maintaining their witness in the sociopolitical sphere. There is at least the realization that Pentecostal mission and evangelism in the twenty-first century ought to be more holistic in approach and thereby strategically interfacing with the public domain whether in terms of organic presence or in terms of initiatives directed toward social transformation.[16]

Yet the fact of the matter is that Pentecostal encroachment in the public square is unfolding not only vis-à-vis social initiatives but also in the specifically political arena. Given the multitude of political contexts across Asia—from communist China and North Korea to Islamic countries in western and southeastern parts of the continent on the one side to Hindu India, Buddhist Japan and Southeast Asia (with the exception of Malaysia), and "Christian" or at least Roman Catholic (in terms of ethos) Philippines and East Timor on the other side—it will quickly be understood that there is no one type of political Pentecostalism to be observed. Those engaged with religious and political ideologies like communism and Islam operate under quite different constraints than those in either more democratic or pluralistic contexts. Yet, even when dealing with specific political environments, Christian and Pentecostal forays into the political are not monolithic. Islamic Pakistan, for instance, with its up to 98 percent Muslim population, is quite different from Malaysia, with its slight Muslim majority, even though both are Islamic states, and these also both contrast with Muslim Indonesia with its philosophy of Pancasila that nurtures religious freedom, in a sense, despite the fact that 88 percent of this island nation's inhabitants are Muslims. The political opportunities and challenges in each of these cases are thereby quite distinct,[17] even as they are also collectively divergent from the emerging forms of political Pentecostalism in other Asian contexts. In the Philippines, as an example on the opposite end of the spectrum, the gradual if not less tangible Pentecostalization or charismatization of this Catholic-majority nation has also had, more recently, felt political effects.[18] These samples demonstrate that while there is no one-size-fits-all approach to understanding the politics of Asian Pentecostalisms, it also goes without saying that any adequate consideration of Pentecostal/Charismatic Christianity in the Asian world cannot avoid assessment of its political as well as social aspects.

The bigger question going forward will be: what does all of this mean for understanding Pentecostal theology in the third millennium? The observation of these developments begs for the articulation of a Pentecostal political theology. The truth to be told, however, is that such a formulation ought to be consistently pluralistic as well: there should be a multitude of Pentecostal political theologies emergent out of the Asian, not to mention Oceanian, horizons, even as these will also then have the capacity to engage, inform, and enrich Pentecostal political theology in global contexts.[19] Just as there is not only one political environment amidst which Pentecostal life is developing in Asia and Oceania, so also there ought not to be one type of political theology emergent in this regard.

ECONOMIC-CLASS DISPARITIES

I will discuss the economic aspects of Pentecostal/Charismatic Christianity separately from the sociopolitical because in our continually evolving postcolonial world, finance is increasingly mattering more than the political even as there are now those who would argue that the day and age of the nation-state is being displaced by the global market economy. Hence it is less and less what kinds of governments are in control that is important and more and more how integrated any locality or region is into the world economy that is crucial for both the quality of life in general and the freedom of religious expression more specifically. Yet even here in this matter, assessment of the economic aspects of Asian and Oceanic Pentecostalisms unveils as much diversity as might be noted on other registers.

What I mean is that if in the earlier twentieth century Pentecostal movements were by and large situated among the lower classes, such generalizations no longer hold in the present time. It is certainly not to say that there are no longer poor and impoverished Pentecostals (there are[20]), but the fact is that Pentecostals now are to be found across the economic spectrum. There are Pentecostal and Charismatic "boss Christians" for instance in coastal China who are investing in large church edifices,[21] perhaps in part following the lead of the largely urban and middle-class Pentecostal/Charismatic phenomenon symbolized in the South Korean megachurch context. The point is that it is now irresponsible to generalize about the socioeconomic status of Pentecostal/Charismatic religiosity, not only on the Asian scale but also worldwide.

Part of the complexity involved relates to the irresistible forces of economic globalization. It is not just that the "prosperity theology" from North America has been exported across the Pacific Rim as much as it is that Asian and Oceanian Pentecostals are agents of their own upward socioeconomic mobility. As Pentecostal migration has intensified over the last few decades,[22] people are connecting from around the world and are adapting whatever they find helpful for their own purposes. Such globalizing dynamics are redistributing wealth, resources, and socioeconomic capital across the Pentecostal polis.[23]

Yet Asian Pentecostalisms are not only being transformed by outside forces; they are also increasingly influencing global trends. On the one hand, the new media, at the vanguard of which Pentecostal Christians have perennially been, is manifesting across the Asian and Oceanian front. Thus, for instance, Pentecostal/Charismatic televangelism is both promoting upward socioeconomic movement as well as reflecting such shifts.[24] On the other hand, Pentecostal/Charismatic entry into the market economy has inspired artistic and musical creativity, if not commodification. Australasian praise and worship, for example, is now impacting the world not only in terms of its peculiar branding but also in terms of overall style, so that the musicalization of Pentecostal spirituality, if I might put it this way, is going hand in hand with economic transformations, even elevations, of this global revival movement.[25]

Pentecostal scholars thus have been more recently attuned to how market forces and globalization trends impact theological reflection.[26] Just as, if not more, important, however, is explicit socioethical consideration of the global economy as it relates to Pentecostal/Charismatic faith and life. If indeed the biblical traditions are rather replete with references to poverty and wealth, then these are not marginal to Christian faithfulness and Pentecostal theologians would be well advised to be intentional about engaging more substantively on these matters than they have to now.[27] Perhaps Asian and Oceanian Pentecostal thinkers shaped and informed by the full spectrum of economic realities across these continents might emerge in due course to not only contribute to but also lead the ongoing discussion.

ECCLESIAL TRADITIONS AND TRADITIONINGS

By this time we recognize that diversity of Asian and Oceanic Pentecostalisms is constituted, at least in part, by the many factors unveiled in the preceding discussion. There are different Asian and Oceanic Pentecostalisms precisely because Pentecostal/Charismatic Christianity across these land masses are shaped by different linguistic, cultural, religious, social, political, economic, and class realities. All of these remain in play when we consider the specifically intra-Christian and even intra-Pentecostal features that characterize the renewal movement across these regions. At least three categories of such distinctions can be made.

First, there are a range of classical Pentecostal churches in Asia and Oceania, defined by Pentecostal scholarship as those ecclesial bodies that trace their roots somehow to the Azusa Street revival in Los Angeles in the first decade or two of the twentieth century. Most of these would have classical Pentecostal roots in some respect in terms of traditional Pentecostal missionaries having traversed the Pacific Rim from North American shores, although in some cases, as in the Oneness Pentecostal movements in East Asia, these were not officially appointed and commissioned by their churches. Yet this important theological distinctive (belief in the oneness of God and in Jesus-name baptism in water) aside, many of the classical Pentecostal churches across both Asia and Oceania today remain remarkably uniform in matters of belief and practice.[28] The Assemblies of God, the Church of God (Cleveland, Tennessee), and the International Church of the Foursquare Gospel, for instance, are more alike than different whether in India, Singapore, the Philippines, or Australasia. Yet such at least recognizable similarities are not immune to the forces of globalization. The emergence of Hillsong from the Australian Assemblies of God (now Australian Christian Churches) is a case in point: such remain in a sense classical Pentecostal, but only by affiliation and not so much in terms of praxis or public perception.

Beyond the classical Pentecostal world, however, is that of the Charismatic renewal in the historic Protestant churches and in the Roman Catholic Church. These, with origins also in North America, have become a worldwide phenomenon at least at two levels. On the one hand, there has been the gradual assimilation of renewal streams into the fabric of these historic traditions. The El Shaddai Charismatic community, for instance, has been enfolded, not easily but nevertheless surely, into the mainstream of the Roman Catholic Church in the Philippines over the last few decades.[29] There were initially other efforts by mainline Protestant denominations also to include streams of Charismatic renewal, but these have led, perhaps inexorably, also to the Pentecostalization and charismatization of such churches at least more recently.[30] In other words, across the historic Christian traditions in the Asian context, churches are exhibiting marked Pentecostal and Charismatic features—both healthy and perhaps not-so-healthy versions—even if they do not go by or understand themselves according to either of these labels.[31]

At a third level, however, we have also witnessed the emergence and growth of indigenous Pentecostal- and Charismatic-type movements throughout the Asian-Oceanian landscape quite unconnected to either classical Pentecostal or Charismatic renewal churches and communities. Revivals especially in the Indian and Chinese contexts have featured Pentecostal and Charismatic expressions, manifestations, and phenomena, and these have developed, on the whole, autonomously from Western Christian missionary initiatives or ecclesial interfaces.[32] To be sure, in the present time the unfolding of an independent and post-denominational mind-set and climate across the Christian world, not only in the West but also in the Asian and Oceanian hemispheres, has fostered non-formally affiliated, although networked, churches and congregations that embrace Pentecostal and Charismatic spirituality even if they do not explicitly self-identify in those terms. The point is that the Pentecostal and Charismatic environment is increasingly overlapping with the evangelical, ecumenical, and generally Christian churches to the point that it is increasingly difficult to talk about these Pentecostalisms without qualification.

AN OVERVIEW OF THE CHAPTERS

Despite the fact that this is a large book, there are many gaps. This is due not only to the fact that it is hardly possible to thoroughly cover the entirety of the Asian-Oceanian continents in one volume, but also to the parameters of the project (given Empowered21 sponsorship, described in the series preface at the beginning of this book), limited connections (for many parts of Asia we the editors did not feel we knew the right people who could write for us), lack of availability (some people we asked to contribute chapters were unable to), and just plain constraints of space and time (the project could not drag on interminably and an already hefty tome could not keep growing). Readers who glance over the table of contents will immediately realize that not all Asian regions are represented (there is nothing for instance on West Asia and we are very thin on North Asia—the one chapter touching this part is actually on North China, not Mongolia, for instance), even as other parts are inequitably discussed or gaping lacuna remain.[33] The editors are well aware that the final product can be improved in a myriad of ways. In any case, surely the volume at hand at least leaves it for others to do better. Other researchers will need to tell the stories that remain untold, and other theologians will have to conduct the analyses that beckon.

Yet when we focus on what is rather than isn't there, we believe that this collection will at least supplement if not advance the conversation, the latter at least in certain key, even if narrow, respects. Many of the various nationally circumscribed studies we feel remain quite helpful for orientation since it is unfortunately still the case that few such overviews are available to researchers interested in learning about Pentecostal and Charismatic Christianity in these parts of the world. While almost all authors heeded the invitation to write about historical and theological developments in a specific context, a few were quite evenhanded in being attentive to both aspects (e.g., Menzies, Xin, Le, Lim, Hymes). A good number of the chapters are more historically or sociologically focused (e.g., Somaratna, Sween, Iap, Hosack/Johnson, Clifton, Hutchinson, Knowles) even as others are more theological in their approach (e.g., Philip, Lee, Tupamahu, Tan), reflecting at least in part, although not exclusively, the disciplinary training and scholarly background that these authors brought to their task. Further, a few of the following essays (e.g., Mathew, Austin, and Grey) break the nation-state mold for the volume and provide transnational coverage that illuminate the crisscrossing of both Asian-Oceanian and Asian-North American borders and boundaries. We should note that at least two more pieces (Maltese/Eßel and Chan[34]) depart from the norm by providing creative and penetrating theological analyses that on the one hand illuminate some of the historiographic issues pertinent to the contemporary state of Pentecostal studies and on the other hand challenge Pentecostal scholars to consider how their work might be pertinent to the future of Pentecostalisms in Asian and beyond looking forward.

While our organization of the book beginning with West Asia and ending in Oceania and thematic discussions is somewhat arbitrary, our goal here was not to tell *one* story but to collect together chapters covering neighboring terrain. At the same time readers certainly can proceed profitably in a sequential manner though this book and in doing so move in an orderly manner through the vast regions of both continents. On the other hand, those who choose to consult specific chapters pertinent to their own interests will find self-contained discussions.

In general this volume is intended to provide a reliable historical guide to Pentecostal and Charismatic Christianity for students and others seeking initial coordination to the various expressions and manifestations of the global phenomenon in the Asian and Oceanian context. More specifically, however, as editors who are also part of the movement that this book seeks to understand, we are confident that scholars and others who identify as insiders of the renewal movement will come to an expanded awareness of the challenges and opportunities before us. If lay members of Pentecostal and Charismatic churches often embrace the idea that the contemporary twenty-first-century church lives out its vocation as the people of God and the fellowship of the Holy Spirit as the twenty-ninth chapter of the Book of Acts, as if following the template laid out in the biblical book's actual twenty-eight chapters,[35] it will be obvious to readers of this book that in many parts of the contemporary movement, theological reflection has yet to catch up to that of the first-century Jerusalem Council described in Acts chapter 15. The point is the much work lies before those who believe Pentecostal and Charismatic renewal is central rather than peripheral to Christian identity and mission.[36] It is precisely for this reason that we accepted the Empowered21 invitation to mobilize not only historical assessment but theological self-reflection and even loyal criticism. May many who read this volume be motivated also to consult the other three companion books in the series and then take up the task to thinking and theologizing renewal for the sake of the church catholic in the twenty-first century.

Part I: South Asia

Chapter 1

Christological Nuances in Bhil Pentecostal Theology

Finny Philip

A DECADE AGO IT was estimated that half of India's 62 million Christians were Pentecostal/Charismatic.[1] By now the proportion will have increased even further, as this decade has seen tremendous and unprecedented growth all over India, especially in North India among the tribal people, Dalits, and lower castes in rural areas, as well as among the middle classes in urban centres.[2]

India's flourishing Pentecostal movement has remained until now underdeveloped in mainline Pentecostal scholarship. This is all the more surprising given Pentecostalism's nearly one-hundred-year history in southern India. Although today it is undoubtedly the most dynamic and fastest-growing movement in India, little has been done to document or to reflect upon this phenomenon. In this chapter we will be focusing on North Indian Pentecostalism, particularly the tribal Bhil Pentecostals[3] by (a) surveying the history of Pentecostal origins in north India; (b) exploring the interconnections between the experience, thoughts, and beliefs that come from real-life situations of tribal Pentecostal believers; and (c) presenting theological nuances, particularly in Christology, within emerging tribal Pentecostalism as they have engaged with their own contexts.

1

EXPERIENTIAL AND DENOMINATIONAL PENTECOSTALISM

Experiential forms of Pentecostal-type spirituality have been widespread in India since the middle of the nineteenth century. The earliest recorded (1860) expressions of Pentecostal phenomena in India, particularly, glossolalia, prophecy and other Charismatic gifts, were evident in revival meetings in the Tirunelveli district of Tamil Nadu in South India.[4] Within a decade the revival extended to nearby Travancore, in Kerala, among Church Missionary Society and Mar Thoma Churches—the predominantly Christian population in central Travancore—paving the way for the Pentecostal movement to grow rapidly in South India. The roots of these revivals can be traced back to the pietistic movement and predominantly to its teachings on the imminent second coming of Christ and hope for the outpouring of the Holy Spirit and spiritual gifts.

However, these awakenings with Pentecostal phenomena were independent of Pentecostalism in the west. The denominational Pentecostalism which came after 1908[5] was instrumental in consolidating the emerging Pentecostal churches. It also brought in classical Pentecostal theology to the South.[6] Being strengthened by denominationalism and a Pentecostal theological framework enabled numerical growth and fervent "mission" activities. The seedbed for Pentecostalism in the south was among the majority Christian population, and thus much of its missional engagements were either defending the movement or "evangelising" and initiating other Christians to the newfound Pentecostal experience.

However, in northern India, missionaries from Wesleyan Holiness and Higher Life teaching persuasions contributed much to the "multiple Jerusalem" experiences.[7] The earliest move of the Holy Spirit happened in northwest India as early as 1895, at a camp meeting in Lonavala near Pune. Later it spread to other places, such as Bombay, Pune, Dond, Aurangabad, and Yeotamal, followed by a revival in Dholka, Gujarat, in April 5, 1905.[8] Among these revivals, the revival at Mukti Mission in 1905 at Kedgaon, near Pune, was chiefly influenced by the Keswick convention.[9]

Simultaneously a revival began in March 1905, among tribal people in the Khasi Hills in the northeast of India (Welsh Presbyterian mission) when Methodist missionaries toured the land for the promotion of holiness.[10] Further, during the second annual convention of Sialkot in Punjab (now in Pakistan) in August 1905, a revival broke out particularly among the Dalits and spread into different parts of Uttar Pradesh.[11] In these revivals the baptism in the Holy Spirit with the restoration of speaking in tongues, a life of holiness, and empowerment for mission were the clear emphases. Concomitant with these revivals was the arrival of Alfred and Lillian Garr in December 1906, the first missionaries to India from the Azusa Street revival, which prepared the ground for Pentecostal revival in Calcutta and nearby regions.[12]

Interestingly, this experiential Pentecostalism in the north did not materialize into Pentecostal churches.[13] There were various reasons for this. First, most missionaries who were involved in the revival message later returned to their home countries and did not develop indigenous leaders to lead the revival from afar. Further, there was a strong anti-colonial-Christian outlook with a right-wing nationalist wave. Last but not least, there remained a strong resistance and suspicion from the mainline churches. As a result, the revival movements in the north declined.[14]

Nonetheless, there were exceptions. The "multiple Jerusalem" continued to manifest in north India, Udaipur, Rajasthan, Jabalpur, Madhya Pradesh, and in Banswara, Rajasthan, among the Bhil Christians.[15] Simultaneously other states, such as Punjab, Orissa,

Bihar, U. P., and Jharkhand, also experienced the spiritual revival among the tribal and Dalit groups.

It was only after the 1960s that the formation of Pentecostal churches happened with the coming of South Indian Pentecostal missionaries to the north.[16] These missionaries came with the Pentecostal message to places where there was some Christian presence and instilled biblical teachings of believers' baptism, Spirit baptism, and the importance of a holy life. With the help of local Christians they moved into the un-evangelized territories and began to establish churches. Consequently several Pentecostal denominations came into existence in the tribal belts of North India.

When these Pentecostal missionaries came, they brought scriptural validation to many of the scattered revival experiences and accepted them as authentic moves of the Holy Spirit. They also equipped native North Indians to lead the new church growth and introduced the classical Pentecostal theological framework to sustain the revival experience. The missionaries harnessed the revival movements into church growth and brought in a missiological shift by engaging with the most spiritually responsive people, viz., tribal people. As a result, tribal Pentecostal churches began to be established.

PENTECOSTAL REVIVAL AMONG THE BHILS

During the 1960s in Banswara, Rajasthan, many of those who belonged to the mainstream churches experienced the move of the Spirit.[17] These experiences, locally known as *Atma ki jagruti* (Revival of the Spirit), had almost all of the Pentecostal characteristics. The visible manifestations of the Spirit in these awakenings included speaking in tongues, singing in tongues, falling down, visions and dreams, confession of sins, and shaking of the body.[18] However, these experiences were shunned as the work of "evil spirits" by the mainstream churches, which quenched the spirit of revival sapping the zeal from the Christian life of the church.

But it was the coming of Thomas Mathews to Udaipur in 1963 that established an important milestone in the history of North Indian Pentecostalism.[19] Mathews visited these places and explained the biblical and theological legitimacy of the Pentecostal experience and harnessed the local revivals into a church growth movement. Some of the young people who experienced Spirit baptism joined him and began to work among the Bhil tribals in Banswara, Udaipur, and other places, and indigenous Pentecostal churches began to mushroom. These gatherings came to be known as *pavitratma vale* (Holy Spirit people—those who were filled with the Holy Spirit) or *anya bhasha vale* (tongues-speaking people) or *hallelujah vali kalisiyas* (hallelujah-shouting churches). It is important to note that these Pentecostals that emerged among these tribal believers in North India began with classical Pentecostal theological tenets but gradually developed theological nuances in their beliefs and practices.

Even from its inception the experience of speaking in tongues was not so much interpreted as the "initial evidence" or the miraculous enabling of the Spirit-baptized believer to speak in languages they did not understand for evangelism. Rather, the outpouring of the Spirit was seen as a sign of *God's visible and dynamic presence here and now.* It was the belief in the Spirit who animated the apostles at Pentecost and who continues to be actively, dynamically, and miraculously present upon those who are filled in the Spirit. This led to a radical openness to God, in particular to an understanding that God was doing something different or new. Everyone who receives the Holy Spirit becomes a *Samarthi Gawah* (powerful witness), inspiring a lifestyle of holiness and igniting a fire for evangelism. Spirit-empowerment meant an empowerment for mission that was tethered to an eschatological expectation. These basic precepts lie behind the new direction of the progressive Christological understanding in Bhil Pentecostal theology.

What is distinct and at the same time conveys the heart and mind of classical Pentecostal devotion, belief, and practice is the functional Christological statement: Jesus as Savior, sanctifier, baptizer with the Holy Spirit, healer, and coming King. The Bhil tribal five-fold gospel succinctly but richly expresses the relationship between Christ and the believer and the holistic work of salvation in the believer.[20] However, what is remarkable about this belief is that this new experience of the Spirit is interspersed with the contextual and daily life situation, thus bringing forth distinctive Christological shades to their confessions.[21] Understanding the Bhil worldview enables appreciation of its implications for Pentecostal theology.

BHIL TRIBAL WORLD VIEW[22]

The Bhil tribal world is very similar to that of any traditional society.[23] Prior to conversion, a Bhil believer comes from a three-tier worldview, based on a close relationship between nature, human beings, and various spirit beings.[24] There is a priority in their life order of material things first, then the spirits, and ultimately a high God, who is known as *Maalik* or *Ooparwala*.[25] Further, their belief in supernatural elements makes them fearful of spirits. The promise of blessing and the fear of vengeance are both involved. This is because the Bhils believe in a number of spirits, both benevolent and malevolent.[26] On the one hand, they consider these spirits as powerful enough to keep their children from sickness, make them fertile, provide rain, and provide for the welfare of domestic animals.[27] Yet while these spirits are thought to protect people in distress, if they are not propitiated, they get angry and are believed to be capable of causing harm to life and property.[28] The fear of these spirits thus motivates the people to worship and offer sacrifices to them.[29] Within the Bhil worldview, the dead are a part of the community and can have either benevolent or malevolent dealings with those who are still alive depending on how they are treated.[30] The material needs or physical problems of the living are thus immediately attached to spirits, and the benevolent high God is sought only as a last resort.[31] Even though tribals believe in a benevolent high God, no offering or sacrifice is made for such a God, as *Ooperwala* does not harm them. Thus, in this worldview much of the interaction happens between the middle and the lower zone.[32]

Every village has a *devara* (shrine) and a *bhopa* who acts as the village priest or witch doctor.[33] The *bhopa* gains power from an intimate relationship with the spirit beings. He exercises great power and authority over the villagers, and his words are heeded. People seek the protection of the guardian spirits of their village. The priests usually ask for alcohol, cockerel, or goats for the ceremonies, or money, and if the people fail to meet these requests, they are threatened with consequences of spirit affliction.

The Bhil believe both that the spirits are responsible for disease and that human beings can induce the healing power of the spirits via ritual performance. When a person in the family gets sick, the first step in the ritual process to find healing is to go to the *bhopa*. Through ritualistic means the *bhopa* determines the cause of the sickness and prescribes a suitable ritual to appeal to the spirit beings.

In addition, magical practices are widespread among Bhil tribal people. The essence of Bhil animism is power—power of magic to control human affairs. Evil spirits (*dakan*) can be mobilized through magic and chants to oppress others. Some people afflict their enemies with sickness with the help of witches or even kill them.[34] Further, they believe that the "evil eye" causes diseases and bad luck. It can destroy family members, ruin the fortune of a person, and bring harm to domestic animals, crops, and houses. For the tribals, sin is understood essentially in relationship to the community and inter-harmony between its members.[35] To break a taboo is sin. It not only results in the provocation of the spirits, but it also incurs penalties dealt by the village council.[36]

Further, the Bhil tribal is categorized socially as India's poorest of the poor.[37] Historically the caste system and untouchability status have pushed them into the fringes of villages, deep into the forests. They have lost their identity in the caste-ridden society due to centuries of social conditioning, deprivation, and injustice. This disfigured social consciousness further works into their worldview.[38]

Thus the Bhil worldview provides us a glimpse into the real-life situation to which the Pentecostal revival arrived. Bhils made a clean break with the animistic past[39] when they encountered the power of the Holy Spirit and accepted the gospel message. With the Pentecostal revival and the messages of the gospel, the story of Jesus enters the lives of Bhil believers, and a new shape is inspired in the content of their Christological reflections.

PENTECOSTAL CHRISTOLOGY
AMONG THE BHILS (TRIBALS)

Although the Pentecostal revival gave great attention to the experience of the Spirit among the Bhils, the movement is inherently Christocentric. However, in the confessional faith the Bhil tribal believer often misinterprets the distinction between the role of Christ and of the Holy Spirit. The Bhil tribal Pentecostals pray to the Holy Spirit as they pray to Jesus, and they consider the Spirit as the healer and deliverer.[40] In spite of such a problem of grayness in understanding the person and work of the Spirit and the relationship of the Spirit to Christ, there is a rich tradition of oral

Christology informed by their Pentecostal experiences and by the transformations they have undergone.[41] They therefore have developed a progressive Christology, moving from a functional to an ontological understanding of Christ. Although many begin by seeing Jesus as the healer, exorcist, provider, and protector, their Spirit experience enables them eventually to acknowledge Jesus as the Savior, Lord, and supreme God.[42]

Jesus the healer (*Yesu Changai deta hai*)

The first Christological moment that is predominant in Bhil Pentecostal churches is Jesus as the healer.[43] Most believers who joined the Pentecostal churches encounter and accept Christ through their healing experience. Healing comes in the name of Jesus, and they confess that Jesus is the healer. Healings affect not only the person who has been healed but also the people close to them.[44] Due to the lack of health care facilities in remote villages, a large majority of people suffer from various sicknesses, while hundreds die from disease annually. Divine healing is thus needed and sought for in this context. Experience of such supernatural healing also empowers a person to reject the old religious practices as well as overcome fears of evil spirits and manipulation by traditional healers.[45] The healing is enacted by the power of the Holy Spirit. The Bhil believers develop an understanding that the healing involves not merely physical recovery or becoming healthy, but life in its totality. Healing is thus an evidence that God loves them and takes care of them. This understanding brings in a new assurance in them, that they are now empowered to heal others.

Jesus as an exorcist (*Yesu Chhutekara deta hai*)

Jesus as an exorcist is a primary faith confession of Bhil Pentecostals.[46] As noted above, they believe that many diseases are caused by spiritual attacks or disseminated by life-threatening evil practices. But the power of Jesus rescues them from the evil influence of wicked spirits as well as witch doctors.[47] Healing in the name of Jesus and deliverance from the evil spirits affects the people's social, economic, and spiritual domains in a positive way.[48] Believers now know that they can also cast out demons in the name of Jesus through prayer and faith. They now have the power to counter the evil forces that harass them.[49] This brings spiritual empowerment and leads them to the confession that Jesus Christ is unique in comparison to any other gods they ever knew.

Jesus as the provider (*Yesu Sambalta hai*)

Drawing on the confessions of Jesus as the healer and the exorcist, another predominant Christological affirmation in the Bhil Pentecostal churches is that of Jesus the provider.[50] This perception expresses a further advanced level of Christological confession. The healing of sickness and deliverance from demonic forces in the name of Jesus impart a new spiritual consciousness among the suffering people. Their newfound experience broadens the spiritual perception of the work of Jesus into other realms of their struggle, including the household, economic, and social domains, enabling them to save their hard-earned resources to provide for life needs. In the midst of extreme poverty, they experience Jesus as the provider. Further, with the Pentecostal emphasis on holiness and constant encouragement to abandon their old ways of traditional tribal life, these believers have become sober, hardworking, and God-fearing people.[51] Thus they fare better than their counterparts in the rural communities. Their change in spiritual perception empowers them to contribute generously to the church.

Jesus as the protector (*Prabhu Yishu ne mujhe Bacchaya*)

Another prominent theme that emerges from the confessional faith of tribal Pentecostal believers is the insight that Jesus is the protector.[52] This perception regarding Jesus also emerges from the intense personal struggle believers undergo. The above-explained notions of Jesus as healer, exorcist, and provider overlap with the understanding of Jesus as protector. Jesus has healed them but also continues to keep them from any possible sickness, preserve them from all possible fears, and guard them from attacks from evil spirits and persecutors. Jesus not only helps them with their struggles of life but also continues to protect their lives, their livestock, agriculture, and finances from being destroyed by demonic forces. For them, Jesus is also the rescuer from caste-ridden social ostracism and oppression, emancipating people and making them part of a caring community.

Jesus as the Savior (*Yishu mera Udharkarta*)

A significant Christological theme that is prevalent among Bhil Pentecostals is the perception of Jesus as the Savior.[53] These believers identify Jesus as the only one who saves them from their sins. The saving act of Jesus encompasses every aspect of their lives: spiritual, physical, material, and social. This concept is derived from the understanding of Jesus as the healer, exorcist, provider, and protector. As a result, they see Jesus the Savior reconciles the relationship that was broken by sinful activities, such as enmity, and establishes peace and unity among the people. In this way Jesus functions as the mediator and reconciler. Hence, Jesus the Savior is a bridge between the functional categories (such as healer, exorcist, provider, protector) and the ontological categories (such as Lord, God). It is both functional as well as ontological.[54]

Jesus as Lord (*Yesu Prabhu hai*)

A further important Christological theme dominant among the Bhil Pentecostals is the notion that Jesus is the only true Lord.[55] The word *prabhu* (Lord) is associated with Jesus Christ and indicates

His lordship over all other gods and thus to be worshipped.[56] The
concept of Jesus the Lord is developed from a reflection by the tribal
believers on the existential categories, namely, healer, exorcist, provider, and protector. Along with these four notions, the believers
also include the idea of Jesus the Savior in their reflective process.
This inclusion brings a new perception of Christ that places Him
above all. Thus, if Jesus heals, delivers, provides, protects, and for-
gives their sins to grant them peace and joy, then He is greater than
all and worthy of worship.

Jesus the supreme God (*Yesu Samprabhu Parmeshwar*)

The final Christological moment is the Bhil affirmation that
Jesus is the supreme God. They exalt Jesus above all gods and consider every other deity they know as inferior to Jesus. Jesus's care
and love, the peace and security He brings, and His extraordinary
power over other deities they followed earlier enable them to elevate
Him to the status of "High God." This "High God," who was earlier
far removed from their life struggles and pain, is now very close
to them in Jesus Christ. This notion, along with Jesus as the Lord,
forms the highest level of Christological articulation.

In summary, the Bhil Pentecostal theology emerges with the
interconnection of themes that move from functional to ontological Christology reflected from the day-to-day life and practice of
the believer. When people are healed of their illnesses or delivered
from demonic attack or possession, they acknowledge Jesus as the
healer and *exorcist*. In this new sense of empowerment they place
their full confidence in Jesus in all of their activities. Thus Bhils
understand Jesus as the *provider*. They also realize that Jesus protects them from external forces. This results in recognizing Jesus as
the *protector*.

This new understanding—Jesus as the healer, exorcist, provider,
and protector—along with the experience of the Holy Spirit and

the passionate worship atmosphere in the community, enable them to elevate Jesus into an exalted position and confess Him to be the *Savior*. Their daily struggles, joys, sorrows, and assurance of Jesus's presence in every aspect of their lives, coupled with preaching and teaching of biblical stories, especially Gospel stories, enable them to proclaim Jesus as the *Lord*. Bhil Pentecostals now proclaim that Jesus is greater than all. Consequently they understand Jesus as the supreme God.

IMPLICATIONS FOR PENTECOSTAL MISSION AND THEOLOGY

It is invaluable to learn from the creative dialogue between the Bhil Pentecostal contextual experience and in their interaction with the gospel. The people who theologize are mainly Bhil tribal people; many of them are illiterate and poor, and the majority are recent converts who hardly have basic Bible literacy. They root their understanding of Christ in the Gospels' stories, especially the Synoptic Gospels, as they are narrated and sung in church, and in their personal experience of Christ through miraculous events. The Christology they express emerges when Gospel stories crisscross with their contextual experiences.

It is interesting to note that the Bhils have individualized and theologized their Pentecostal faith by drawing from their own experiences, categories, and values. The danger of the Bhil spirit worldview is that it may become a vehicle that traps people and communities if it is overemphasized theologically.[57] The above discussion suggests that the Bhils have not been content with a stagnant Christology. Rather, their formulations have moved from an elementary stage to more advanced categories to accommodate and respond to changing life situations. This pattern of progressive movement is apparent also in the New Testament tradition.[58]

Therefore it is significant to search for those essential factors that are lacking in any Christology, including the Bhil articulation, with a view to making it more comprehensive and enduring.

Power encounters are important for Bhil Pentecostals. As a result they have a very high view of the divinity of Jesus. For a Bhil Pentecostal believer, Jesus is all powerful: able to heal, to deliver from evil spiritual and social forces, and to provide and save them from their struggles. Jesus is thus greater than all gods or the gods they worshipped, and therefore He is God. Yet in practice, the result is that the divinity of Jesus is emphasized at the expense of the humanity of Jesus. Their Christology is normally "from above," stressing Christ's divinity almost to a docetic neglect of His humanity. This unbalanced understanding may hinder them from imitating Jesus and carrying out Jesus's ministry in their surroundings, which would be harmful to the growth of the movement in its future direction.

Further, since contextual engagement determines the nature of Bhil Pentecostal Christology, the role of Jesus as the coming King is generally missing. Originally, when the revival hit the Bhils, the Pentecostal eschatology was prophetic in outlook. The movement interpreted itself as a sign of the end, the last and greatest revival before the Lord's return. But now Jesus as the coming King is a missing element in the theology of an ordinary Bhil Pentecostal, which will potentially if not actually affect the vitality of the movement in its missiological urgency.

CONCLUSION

With Pentecostalism in North India emerging forward, the Spirit revival is continuing to grow and is making its mark on Indian Christianity. We have looked into its historical origins, particularly the early revivals, and the South Indian connections in terms of revitalization and consolidation of the movement into Pentecostal communities. It is revealed that the Bhil believers' context, history, and personal and communal experiences have impacted their Christological articulations. Although these Christological themes are consonant with the larger Pentecostal tradition and with the progressive Christology and the testimony of the New Testament, a critical engagement with the larger scholarship in Pentecostalism and the broader Christian tradition is needed to rescript the Bhil Pentecostal Christological categories so that these first-generation tribal Pentecostals can build their Christian faith on more enduring ground.

Chapter 2

Pentecostalism in Sri Lanka

G. P. V. Somaratna

THE PENTECOSTAL MOVEMENT, which began in the first decade of the twentieth century in America and Europe, had an early beginning in Sri Lanka. It arrived in Sri Lanka from a number of sources and became solidified in the 1920s by the formation of the Ceylon Pentecostal Mission (CPM) and the Sri Lanka branch of the Assemblies of God. It remained a small group within the Christian minority, deriving its membership mostly from the existing Christian denominations for about half a century. It was after the 1970s that the Pentecostal churches began to experience a significant conversion growth from a non-Christian background. Important growth was seen in this period with the influence of the Charismatic movement where independent Pentecostal churches as well as the traditional churches began to wield a significant potential for growth. As a result, Pentecostal spirituality was a lifestyle no longer limited to the classical Pentecostal churches.

An attempt is made to analyze the causes for the slowness of initial growth and stagnation in the first period and the reasons behind the relative success of Pentecostalism in the second period. The non-indigenous expression of Pentecostalism and repetition of some of the mistakes made by the missionaries in the nineteenth century stand out as factors deciding the fate of Pentecostalism in the country.

The Pentecostal/Charismatic movement injected new vigor into the mainline churches, something they were lacking up to the last decades of the twentieth century. The Pentecostals emphasized the gifts of the Spirit, which they said had been neglected by the mainline denominations. They utilized the Christian cultural infrastructures already existing as their base. They built on the foundation that was provided by the traditional church but added "the excluded middle" within their praxis.[1]

HISTORICAL FOUNDATIONS AND GEOGRAPHICAL FACTORS

Roughly 10 percent of the Christian population in Sri Lanka professed the Christian faith at the time the classical Pentecostals began work in Sri Lanka in the first decade of the twentieth century. Of that number about 10 percent were Protestants who belonged to the Anglican, Methodist, Baptist, American Presbyterian, and Salvation Army denominations.[2] The major portion of the Christian community was Roman Catholic. All these churches had their own schools that the believers of their own denomination could attend. The education they provided was the passport for secular advancement. Christianity was taught in these schools; therefore the Pentecostals who came with "views of spiritual warfare" could use it as the base for their teaching community. Christianity being a religion that arrived with a colonial imprint continued to be guided and led by the leaders and policy makers in the metropolis in Europe and America.

Sri Lanka was in the British Empire until 1948, and the English language was used for administration. About 5 percent of the population, mostly middle class, spoke English in this period. Most of them professed Christianity. The early Pentecostals, who were American and British, found fertile ground in Sri Lanka to convey their message in the English language. Even evangelists who came from the Scandinavian countries were familiar with English.

Sri Lanka gained independence in 1948. The denominational Christian schools, which received assistance from the government until 1961, were nationalized in that year.[3] The percentage of Christians in the country therefore declined from about 10 percent to less than 8 percent. The total Christian population in Sri Lanka according to the national census of 2012 is 7.65 percent. Of that number about 85 percent are Roman Catholics. Protestants are about 1.5 percent of the total number. The Pentecostals would be less than 0.5. It is a minority in a minority religious group. Pentecostals are also divided into hundreds of small groups. Remarking on this division, a Hindu is supposed to have said, "We have over 330 million gods, and they are in one place of worship. On the other hand, the Christians have only one God, but you cannot worship Him together in one place."[4]

One factor was that Sri Lanka was located in a strategically important place of travel in the Indian Ocean. Those itinerant Pentecostal evangelists who traveled to New Zealand and Australia from Europe had to stop in Colombo after the Suez Canal was opened in 1869.[5] The other factor that helped the Pentecostals come to Sri Lanka was the nearness to South India, where most Pentecostal evangelists were active in the early years of the twentieth century. These evangelists found it easy to travel to Sri Lanka from South India and find a group of people who spoke Tamil, which is an important South Indian language. Some evangelists used Sri Lanka as the springboard for their missions in neighboring India.

ITINERANT AND LOCAL EVANGELISTS

The traditional Protestant denominations were introduced officially by missionary organizations located in Europe and America.
Their missions were maintained by the missionaries sent from the
mother church. Pentecostalism did not begin like that. Itinerant
evangelists were the primary agency by which Pentecostalism
spread in the early years. These traveling evangelists brought the
gospel to the believing community and stayed a few days or weeks
before moving on to another country. Among them Sadhu Sundar
Singh (in Ceylon May–June 1918) was significant.[6] Though he was
not a Pentecostal, his mysticism drew large crowds to his meetings.
Healing and miraculous occurrences were reported in the meetings
during his six weeks' stay. He held meetings in Jaffna, Colombo,
Kandy, and Galle. His meetings at the Methodist church in Galle in
particular made a deep impression upon the young Alwin de Alwis
(ca. 1901–1967), which shaped the latter's concepts of a radically
indigenous ministry that later found expression in the founding of
the Ceylon Pentecostal Mission.

An Anglican spiritual healer named James Moore Hickson
(1868–1933), who had a remarkable healing gift, arrived in
November 1920 in Colombo and sought to restore the healing ministry to the church at large.[7] Smith Wigglesworth (1869–1947) was
an Englishman who traveled to several countries as an itinerant
evangelist. He arrived in Sri Lanka on his way to Australia and
conducted a number of meetings in Galle and Colombo in January
and February 1922. On another visit in 1926 the campaign began on
March 5. Walter Clifford (1887–1973), who was there on these occasions, wrote: "Many people were helped by rising from their seats
in faith and saying, 'Jesus healed me,' without the prayers of the
evangelist at all. One woman, who had eruptions on her arms and
burning sensations caused by these eruptions, was healed as she

sat in her seat. Truly these were wonderful days. God's Spirit was poured out and Jesus was glorified. Brother Wigglesworth has been with us in Colombo, ministering for two weeks."[8] He came again in 1927, which impacted several who later became the leaders of the Assemblies of God.

Early local evangelists like D. E. Dias Wanigasekera, S. A. de Alwis, and Charles F. Hettiaratchy were ministers of the Church Missionary Society (CMS) who were convinced by the Pentecostal message. They had sought the baptism of the Spirit even though the CMS did not subscribe to such contingencies. The three of them separately commenced a ministry of their own in the Kandy area. Wanigasekera was converted to Pentecostalism in India in 1907. Charles F. Hettiaratchy was influenced by the Beruldsen family, who pioneered the Pentecostal ministry in Edinburgh, Scotland, in 1910.

RESIDENT EVANGELISTS

William David Grier (1888–1965) and his wife were the first recorded Pentecostal missionaries to Sri Lanka. They arrived in 1913 and returned to America in 1917. He traveled to major cities of the country conducting evangelistic meetings. The fruits of his ministry were picked up by the later arrivals. S. A. de Alwis stated that W. D. Grier was responsible for his conversion to Pentecostalism in 1913.[9]

A Danish actress, Anna Lewini (1876–1951), who was radically converted under the ministry of Thomas Barratt (1862–1940), came to Sri Lanka from Denmark for the first time in 1919 with two other missionary ladies, Sisters Pauline and Margaret, about whom nothing else is now known. She returned to Denmark in June 1920 after more than one year's work in Sri Lanka. She returned from Denmark to Sri Lanka in 1923. Lewini welcomed the arrival of Rev.

Walter Clifford, who was instrumental in founding the Assemblies of God (AG) in Sri Lanka, and cooperated with him.

She became the channel of converting some significant people who later became very active as Pentecostal leaders. John Samuel Wickramaratne, a customs officer and Baptist laypreacher, and father of Rev. Colton Wickramaratne, was one of them. Another Baptist laypreacher, J. J. B. de Silva, and the founders of CPM, Alwin de Alwis and Ramankutty Paul (1881–1947), are well-known converts of Lewini. Wickramaratne and de Silva eventually took charge of the work in the outstations.

The output of the women missionaries in the foundational years of Pentecostalism is significant. Anna Lewini, Lilian Everett (d. August 1972), and Grace Watson (d. April 1972) were active missionaries from the very beginning of the Pentecostal missionary work. The latter two were ministering at the Bethany Mission, Nugegoda. In the 1930s Kathleen Long and Rosa Reineker arrived. They took up the work in Galle and Jaffna respectively. They are especially important for the work they did to start Sunday schools in the AG church on the island.

Walter Clifford first came to Colombo in November 1923 as an itinerant evangelist and held meetings for about five months. Before he left Sri Lanka in April 1924, the first Pentecostal Assembly was formed in Colombo. When Clifford received a definite invitation to return to Ceylon later in 1924, Wickramaratne[10] and de Silva, who were disciples of Lewini, had already started centers in Colombo, Jaffna, and Kandy.[11]

MISSIONARIES

In the early years the Spirit-led cooperative network of ministries with input from Scandinavia, Britain, Australia, India, and America contributed to the formation of a small group of Pentecostals in Sri

Lanka. They did not represent a missionary organization. The situation changed with the official affiliation of the work by Walter Clifford with the Assemblies of God in Springfield in America in 1929.

Walter Clifford, who worked with Anna Lewini at the Glad Tiding Hall in Colombo, became the founder of Assemblies of God Sri Lanka in 1924. When Clifford arrived in 1925 on a permanent basis in Colombo, Anna Lewini willingly handed over the leadership of work begun by her. This became the beginning of the Assemblies of God of Ceylon.

Initially the Assemblies of God in Ceylon was organized as part of the South India and Ceylon District Council in 1929. Thereafter the work of the itinerant Pentecostal evangelists came under the sponsorship of the Assemblies of God. In addition, the mother mission in America also sent missionaries to assist Water Clifford, who was their agent in Sri Lanka. However, Clifford as head of the work in Sri Lanka had served more than two decades. By 1947 AG Ceylon was incorporated by an Act of Parliament and became an independent entity recognized by the government of Sri Lanka. It had three tabernacles, eight outstation churches, six missionaries, twelve local full-time workers, and about fifteen hundred believers.

The Assemblies of God by and large followed the principles of the other Protestant missionary organizations. These evangelists were guided by the rules of the Assemblies of God headquarters in Springfield. They were not allowed to marry the local non-Europeans. They were expected to retire at a certain age and return to their home countries if they were willing. The gap between the locals and European evangelists of the Pentecostal church was similar to other European missionaries. There was no incarnational aspect in their ministry, thus making it another foreign Christian institution. It was more foreign than the traditional Roman Catholic and Protestant denominations. The Assemblies of God remained a part of the American mission. However, Clifford, as the head of the work in Sri Lanka, had served more as a pastor than as an administrator. By this time the traditional Christian denominations had considered employing more indigenous workers and placed some of them in leadership positions. The Assemblies of God, on the other hand, remained foreign managed, even after national independence. The Assemblies of God was small and not very significant as a body of Christians in Sri Lanka.

CEYLON PENTECOSTAL MISSION

The Ceylon Pentecostal Mission, which was founded in 1923,[12] was an indigenous Christian sect. The founding fathers of the group were Alwin R. de Alwis and Ramankutty Paul.[13] This group is regarded as a breakaway from the fellowship under Anna Lewini at Glad Tiding Hall. When Walter Clifford arrived in September 1925, the rift between the Glad Tiding Hall of Anna Lewini and the founders of the CPM had already taken place.[14]

From its inception the administration of the CPM was very simple. The members emphasized an ascetic approach to Christian living. They insisted that those who believed that they had a calling on them to the full-time ministry be celibate. Men and women who joined the ministry on a full-time basis lived in faith homes[15] in separate compartments. The leaders of the faith homes were always men. They also held all their assets in common in their faith homes. The private ownership of property was discouraged.

The Sunday worship service and other religious gatherings were conducted in the hall of these faith homes. All three national languages were used in ministry; therefore every worker of CPM had to be familiar with Sinhala, Tamil, and English. As time passed, they began to have a hierarchical gradation known as believer, worker, pastor, chief pastor, and senior pastor.

Their exclusive tendencies made it difficult to attract believers from non-Christian backgrounds. The CPM insisted on divine healing and therefore discouraged the use of medicine. Fasting and prayer was used instead of medicine. Many who came from a Buddhist background for healing did not wish to come back for regular worship even if they experienced healing. The popular religious practices within the Buddhist and Hindu religions had healing rituals, which they considered the work of the lower pantheon of the celestial hierarchy. They equated Pentecostal practices with this form of their religion for which they made payments. Pentecostal preaching was unintelligible to the non-Christians as the preaching was targeted to those who were already familiar with basic Christian teachings and familiar with Christian Scripture. Preachers randomly quoted the Bible in their sermons. Those who were not familiar with the Bible could not follow the sermons, which were the main part of their worship service.

The Ceylon Pentecostal Mission, like the Assemblies of God in 1948, had about fifteen hundred believers throughout the country. The majority of the believers of these two denominations had come from various Christian denominations. They were already Christians but were seeking a teaching that they believed to be closer to that of New Testament times. The Ceylon Pentecostal Mission called itself a full-gospel Pentecostal mission. They also appreciated the emphasis on the display of spiritual power in the Pentecostal churches. In both cases the CPM teaching was not intelligible to the non-Christians. Their practice of austerity and rigid discipline discouraged the recruitment of new believers.

LOCAL BARRIERS FOR GROWTH AND FOREIGN DEVELOPMENTS

The Pentecostals in the period prior to independence were confined mostly to English-speaking communities. English-educated middle class Sinhalese, Tamils, and Burghers were attracted to the early Assemblies of God. The Ceylon Pentecostal Mission was an indigenous organization. Even there, under the influence of Alwin R. de Alwis, the English-speaking middle class had the upper hand. However, Ramankutty Paul, being a Malayali, attracted the local Malayalis and to a certain extent Tamil-speaking believers to the church. The exclusive nature of the CPM did not attract large numbers of believers to their church on a permanent basis.

The early Pentecostals placed a high value on religious experience and showed a preference for oral communication. Hence CPM did not have any educational institutions to instruct the children of their believers. On the other hand, the traditional missionaries could attract people through their schools. The classical Pentecostals, in fact, rejected education. Even the AG contemplated starting a Bible school only more than three decades after it came into existence. Neither the CPM nor the AG had a system of schools similar to traditional Protestants who used these institutions to mold and instruct their children. They did not apply for assisted status for maintenance of schools from the government, which was freely available to Christian educational establishments in this period.

Unlike the mainline denominations, the CPM did not receive foreign funds for its maintenance or personnel for its guidance. Yet it had sufficient funds even to embark on missionary activities abroad. Although the number of believers in the CPM was limited, they insisted on the payment of tithes by all believers. The English-speaking believers who were in government employment and held entrepreneurial positions were able to support the church and even

25

to embark on a program of foreign missions. The Buddhists and Hindus who attended their healing meetings often contributed lavishly if they felt that their problem was answered. Under Alwin de Alwis the CPM was able to open faith homes in Malaya and South India. In addition, through the Sri Lankan migrants, faith homes were introduced in the United States, the United Kingdom, Canada, France, Switzerland, and Jamaica. One can notice more attention given to foreign work in the CPM than local work. This seems to be mostly because of the sensation attached to it. The same kind of ascetic practices were introduced to the faith homes abroad. CPM insisted that a core of Christian believers who were prepared to be the bride of Christ remain as a small group in all these countries. Their contribution to the Christian faith in Sri Lanka therefore was limited within their group. Their impact on the nation was marginal.

THEOLOGICAL TRAINING

Although the CPM rejected any formal theological education for its workers, it insisted on the study of the Bible and prayer. It did not have any foreign support. It did not maintain a bank account. It did not maintain any documents pertaining to its activities throughout its history. Therefore there is no archival material available. Each faith home was financed and governed indigenously. Rules and regulations of the mission were given by word of mouth, and some of the traditional practices have been developed on the way. The leader of the group until 1962 was Alwin R. de Alwis. His ability to utilize English books helped him to guide the mission. Its main method of giving religious instruction was through the annual conventions where the believers of the entire CPM were gathered in one place.

The practice of transferring pastors and workers from one faith home to another was helpful in preventing the teachings of one person dominating in an atmosphere where oral instruction was emphasized. Prophesies and words of knowledge often became the guiding post of these teachings.

The early missionaries of the Assemblies of God also were simple believers with a heart for mission. Even they did not have any theological education as they were not appointed by a missionary organization. Most of them were individuals who came to the island as evangelists without theological qualifications. Carl Graves may be regarded as the first Assemblies of God missionary in Sri Lanka who had a theological degree from a theological seminary. When he arrived in 1931, he embarked on a program of training a limited number of pastoral assistants. For that purpose he opened a Bible college in Galle in 1934 even though the AG began missionary work in Sri Lanka in 1914. The number of students who entered the school was few. It had a zigzag history. In fact, the first batch of nine students graduated only in 1951. Even then this Bible college was discontinued in 1959.

The mainline churches shunned the Pentecostals after an initial period of cooperation. They blamed the Pentecostals for "sheep stealing." It is true that most of the followers of the CPM and AG came from individuals who left the mainline churches looking for a more tangible form of Christianity. Very few Buddhist, Hindu, and Muslim converts were won. Many believers from mainline churches attended meetings of the Pentecostal churches for specific needs. This was usually done without allowing it to be known by their own churches. Those who were caught were often disciplined.

The two Pentecostal churches in Sri Lanka in the period before independence derived their membership mostly from the mainline Protestant and Catholic churches. Therefore they could not contribute to the growth of Christianity in this period in Sri Lanka. Pentecostalism under the CPM and AG failed to make an impact on the mainline churches because of their exclusive nature. The absence of elementary and secondary schools among these Pentecostal churches discouraged those parents who were interested in the education of their children.

Among these two Pentecostal bodies the CPM had created a secluded society. It typically involved separation from the community at large. Theirs was a devotional practice of individuals who lived ascetic and cloistered lives dedicated to Christian worship. Therefore their impact was limited to their own believers. The inadequate training of the pastors other than in the use of the English translation of the Bible together with the Sinhala and Tamil translations was limited. Their teaching of the believers was inadequate because they spoke only to the believing Christians. There was no attention to the non-Christians in their teaching.

The Assemblies of God has been an organization that depended on lay leadership. They had the imprint of the mother church in America just like the other Protestant churches serving in Sri Lanka. The leadership was in the hands of English-speaking foreigners and some local individuals. Therefore they remained a small and alien body.

SECOND PERIOD

After Sri Lanka gained independence in 1948, the inhibitions that the local Christians had regarding the management of the church gradually dissipated. The missionaries slowly loosened the grip they had on the traditional churches, and their leadership came under the nationals. The leader of the Assemblies of God, Walter Clifford, left Sri Lanka in 1948, the year of independence.

In the meantime, the missionaries were being criticized in the public media and nationalist political forums. The independence of the country also took away the freedom to act in the manner that the missionaries had done under the British Raj. The mother missions were also unable to spend on missions as a result of the destruction caused by World War II. Therefore the missionary output in the post-independence era became less and less significant. The elections of 1956 brought a populist government under the leadership of Prime Minister S. W. R. D. Bandaranaike.[16] The Buddhist lobby forced him to curtail missionary activities. He went to the extent of prohibiting the hospital work done by the Sisters of the Holy Family, whose compassionate care encouraged many to embrace Christianity. In 1961 the Sri Lankan government nationalized the Christian denominational schools, asserting that they were agencies for conversion. In 1963 a coup d'état organized by some Christian leaders in the armed forces against the government was discovered. That paved the way for the suppression of most of the privileges enjoyed by the Christian missions. The visas of the missionaries also came under restrictions.

New Pentecostalism

Defining Pentecostalism in this period is a difficult task. Theologians and historians have used very broad definitions. The term has been applied to all churches and movements that emphasize the working of the Spirit both on phenomenological and theological grounds.[17] The new Pentecostals are often called Charismatic Christians and occasionally renewalists. Charismatic Christianity is often categorized into three separate groups: Pentecostalism, the Charismatic movement, and neo-Charismatic movements. There is a considerable overlap among these groups. This is a form of Christianity that emphasizes the work of the Holy Spirit, spiritual gifts, and modern-day miracles. This adoption of Pentecostal beliefs by those in the historic churches became known as the Charismatic movement. Charismatic believers have shared with Pentecostals an emphasis on the gifts of the Spirit but remained a part of their mainline churches. They are like Pentecostals in many ways, but there are some who do not believe that glossolalia is an essential evidence of Spirit baptism. Early Pentecostals were often marginalized within the larger Christian community. However, Pentecostal beliefs have penetrated within the mainline Protestant denominations since the 1970s in Sri Lanka. The same experience was noticed in the global Roman Catholic Church from 1967, and its impact in Sri Lanka has been noticeable since 1972.

Pentecostal and Charismatic Christian churches have experienced a tremendous growth since the 1980s in Sri Lanka. Almost every important village and city has at least one center of worship conducted by a person converted from the same community. On average these worship centers vary from about thirty to one hundred believers.

DEPARTURE OF MISSIONARIES FROM THE ASSEMBLIES OF GOD

All the missionaries of the Assemblies of God left Sri Lanka in the 1960s. This allowed the local leaders to take the mission into their own hands and contextualize the Christian message to suit the situation in Sri Lanka. The leadership of Colton Wickramaratne that began in the 1960s with the departure of the missionaries paved the way for the expansion of the Assemblies of God church in all parts of the country. By 2010 the Assemblies of God had more members than the biggest Protestant church, the Anglican Church in Sri Lanka.

In 1950 the presence of Swedish Pentecostal missionaries paved the way for the formation of the Fellowship of Free Churches. Some Swedish missionaries who were expelled from China in the 1950s came to Sri Lanka as evangelists. Their work in the 1950s was significant because they trained local leaders while engaged in itinerant evangelism. In 1974 they started a Bible school in Kandy to train pastors locally. Swedish Pentecostal churches were established in Jaffna, Batticaloa, Kandy, Nuwara Eliya, and Colombo. Through these main churches hundreds of branch churches have emerged all over the country.[18]

In the 1980s a number of American Pentecostal churches began to act through local evangelists to establish their own brand of Pentecostal churches. The Foursquare movement began through a missionary named Richard Kaiser in 1979.[19] It was a small group when he left Sri Lanka in 1983. However, under the leadership of Leslie Keegal who is a Sri Lankan, the church has grown in all parts of Sri Lanka. In 2010 the estimated number of Foursquare churches was more than five hundred.

There are many other American Pentecostal groups: the Church of God (Cleveland, Tennessee), Wesleyan Methodist, Church of God in Christ, Nazarene Church, and Apostolic Faith Church, to name but a few. The Apostolic Church, however, is a Pentecostal denomination with affiliations to the apostolic church in England. There are some Pentecostal churches with affiliations to some churches in India. In addition to these foreign affiliated churches, a large number of independent churches are scattered all over the island. Some of them have branches in other parts of the country. The number exceeds one hundred; therefore it is not possible to name all of them. All these groups have experienced growth since the 1980s. Most of the growth may be attributed to tangible results to prayers and koinonia fellowship in these churches.

Proliferation of Bible Schools
and Megachurches

Neo-Pentecostal groups in Sri Lanka have focused most of their attention on evangelistic work and on the training of Indian evangelists and pastors. The Pentecostal and Charismatic churches there have started a large number of theological training institutions in the country. The Assemblies of God Bible College (1974),[20] Lanka Bible College (1974), Calvary Bible School (1983), Homsa Theological Seminary in Hatton (1990), Colombo Theological Seminary (1994), Calvary Theological Seminary (1998), Baldaeus Theological Seminary in Trincomalee (1999), Foursquare Bible School (2002), Pentecostal Bible Seminary (2006), and Galle Bible School (2002) are some theological institutions that award theological degrees. Some are affiliated with the Asia Theological Association. Although all of them do not carry the label Pentecostal, the majority of their students are Pentecostals. They believe in Charismatic gifts such as prophesy, glossolalia, glossographia, and interpretation of tongues; other Pentecostal phenomena, including prayer for the sick, falling down and shaking, as well as restoration of the offices of apostle and prophet, are present. There are many theological schools that have not received any accreditation from an authorized body. In addition there are a large number of pastor training institutions all over the country.

There is a tendency among new and old believers of the Christian faith to seek something different, new, and exciting in their worship. It appears that the megachurch is a wonderful fantasy, a spiritual dream-come-true to some. These are not simply large churches, but have regular weekly attendance from one thousand or more. The Pentecostal/Charismatic movement has contributed to the formation of several megachurches in Colombo. The People's Church of Narahenpita of the Assemblies of God, Calvary Church at Kirulapone, Living Way Foursquare Gospel Church at Delkanda, and King's Revival Church in Ratmalana are noteworthy. These churches accommodate more than one thousand in one session of worship on a Sunday. Critics have complained that there is no intimate fellowship in these churches. Some of these churches have introduced the cell-group method to put the responsibility for discipleship outside the church campus, in homes, where intimate contact and ministry are possible. One-on-one is the other method that they have adopted to develop relationships.

CATHOLIC PENTECOSTALISM AND ECUMENICAL REACTIONS

In the Roman Catholic tradition there is clear evidence of sporadic outpourings of the Holy Spirit. There are Catholic groups with Pentecostal-like experiences and a common emphasis on the Holy Spirit that have no traditional Pentecostal or Charismatic denominational connections. The Roman Catholic Church in Sri Lanka came under Pentecostal influence in 1970. Father Oscar Abeyratne, spiritual director of Pubuduwa (revival), has led the Catholic Charismatic renewal movement since the early seventies. This has grown to the extent of forming Catholic groups similar to megachurches. The meetings held at the Hall of St. Peter's College in Colombo under the leadership of laypersons attract thousands of Catholics for weekly worship services where Pentecostal kinds of practices are encouraged.

The growth of Charismatic and Pentecostal churches has brought opposition from some sections of the traditional Christian denominations. The Roman Catholic Church has been one of most powerful opponents against new Protestant Charismatic churches in Sri Lanka. It has gone to the extent of siding with Buddhists and Hindus, even to the extent of supporting the anti-conversion bills brought before the Parliament on several occasions. The Catholic Church's argument is that it has lost more than 10 percent of its believers to the Pentecostal and Charismatic churches since the 1980s. However, the critics within the Catholic Church itself have stated that the Charismatic churches have won the Catholics because of the failures of the Catholic establishment to provide sufficient spiritual nourishment. However, there has been a Charismatic and Pentecostal type of worship service conducted in the Catholic Church under the name *Pubuduwa* (revival). Some Catholic fathers have objected to even this development because the believers now go around praying for the sick, blessing houses, and so on, thereby making the Catholic priests less important. Therefore the policy of the Catholic Church has varied from diocese to diocese.

There is a very small minority of Christians who have been influenced by the modern Western scientific worldview and liberal theology. As the adage indicates, "Anglicanism is a unity in diversity."[21] Though they are a small number, they make a big impression in the public because of the ability to get their views published in the media. The Church of Ceylon also had a hostile attitude to the Charismatic movement even within the Anglican church, until the appointment of the new bishop, Dhiloraj Ranjith Canagasabey, in 2010.

NON-CHRISTIANS

Buddhist, Hindu, and Muslim opposition to the Charismatic churches also has increased since 1980 in a significant way.[22] The Buddhists have been more hostile to Pentecostals and Charismatic churches because of the conversion of a large number of Buddhists to Christianity. There is a good representation of Buddhist monks among the converts; many of them have become pastors of new congregations. The Buddhist lobby has accused the Pentecostals and Charismatic groups of using unethical methods for the conversion of Buddhists, such as offering money, jobs, and other material benefits to convert people. Christians have denied those allegations.

Despite their opposition, the Buddhists have not been able to curtail the tide of conversions in rural and urban areas of Sri Lanka. Therefore they have resorted to numerous actions to stop and even to eradicate the growth of Christianity among the Buddhists. They have burned and destroyed worship centers, assaulted pastors and their families, and have displayed posters accusing the Christians of using nefarious means to convert Buddhists. The Buddhist criticism of Christian charity is based on the differences in the world-views of the two religions. Buddhists look at issues through the karmic concept where religious activities are done in order to gain merit, whereas Christianity is based on a personal relationship with God, and Christians do charitable works because of the commandment to "love your neighbor."

The Buddhists have tried vilifying Christians in every possible way, and failing in all these means, they have made several attempts to make conversions to a religion other than the religion of the parents illegal. These legal enforcements also have failed to receive the approval of the Parliament. Nevertheless, there is the difficulty of building new Christian worship centers because of the extra-parliamentary actions. Religious instruction in schools in Sri Lanka is compulsory. However, the education of children in the Christian religion has been curtailed as the government schools enforce Buddhism on the children in the school curriculum.[23]

GROWTH AND GOVERNMENT AND QUASI-GOVERNMENT ACTION

The statistics maintained by the Evangelical Alliance of Sri Lanka (EASL) show that there are over one thousand churches registered with the EASL. The rival organization known as the National Christian Fellowship (1999) has about two hundred church bodies registered under it. The Shepherd's Fellowship (2000) is another such organization, which has about two hundred churches and organizations. However, there is an overlapping of membership in these three organizations. According to them, these organizations have been formed for security purposes. In addition, in each of the twenty-five administrative districts there are Pastors' Fellowship organizations. These are ad hoc organizations that meet mainly for fellowship, prayer, cooperation, and to discuss the issues in the area. This kind of fellowship has become a source of strength to the threatened churches because of the recurrent harassment coming from Buddhists and other organizations. Since most of these churches are based on individual pastors, they need such a gathering to give them social support. The majority of pastors scattered all over the country have no connection with any organization to advise them on doctrinal issues. They are based on personalities rather than doctrines. Therefore the organizations of Pastors' Fellowships, which cut across all denominational boundaries, have been useful. There is a remarkable unity among the two ethnic groups in these Pastors' Fellowships.

Yet with growth, over the past several years Sri Lanka's Christians of all varieties, Pentecostals, Catholics, and Protestants, have suffered severe persecution at the hands of militant Buddhist groups. Pastors and believers have been harassed and churches vandalized. Pentecostal and Charismatic churches have been burned, and Bibles have been destroyed. Christian suffering is not uncommon in Sri Lanka. The parliamentary democracy where the popularity with the majority counts has become a hindrance to the Pentecostal movement in Sri Lanka. The parliamentarians who seek a major quota of electoral votes have a tendency to please the Buddhists. In 2004, when the United National Party was in power, there were a number of Roman Catholics, Anglicans, and several powerful Pentecostals in the ruling party in the Parliament. It was during that period that the Buddhist militia went around the country destroying churches and intimidating the believers. The Christian members of the ruling party did not have any significant voice to make their protest known, believing that they would lose their votes.[24]

When it comes to the local levels, there is also hostility from the government officials and even the police. Nationalist Buddhist groups such as Bodu Bala Sena (Buddhist Force) and Ravana Balaya have campaigned against religious minorities in Sri Lanka. Although they say they are nonviolent, they systematically attacked Christian churches and prayer centers in the recent past.[25] The complaints of the Christians with regard to harassment have not often been taken into account. Some officers in charge of law and order have shown hostility to new Christian worship centers.[26] Christians have found it difficult to get legal approval from the local government agencies for plans to build new churches.

FUTURE OF PENTECOSTALISM IN SRI LANKA: LITURGY, ETHICS, AND CLASS DIFFERENCES

The growth of Pentecostal churches in Sri Lanka resulted in the necessity of pastors and workers to disciple the new believers and to look after the existing Christian community. Because of the urgency of the need there has been an influx into these new churches of pastors who have had very little training to be pastors. Most of them are first-generation believers whose religious background is Buddhist or Hindu. Among these pastors there are quite a number who are school dropouts; therefore they have very little academic training to equip them to bear the burden of the pastoral work. The idea of "calling" for Christian servanthood is misunderstood in these new churches. It is often mistaken for a glamorous profession. There is a dependence on miracles and seeking prosperity through Christian ministry. Many of the pastors seek financial gain, prestige, and power through the pastoral profession.

The leadership of the Pentecostal churches is in the hands of urban English-speaking middle-class persons. Their work in the local languages is very poor. There is a tendency for dependency on foreign funds by rural as well as urban leaders. There is a display of strong individualism among the Pentecostal pastors; therefore there is a proliferation of independent churches. Disciplining such pastors has been a difficult task, and so personal failures are very common. For example, one pastor praised God in the testimony time in his church for his son's successful entrance to Australia by illegal means.

The Pentecostal and Charismatic worship services follow the same pattern everywhere. Although they say that they do not believe in liturgy, their own liturgy is to have an average of a half hour of singing, notices, one hour of sermon, followed by prayers for individual needs. In their worship services one would notice spontaneity in personal conduct as well as in corporate worship. Very often repetitive words are uttered in between singing. The absence of traditional liturgy seems to create chaos in these worship services. Similarly, disregard for local customs has created hostilities and misunderstanding among the nonbelievers. One can notice the absence of traditional respect for the things associated with religion. Lack of religious symbols in the worship services and the places of worship have a tendency to reduce the respect and honor due to God and Christ.

Lack of ethical teaching while giving emphasis to miracles has eroded the moral aspect of Christianity. The new believers have lost their Buddhist ethical teaching that they followed earlier. The Pentecostal churches do not have any place for the Ten Commandments, the Lord's Prayer, or any kind of credal statement in their Sunday worship. Many of the new pastors do not know even the Ten Commandments, which is the base of Christian morality. As a result there is an erosion of respect for parents and elders among the new Christians. The habit of prostrating before parents that children do before going to school or at any other important time has been given up by interpreting it as worship. While taking away the Buddhist moral base, the Pentecostals have left a vacuum in the moral life of the new Christians that they bring into their fold.

Criticism of other religions in Pentecostal meetings has created hostility against the Pentecostals. Their critical attitude to Roman Catholicism and other forms of traditional Christianity bewilders the Buddhists and Hindus who treat all Christian groups as one.

Pentecostal churches from the beginning have had the social class difference on account of the language used. The Pentecostals united in many ways irrespective of the ethnic lines that have divided the Sri Lanka nations in recent years. What hinders the growth of the movement is its domination by small groups of English-educated urban middle-class Christians. The leadership is in their hands; therefore decisions are made by them. The noteworthy factor is that they subscribe not only to Western forms of worship but also to Western social habits. Birthday parties, large-scale wedding ceremonies, anniversaries, and other forms of tamashas are very common. The rural Christians who come from non-Christian backgrounds and are not used to these kinds of activities get hooked onto these habits. The lack of knowledge of Sinhala and Tamil among the leadership of the Pentecostal church is very much prominent in the hymns, musical instruments, and forms of social address in their meetings. In this manner division found in the colonial era between the elite and the rest is continued, thereby hindering the indigenization of the Christian faith.[27]

ANALYSIS

The new Pentecostal churches are found in all parts of the country. They cover all ethnic groups found in Sri Lanka. One may find all ethnic, caste, and social groups in one congregation. Liberal giving by the believers makes it possible to maintain the pastors and the work, even in rural areas.

The Pentecostal/Charismatic movement in Sri Lanka is by no means a cohesive one. However, there are some things and beliefs that are commonly shared. Yet even within this cohesion there can be wide-ranging positions. The churches identified with this movement would in general be theologically conservative. But this conservatism can range from rigid fundamentalism to open evangelicalism. Almost all the churches in the movement tend toward less structured and free worship, but some would take the best of other spiritual and liturgical traditions with much more seriousness than others. All would be open to the speaking of tongues. But some would follow the classical Pentecostal doctrine of insisting on a post-conversion experience of the Holy Spirit.

The Pentecostal churches scattered all over the island often get foreign support to carry out their work. However, this is sporadic and targeted to a special task. There are foreign individuals and Sri Lankan expatriates who send love gifts to various Charismatic churches. Since these gifts are sporadic and ad hoc, churches cannot depend on them to build their ministries.

Although the reading of the Bible is lacking in the Sunday worship services of the Pentecostal churches, ordinary believers are encouraged to read the Bible daily and pray. However, there is a necessity to improve the reading habits. These churches are Bible based and miracles oriented; therefore people are inclined to read the Bible. This is possible in Sri Lanka, where literacy is above 95 percent.

Pentecostal churches have several problems in Sri Lanka because every religious group is trying to marginalize them. This includes traditional Christians. They have been able to overcome most of this opposition with prayer and fellowship. Most of these churches are led by people who were born and bred in the locality; therefore they do not run away in the face of opposition.

Pentecostal believers are scattered in the country in villages and cities. Therefore they are not concentrated in one area like the Muslims. This makes it difficult to get their children even a rudimentary Christian education in schools. There is a heavy responsibility on the parents and pastors to educate their children in the newfound Christian faith.

There is a criticism that some of the Pentecostal churches display an anti-national attitude. They do not hoist the national flag on national days of importance. They do not sing the national anthem on their festivals and special occasions. They do not seem to take pride in their national heritage. This needs serious attention when the country is moving toward national integration. The leaders of Charismatic churches do not seem to have a knowledge of national history or of church history of Sri Lanka.

They seem to have a kind of persecution complex where they even go to the extent of inviting persecution. For example, the noise in their worship services and the habit of destroying statues and other religious objects have repeatedly brought the wrath of the Buddhists and Hindus. Yet the practices have continued without any learning from the past.

In the third millennium the universal church is likely to find the majority of its adherents living in the two-thirds world in the

Southern Hemisphere and practicing a Pentecostal spirituality. Pentecostal missionary efforts reflect a spirituality that is characterized by an absence of the heritage that built it during the last two thousand years. The absence of a liturgy and the dependence on popular songs and lengthy sermons may not quench the spiritual thirst of the believers in the two-thirds world.

CONCLUSION

The Pentecostal movement in Sri Lanka is nearly one hundred years old. However, its impact on society and the Christian church at large was limited in the first half century of its existence. Both the Ceylon Pentecostal Mission and Assemblies of God were exclusive bodies. In the period after independence, however, the Pentecostal teaching has been able stop the tide of decline of the Christian community. The Protestant and Roman Catholic Churches that took the Charismatic movement as a challenge have also injected the vigor of Pentecostal form of worship and practice into their churches. The new Pentecostals have been able to stop the decline of the percentage of Christianity in the population of Sri Lanka. In 1981 the percentage of Christians was 7.5. The prophets of doom forecasted the possibility of disappearance of Christians from Sri Lanka. Their hope has been shattered as the 2012 census shows the Christian percentage as 7.65 despite the possible under-enumeration. We shall see what happens next.

Chapter 3

Indian Pentecostalism in Kerala and the Diaspora: Living Locally Defined Holiness in a Globalized World

Thomson K. Mathew

ERALA, THE SOUTHWESTERN state of India on the coast of the Arabian Sea, is the cradle of Indian Pentecostalism. Although it is deeply connected to the Azusa revival, Indian Pentecostalism traces its history more directly to the pre-Pentecostal revivals in India and Panditha Ramabai's Mukti Mission in North India. Headquarters of all major classical Pentecostal denominations in India are still in Kerala, the state that is the home of Saint Thomas Christians, ecclesiastical descendants of the disciple of Jesus who is believed to have arrived in India in AD 52 (AD 57 by some accounts), evangelizing the Hindus and establishing Christian churches.[1]

This essay attempts to trace the history and global growth of the Indian Pentecostal movement with a particular focus on its origins in Kerala. Current challenges facing the classical Pentecostals, particularly Keralite Pentecostals, in light of the explosive growth of the wider Spirit-empowered movement deserve study. This chapter reviews the major challenges discussed in bilingual (Malayalam and English) sources within the classical Pentecostal movement. Certain issues underlying these challenges are identified in this

process and analyzed from a historical critical perspective, producing some recommendations that might open the movement for
renewal.

INDIAN PENTECOSTALISM IN KERALA

Western missionaries sent by both private and denominational sup-
porters were instrumental in the establishment of Pentecostalism
in Kerala. The Assemblies of God and Church of God (Cleveland,
TN) missionaries played major roles in the establishment of early
Pentecostalism in India. The most influential among them in Kerala
was Robert Cook, who started as an independent missionary, joined
the Assemblies of God, and then became independent again, later
to affiliate with the Church of God (Cleveland, TN).[2] The work of
the missionaries continued successfully under their denominational
banners with supervisory connections to their respective Western
headquarters offices, but post-independent India provided the extra
momentum to propel the indigenous Pentecostal movement further, creating leaders such as K. E. Abraham and P. J. Thomas and
denominations like the India Pentecostal Church (IPC) and Sharon
Pentecostal Church.

Started with scattered congregations in Kerala that were loosely
connected to each other, K. E. Abraham's network of churches grew
beyond Kerala and became the South India Pentecostal Church first
and later expanded to become today's India Pentecostal Church.[3]
Divisions based mostly on leadership issues created several similar
organizations, but IPC remains the largest Pentecostal denomination in India today, with over six thousand churches across the
nation and around the world.[4] There is still no noticeable harmony
or cooperation between the various Pentecostal denominations in
Kerala.[5]

The first seventy-five years of the history of Pentecostalism in

India is mostly about classical Pentecostals. The more recent history, however, is about the growth and development of the Charismatic movement, generally known in India as new generation churches. According to one report, Charismatics outnumber classical Pentecostals by 400 percent.[6] This includes Catholic Charismatics whose retreat centers host masses of believers each year and independent Charismatic ministries in major cities with outreaches all over India.[7] The relationship between classical Pentecostals and Charismatics in Kerala is still one of mistrust and disapproval.[8] New generation churches are labeled as centers of false doctrines whose members do not practice "separation from the world." Pentecostal leaders who associate themselves with Charismatic churches and ministries are viewed with suspicion and considered theologically "unsteady."[9]

Locally grown Pentecostal churches are seen all over India. However, Pentecostals from Kerala claim to have been instrumental in the growth of Pentecostal churches outside their home state. Some among the new generation of Pentecostal believers outside Kerala accuse Keralite Pentecostals of being elite and patronizing in this claim. However, it is true that pioneering work in many parts of India was initiated by Pentecostal missionaries from Kerala, some suffering great hardships.[10] Due to the rural nature of Kerala and the lack of development in the past, English-speaking Keralite masses—thanks to the British legacy of higher education—had to leave Kerala for better employment in North Indian cities. These Keralites started churches for themselves first, and later reached out to their local communities. In fact, Pentecostal missionaries from Kerala were found even in Pakistan prior to India's independence and the Indo-Pakistan partition in 1947.[11]

KERALITE PENTECOSTAL DIASPORA

The search for jobs took Keralites outside India to the Middle East, the United States, and Canada.[12] Many migrated to Australia and several European countries. Both professionals and laborers were in these groups. Pentecostals among them started home-style churches in their newfound homelands.[13]

Pentecostalism encountered great opposition in its early days in Kerala from society in general and traditional Christian churches in particular. Early converts to Pentecostalism, especially several key leaders, were from Mar Thoma and Orthodox churches.[14] These historic churches did not take their defection lightly. Public debates, tests of orthodoxy, and ex-communications were common practices in those days.[15] A number of early Pentecostal leaders made their way to Pentecostalism by way of the Brethren church, which was very prominent in Kerala in the early twentieth century.[16] Many of the classical Pentecostal teachings—such as teaching against wearing ornaments—were highly influenced by Brethren practices.[17]

Pentecostalism in Kerala did not develop in a religious vacuum. It had to accommodate itself to the prevailing religious ethos. As a result, some cultural trappings were strongly attached to Pentecostalism. These would turn out to have a significant impact on the movement a hundred years later.

Keralite Pentecostals were world travelers from the very beginning. Autobiographies of early leaders give colorful descriptions of their travels worldwide. Travels to Europe and the United States began as early as 1936. For instance, K. E. Abraham's autobiography describes his thirty-two-day trip by ship to New York from Colombo, Ceylon (now Sri Lanka), to preach the gospel. These travels were before the liberalization of US immigration laws, and most of the pre-1964 visitors returned home and continued their domestic ministries. The early travelers paved the way for others to come to America, primarily to study theology. They joined Bible colleges in New York, Chicago, and other cities. The new immigration laws made it possible for many of them to stay in America.

Simultaneously, a shortage of professional nurses expedited the immigration of Indian women to America.[18] Stanley Jones, the well-known missionary to India, is credited with opening the American medical field to Indian nurses. With what began as an exchange program, the nurses were later given opportunities to immigrate, and they settled in the major cities of America. Many of the nurses were Keralite Pentecostals who were trained in North Indian nursing schools and hospitals. Nursing was not considered a profession of prestige at that time in India. Girls from poorer homes went to become nurses. (This has since changed. Admission to nursing schools is highly competitive nowadays. Private nursing schools are charging market-driven tuition rates.) Earlier Pentecostals in Kerala struggled with the idea of sending their daughters to nursing schools since most of them were against offering medical care to the sick, but the potential for economic advancement prevailed and a large number of Pentecostal women became nurses.[19] The young men who came to study theology in America married the Indian nurses and settled as permanent residents in the States. Later they brought their families to America through the family reunification provisions of the immigration laws, and the population grew.[20]

The first Pentecostal prayer meetings among Keralites in America took place in the New York/New Jersey area among the nurses. Pastor C. M. Varghese is credited with starting this ministry.[21] The first Keralite Pentecostal church in America was organized in New York City. The first meeting of this church—the India Pentecostal Assembly—took place in Manhattan on February 18, 1968.[22] It was the beginning of the significant growth of Indian Pentecostal churches in America as the 1970s and 1980s witnessed the arrival of increasing numbers of Keralite immigrants. New York City, Philadelphia, Chicago, Atlanta, Dallas, Houston, Los Angeles, and the tropical cities of Florida attracted Keralites. Churches were established in all these cities. There are about fifty Keralite Pentecostal churches in New York City alone.[23] There are thirteen churches each in New Jersey and Pennsylvania. A number of churches have also been established in the various provinces of Canada.[24] Indian Pentecostal churches have thrived in North America. There are networks of churches organized now at the national level based on denominational affiliations.[25]

An interdenominational Indian Pentecostal conference was held in Oklahoma City in 1983, with three hundred attendees. The conference, now known as the Pentecostal Conference of North American Keralites (PCNAK), has been held annually ever since and has enjoyed attendance of up to seven thousand persons.[26] A similar Western Pentecostal Conference is also held annually for Keralites living in Northwest USA and Canadian provinces.[27] Additionally, national conferences are now held annually by the major Indian Pentecostal denominations.[28] Generally speaking, the Keralite Pentecostal churches in North America are affiliated with their respective head offices in Kerala. That means the Assemblies of God churches of Keralites in the United States are more directly connected to their headquarters in Punalur, Kerala, rather than Springfield, Missouri. There are also several independent and denominational youth organizations active in the Keralite community in North America.[29] The Sunday Schools of North American Keralites (SSNAK) is another organization focused on the spiritual development of Keralite Pentecostal children in America.[30]

Keralites in North America have been active in literature ministry. There are several bilingual (Malayalam-English) periodicals in circulation. Most of them are published from Kerala, available by mail and online. There is a Keralite Pentecostal Writers' Forum that promotes bilingual writing in America.[31]

As the number of Keralite immigrants increased in America, even more Keralites were finding employment in the Middle Eastern countries, especially in the oil-rich United Arab Emirates. Although property ownership and citizenship are not guaranteed in the Middle East, Keralite Pentecostals there established their churches everywhere they could. Underground church groups were formed in places where churches could not exist legally. Testimonies of soft-singing undercover churches in soundproofed apartments in Muslim neighborhoods of certain Middle Eastern countries are well known. Because of the proximity to India and the difficulty of local assimilation, the Middle Eastern Keralite churches are very similar in their worship style to Pentecostal churches in Kerala.

A major problem facing the diaspora church, especially in North America, is language of worship. Unlike their Middle Eastern counterparts, American-born Keralites (ABKs) do not speak Malayalam, their parents' heart language, and prefer English language for worship. This has caused ongoing conflicts in these churches. Most churches now have bilingual services or separate services in English for young people.

Twentieth-Century "Mistakes"

Classical Pentecostalism in Kerala is facing a season of significant challenges. Samkutty Chacko, editor of the prominent weekly *Hallelujah*, recently predicted several outcomes if the status quo continues in the Pentecostal churches. He predicts the following changes in the next twenty-five years:

- Kerala Pentecostal churches could look like today's European churches in the next two decades because young people are not engaged in the life of the church.

- New generation churches will grow independently, and most of them will not affiliate themselves with mainline classical Pentecostals.

- More church buildings with modern facilities will be built.

- Church politics will get worse with intra-denominational disputes going to the secular courts in higher numbers. Many Bible colleges will be closed. Many are already struggling for enrollment due to the declining population in Kerala resulting from the implementation of a stringent popula-tion control program promoted by the central government.

- Pentecostal youth movements will decline.

- Shorter services with globalized (westernized) wor-ship music will prevail.

- There will not be any increase in cooperation between classical Pentecostal denominations.

- Mission work will be more centered in local churches instead of being led by centralized denominational mission boards

- Church governance will change in Kerala with more Pentecostal churches adopting the Episcopal style of polity and governance.[32]

It is hard to tell how many of these predictions will come to pass, but the concerns of a major periodical regarding classical Pentecostalism in Kerala is obvious in these predictions.

In a number of articles from July 2013 through November 2013, *Hallelujah* followed up with a series titled, "Ten Foolish Mistakes of Pentecostalism in Kerala," reflecting on the first hundred years of Keralite Pentecostalism. The ten major "mistakes" are listed here:

1. Abandoning the Charismatic movement by not discerning the work of the Spirit within that movement ("When the masses of people were filled with the Holy Spirit in the Catholic and Orthodox churches and looked for guidance and mentoring, the classical Pentecostals acted like a fisherman facing a large school of fish with a torn net!")

2. Neglecting higher education by not establishing degree-granting regular colleges; not following the example of other Christian traditions

3. Not encouraging Pentecostals to enter state and federal government services to occupy positions of influence

4. Blindly implementing the rigid family planning program of the Indian federal government, resulting in a diminished population of Christians in certain key areas of Kerala with significant political and religious implications

5. Making rejection of ornaments a doctrine and then relaxing the rules for some non-Keralite Pentecostals outside Kerala

6. Not strategically grooming Pentecostal leaders for the future as former leaders mostly used their organizational power to enhance their own ministries and other enterprises (television, Bible schools, etc.)

7. Lacking a strong Pentecostal theology and the abundance of honorary doctors among unschooled leaders

8. Moving water baptisms from public venues to private church-based baptisteries, thus losing opportunities for public witness in a non-Christian culture

9. The "Brethrenizing" of Keralite Pentecostalism, which promoted a legalistic mentality that undermined Pentecostal freedom in worship and other practices ("It appears that we only need to believe that there is a Holy Spirit. Pentecostal churches have preachers, Bible school teachers and even pastors who hold Brethren ideas about the Holy Spirit. Speaking in tongues and noisy worship are considered out of fashion. These are spokesman for legalism.... Only about 50% of Keralite Pentecostals consider themselves Spirit-filled."[33])

10. Eliminating the image of the cross from everything as if having the symbol of the cross in any form anywhere is idolatry

TWENTY-FIRST-CENTURY CHALLENGES

It appears that Samkutty Chacko considers three "mistakes"—(a) the neglect of the Charismatic movement, (b) making the rejection of ornaments a litmus test of holiness, causing cultural conflicts and family hostilities (by forcing women to abandon their wedding rings to be baptized in water!) and significant hindrance to evangelism, and (c) lack of leadership development—as the major causes of Pentecostalism's loss of dynamism in Kerala. While Pentecostals in Kerala generally have reached higher economic status—mainly due to foreign currency coming from expatriates—and political recognition in Kerala, their movement has stagnated. Sociologists are not surprised by these developments. They believe that movements and organizations are on a predictable track to decay unless proper interventions take place to improve their health and growth.[34] It does not seem that proper intervention is taking place in the case of Pentecostalism in Kerala.

Keralite Pentecostalism in diaspora has been a true reflection of its home-grown version. The domestic "mistakes" had their impact on diaspora Pentecostals, only with added complications due to the additional contextual issues. The language issue has been mentioned above. Generational conflicts, impact of affluence, desire of the first-generation immigrants to preserve their imported religious practices and cultural norms, impact of globalization, conflicts regarding hiring of American-trained pastors vs. importing pastors from Kerala, etc., complicate the matter among diaspora Pentecostals. These are acute concerns in North America. To a lesser degree, these issues show up in the Middle Eastern churches, although cultural conflicts are of less intensity, due to the fact that Keralites preserve their culture in the Middle East to a much higher level because of low acculturation and poor assimilation within the Muslim culture there.

Some of the major symptoms of Indian Pentecostalism afflicting the diaspora churches are listed here:

- The issue of ornaments remains a highly charged one in the Pentecostal churches in America and Canada. There have been church splits and leadership changes because of this issue.[35]

- Denominational leadership elections are highly controversial and often accused of major corruptions, such as vote-buying, fraudulent campaigns, etc.

- A majority of the congregations are still importing their pastors from India. American seminary graduates are not given the opportunity to lead the churches.[36]

- Bible schools in Kerala are declining in enrollment and maintaining substandard academics.[37] The American Keralite churches have no Bible school of their own.

- There are no major or coordinated outreaches to evangelize India. Evangelism and missionary work do not seem to be a priority in most American congregations.

- There are not many women in leadership at the Indian Pentecostal churches.

- New generation (Charismatic) churches are not embraced by Pentecostals in the United States.

- Conflicts regarding worship styles and music are major generational problems in many congregations.[38]

- North American churches are not welcoming places for non-Indians.

- There is no evidence of developing a strategy to groom a new generation of leaders capable of fully adapting to the American context.

OUTLINE OF A HISTORICAL-CRITICAL ANALYSIS

The symptoms of the malady currently afflicting Keralite Pentecostalism deserve closer scrutiny and deeper analysis. The following is an outline of such an analysis.

Rural vs. urban

Pentecostalism in Kerala was a rural movement. Indian Pentecostalism developed in the rural areas of the country and spread to the cities through native missionaries and the mobility of an educated employment-seeking populace. Most of the world now lives in cities, but Pentecostalism's cultural trappings are still rural in nature and in need of review in the urban world. A globalized world with its technology, speed, and universal tastes and fashions challenges the rural cultural trappings of Pentecostalism. Today's entertainment looks like yesterday's sin. Modern lifestyle looks like old-time backsliding. A new generation of urban Pentecostals finds it hard to fully comprehend a rural view of faith and practice. This is a real challenge both in India and abroad.

Indian immigrants in America, like any other immigrant group, are under strong pressure to adapt to a new country and culture. The pressure to survive and the desire to succeed are difficult to handle without assistance. Pentecostal immigrants look to their faith for strength and courage to face this pressure, but a faith with inflexible rules developed in a rural past in a faraway place is not a sufficient resource. More than their parents, the ABKs find it hard to accept. No wonder they are leaving traditional immigrant churches in large numbers. This writer knows two pastors who attempted to study this phenomenon with much concern as part of their doctor of ministry studies.[39]

Some of the rules and regulations implemented in the Pentecostal churches in Kerala made perfect sense when they were initially developed. Women wearing saris made sense in tropical Kerala. Avoiding ornaments for simplicity as a preference made sense in a culture that displays excessive ornaments. Women and men sitting in different sections of the sanctuary made sense in the Indian context. Holding cottage meetings in the homes of small-town people made sense. Pastors' expecting to attend every family event of all church members was workable in smaller churches in rural communities.

Requiring women to wear saris in subzero temperatures in New York City, while men are happily clad in three piece suits and overcoats, does not make sense. Making the avoidance of ornaments a doctrine in practice that applies only to Keralite Pentecostals does not make sense to people in the diaspora. Forcing husbands and wives to sit apart from each other in large Pentecostal conferences held in huge facilities in the American context does not make sense. Indian Pentecostalism's rural cultural trappings need a close examination.

Local vs. global

Pentecostalism in India in the twentieth century was a global enterprise because of the influence of Western missionaries. Many Pentecostal practices had their roots in American and British Pentecostalism. Pentecostalism practiced by local people, however, had local cultural flavor. Pentecostal worship style was characteristically Indian. Pentecostal songs had Indian tunes and followed the tradition of pre-Pentecostal revivals in India. This was not the case with the Anglicans in India, for example, or the Pentecostals in Korea. The order of worship and the music used in worship are clearly Western in these traditions. The Anglicans sang English songs in India. Korean traditional music took a backseat to American tunes in Pentecostal churches in Korea. This was not the case in Kerala. Global connections of early Keralite Pentecostals did not impact the style of their worship. That remained local.

Only a few people traveled outside India in earlier days. People's understanding of Pentecostals in other parts of the world was limited to the secondhand reports of these travelers. This has changed. India is a global market leader today. Even rural people have access to technology and multiple means of communication. They know how believers in other parts of the world work, worship, rest, and play. This has an impact on Pentecostals in Kerala itself, but the church has not adapted well to this reality. Young people are leaving inflexible Pentecostal churches for new generation churches in Kerala.[40] The tension is higher among diaspora Pentecostals. The leaders do not find it easy to enforce strict traditional lifestyle, worship, and spiritual practices. How does one adopt the new ways of worship? How does one update classical Pentecostalism's cultural trappings? How can one embrace the new and not abandon the best of the past? How does one contextualize Indian Pentecostalism outside India? These are questions facing Keralite Pentecostal leaders all over the world.

Poor vs. rich

While Pentecostalism in the West was born on the wrong side of the cultural track, it belonged to the really poor in India. Indian Pentecostalism's cultural trappings and spiritual practices were influenced by the social location and economic status of its pioneers. How much of the Indian Pentecostal lifestyle was an imitation of Hindu *sadhus* (spiritual men) who were seeking *nirvana* through self-rejection? India's economy has changed. The poor are still there, but a large middle class is amassing wealth, much of it coming from and through expatriates in the Middle East and America. Globalization with its outsourcing and technology development has brought much wealth to India. Millions of rickshaws have been replaced by auto-rickshaws. Auto-rickshaws are now being upgraded to Nano cars. India now owns the Jaguar Land Rover! Television screens are illuminated in millions of Indian huts and even in slum tents. India is seen as an economic power of the twenty-first century, massive corruption notwithstanding. A starving India of fifty years ago has been replaced by an India that exports food! Pentecostals in India, particularly in Kerala, have experienced a social lift. Pentecostal religious gatherings have political ministers addressing them now because they have become a strong voting bloc, while severe persecution of Christians takes place outside Kerala. In a state with strong communist influence, the Congress Party woos all Christians, including Pentecostals. Pentecostals may not have their own universities in Kerala, but they are highly educated and well connected economically.

Listening to the radio was a sin once. Watching television became the next sin. Consumer goods and services, which used to be sins in the past, are now in almost every home. Are they still sins? Were they ever? Or were the rules there because they could not afford to have these things? Poor and rich are worshipping together in the Pentecostal churches of Kerala, but the rich are setting the standard. The theological conflict that results from the new arrangement has not been properly addressed. The consequences are seen in India and abroad.

Expatriates are bringing money and many foreign customs to Kerala. Many Keralite Pentecostals are financially better off and are comfortable with "foreign Pentecostal practices." The Pentecostalism of the poor now has to cater to the spiritual needs of the rich. This causes tension within Kerala churches at different levels. In a well-connected world where ministers are traveling back and forth and pastors for American congregations are imported from India, these tensions affect the diaspora church.

Postcolonialism vs. independence

India was in the throngs of her struggle for independence when twentieth-century Pentecostalism took root in Kerala. Mahatma Gandhi was leading the political struggle, modeling a leadership style characterized by simplicity and personal sacrifice. Gandhi was the symbol of freedom and the power of powerlessness. Simplicity was not a Pentecostal virtue in India at that time. It was an Indian virtue symbolized by Gandhi, a devout Hindu. Indigenization was not just a missiological concept in mid-twentieth-century India— it was a statement. It is noticeable that the indigenous Pentecostal denominations like the India Pentecostal Church had a significantly higher growth rate than the denominations that had direct supervision from the West. Was it partly due to postcolonial reactions?

Modern India is an emerging economy and a potential superpower. Indians' self-identity has changed since independence. The largest democracy in the world that has never had a coup does not glorify simplicity anymore. No wonder modern urban Pentecostals are questioning early Pentecostal rules about rejecting ornaments and seeking medical care, and any practice reminiscent of colonialism and postcolonial reactions. (The medical care issue disappeared with the flow of Keralite young women to the nursing profession.) Kerala Pentecostalism is challenged to adjust to this reality. This challenge is magnified among Keralite Pentecostals in more advanced nations.

That world vs. this one

Indian Pentecostal preaching of the mid-twentieth century was highly other-worldly. Much of the teaching and singing was about the second coming of Christ and the world to come. Prophetic teachers with their custom-made charts of world events and biblical calendars traveled across Kerala, conducting month-long study classes on Daniel and Revelation. Jesus was coming back any day, or at least in the very near future. Geopolitical incidents were clear fulfillment of prophecies to these teachers. Gog and Magog and the European Union all had their place in their prophetic schemes. The Antichrist was identified as people in different political positions at different times. Social concerns were not on their agenda. Politics were left for heathens and other sinners, but every believer was an evangelist. This is not the case now.

Politicians are on Pentecostal convention platforms. Pentecostal charitable societies are active today. Preaching about the world to come has been replaced in many places with some version of the prosperity gospel. Accumulating wealth and experiencing material blessings are fine now. The air-conditioned world here below is not too bad. Indian Pentecostalism is at the crossroads now. It needs to find a way to recalibrate its practical theology to a much-changed global world.

Megaphone vs. multimedia

Open-air evangelistic meetings conducted by Pentecostals were very common in twentieth-century Kerala. These were conducted at marketplaces and other noisy venues. The megaphone was used to amplify the preaching at these meetings. Megaphones were the poor man's loudspeaker system. Today, Indian Pentecostals have much advanced technology. Traditional musical instruments have been replaced with modern equipment. Increased life expectancy has brought together multi-generations to worship services. Pastors have to address widely differing spiritual needs of multi-stratified congregations. Disagreements about the length of services, use of technology, and type of music used in worship abound.[41] Arguments about watching movies or using arts in evangelism are also common. How much technology should be allowed in church? How should multimedia be used in evangelism? Should Bollywood movie makers be used for evangelistic purposes? Fast-changing technology has theological implications.

Orthodox vs. holiness

Many pioneer leaders of the Pentecostal movement in India were members of the historic Orthodox churches of Kerala. Some belonged to the Jacobite Orthodox Church, and others came from the Mar Thoma Church. A few were studying for the priesthood in the Orthodox tradition when they encountered the Pentecostal message. A number of the early leaders made the journey to Pentecostalism via the Brethren movement, which was strong in Kerala in the 1920s and '30s. These pioneers in their historical location had to differentiate themselves in theology and practice. On the one hand, they were Indian citizens, but non-Hindus. On the other hand, they were non-Orthodox Christians, but "separate" from the non-Pentecostal Brethren. Finding the right religious expression at that time was not easy, especially in the middle of a flaming revival and political struggle against colonialism. The Brethren group put the most pressure on the Pentecostals in the area of separation from the world and holy living. The Pentecostals could not possibly appear less holy than the Brethren!

The pressure from the Brethren may have been the real reason behind the rules about ornaments and other separation-from-the-world-oriented cultural teachings. It is hard to tell the role the Western missionaries played in establishing these early Pentecostal teachings. In any case, the rules of locally defined holiness have become hindrances to evangelism in India and magnified challenges to the new generation in diaspora. Definitions of holiness and expressions of the same remain unresolved among Keralite Pentecostals, impacting the growth of Pentecostalism in negative ways in a globalized world.

Natives vs. expatriates

Pentecostalism's adjustment problems are more serious among expatriates because of the additional issues they are dealing with, especially in North America. Language issues, first-generation immigrant concerns about preserving their culture and legacy, generational differences in needs and tastes within congregations, economic and educational levels of members, and lack of opportunities for leadership for theologically educated church members complicate the issue in the West. Pressure from the local culture and faster assimilation of ABKs due to professional and economic advancement make it more difficult for young people to accept the status quo.

ABKs pressured their churches to change the language of worship. Starting with only translating the main sermon from Malayalam to English, now there are churches worshipping fully in English or conducting separate services for people who prefer English. The rest are bilingual with significant portions of the services being in English. Wedding bands are worn by many ABK couples now even though they are still not a part of the official wedding ceremonies. There are conflicts regarding these matters, especially in congregations with a higher percentage of more recent immigrants.

The fact that Keralites prefer to import their pastors from Kerala perpetuates a number of these problems. The continuous circulation of visiting preachers in US churches who benefit from the status quo make the changes harder to implement. Although pastors who are trained in Indian Bible schools demonstrate good understanding of Pentecostal doctrines, they are not in a position to minister to the ABKs with the depth and cultural understanding they require.

INITIAL RECOMMENDATIONS

Keralite Pentecostals of the twenty-first century who claim the St. Thomas tradition of Christianity hold much potential for the expanding Spirit-empowered movement. They are proud holders of a great legacy of Pentecostal missionary work within India and abroad. However, the cultural trappings of early Keralite Pentecostalism have become a hindrance to the dynamic growth of the Pentecostal movement within Kerala, and especially in the diaspora. Some adjustments must be made to make room for a fresh move of the Holy Spirit.

Based on the observation of Samkutty Chacko and the analysis previously given, three small changes can produce a large positive response and reduce much stress within Kerala Pentecostal churches: (1) reach out to the Charismatic and new generation churches and movements in Kerala and engage with them in creative ways to promote evangelism and missions; (2) explicitly make the requirement of avoiding ornaments a preference rather than a doctrine for Pentecostals in and out of Kerala, leaving it as a matter of taste and heritage; and (3) encourage the appointment of American-educated ministers as senior pastors in the diaspora churches, reducing the number of imported pastors. Other changes can follow.

Although individual congregations can implement these suggestions, some kind of an organized forum of recognized leaders and representatives to discuss the issues and recommend these changes will empower the pastors and multi-denominational congregations to make the changes simultaneously. If representatives of the prominent Pentecostal denominations would lead the way, no one denomination would suffer internal conflicts or loss of members. Today's globalized world requires a separation of the wheat from the chaff in terms of the word of truth and twentieth-century cultural preferences. The postmodern young people who seek authentic leadership, true mentoring, and a new "vocabulary" of faith will truly appreciate any move in this direction.

Part II: East Asia

Chapter 4

Pentecostals in China

Robert Menzies

From the East Coast to the West Coast
The wind of the Holy Spirit will blow everywhere

From the East to the West
The glory of the Holy Spirit will be released

Good news comes from heaven
Good news rings in the ear

Causing dry bones to become moist
Frail bones to become strong

Full of the Holy Spirit, we will not turn back
Step by step we go to distant places

The lame skipping
The mute singing

The fire of the Holy Spirit
The longer it burns the brighter it gets.[1]

IT IS NOW apparent that since the early 1980s the church in China has experienced unprecedented growth. Once viewed as an essentially foreign faith, Christianity has taken root in Chinese soil. And it has blossomed. If the trends of the past three decades remain constant, by 2020 there will be more evangelical Christians in China than in any other country in the world.[2]

Researchers are agreed that the form of Christianity that has emerged in China is both evangelical in character and Chinese in expression.[3] It is evangelical in that the vast majority of Chinese believers exhibit a firm belief in the authority of the Bible, faith in Christ as the sole means of obtaining salvation, and the necessity of evangelism.[4] And yet this evangelical faith has been expressed in ways that are especially appropriate to the Chinese context. Church life is often experienced in small groups that feature close relationships and family ties. There is a strong emphasis on the miraculous, with prayer for healing taking on an important role in the life of faith. The experiential dimension of Christian spirituality, expressed in earnest prayers and emotionally charged worship, is significant to many Chinese believers. And the vast majority of Christians in China worship in "house churches" that are independent of state or foreign control.[5]

Indeed, the strong experiential nature of Protestant Christianity in China, and particularly the emphasis in the house churches on healing, exorcism, and prophecy, has led many to describe the dominant form of Protestant Christianity in China as Pentecostal. While Tony Lambert describes Chinese Christianity as "biblical supernaturalism," others, such as David Aikman, Gotthard Oblau, Edmond Tang, and Chen-Yang Kao speak of the specifically Pentecostal features of the church in China.[6] Although sociologists like Oblau and Kao tend to minimize the significant role that the Bible or theological convictions play in shaping the praxis of these Chinese Protestants, they do helpfully highlight the Charismatic orientation of their spirituality. Regardless of whether or not these groups can truly be categorized as Pentecostal,[7] this general Charismatic orientation is widely acknowledged as the key to the rapid growth of the Chinese church.[8]

In the following essay I hope to shed light on this significant sector of the global church: the Pentecostal churches of China. I shall begin by offering a brief overview of the historical development of Pentecostal churches in China, including the fascinating story of how churches with direct links to the Azusa Street Revival (1906–1909) were established. I shall then offer evidence for the Pentecostal nature of the house church movement that has grown so rapidly in recent decades. While, as we have noted, some scholars downplay the role of the Bible in shaping Pentecostal practice in China, and thus they also deny that Chinese Pentecostals possess a clear theological identity, I will challenge this judgment. Certainly not every Christian that prays for the sick, exorcises demons, or prophesies would affirm a baptism in the Spirit distinct from conversion that is marked by speaking in tongues. Nevertheless, there is a significant number that do.[9] And their influence, as well as the clarity of their biblical convictions, should not be underestimated. The common thread that unites Pentecostals in China with other Pentecostals around the world is their sense of connection with the apostolic church as reflected in the Book of Acts. Chinese Pentecostals pray for the sick, worship with joyful abandonment, speak in tongues, and seek the enabling of the Spirit for bold witness in the face of persecution because they find all of these experiences described in the New Testament. The message and methods of the early church are models for their lives and ministry. We shall seek to demonstrate that this is the case in two of the largest networks in China. Finally, I will identify some of the key questions that confront Pentecostals in China as they face an exciting but uncertain future.

THE EARLY YEARS (1908–1949)

One of the striking aspects of Christianity in pre-1949 China was the emergence of strong, vital indigenous churches. These churches were founded and led by Chinese Christians. They were established and operated entirely independent of foreign finances, control, and leadership. Although these groups were largely overlooked by missionaries and have been neglected by historians, it is evident that these groups were extremely significant. More recently Daniel Bays, a noted historian of Chinese Christianity, has highlighted the significance of these groups. Speaking of these independent Chinese Christian groups, Bays writes, "I believe that this sector [of the Christian church] was far more interesting and significant than it might have been thought."[10] Bays estimates that by the 1940s these indigenous groups accounted for between 20–25 percent (or 200,000 believers) of all Protestants.[11] Furthermore, Bays notes that these groups have exerted a tremendous influence on the Christianity that has flourished in China since the 1980s.[12]

The largest of these groups, the True Jesus Church, was and remains Pentecostal in character. Bays and Iap Sian Chin have established important links between the Azusa Street Revival and the key founders of the True Jesus Church. Alfred Garr, one of the first pastors at the Azusa Street Revival to receive the baptism of the Spirit and speak in tongues, felt called to go as a missionary. He and his wife arrived in Hong Kong in October of 1907. The Garrs were joined by a small group of Pentecostals, and they began to minister in Hong Kong. Garr's interpreter, Mok Lai Chi, was baptized in the Holy Spirit and spoke in tongues. Mok became the founding editor of a Chinese monthly paper, *Wuxunjie zhenlibao* [Pentecostal Truths], which was first issued in January of 1908. This paper "directly influenced the North China founders of the first major Chinese Pentecostal church, the True Jesus Church."[13]

Another link between the Azusa Street Revival and the True Jesus Church can be traced through Bernt Berntsen, a missionary serving in China who was profoundly impacted by his experience at the altar of the Azusa Street Mission. After his baptism in the Spirit at Azusa Street, Berntsen returned to China and, along with a small group of Pentecostals, opened an independent mission station in Zhending (just north of Shijiazhuang) of Hebei Province. In 1912 this group began to publish a newspaper, *Tongchuan fuyin zhenlibao* [Popular Gospel Truth]. This paper, along with the Hong Kong paper noted above, provided inspiration for the early founders of the True Jesus Church. Additionally, two of the key Chinese founders of the True Jesus Church, Zhang Lingshen and Wei Enbo, were impacted in Beijing by members of the church Bernsten's group had founded, the Faith Union (Xinxinhui).[14] Berntsen, who was increasingly drawn to the non-trinitarian Oneness position and eventually left the Assemblies of God, appears to have exerted considerable influence on these leaders. It is notable that the True Jesus Church (as did the Jesus Family noted below) followed in this non-trinitarian path.[15]

Zhang Lingshen and Wei Enbo, along with Barnabas Zhang, all of whom had Pentecostal experiences that included speaking in tongues, determined that they would form a Pentecostal church in China. They founded their first church in Tianjin in 1917. The church grew quickly and spread to Shandong, Hebei, Henan, Zhejiang, and other provinces. Its key areas of strength were in Hunan, Fujian, and Henan. In *Protestantism in Contemporary China*, Alan Hunter and Kim-Kwong Chan note that the church's "estimated membership was at least 120,000 by 1949," with seven hundred churches throughout China.[16] The True Jesus Church remains a strong force today in Taiwan and in China.

The Jesus Family was another large, indigenous Chinese church that was Pentecostal in nature. The Jesus Family was founded in the 1920s by Jing Dianyin in the village of Mazhuang (Taian County), in Shandong Province. Jing formed a friendship with Assemblies of God missionary Leslie M. Anglin and quickly embraced Pentecostal doctrine.[17] Thus, the Jesus Family's worship was marked by an emphasis on baptism in the Spirit, speaking in tongues, prayer for healing, prophecy, and other spiritual gifts. The Jesus Family also featured a communal way of life in which everything was shared. The Jesus Family was especially strong in the poorest parts of China. Hunter and Chan provide a wonderful description of the church from a present-day believer's perspective: the church was "a love fellowship, a meeting-place for the weary and a place of comfort for the broken-hearted...where you are, there is our home, and our home is everywhere."[18] In its heyday in China the Jesus Family totaled over a hundred communities and around six thousand members.[19] Although the church still exists today in a non-communitarian form in various parts of China, it is quite small.

There were other indigenous churches that were non-Pentecostal in character, such as The Little Flock (Xiao Qun) established by Watchman Nee (Ni Tuosheng) in the mid-1920s. And there were certainly a number of non-Pentecostal Chinese church leaders of stature. Wang Mingdao, for example, apparently had a Pentecostal experience in 1920, but later "backed away from full Pentecostalism."[20] Nevertheless, the fact remains that of the three largest independent Chinese churches that sprang up in the early part of the twentieth century (the True Jesus Church, The Little Flock, and the Jesus Family), two were Pentecostal. And one of these Pentecostal groups, the True Jesus Church, was by far the largest single indigenous Chinese church group of that era. This fact, coupled with the significant impact of the Pentecostal form of revivalism that swept through China in the 1930s, indicates that the majority of Chinese Christians prior to 1949, when able to develop their own Christian identity, gravitated to Pentecostal forms of worship and doctrine. It is worth noting, then, that indigenous Chinese Christianity was predominantly Pentecostal.

Of course many Pentecostal missionaries served in China during this period, planting churches and training Christian leaders. The Pentecostal Missionary Union, established in the United Kingdom in 1909, and the Assemblies of God, established in the United States in 1914, were early Pentecostal missions agencies that sent missionaries to China. By 1915 there were approximately 150 missionaries serving in roughly thirty locations around China.[21] These remarkable early pioneers left a lasting legacy. Although this group is too numerous to list, Mattie Ledbetter serves as an outstanding example of their dedication and impact. A single lady, Mattie was ordained a missionary to South China in 1911. She served for many years in Fat Shan (Foshan in Guangdong Province), establishing two outstations and serving in an orphanage. She often traveled by horseback from village to village distributing Bibles and preaching. In a letter dated November 30, 1920, she offers a vivid picture of her prayer life. She writes, "Once recently at morning prayer...I sunk on the floor under the power of God and lay there three hours. Every little while the power would shake me from head to foot and the Lord would give me a prayer or a song or reveal something to me...and Oh how sweetly Jesus spoke to my soul. I was melted in love."[22] In 1928 Mattie, suffering from exhaustion, traveled to Hong Kong for a time of rest and recuperation. Little did she know that God would use her to preach evangelistic crusades in a tent and in this way pioneer a vibrant church in Hong Kong. Hong Kong First Assembly of God now numbers close to one thousand believers. Mattie died of dysentery in Hong Kong on March 2, 1938, at the age of sixty-seven.[23]

Tony Lambert points out that today the church in China is generally strong in those areas where historically the missionaries were most active; that is, in the eastern coastal provinces of Fujian, Zhejiang, and Jiangsu. However, Lambert goes on to note that the Chinese church is also very strong in some provinces where the missionaries were not as active, provinces like Henan and Anhui. He offers no rationale for the growth of the church in these regions, but does note that "the witness of independent, indigenous churches, such as the Little Flock and the Jesus Family, are also vital factors to be taken into account."[24] What Lambert does not state, but what is especially striking, is this: strong, indigenous Pentecostal churches were active in these regions prior to 1949, and today, strong, indigenous Pentecostal churches have blossomed in these same regions. It is difficult to deny that the legacy of these early indigenous churches lives on in the Christians and churches birthed in the revivals of the 1980s.[25] This legacy is conspicuously Pentecostal, and it is to this legacy that we now turn.

EXPLOSIVE GROWTH (1949–PRESENT)

When Mao Zedong established the People's Republic of China in 1949, the Chinese church entered a new and uncertain era. Although the government's attitude toward religion often featured hostile repression, the striking fact remains that under the first three decades of communist rule Protestant Christianity in China grew by leaps and bounds. As Kao notes, "After the long period of eradication measures from 1956 to the late 1970s, the number of Catholics and Muslims remained the same, while the number of Protestant Christians rose from 0.8 million to 3 million."[26] Even though, as Kao acknowledges, these official figures represent an absolute minimum, since they do not include underground Protestants, they still bear witness to exceptional growth.[27] And by all accounts, this remarkable growth, which continues to this day, has been fueled by the emergence of Pentecostal churches or groups with Pentecostal-style patterns of worship and outreach.

Nevertheless, as we have noted, many scholars are reluctant to describe these churches as possessing a clear Pentecostal identity—one that is rooted in their reading of the Bible. A host of other factors are offered in an attempt to explain why Chinese Protestants have gravitated toward Pentecostal forms of belief and praxis. For example, Hunter and Chan point out that Pentecostal values resonate with important features of Chinese folk religion and thus meet the felt needs of many Chinese believers.[28] Fenggang Yang argues that the vicissitudes in China created by the transition to a market economy have created a new kind of angst and the need for a new worldview "to bring sense and order" to peoples' lives.[29] Pentecostal spirituality helps meet this need. Chen-Yang Kao argues that the Cultural Revolution (1966–1976) paved the way for the emergence of "practice-led Pentecostalism" by stripping away various forms of ecclesiastical authority that, without the strident persecution that characterized this era, would have been present; thus, "there was no Christian authority that was able to provide a doctrinal framework or institutional regulation for discouraging those ecstatic experiences and the exercise of Charismatic power…"[30] While all of these explanations may help us in varying degrees understand more clearly why China, like so many places around the world, has been such fertile ground for Pentecostal church growth, they all fail to account for the central dynamic: the biblical record. Yes, the Pentecostal faith, with its openness to the supernatural, provides spiritual resources for significant felt needs. Yes, the Pentecostal message, centered as it is in faith in Christ, provides stability in the chaos of moral confusion. And certainly Pentecostal faith thrives where there is limited ecclesiastical structure. But none of these explanations take us to the heart of the matter. Pentecostal faith is rooted in the Bible and flows from the conviction that the stories in the Book of Acts are our stories: stories that provide models for life and ministry. Is it not significant that the Pentecostal movement in China was given first breath through the printed page? Why should we imagine that it is any different today? Indeed, even among largely illiterate Pentecostals, the stories of the Bible, passed on orally, serve as models for their faith and praxis. As we shall see, China at this point is no exception.

It is perhaps easy to forget that the Pentecostal movement was birthed in a Bible school. Around the world Pentecostals have always been quick to establish schools that highlight the study of the Bible. Although Pentecostals feature a simple, narrative approach to the Bible and their hermeneutic is void of the angst over miracle stories and apparent contradictions that characterize many in the West, they emphasize the Bible just the same. This is certainly true of the Pentecostal house church networks in China, who have established an impressive array of training centers in the face of staggering obstacles. As one Pentecostal church leader from Wenzhou stated, "We act strictly in accordance with the Bible. The Bible is the standard for our faith and way of life. We are not evangelical. We emphasize the full gospel."[31] Another Chinese evangelist framed the issue in a slightly different way, choosing to highlight the different approach to Scripture that marks many Chinese believers. He said to me, "When Western Christians read the Book of Acts, they see in it inspiring stories; when Chinese believers read the Book of Acts, we see in it our lives." Of course his point was clear: Chinese believers tend to read the Book of Acts with a sense of urgency and desperation, with a hunger generated by their need. This type of reading generally leads to a Pentecostal approach. This is certainly the case in China.

A survey of the larger house church networks in China reveals that a majority is Pentecostal in theology and practice. The Fang Cheng (or China for Christ) Church, the Li Xin (or Zhong Hua Meng Fu) Church, the Ying Shang Church (Anhui), and the True Jesus Church are all strongly Pentecostal groups. The China Gospel Fellowship (CGF) should probably be categorized as neo-Pentecostal, although it is home to many Pentecostals as well.[32] The Wenzhou church established by Miao Zhitong might also be described as neo-Pentecostal. Non-Pentecostal groups would include the Word of Life (or Born Again) Church, established by Peter Xu, and Watchman Nee's Little Flock (or Xiao Qun), as well as a number of smaller groups that are largely reformed in theology and follow the cessationist teaching of Indonesian-based Chinese pastor Stephen Tong.[33]

An analysis of two of the larger house church networks indicates that Chinese Pentecostals have, for the most part, a clear understanding of who they are and that this sense of identity is rooted in their reading of the Bible, particularly the stories in Acts.[34]

CHINA FOR CHRIST (FANG CHENG)

We begin our brief survey with what was the largest of the house church networks operating in China in the 1990s, China for Christ (sometimes called the Fang Cheng Church). The China for Christ Church began in the Fang Cheng district of Henan Province. It grew very rapidly in the 1980s and constitutes a large network of house churches that span the length and breadth of China. Zhang Rongliang, recognized as the church's main leader, described a key turning point in the life of the church: "In 1980, we received our very first Bibles from outside China. We held them in our arms and kissed them delicately, with tears in our eyes. They were the fulfillment of many years of fervent prayer and longing."[35] Decades of oppression had created a great longing and desire in the hearts of people for spiritual truth. In this explosive setting Zhang Rongliang and other Fang Cheng leaders, such as Sister Ding Hei, began to preach the gospel with great boldness. Despite tremendous hardships the church began to grow exponentially. From 1980 to 1990 Zhang was a fugitive on the run from the authorities. He traveled throughout the country preaching and led many to Christ. He also trained a group of eighty men and women who became the core leaders of the Fang Cheng Church. The church network grew from five million in the early 1990s to ten million in 1999.[36]

Another key moment in the life of the Fang Cheng Church occurred in 1988. Dennis Balcombe, an American missionary based in Hong Kong, traveled into Henan and for the first time met with the Fang Cheng leaders. Balcombe's humble bearing and Pentecostal message resonated with the Fang Cheng believers. Sister Ding Hei described Balcombe's influence: "Before Pastor Balcombe came to Henan, some house churches here were already Spirit filled. However, their believers generally didn't speak in tongues, clap hands, or dance during worship.... After two to three years, all our Fang Cheng house churches, except for a few, accepted the Spirit-filled teaching."[37]

Some years ago (November 26, 2002) I met Zhang Rongliang in Southwest China. We discussed various matters for about an hour and a half and then shared a meal together. While we were eating, Sister Ding, the second highest leader in the China for Christ Network, joined us.

During our meal Sister Ding, who was sitting next to me, raised a question about a book on Pentecostal doctrine that I had made available to them.[38] She suggested that baptism in the Spirit, although possibly an experience subsequent to conversion, could also take place at the moment of conversion. She felt the book implied that Spirit baptism must take place after conversion. I assured her that we were all in agreement on this point and that when most Pentecostals speak of baptism in the Spirit as subsequent to conversion, we actually mean that it is logically subsequent to conversion, a distinct work of the Spirit. Temporally both could occur at essentially the same moment, as with Cornelius and his household in Acts 10. We continued our discussion and Sister Ding indicated that their church was Pentecostal in nature.

Sister Ding then stated emphatically that their church came to these classical Pentecostal conclusions, not on the basis of receiving this tradition from others, but rather as a result of their own experience and study of the Book of Acts. She indicated that in the 1970s and 1980s they were quite isolated and experienced considerable persecution. In this crucible of persecution they developed their classical Pentecostal orientation. At this time their church began to grow rapidly and was widely recognized as the largest house church group in China.

As I reflect back on this conversation, I can now see that there are several streams of Pentecostal influence that have impacted China's house churches. First, it is clear that there were seeds of Pentecostal teaching and revival planted by the indigenous house churches that were so prominent in China prior to 1949. Additionally, Sister Ding's testimony also points to the Chinese believers' sense of solidarity with the persecution and power of the apostolic church. Their context of suffering encouraged their own Pentecostal reading of the New Testament.[39] Finally, Dennis Balcombe's influence and teaching have served to encourage and give further impetus to Pentecostal revival in China. It is probably difficult to overstate the impact of Balcombe's example and teaching on the Pentecostal churches in China. Clearly, as Sister Ding notes, Pentecostal influences were already present in the Fang Cheng Church. Nevertheless, there can be little doubt that Balcombe was a key instrument that God used to fan the flames.[40]

Toward the end of my time with Zhang and Ding, I asked them if they felt the majority of Christians in China were Pentecostal. Brother Zhang answered that apart from the government-recognized (TSPM) churches and various smaller house church groups, the vast majority were indeed Pentecostal. He considered, in addition to their own church, the China Gospel Fellowship, the Li Xin Church, and the Ying Shang Church to be Pentecostal.

On another occasion late in 2002 I had the joy of teaching in an underground Bible school associated with the China for Christ Network. During one of the breaks the leader of the school showed me around and introduced to me some of the other faculty members. In the midst of our conversation I noted that their theological tradition was similar (*lei si*) to mine (he knew that I was an Assemblies of God minister). He stopped, looked at me, and said emphatically: "No, our theological traditions are the same (*yi yang*)." Later, with great excitement, he spoke of the hunger for the things of the Spirit in the churches in the countryside.

THE LI XIN (ZHONG HUA MENG FU OR "CHINA IS BLESSED") CHURCH

In March of 2014 I met with several leaders of this large Chinese house church network. The Li Xin (China Is Blessed) Church was established in the early 1980s in Anhui Province. It has grown rapidly over the past twenty years and now has churches all over China. The founder and leader of the church, Uncle Zheng, shared with me his fascinating story.

Uncle Zheng became a believer in 1978 in his home village in Li Xin County of Anhui Province. His mother was sick and afflicted by a demon. His brother was also not well, and his father died of an illness when Zheng was thirteen years old. Six or seven other sick people in the area had become Christians. They had no Bible and they were illiterate, but Christian stories and traditions had been passed down to them orally. This small group would often come and pray for Zheng's mother. Zheng remembers that he liked this because when they came, they would share their food with him. In those days he was often hungry.

This small group of believers had a strong influence on Zheng. He watched them as they prayed for his mother and worshipped together. They asked Zheng to help them understand some worship songs that they had received in written form. Since they were illiterate, they needed him to help them understand the content of the songs. As Zheng read the songs to them, he was touched by the message. These early events led to his conversion as a young, sixteen-year-old boy. Eventually Zheng's mother was also wonderfully healed and set free.

Zheng indicated that the church in those days was like the church in the Book of Acts. They relied heavily on testimonies, miracles of healing, and the casting out of demons. And the church grew rapidly. He told of one lady who was baptized in a river near the church. She took a bottle with her and filled it with "holy water" from the river when she was baptized. She then took this water back to her husband, who was very sick, and told him to drink it. He did and was wonderfully healed. Zheng and the others said that they had many stories like this.

An important event took place in 1983. The police were pressuring Zheng to stop his church meetings and close down the church. Finally he said that he would, but that he wanted to meet with the believers one last time. When he returned home, his mother, who at this time was still possessed by a demon, began to laugh in a loud, demonic voice. When Zheng heard this demonic laugh, which seemed to symbolize Satan's triumph, he felt prompted by the Holy Spirit not to give up and close down the church. Zheng indicated that this was the beginning of a period of many miracles and rapid growth in the church.

The Pentecostal message, complete with an emphasis on speaking in tongues, came to the church in 1988. Two Christian brothers were released from prison after spending fifteen years in a labor camp. Zheng noted that the earlier generation (1950s to '70s) of evangelists spent many years in labor camps; his generation (1980s and '90s) represented the "short-term" generation, because they only spent a few years in prison. These two brothers encouraged Zheng and his church to consider the role of speaking in tongues in their own worship and prayer lives. They also introduced them to a Romanian missionary, Brother Matthew, who brought to them the Pentecostal message of tongues as the sign of baptism in the Holy Spirit. They said from this point on they began to emphasize the work of the Spirit and speaking in tongues.

Dennis Balcombe visited the church in 1988, and his influence was also significant. Uncle Zheng and his colleagues spoke of Balcombe's ministry and influence with great appreciation. In fact, they began to receive Bibles in 1985; this was largely due to the ministry of Balcombe's church in Hong Kong.

The church began to grow rapidly and spread beyond the borders of Anhui Province beginning in 1990. A catalyst for this came in 1993. The police attempted to arrest Zheng, and their efforts forced him into an itinerant mode of ministry. From 1993 through 2002 he traveled widely through many provinces, preaching and evading the police. Although Zheng stated that their church does not face strong opposition or persecution now, this earlier period was an important time of church growth, stimulated by persecution. He noted that this was also the experience of the early church in Acts.

I asked Zheng and the other leaders how they would compare the church today with the church of the earlier years (1980s). They said that the church of the early years was largely a village church and that the gospel moved from the villages to the cities. Now, they said that the church is taking root in the cities and the gospel is now moving from the cities to the villages. They feel that this transformation of the church from a largely rural context to a largely urban context is a part of God's plan. While they noted that the village church emphasized spiritual life and the urban church highlights spiritual gifts, they also observed that some in recent years are not as committed as those in the early years; generally they feel that the church today is vital, committed, and strong. In fact, they noted the parallels with the growth of the church in the Book of Acts: the church began with uneducated fishermen like Peter, but as it expanded into the Gentile world, God used an educated man like Paul to help the church expand. So also in China; God used illiterate villagers to establish the church, now He is using university graduates to take the gospel to those in the cities and beyond. They noted that their church now emphasizes planting churches among the university students of the cities because they see this as the future of China's church.

Zheng viewed the early days, when they did not have a Bible and people experienced miracles in a way that might be viewed as superstitious, in a positive way. He noted that in those days, "We did not begin our presentation of the gospel by talking about sin and the need for forgiveness." These were concepts that the villagers would not readily understand or feel significant. Rather they began by talking about Jesus's power to heal and to free people from demonic bondage. In time people came to understand other elements and implications of the gospel, but this was God's way of reaching down and touching people at their point of need. I found this striking, for it reminded me of the ministry of Jesus. Zheng and his colleagues did not view the focus on the miraculous as superstitious; rather, they understood these experiences as God graciously accommodating His work to their situation and needs—a divinely inspired contextualization of the gospel.

Zheng highlighted that their churches continue to emphasize and experience the Holy Spirit's power and gifts, such as speaking in tongues. Zheng put it this way: "While we believe that the apostles are gone [limited to the Twelve], the Spirit of the apostles is still the same." He also said that, "Acts is the pattern for the mission of the church. If the church does not follow the path of the early church, we will lose our way."

THE HOUSE CHURCH STATEMENT OF FAITH

On November 26, 1998, a group of four house leaders, including the leaders of the Fang Cheng Network and the China Gospel Fellowship, signed a statement of faith that they had forged together during meetings convened throughout the previous days. This statement represents the most significant theological statement issued by house church leaders to date. It is thoroughly evangelical and organized around seven key headings: On the Bible; On the Trinity; On Christ; On Salvation; On the Holy Spirit; On the Church; and On the Last Things. The statement on the Holy Spirit is especially significant for our purposes. It reads:

> On the Holy Spirit: We believe that the Holy Spirit is the third person of the Trinity. He is the Spirit of God, the Spirit of Christ, the Spirit of truth and the Spirit of holiness. The Holy Spirit illuminates a person causing him to know sin and repent, to know the truth and to believe in Christ and so experience being born again unto salvation. He leads the believers into the truth, helps them to understand the truth and obey Christ, thereby bearing abundant fruit of life. The

Holy Spirit gives all kinds of power and manifests the mighty acts of God through signs and miracles. The Holy Spirit searches all things. In Christ God grants a diversity of gifts of the Holy Spirit to the church so as to manifest the glory of Christ. Through faith and thirsting, Christians can experience the outpouring and filling of the Holy Spirit. We do not believe in the cessation of signs and miracles or the termination of the gifts of the Holy Spirit after the apostolic period. We do not forbid speaking in tongues, and we do not impose on people to speak in tongues; nor do we insist that speaking in tongues is the evidence of being saved.

We refute the view that the Holy Spirit is not a person of the Trinity but only a kind of influence.[41]

This statement contains several significant declarations that highlight the Pentecostal leanings of its framers. First, the notion that Charismatic gifts were given only for the apostolic period (cessationism) is explicitly denied: "We do not believe in the cessation of signs and miracles or the termination of the gifts of the Holy Spirit after the apostolic period." Thus, it is not surprising that the statement also declares that the Holy Spirit "gives all kinds of power and manifests the mighty acts of God through signs and miracles." This statement, at the very least then, identifies the framers and the house church groups they represent as Charismatic.

However, there is more. This statement contains another significant declaration: "Through faith and thirsting, Christians can experience the outpouring and filling of the Holy Spirit." Since this "outpouring and filling" may be received by Christians, this phrase must refer to a work of the Spirit subsequent to (at least logically, if not temporally) the regenerating work of the Spirit experienced at conversion. Although the purpose or impact of this gift is not explicitly stated, it is interesting to note that the language used to describe the experience (i.e., "outpouring and filling") is drawn from the Book of Acts.[42] It seems obvious that a strengthening or empowering of the believer by the Spirit in accordance with the experience of the early church as recorded in the Book of Acts is in view here. The only prerequisites for receiving this gift that are listed in the statement are "faith" and "thirsting." Surely this is another way of saying that this gift is available to all earnest believers who desire it. This statement then speaks of an empowering by the Spirit that is distinct from conversion and available to every believer. It thus identifies the framers as not only Charismatic but Pentecostal as well.

Finally, let us examine the reference to tongues: "We do not forbid speaking in tongues, and we do not impose on people to speak in tongues; nor do we insist that speaking in tongues is the evidence of being saved." The phrase "we do not impose on people to speak in tongues" probably should be taken in light of what follows to mean that they do not force believers to speak in tongues by means of emotional or psychological coercion (e.g., by declaring tongues to be a sign that they are truly believers).[43] It is highly unlikely that the framers, with this phrase, were consciously renouncing the initial evidence doctrine of classical Pentecostalism. This seems to be an obvious conclusion in view of the fact that one of the four cardinal framers (Zhang Rongliang) is the head of an overtly classical Pentecostal group, the Fang Cheng Church.

The only doctrine that the statement specifically rejects and that is relatively common in evangelical circles in the West is the doctrine that denies the current validity of speaking in tongues. The statement is very clear: "We do not forbid speaking in tongues." The statement, of course, also rejects the relatively rare notion that tongues-speech is a sign of salvation.[44]

In short, the statement on tongues does not appear to be a rejection of the classical Pentecostal position. However, it does not affirm this position either. It reads like a very diplomatic attempt to steer a middle path between two extremes. It rejects the position of those who would seek to forbid tongues, and it refutes those who would seek to use manipulative means to force believers to speak in tongues. In fact, the careful way in which this statement is framed suggests that it is a wise compromise that accommodates both classical Pentecostals on the one hand and Charismatics on the other.

THE FUTURE OF PENTECOSTALISM IN CHINA

Pentecostal churches in China have experienced exhilarating growth over the past decades, but as they look to the future, they face a number of new challenges:

First: In the past, Pentecostal churches have been strong in the rural areas. With the economic changes that are transforming China, they will need to impact the cities if they are to experience continued growth. Will Chinese urban centers prove to be fertile soil for Pentecostal ministry?

Actually, the outlook here is bright. Strange as it may sound, the process of modernization and development may represent a major factor in creating a context conducive for the growth of Pentecostal Christianity. Ryan Dunch, in a very perceptive article, notes that modernization does impact the religious makeup of a nation. However, he suggests that rather than "producing a straightforward decline in religion," modernization tends to change its nature. More specifically, Dunch suggests that religion, as it meets modernization, tends to become more voluntary (rather than acquired at birth), individualized, and experiential. These shifts in turn force religious institutions to change accordingly. Dunch views the Pentecostal movement as especially well suited to minister to the needs of people in societies, like that of China, which are shaped by industrial market economies.[45]

Second: China's Christian population was isolated for decades. During this period the Pentecostal churches exploded. Now that the influence of foreign churches, many with different theological perspectives, is on the rise, do Chinese Pentecostals have the theological resources to compete in the marketplace of ideas?

This is a question that remains to be answered, but there are promising signs on the horizon. Largely due to the gifted and tireless labor of Robert Yeung and his colleagues at the Synergy Institute for Leadership based in Hong Kong, a number of significant Pentecostal books have been translated into Chinese. Furthermore, Pentecostal Chinese scholars like Aaron Zhuang, Timothy Yeung, and Iap Sian Chin have produced important works in Chinese as well. Additionally, the leaders and faculty of Ecclesia Bible College in Hong Kong, an Assemblies of God Bible school, next year will launch the *Chinese Journal of Pentecostal Theology*, the first Chinese language journal of its kind. Asia Pacific Theological Seminary, located in Baguio City of the Philippines, is also offering master's-level theology degrees in Chinese. David Wang of the Hosanna Foundation is partnering with Jack Hayford's King's University to provide master's and doctor of ministry programs for house church leaders in China. These positive developments bode well for the future of the Pentecostal movement in China.

The challenges are very real, however. In my recent interview with Dennis Balcombe he stated that the primary challenge Pentecostals in China currently face comes from the virulent attacks from the Indonesian-based pastor Stephen Tong. Balcombe likens Tong's theology, laced as it is with cessationist polemic, to "rat poison," which combines much that is good with a little that is deadly. Balcombe cites several examples of churches that have been destroyed after embracing Tong's teachings.[46]

Nevertheless, in spite of the critiques of Pentecostal theology and praxis offered by Stephen Tong, I find it hard to believe that this sort of cessationist teaching, rooted as it is in an elaborate and opaque philosophical system, will win the hearts and minds of many Chinese Christians. It should be noted that one of the great strengths of the global Pentecostal movement is its simple, straightforward approach to the Bible. Chinese Pentecostals love the stories of the Bible. They identify with the stories that fill the pages of the Gospels and Acts, and the lessons gleaned from these stories are easily grasped and applied in their lives.

In a country still populated by a large group of semi-literate people, the simplicity of the Pentecostal approach, rooted as it is in the biblical narrative, is a huge asset. The stories of the Bible and the stories of personal testimony often play an important role in Pentecostal worship and instruction. These stories make the communication of the message much easier, especially when cultural barriers need to be hurdled. This is particularly so when the stories connect with the felt needs of the hearers, as is generally the case with stories of spiritual deliverance, physical healing, and moral transformation. In China, a narrative approach that takes seriously the spiritual needs of people and the miraculous power of God is destined to win a hearing.

Third: Can Chinese Pentecostals, who have thrived under intense persecution, survive in a context of increased freedom and growing affluence? This may be the most difficult challenge of all. The experience of Chinese Pentecostals has taught us that Pentecost brings with it a double promise: the anointing of the Spirit brings both power and persecution. It is hard to maintain one without the other.[47]

CONCLUSION

The story of Pentecost in China is remarkable. It begins with ordinary people, like Alfred Garr and Mok Lai Chi, who were caught up in the fire of Pentecostal revival. The spark they released ignited into a flame that swept through the indigenous churches, groups like the True Jesus Church and the Jesus Family, which in turn shaped the ethos of the dynamic house church movement that has registered explosive growth in the face of mind-numbing opposition. Now, as China is undergoing rapid and massive transformation, Pentecostals in China face new and significant challenges. But we well may find that these challenges in reality represent fresh opportunities. If the last six decades in China have taught us anything, they have surely taught us never to underestimate the power of the Holy Spirit.[48]

Chapter 5

Bernt Berntsen: A Prominent Oneness Pentecostal Pioneer to North China

Iap Sian-Chin

IN CHINESE CHRISTIAN history recent studies of Christian mission movements have taken a crucial new direction. However, there is still a relative lack of related historical study with regard to Pentecostal missionaries in this area.

In this essay I attempt to explore the work of an earlier Norwegian American Pentecostal missionary to North China—Bernt Berntsen, who influenced the earliest founders of the True Jesus Church (TJC), the largest Chinese independent Pentecostal-like church today. This essay will introduce Berntsen's life and thought by comparing his Chinese periodical, *Popular Gospel Truth*, with other secondary publications. I will then address his concept of Oneness. With the connection between Berntsen and TJC's "pioneers," the origin of the latter's Oneness purpose can clearly be traced.

It is well known that theologically the TJC has always distinguished itself from other Protestant churches. Initially TJC proclaimed that it is the only true church providing salvation. In keeping with this proclamation, as we can see, they named their church the "true" church. Secondly, they opposed the traditional Trinitarian doctrine, asserting the oneness of the Godhead. They also baptize people in Jesus's name and generally advocate that the identical nature between "regeneration in the Spirit" and "Spirit baptism" is different from the Pentecostal "two-stage" or "three-stage" model. In these matters TJC seems to be very similar with American Oneness Pentecostals.

BERNT BERNTSEN AND THE PENTECOSTAL MOVEMENT

Bernt Berntsen was born in 1863 in Larvik, Norway. He immigrated to the United States in 1893, settled in Chicago, and worked as a store-keeper in a local grocery store. He married Nagna Berg, and they had two children.[1] In 1904 he joined a nondenominational Norwegian mission society—the South Zhili Mission (南直隸福音會), founded by Horace William Holding. Berntsen came to China at the age of forty and started his mission work in Damingfu, Zhili Province (today's Daming, Handan, Hebei Province).[2] In 1906 he came across an issue of *Apostolic Faith* and learned the news of the Azusa Street Revival, which interested him.

In 1907 he traveled to the Centennial Missionary Conference in Shanghai, expecting to meet someone who had experienced the Pentecostal gift of tongues; however, all the people he met told him that it was "the work of demons." Upon his returning to the mission field, Berntsen received a letter from a friend in Chicago who claimed that she had been baptized in the Holy Spirit. With this incentive Berntsen determined to go back to the United States to experience the revival. In the same year he traveled to Seattle, where he met Martin L. Ryan, whose team was holding group prayer meetings. Here Berntsen sought for the Spirit baptism in the meetings but did not receive it. He then traveled to Oakland, California, where he attended prayer meetings held by William F. Manley, again without receiving the tongues-attested Spirit baptism. Finally he visited the Azusa Street Mission in Los Angeles, where he was baptized in the Spirit and finally spoke in tongues.[3] The September 1907 issue of *Apostolic Faith* reported this event.[4]

In the January 1908 issue of *Apostolic Faith*, Berntsen's Spirit-baptized experience was published, wherein he mentioned that five years before, a burden came upon him for "more of Jesus," although he was convinced that he had been "sanctified" years before. This, however, did not satisfy him. When he returned to China, the "more-of-Jesus" burden became stronger, and Berntsen said he had been hungry for a "melting power in the Holy Spirit." He also reported that as his wife read the above-mentioned letter to him, the "melting power" for which he had been praying came upon him, and he fell down on the floor crying out, "God's wonderful mercy." According to him, he was baptized in the Spirit on Sunday, September 15, 1907, the third day after his coming to Azusa Street.[5] On this pilgrimage trip to Azusa Street he not only received the Pentecostal experience but also established his connection to the Pentecostal movement.

At the end of the same year Berntsen again went to China, with eleven new workers whom he had recruited in Seattle, and planned to find a place to house a number of orphans for whom he had been caring. At the same time he encouraged other Pentecostal missionaries to remain with him and help with those missionary candidates whom they considered to have a genuine call sufficient to sustain them in long-term missionary work in China.[6] Soon after, he moved his base to Zhengding, Zhili, southwest of Peking (Beijing), which became his first mission station.[7] He then stayed in Zhengding until he moved to Peking in 1917.[8] In 1910 Berntsen left for his hometown in Scandinavia after a short time in the United States. While in Scandinavia he recruited twelve Norwegian missionaries to accompany him back to China.[9] Reporting in 1911 on his mission stations based in Zhengding, the *Pentecostal Testimony* of the North Avenue

Mission (in Chicago) established by William Durham told about several missionaries and an orphan house there and how he kept his home open as a receiving station for missionaries, who, upon their arrival in China, needed a place to rest and study languages and to gain some knowledge, in a practical way, of the work in China.[10] The previous issue of the *Pentecostal Testimony* claimed that Berntsen and his family were "their missionaries" and promised, "We will forward 100 cents on every dollar sent to us for any missionary, anywhere."[11] In 1912 Berntsen established a Chinese language periodical, *Popular Gospel Truth* (通傳福音真理報), in order to spread his Pentecostal beliefs. It is said that this newspaper influenced the earliest TJC pioneers.[12]

BERNTSEN'S AFFILIATION WITH DIFFERENT GROUPS AND THE SHIFT IN HIS THINKING

Since Berntsen's visit to Azusa Street in 1907, his work had also been supported by other Pentecostal mission societies. After his first visit Azusa Street started to support his mission to China; hence, he used the name the "Apostolic Faith Mission" (AFM) when he came back to China. The AFM in China was a loose association of early American Pentecostal missionaries influenced by the 1906 Azusa Street Revival, mainly active in North China. Years later, many of the AFM missionaries in China became affiliated with the Assemblies of God (AG). By 1936 E. L. Brown was the sole AFM representative in China.[13] One can see Mr. and Ms. Berntsen's names as ministers listed in the Minutes of the General Council of the Assemblies of God at the AG meetings held in Hot Springs, Arkansas, and Chicago, Illinois, in 1914.[14] In fact, besides the AFM, several weak Pentecostal mission societies also became affiliated with the newborn Assemblies of God.

It is worth noting that Berntsen changed his church's name four times. At the beginning he used the name *shitu xinxinhui* (Apostolic Faith Mission) or *xinxinhui* (Faith Union). When he moved to Beijing in 1918, his church was called *Fu yintang* (Gospel Hall). The next year, along with moving to Caoyangmeng nei Liangjiadayuan, Beijing, his church was renamed *Zhenshenjiau xinxinhui* (The True God Faith Union). After this it was changed to *Shenjiaohui* (Church of God). As it relates to the name *Shenjiaohui*, it was speculated that this church was not of the Pentecostal denomination (Church of God, Cleveland, TN). In Tiedemann's opinion, this Church of God was a branch of the Adventists, since he found a record of the Church of God in the *Peking Who's Who*, and discovered an "Elder Bernstein" supervising a "Church of God" in Beijing in 1916.[15]

No further references to Berntsen's missionary activities were listed until 1933, when his name appeared on the list of the "seventy to go forth two by two, all Church of God elders."[16] However, he did not abandon his Pentecostal faith. On the other hand, Tiedemann pointed out a salient point: in 1920 Bernsten's son, Henry, married Helga Nathalia Hansen (daughter of Pentecostal missionaries George and Sofie Hansen), and Bernt Berntsen was authorized by the Pentecostal Assemblies of the World (PAW) to perform the ceremony. Hence, to some extent, it shows a certain connection between Berntsen and the Oneness Pentecostals. Interestingly his passport application of August 25, 1919, lists both the PAW and the Church of God.[17] Affiliating with these two groups seems to satisfy his dual identities: Pentecostal and Adventist. We will talk further about his doctrinal perspective on these two issues. According to TJC's writings, Berntsen was regarded as an AG minister, but after being affiliated with the AG, he had left them before encountering the earlier TJC leaders. The reason why his church was called AG was probably in relation to his membership with the PAW, for this denomination in China was called "Assemblies of God Gospel Hall"—神召會福音堂 (*shenzhaohui fuyintang*).[18]

Bernt Berntsen's daughter, Ruth Ester Berntsen, carried on his work at Zhengding in the 1930s, evidently in the Oneness tradition. In August 1946 excerpts of a letter she had received from Chang Ying Shi (張應喜), who had been trained by her father and had subsequently been in charge of the work in China, were published in the *Pentecostal Herald*, the official publication of the United Pentecostal Church.[19] According to TJC's document, this Chang was a native of Shanxi, leading the "Oneness Assembly of God"—位神召會 (*yiui shenzhaohui*)—and converted several TJC members into this church. The document also shows that this church was named by Berntsen[20] and may be another reason why Berntsen's church was called AG.

THE INTERACTION BETWEEN BERNT BERNTSEN AND CHINESE CHURCH LEADERS

The connection between Berntsen's Faith Union and TJC's earlier pioneers has been pointed out by several scholars, while even TJC members also admit to this connection. Their three major founding pioneers, Paul Wei (Wei Enbo), Zhang Ling-Sheng (Zhang Dianju), and Barnabas Zhang (Zhang Bin), all had contact with Berntsen. Upon receiving Spirit-baptism through AFM in Shanghai in 1909, Zhang Ling-Sheng went to Beijing in 1917, where he was ordained as an elder by Berntsen and Elder "Qui" (奎長老).[21] However, scholars state that Zhang was ordained by "elder Peterson," and Zhang persuaded this Peterson to keep the Sabbath;[22] I believe it was Berntsen. The writings of TJC claim that Zhang had persuaded Berntsen to keep the Sabbath. Although Berntsen once accepted this suggestion, he subsequently changed his worship day to Sunday again. Because of this, Wei blamed Bernsten for being weak in his faith.

This account is very similar to the description of "Elder Peterson."[23] *Popular Gospel Truth* recorded the testimony of Barnabas Zhang's Spirit baptism, which shows his association with Berntsen's organization.[24] Besides, Zhang also describes his contact with Berntsen, and Zhang was asked to operate the church together.[25]

Paul Wei had a stronger tie to Berntsen than Zhang. In Wei's autobiography he mentioned his recovery from being sick through the prayer of *Xin Shengmin* (新聖民),[26] and through him he was acquainted with Berntsen. They became close friends. Berntsen helped Wei very much in his faith formation.[27] However, their friendship did not last long since Wei, who opposed the legitimacy of denominations, kept experiencing many "revelations," one of which led him to insist on revoking the title of pastor, because Jesus said, "Do not be called teachers."[28] He also had other "revelations," such as practicing facedown immersion baptism, canceling every denominational name, and changing the name of his group to the "Universal Correction Church" (萬國更正教). Wei also informed many mission church leaders to do the same. Wei then established the True Jesus Church in 1917, which meant that he officially severed his relationship with Berntsen's church.

Another event reinforced the tension between Wei and Berntsen. According to Wei, Berntsen's AFM had a bank account at the Tianjin Bank. When Wei needed to borrow money in order to open another branch of his fabric store, he went to Berntsen for a loan; however, Berntsen required 2 percent interest on the loan. When Wei was not able to pay back the loan on time, Berntsen not only wrote to request the payment but also sued Wei, with Zhao Deli and Xin Shengmin. Gradually Wei's attitude toward Berntsen became bitter, and Wei condemned and rebuked Berntsen, both in his speeches and many times in his writings. Wei constantly described Berntsen as a mammonist. However, we can see different descriptions of the

transaction through a comparison to Wei's report. For example, by
contrast, Barnabas Zhang, one of the three major pioneers of TJC,
reported that Berntsen loaned the money to Wei to earn interest.
When Berntsen became aware of Wei's failing business, he wanted
to withdraw the money he had loaned; however, Wei was unable
to repay the funds. Therefore, the case was brought to court for a
resolution of the matter.[29] In summary, Barnabas Zhang's account
offers another perspective on this event.

It is said that when Paul Wei was dying in September 6, 1919,
Berntsen visited him. They shook hands and emotionally cried
loudly in united forgiveness. During the visit Wei queried Berntsen
again about his willingness to accept facedown baptism. Berntsen
replied, "If the Holy Spirit does so proclaim it, then you may
enter the 'Holy of Holies.'" Wei died later that day amidst his own
laughter, when he proclaimed, "Behold, the Angel has come."[30]

Besides TJC's earlier leaders, Wang Mingdao (王明道) might
have met Berntsen. Wang mentioned that he was expelled from a
Presbyterian school in Baoding in 1921. At that time he was strongly
influenced by some AFM missionaries who proclaimed that being
baptized by immersion was the biblical way. According to Wang,
"Those AFM ministers once 'disturbed' Presbyterian churches."[31]
Wang was subsequently rebaptized by immersion by AFM pastor
Zhu Dingchen. Zhu also led other students to seek Spirit baptism.
Although Wang claimed to receive this experience, in reality he
was suspicious of its moral justification.[32] When Wang returned
to Beijing years later, he again attended Zhu's meetings. He said
that the church had been called "Faith Union" but was changed to
"Church of God" (Shen de jiaohui). The leader was a Norwegian
old man, and since they did not have a regular chapel, meetings
were held at this old man's reception room. Wang also said that the
"Norwegian old man" lived in a courtyard.[33] What Wang described

fits Berntsen's characteristics, his living conditions, and his manner of functioning. When Berntsen moved his base to Beijing, his church did change its name to "Church of God," and he was in his sixties at that time. As for the description of the meeting place, we can refer to what Henry Berntsen mentioned, "We do not rent houses to establish Gospel Halls…we should follow those disciples, to preach and establish church in a believer's home, everywhere."[34] Additionally, the location this periodical calls "*Liangjia dayuan*" was identical to Wang's description. Therefore, I think this "Norwegian old man" was Bernt Berntsen.

BERNTSEN'S ONENESS PENTECOSTAL AND SABBATH BELIEF

Berntsen's Pentecostal experience can be traced to the Azusa Street Revival. Nevertheless, if one reads Berntsen's periodical carefully, he will find that his belief was not identical with those of Azusa Street; rather, it was very similar to the Oneness Pentecostals. As we have seen, the Oneness wing of Pentecostalism assumed the identification between "regeneration in the Spirit" and "baptized in the Spirit," as well as the oneness of the Godhead. This implies that they refused both the two-stage and the three-stage model. Rather, they followed the function of Acts 2:38. While they viewed conversion, baptism in water, and baptism in the Spirit as a complex unity, they still insisted on the initial evidence doctrine. In other words, speaking in tongues was a condition for salvation.[35] African American Oneness Pentecostal leader G. T. Haywood thought that the "rest" quoted in Matthew 11:28 should be understood as "the full salvation," and he connected this verse with Isaiah 28:11–12, claiming that by being baptized in the Spirit and speaking in tongues, one acquires "the full salvation."[36] It has been said that those from the Oneness camp have their roots in William Durham's teachings. Frank Macchia emphasizes that Durham challenged the three-step model advocated by early Wesleyan Pentecostals of justification, entire sanctification, and Spirit-baptism.[37] Since Christ's "finished work" on the cross and in the Resurrection is sufficient to completely save us, one must be born again and entirely sanctified at the moment of faith in Christ, which can be called "single-work perfectionism." Durham, however, did not include Spirit baptism within the fullness that is achieved through faith in Christ and His finished work. The Oneness Pentecostals who came from Durham's wing, however, did take Durham's position in this direction.

In 1916 Berntsen announced "Statements of Zhengdingfu Xinxinhui" on the front page of issue 13 of *Popular Gospel Truth*, which intended to explain their basic beliefs. The first article, "Baptism by Immersion in the Name of Jesus Christ," was apparently related to the statement of the Godhead.[38] According to this statement, we can see that Berntsen's doctrine of the Godhead was obviously not traditionally Trinitarian. Berntsen also pointed out elsewhere that the Father gave His name to Jesus; hence, Jesus is the true God. Besides, he enumerated other verses to demonstrate his arguments; for example, he thought that "the glorious riches of this mystery, which is Christ in you, the hope of glory" (Col. 1:27, NIV) means the indwelling of the Spirit; hence, Christ is the Spirit. In Colossians 2:9 (MEV), "For in Him lives all the fullness of the Godhead bodily," he claimed that everything of the Father, Son, and the Holy Spirit is fulfilled in Jesus Christ, for Jesus represents the Father, Son, and the Spirit.[39] To sum up, it is the Holy Spirit, and only one Spirit shares three names.

As for Spirit baptism, Bernsten was also obviously familiar with Oneness Pentecostals. He frequently argued that receiving "baptism in water and the Spirit" can be regarded as effective salvation. By quoting John 3:5 and 1 Corinthians 12:13, he argued that being baptized by the Spirit into one body, which can be viewed as the body of Jesus, qualifies one to ascend to heaven with Jesus. Obviously Berntsen's perspective in Spirit baptism distinguishes him from the majority of Pentecostals.

Simultaneously Berntsen also emphasized the doctrine of "initial evidence" by quoting so-called "key passages" in the Book of Acts, while connecting it to the process of salvation.

Among the earlier three pioneers of TJC, Wei was considered the key person in establishing the organization and teaching its doctrines. When he initially engaged in Pentecostal beliefs, he was very close to Berntsen. Compared to what Wei stated in 1917 about doctrines of revelations from the inspiration of the Holy Spirit, we can discover the similarities with Xinxinhui's statements of faith established by Berntsen. Wei claimed that the Holy Spirit directed him to preach the following "Correction of the church's principles":

1. Must seek baptism in the Holy Spirit, for if one is not born of water and the Spirit, he cannot enter the Kingdom of God.

2. Must receive baptism by complete immersion in water, for Jesus was baptized in the same way.

3. Be baptized in the name of Jesus, rather than in the name of the Father, Son, and the Holy Spirit.

4. Must keep the Sabbath, and one should not keep the Sabbath on Sunday.

5. Revoke the title of pastor, for we only have a master, which is Jesus Christ.

6. Do not call God as Shangdi 上帝 or Tianzhu 天主; instead, call God Shen 神 or Zhenshen 真神.[40]

Except for the last two articles, the revelations he claimed to have received from God were actually not different from the messages preached by Berntsen. Subsequently TJC added foot washing as one of their "Ten Main Doctrines and Beliefs." Briefly we can say TJC's beliefs were related, to some extent, to Bernt Berntsen.

Concerning the link between Berntsen and the Oneness Pentecostals, there are some connections that must also be noted. As mentioned earlier, in 1910 Durham's North Avenue Mission stated that Berntsen was a missionary sent out by the church. Furthermore, Durham's "finished work" theory became a crucial element to subsequent Oneness Pentecostals. Durham himself had been a Pilgrim to Azusa Street too, but his "finished work" perspective in sanctification soon conflicted with the Azusa Holiness "three-stage" statement and resulted in a separation between the two parties. Berntsen determined to stay with the North Avenue Mission, which might have brought about a change in his thinking. According to his testimony in Azusa Street, he claimed to be sanctified before Spirit baptism, which was a typical holiness-Azusa Street's view. *Popular Gospel Truth* also shows Berntsen's position in the Oneness wing, which had gradually departed from the main lines of the Azusa Street tradition. Additionally we find that he published subsequent Oneness Pentecostal leaders such as G. T. Haywood[41] and Frank Ewart,[42] both of whom were followers of Durham.

As we noted earlier, Mr. and Mrs. Berntsen had been listed in the AG ministerial list in 1915.[43] At this point it is clear that Berntsen was a certified AG minister. It is worth noting that 1915 might be the climax of the Oneness issue raised in AG and Pentecostal communities. In the same year the headline of the *Weekly Evangel* was, "The Sad New Issue," which intensely criticized the Oneness view. Interestingly Berntsen's mission field report in North China appeared on page 4 of this issue of the newspaper. Compared to the headline, Berntsen's viewpoint should be what the official position condemned. During the same year the *Minutes of the General Council of Assemblies of God* mentioned the model of baptism, which refused the ongoing tendency of re-baptism; verily, the emphasis here is connected with the issue of the Godhead.[44] The same minutes increasingly made some statements of faith, which were apparently directed toward the "new issue," which referred to equating rebirth with Spirit baptism as an unbiblical teaching. Then it stated that the Spirit and the blood, the Father and the Son, and Christ and the Holy Ghost cannot be confused.[45] The minutes of 1916 spent two pages stating that AG observes the traditional Trinitarian view.[46] William Menzies described "considerable tension in the air" in the 1916 General Council where all preachers and churches were forced to take a stand on the new issue. The council began with the Trinitarians at a decided advantage: they regained some of the leaders who had been participating in the Oneness wing.[47] With the "Jesus only" issue, the AG lost more than 150 ministers.[48] After this event we no longer see Mr. and Mrs. Berntsen's names on the ministerial list for 1917. It is possible that he reconfirmed his position in this issue and determined to leave the Trinitarian AG.

Besides the Oneness Pentecostal agenda, Berntsen had another view that is worth noting—the Sabbath. At this point Berntsen's views seem to be very similar with TJC. In issue 13 in 1916 of *Popular Gospel Truth*, Berntsen declared that from July 1, 1916, onward his church would worship on Saturdays instead of Sundays, for it had been three days and three nights from Jesus's burial to His resurrection. He then said Jesus died on the preparation day of the Passover, which should be Wednesday, and Jesus was resurrected on a Saturday night; hence, we should worship on Saturdays (three days from Wednesday).[49] In the same issue of this newspaper

Henry Berntsen mentioned the reason his father had, overnight, changed worship day from Sundays to Saturdays, which he had been thinking about and praying about for thirteen years. Berntsen had received an earlier publication talking about Jesus being resurrected on Saturday and was almost persuaded at that time; however, on reflection, he also worried about his Xinxinhui companions possibly blaming him (and discontinuing their financial support to him) for the change. However, he ran into Xin Shengmin, who had kept Saturdays as the official worship day and who claimed he received a revelation about this truth from the Holy Spirit at the same time Berntsen made his decision, which appeared to Berntsen as a confirmation of the "truth." Thus, commencing on July 1, 1916, he determined to worship on Saturdays. He also wrote to his son, Henry, who was in Sunjiazhuang at the time, and told him to also follow his decision.[50] Regardless, the next year he abandoned his change of keeping the Sabbath and declared that worshipping on the Western Sabbath day is equivalent to worshipping on Sunday in China, because of the eighteen-hour time differences between China and the Garden of Eden.[51] But in 1919 Berntsen announced in *Popular Gospel Truth* that he would keep Saturday as the Sabbath again.

As mentioned above, the Sabbath was also one of the core beliefs for TJC. Tiedemann argued that these encounters between Berntsen and the TJC pioneers had a bearing on the development of Pentecostal-Sabbatarian elements in TJC.[52] According to TJC's statement, in 1916 Zhang Lingsheng advised Berntsen to observe the seventh-day worship, and Berntsen was persuaded by Zhang and he announced it in *Popular Gospel Truth*.[53] Furthermore, according to Barnabas Zhang's account, in 1917 Zhang Lingsheng left for Tianjin to cope with personal issues. On this trip he stopped in Beijing to discuss the issue about the Sabbath with Berntsen.[54]

Nevertheless, the Berntsens said that he had, for more than ten years, already thought about keeping the Sabbath. Moreover, at that time he had not been engaged in the Pentecostal movement. Yet they never mentioned Zhang Lingsheng's persuasion. Judging from this time element, Zhang Lingsheng started to keep the Sabbath earlier than Berntsen, and the first time they met each other was in 1914. Barnabas Zhang also announced that he had kept the Saturday Sabbath before encountering Berntsen.[55] By his record it happened in the spring of 1915, before Berntsen announced keeping the Sabbath. In addition, Paul Wei was reported receiving Seventh-Day Adventist's teachings in 1915.[56] To sum up, it seems impossible for TJC's pioneers to be influenced by Berntsen on the issue of the Sabbath. At the same time, only minimal information can demonstrate that Berntsen was persuaded by TJC's pioneers to keep the Sabbath.

A salient point worth noting is the root of the Adventist "Church of God." Tiedemann discovered that the record about "Elder D. Bernstein in the Church of God, Beijing" was in 1916, which was precisely the year Bernsten announced the precept to keep the Sabbath. Interestingly, in the meantime he kept preaching the Pentecostal beliefs, in spite of his involvement in the Sabbath-Adventist movement. According to his newspaper, Berntsen's church had actually been changed into the Church of God. Tiedemann indicated that this church should be in the Sabbath-Adventist tradition. As I noted above, Berntsen was simultaneously affiliated with the PAW. It seems that the connection with these two denominations satisfied his dual identity: Pentecostal and Sabbath-Adventist. Berntsen might have been equally comfortable with these beliefs.[57]

In summary, with respect to the Sabbath beliefs, we can conclude that TJC's Sabbath announcement might not have come from Berntsen. On the other hand, TJC's one-sided statement claimed that Berntsen was influenced by the former to keep the Sabbath; however, there is no direct evidence to prove it. In issue 18 the report of *Popular Gospel Truth* seemed to exclude the influence of TJC. It is also possible that both parties had held the idea of seventh-day worship before they met each other. For Berntsen, who had never announced the idea in public, the encounter with Zhang Lingsheng simply reinforced his idea that worshipping on Saturdays was the truth. It is also possible that Berntsen deliberately lowered the degree of Zhang's influence.

CONCLUSION

To summarize from Berntsen's biography, first, Berntsen emphasized doctrines that were inconsistent with the contemporary phenomenon of Pentecostalism. He kept revising his beliefs and always had the courage to reflect and adjust his ideas when he felt that was biblical. From another perspective, he may have been thought of as being unstable. However, to his credit, he freed himself from the bonds of tradition in pursuit of the truth. Berntsen marched according to his own convictions.

Second, similar to other missionaries who "plunged" into the Pentecostal movement, Berntsen's mission enterprise was given impetus and deepened by his experience of the Spirit. His mission work in North China directly contributed to the establishment of an influential Chinese independent Pentecostal denomination, The True Jesus Church. His position in Chinese Christian history should be reappraised.[58]

Contemporary Expressions of a Spirit-Led Christian Movement: A Chinese Case Study

Yalin Xin

A CHRISTIAN MOVEMENT KNOWN as the Word of Life (here-after, WOL) that started in rural China about four decades ago has grown dramatically and unexpectedly.[1] Why? While a variety of perspectives can be brought to answering this question—i.e., church growth, missiology, and social movement theories—this chapter responds from the perspective of Howard Snyder's biblical, theological, and historical model, more specifically, his theory regarding the five dimensions of Pentecost: (1) harvest of the firstfruits, (2) time and history, (3) peoplehood and witness, (4) sovereign action of the Holy Spirit, and (5) the eschatological promise of new creation.[2]

The WOL movement may not be a typical case within the commonly accepted framework of Pentecostal studies and is even classified as "non-Charismatic" by one of the studies on Chinese Pentecostalism.[3] It is, arguably, a Spirit-led Christian movement, vibrant and dynamic, as this study reveals, and deserves to be regarded as "one of the most powerful, sustained revivals in church history."[4] Rather than attempting to explain WOL as a supernatural encounter of the Spirit of God, this chapter will seek to uncover, record, and analyze the inner dynamics of the movement, in particular the human response to the perceived leading and working of the Spirit. Such signs of the Spirit in the Chinese context can be recognized through believers' reflections on the Word of God amidst their practice in ministry, prayer, witness, house church structure, networking, fellowship, discipleship, and strategic initiatives.

Snyder's five-dimensional model of Pentecost provides a biblical and holistic framework through which this Chinese Christian movement is discussed. It is only natural that some of these dimensions engage the dynamic of the WOL movement more closely than others because "'Pentecostal' movements of various sorts typically stress one or two of these themes," as Snyder explains, but all these dimensions are "part of revealed Scripture" and "all contribute to the dynamic of revitalization."[5] For the theological aspect of this study I will add a sixth dimension, the Spirit's empowerment for evangelistic witnessing that is both biblical and closely relevant to the Chinese context.

A BRIEF HISTORY

The WOL movement originated in Henan Province in central China. It had a humble beginning as a rural house church in one of the poorest areas of China, but it rose up as one of the most dynamic recent Chinese Christian movements. Starting with the evangelistic zeal of a handful of faithful believers four decades ago, this house church multiplied and spread all over Henan and into other provinces. Farmers, as marginals of Chinese society, were empowered by the Spirit to be dynamic leaders of the movement that impacted a significant part of China's rural population with the gospel.[6]

Under the leadership of Peter Xu, founder and leader of the movement, and characterized by its indigenized theology and structure, the WOL distinguished itself as a significant house church movement from the mid-1980s onward. Not only did it bear witness to the power of the Spirit of God in China, but also believers structured themselves in response to the Spirit's leading in such a way that contributed to the movement's sustained growth and dynamic:

> (1) The WOL structured itself in different levels of coworkers' meetings and conferences, whereby house churches in different areas and regions were connected and interlinked in organization and fellowship; (2) it developed its own theological training system, through which all new converts went through some form of basic discipleship training program before some were selected for further training in the underground seminaries in preparation for full-time ministry; (3) by studying and reflecting on the Word of God, and summarizing its experience in ministry, the WOL was able to produce its own training manual, the *Seven Principles*.[7]

As a strong community of faith grounded on the Word and Spirit, informed by its contextual theology, developing along the lines of its theological training system, WOL Christians made use of the opportunities given in their historical context as the movement continued evangelistic outreach to the communities in the neighboring provinces. One of the key dynamics of the WOL movement was its three constituent aspects, or its basic structure, namely, established churches (or local congregations), theological education (or training centers and underground seminaries), and the Gospel Band (or mission agency), which started to take shape from the mid-1980s. These three features of the WOL have been working coherently together, undergirding the growth of the movement. This structure expresses what Patrick Johnstone, author of *The Future of the Global Church* (2012), calls "The Ministry of Jesus/The Early Church" and what he suggests is "A 21st C Missional Church/Congregation" model.[8] By the end of the 1980s the WOL movement had established more than three thousand house churches across the country.[9]

The 1990s saw the incredible expansion of the WOL movement to the various regions of the country as believers devoted themselves to the work of evangelism as "Messengers of the Gospel" (hereafter, MGs).[10] It established house churches across the country, and its network touched every province in China with the gospel. Statistics show that, by the end of the twentieth century, the WOL had established approximately fifty thousand house churches throughout China.[11] The movement has continued to cross national boundaries and has established churches, training centers, and fellowships overseas, contributing its part in following the biblical mandate of spreading the gospel toward the ends of the earth.

The WOL can be understood as a story of how the Spirit of God inspired and guided faithful followers of Christ and how those believers responded in faith, discernment, and action, structuring themselves according to what they felt was impressed on their hearts and minds by the Spirit. It is a story of faithful believers: plowing, planting, weeding, and gathering, trusting the power of the Spirit of God to bring their labor to fruition, to convict and convert, to touch and change lives, and to empower achievement of great things for the kingdom.

HARVEST OF FIRSTFRUITS

Pentecost, the Feast of the Weeks as in the Old Testament, is associated with the celebration of the firstfruits (Num. 28:26), "a celebration of real physical, edible grain," which also symbolizes God's faithfulness in His covenantal relationship with His people and the land.[12] "The Feast of Weeks thus celebrated God's gracious provision of the land and the harvest. Israel's well-being depended upon God's blessing of the land and upon Israel's fidelity in serving God and nurturing, and being nourished by, the land"; "By its very nature Pentecost as a harvest celebration points to the future," linking "past and present with God's yet-to-be-realized promises. Fruitfulness, and ever-increasing fruitfulness, is part of the promise of Pentecost."[13]

So, in this respect, Pentecost and what is associated with it in Acts 2 can also be understood as manifestations of the firstfruits, testifying to and symbolizing the fuller manifestation of the power of the Spirit in the future. "It testifies to the materiality and goodness of the creation, both human and nonhuman, and it witnesses to God's covenant relationship with his people and the earth. Seedtime and harvest sowing and reaping is thus a key biblical theme even if not tied specifically to Pentecost in the New Testament."[14] Sowing the gospel seed and reaping a harvest of souls has become a prominent theme in many evangelical missionary and evangelistic movements.[15]

Themes of sowing the gospel seeds were easily recognizable in the WOL movement: the emphasis of its theology, the structure, for instance, all point to the ultimate goal of sowing the gospel seeds for soul harvest. The introduction to one of the lessons in their *Truth Practice Curriculum*, the WOL theology and training manual, appeals, "in this time of the Holy Spirit, Messengers of the Gospel should not waste any time in sowing and harvesting, holding high the banner of the cross and preaching Christ."[16] Of course this theme is not unique to the WOL movement. Other house church networks share a similar accent, reflecting a continuity of the earlier fundamentalist tradition brought in by Western missionaries.

Historical continuity

For the WOL movement we could trace the influence from Marie Monson, a Norwegian Lutheran (evangelical) missionary to Henan during the first three decades of the twentieth century, who recognized the difference between head knowledge and owning new life among missionaries to China and Chinese coworkers. Monson realized that:

> ...the revival she anticipated would be the result of long-term work...in order for people to understand salvation, teaching them how to read the word and planting the seeds of the Word of God into people's hearts was the priority. When the time came, the Spirit of God would turn the Scripture hidden in the hearts into light, and the Word became life, and true help in life.[17]

Monson was well known in Henan where she was based, training Bible women and leading revival meetings, and was responsible for influencing the earlier Chinese believers with her Pietistic and conservative theology, among whom were grandparents of some of WOL Christians.

Embracing Monson's heritage, the WOL movement placed the reading and preaching of the Word of God as the first priority in ministry and discipleship. Reading of the Word of God was part of the daily personal devotion for believers. At all levels of training and underground seminaries, reading and memorizing the Scripture became part of the routine of the whole training period, whether it was two weeks, three months, or six months. Common among WOL believers, prayers consisted of significant amount of scriptural reading, reflection, and recitation, as they taught, "Eat the Word, chew it, and regurgitate it in prayer." As one of the exercises in underground seminary training, trainees would join in prayer with fellow students and teachers after each lesson to "regurgitate" (with reflection) what they had just learned from the Scripture and the lesson. This would also become a significant part of the practice that reflects the peoplehood of the movement (which will be dealt with later).

Structural emphasis

The WOL system of training emphasizes sowing the gospel seeds in preparation for the harvest of souls at the end of days. Salvation through the cross, the first principle in the WOL contextual theology, is regarded as the entry point to Christian faith. Systematic study of the topic is undertaken at various levels: evangelistic meetings, life meetings, truth meetings, and underground seminary training of different lengths. This has become foundational to establishing a solid faith in Christ and owning "life" through the rebirth experience, evidenced in transformed lives and empowered ministry. Dedication for full-time Christian service is highly encouraged via different levels of training for those selected to work as MGs, or itinerant evangelists, the backbone in the continuous growth and expansion of the movement.

The training system starts with evangelistic and revival meetings; continues in life meetings and truth meetings; and moves on to short-term or pre-theological education training (Pre-TE), TE-1, TE-2, and, for some, shifts to TE-3 and graduate class. Typically, evangelistic and revival meetings are organized and facilitated with the house churches by the MGs in the area. These meetings often last from three to fifteen days, when "seekers" and believers are gathered in one place for the duration of the session to encounter the new reality of the Christian faith through worship, prayers, singing praises, preaching, confession, repentance, meditation, and counseling.

Theological education (TE) at all levels is more centralized in undisclosed locations for a longer period of time. For example, TE-1 normally lasts three to four months in practice, while TE-2 lasts about six months. Trainees are closely involved with ministry practice so they can immediately apply knowledge in ministry, reflect on their successes and failures, and contribute to the community's hermeneutical understanding of the Christian faith. Upon graduation from TE-2, trainees are assigned to the "Gospel Band," one of the three constituents of the WOL movement, where strategic sending takes places for frontier evangelism, establishing house churches, training believers, and recruiting to the Gospel Band. And the cycle continues.

The explosive growth of the WOL community testifies to the biblical theme of seedtime and harvest, which was explained by Jesus in the parables as a *musterion* (secret) of the kingdom of God: "Some of the seed reproduces extravagantly—'thirty and sixty and [even] a hundredfold'—the key, apparently, to kingdom fruitfulness (Mark 4:20; cf. Mk. 4:27–29)."[18] Maybe the good soil needs to be prepared, attentive to local factors such as geography, weather, and culture. Maybe the sower needs to attune to the Spirit to be prepared to address local needs. In *Models of the Kingdom* (1991) Snyder explains:

> The kingdom is a mystery because it is God's action and yet involves human participation or response, because in some sense its reality is accessible only by faith and because it is in some way bound up with the mystery of the incarnation.... Further, the kingdom involves the mystery of human history, personality, and culture, none of which is yet fully understood.[19]

At any rate, the Chinese experience witnesses to the Harvest of Firstfruits, presenting itself as a current manifestation of how the Spirit works in bringing fruition historically and globally. It is a celebration of the "real physical, edible grain."

TIME AND HISTORY

Howard Snyder writes, "God has instituted a historical process, or rather a journey, toward a larger goal of universal shalom" and Pentecost is part of the process as "a ritual reminder of God's goodness now, his provision in the past and his promise for the future."[20] In this sense, "time and history" naturally receive rhetoric emphasis in renewal and revitalization movements historically. Snyder continues: "Renewal movements generally see themselves either as the fulfillment of time and history (prophetic and eschatological accents), or a major rupture of history (apocalyptic accents). The degree of historical continuity or discontinuity varies according to the ideology and the context of such movements."[21]

The WOL movement has a prophetic message that resonates for their times and contexts. The history of Chinese Christianity during the first three decades after 1949 was pale indeed. In Peter Xu's words, "some died for the sake of the Lord; some were imprisoned; some escaped from China; some compromised their faith in fear; some betrayed the Lord and friends. Few dared to openly confess that Jesus is Savior."[22] In the very early stage of the formation of the WOL movement, believers saw themselves as vessels used by God to stir up the fire of true life in Christ in the midst of decline of Christian morale.

"Life" became the issue at stake—life attained through rebirth in Christ, something that would sustain believers in the trials of the day. Christian leaders felt called of God, and empowered by the Holy Spirit, as God's messengers, (1) to speak out to the decline of the health of the church, (2) to stress salvation through the cross as foundation to true Christian faith, and (3) to encourage Christians in suffering with the examples and teaching of Jesus. They started "furnaces of revival,"[23] something uniquely Chinese, to draw people from the dark and cold night of suffering and hopelessness to the light and heat of hope of salvation.

The WOL theology is influenced by the conservative evangelicalism inherited from Pietism of earlier missionaries, such as Marie Monson, the Norwegian Lutheran missionary to Henan. To a certain degree, the WOL is apocalyptic in its theology, believing the end of the age is soon to come. The urgency of saving souls is reflected in the whole training and sending system of the WOL, a dynamic and cycling missional expansion. As such, the WOL serves as a force of renewal within historical Chinese Christianity.

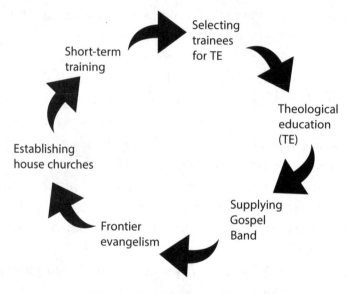

DIAGRAM 1: WOL MISSIONAL MODEL

PEOPLEHOOD AND WITNESS

Howard Snyder writes further that, "Pentecost is a corporate experience, not a private or primarily individual one.... Witness is given to the whole people of God not just to the few," and therefore a biblical model of Pentecost identifies "what God is doing in forming a missional people for his own purposes."[24] This sense of being a distinct people called to be witnesses to a new, inbreaking reality seems also to be a constant in revitalization movements, though in varying ways.[25] This communal self-understanding has been one of the key features of the movement. From the early 1970s new forms of community started to emerge among the house churches in central China—the "furnaces of revival"—which connected Christians for fellowship and attracted nonbelievers.

> Following the New Testament model of Christian life, the WOL house church structure offers us a picture of organic movement of messianic community, linking believers together in close fellowship, practicing *koinonia*, engaging in evangelism, witnessing in worship and service, and thus transcending the traditional Chinese family-centered solidarity. The presence of this new community of faith alone bears powerful witness in its surrounding.[26]

Theologically speaking, the gifts of the Spirit and the priesthood of believers have played important roles in this new form of community. "Anyone—women, the poor, the uneducated, the young—may be lifted by the Spirit to a place of leadership," and a "universal 'mobilization' of all members in behalf of a movement's mission powers its renewal dynamic, its revitalizing impact."[27] The WOL system of training fleshes out how theological concerns are practiced in reality. In the initial and continuous development of WOL theology and training materials, conscientious measures were taken to ensure the participation of the community of believers in the process so that it would not be the work of only a single person or even a small group of people. Here's what happens in the short-term and TE trainings:

> The teachers teach from the materials we developed. After each lesson, all the students kneel down together to reflect in prayer what they have just received. When one is engaged in

prayer, all other twenty-nine students listen. After everyone
has prayed, everyone has listened twenty-nine times to what
has just been taught in the lesson, and yet with different
emphases. At each phase of training, there will be an opportunity for each of the students to lead a teaching session, at the
end of which, others confirm, critique, add to his/her teaching
frankly in the Lord.[28]

These practices nurture the fruit of the Spirit among the community. Now theological jargon becomes reality. People have a sense
of ownership of what they believe and do because they experience
the power of the Spirit breathing over their work. They perceive
themselves as the proud sons and daughters of the living God, the
"people of God," called to accomplish great things for God through
the Holy Spirit.

SOVEREIGN ACTION OF THE HOLY SPIRIT

Snyder writes: "Pentecost concerns the compete dependence of
God's people on his sovereign action as well as the people's openness and response to that action; their willingness to be witnesses
of and for the divine purposes. In the Old Testament it is God who
provides the harvest and guides his people, but it is the people who
do the actual work of sowing, reaping, and gratefully worshiping
God."[29] Further, "A fully biblical Pentecostal movement will seek
to discern where God is leading and to be faithful to that vision."[30]
Here the human response is inseparable from dependence on God's
sovereign action. And it is through these human responses and the
fruit of them that we also identify the "signs of the Spirit."

The joint "Confession of Faith of House Churches in China,"[31]
in which the WOL was a part, affirms the nature of Holy Spirit as
such:

The Holy Spirit illuminates a person causing him to know sin and repent, know the truth, and to believe in Christ and so experience being born again unto salvation. The Holy Spirit leads believers to the truth, and gives them understanding of the truth, and enables them to obey Christ, thereby bearing abundant fruit of life. The Holy Spirit gives all kinds of power [to His servants] and manifests the mighty acts of God through signs and miracles. The Holy Spirit enables and searches all things.

In Christ, God grants a diversity of gifts of the Holy Spirit to the church so as to manifest the glory of Christ. Through faith and thirsting, Christians can experience the outpouring and the filling of the Holy Spirit.[32]

In an interview by one of the overseas Christian producers, Peter Xu was asked to reflect on the causes of the revivals in China. He responded:

The revival of the Chinese church had nothing to do with structure of the traditional church, nor did it have to do with the TSPM, nor did it have anything to do with the support of the regime, nor did it have to do with overseas support, nor did it have direct relationship with the leaders of the church. It was the direct work of the Holy Spirit.[33]

Because God chooses to partner with His people to fulfill His good purpose, the roles WOL believers play are also important. WOL believers are sensitive to the Spirit of God, through prayer, Bible study, and fellowship, and able to identify and respond to the leading of the Spirit. These responses can be noted in all aspects of the movement, especially the three constitutive parts: established churches, theological education, and the Gospel Band. They include:

1. Rediscovery of the gospel

The development of the WOL theology was an act of responding
to the needs identified in context as believers "rediscovered" what
was important for the church and its mission in the world. Two
stages of such "rediscoveries" were prominent in the history of the
WOL movement: (1) the identification of the centrality of the cross
in the life and ministry of the church during the 1970s, and (2) the
realization of the important biblical principle of unity of the body
and united witness in the mid-1990s. Both of these rediscoveries are
reflected in the WOL theology and training curriculum.

2. The WOL structure

In identifying the principles of the body of Christ, Christians
structured a multilevel coworkers' meetings throughout the network, i.e., seven house churches formed a coworkers' meeting, and
seven coworkers' meetings formed an area coworkers' meeting,
etc. The significance of this structure is its obvious emphasis on
"interlink and fellowship," one of the seven principles in the WOL
theology, a biblical mandate important for sustaining such a large
network of house churches, coordinating ministry in all levels,
guiding against heretic teachings, and channeling the revival
throughout the network.

Stories of MGs who labored in frontier evangelism speak of their
dependence on God to supply their needs; empower their message;
and convict, convert, and transform lives; and testify to their reli-
ance on the Holy Spirit. The expansion of the movement testifies
to the faithful responses of this community of believers. Marie
Monson said it well as she reflected on her experience in the well-
known Shantung Revival in China in the 1930s: "This was God's
plan, the method of His choice. He needed to have all these fellow-
workers with Him rightly related to Himself, before He could send,
or we receive, the revival that was a work of the Holy Spirit."[34]

THE ESCHATOLOGICAL PROMISE
OF THE NEW CREATION

Pentecost, in both Testaments, according to Snyder, *"points ahead* to the future."[35] The outpouring of the Holy Spirit empowers believers for witness to the "full coming of God's kingdom (Acts 1:2–8; 8:12–19; 20:22–25) and with the final 'restoration of all things' (Acts 3:21, ASV)."[36] "The initial fulfillment" can be seen as "a sign of the later fulfillment," and *"prepares the way for,* and in some sense *actually begins to effect* or accomplish the final fulfillment."[37] "A key question, of course, is the degree to which this eschatological vision is thought to be possible within present history, or is expected only after the end of the present order of things."[38]

From the perspective of its ministry focus, the WOL eschatological vision pertains more or less beyond the present age. On the one hand, its theology of the cross based on a premillennial understanding of the *parousia* provides hope and assurance for those who were experiencing external suffering in forms of opposition; on the other hand, saving souls occupies a more prominent place in the WOL understanding, as is evidenced in the movement's missional-oriented structure. The outpouring of the Holy Spirit in Acts is primarily taken as empowerment for ministry as the movement trained and selected young men and women for frontier evangelism to the unreached peoples and regions. The Back to Jerusalem ministry, as part of the ministries of the WOL movement, envisions "taking the gospel back to Jerusalem, thus completing the Great Commission and hastening the return of our Lord!"[39] The concept of China's responsibility as the anchor runner in this "gospel relay race" taking the baton back to Jerusalem is pervasively accepted, and this explains, at least in part, the emergence and growth of the Back to Jerusalem Movement, which includes multidirectional routes throughout Asia.

The movement's emphasis on the "harvest of souls at the end of times" naturally causes imbalance. The obvious extended interim between now and *parousia*, given the WOL generally accepted understanding that Christ would not likely return before the gospel is preached all the way back to Jerusalem, presents questions that need to be addressed. These and other questions already have been emerging within the WOL community in the last decade. This is an area worthy of extensive research.

One of the practical challenges facing the movement after the WOL hit its plateau of expansion and growth in the late 1990s was the lack of support system for families left behind by the young MGs (evangelists). The fact that the WOL was primarily a rural Christian movement made this situation especially difficult for families with young adults away from the family farm work for extended periods of time. This lack of support was also evident in the Gospel Band that was responsible for sending the MGs to various parts of the country. When the WOL engine was in full power toward frontier evangelism, saving souls, and establishing house churches, there was no time to pause and think about the long-term impact on MGs and their families. As a special force in the movement, all MGs abided by the covenantal agreement, which included forbiddance of dating while in service. Those who dated were disciplined and sometimes called back from their ministry.

This pastoral issue is in need of further theological reflection. With all the positive contributions from the community of believers to the WOL theology through all levels of theological education (as delineated above), this area is insufficiently addressed. The influence of premillennial eschatology deflected attention from important areas of life and ministry. This raises a larger question for believers to think about: How will the WOL movement continue to effect or accomplish the final fulfillment of the kingdom of God?

THE SPIRIT'S EMPOWERMENT FOR EVANGELISTIC WITNESSING

The Pentecostal coming of the Spirit highlighted its power and ministry in convicting people of their sins and converting them to Christ. "Tongues" were given to the disciples so that they could preach the truth about God in people's vernaculars, but the Spirit illuminated the truth and convicted the heart. Or, in the apostle Paul's warfare language, the Word of God is "the sword of the Spirit" (Eph. 6:17, MEV). "When the people heard this, they were cut to the heart and said to Peter and the other apostles, 'Brothers, what shall we do?'" (Acts 2:37, NIV). About three thousand were converted and "added to their number that day" (Acts 2:41, NIV). What's more, the same empowerment is promised to all believers who repent and are baptized unto Christ Jesus for the forgiveness of sins (cf. Acts 2:38–39).

In its theology and ministry the WOL movement prioritizes the power of the Spirit to convert and grant new life. Possessing the new life born of the Holy Spirit is essential to the Christian who "walks the way of the cross."[40] "As prophesied in the Old Testament, when the Spirit is poured upon all people, it indicates the coming of the last days. In God's eternal plan, the ministry of the Holy Spirit at this age is to convict and cause to repent in order to receive life."[41] This power to convert and grant new life does not diminish the power to heal and drive out evil spirits; neither did it diminish the power to bring change in people's lives, to empower MGs for frontier evangelism, to open doors for them, to provide for all their needs, to protect them from harm, to establish new house churches, all of which derive from total trust upon the Holy Spirit of God!

> He [the Holy Spirit] will execute salvation, which was prepared by the Father and fulfilled by Christ, unto sinners. All the work of the Holy Spirit revolves around Jesus Christ, and

> he is to reveal Christ to the world, and testify to Jesus through the Word,...In other words, in order that a person receives salvation through obedience to the Holy Spirit, he will need to hear the Word of God, when the Holy Spirit illuminates his heart by means of the word of truth (which is the gospel of salvation).[42]

Snyder's biblical exposition of the role of the Holy Spirit coincides with the WOL experience: "salvation is the work of the Holy Trinity, and that the Holy Spirit is to testify to Jesus Christ, to lift him up and make him real in our experience, the focus of our discipleship, and basis of our ethics."[43]

Examples of how the Spirit works in convicting and converting people are abundant through the ministry of the WOL movement. In the early stage of the movement revival meetings were often spontaneous instead of planned events. The unique rural context provided that flexibility for leaders to follow the moving of the Holy Spirit, which meant prolonging meetings to as many more hours and days as needed. Peter Xu reflected after one of the revival meetings in which he preached for five days in the 1970s:

> The Holy Spirit worked mightily, imprinting His own word on the hearts of the people, who, when understanding the love of God in Jesus and seeing the sins of their own, wept heartily, confessing their sins, and repented. When they wept, we leaders went to kneel beside them and see how the Holy Spirit was moving them, for example, when they felt the love of God and their own sinful nature, we reminded them of the work of Christ on the cross and declared to them God's forgiveness of sin. When they received the confirmation of their sins being forgiven in the Word of God through our declaration, they were comforted in the heart through the work of the Holy Spirit. Together we witnessed the work and power of the Holy Spirit, delivering many and giving them peace, joy, and comfort.[44]

Female MGs (evangelists) often present testimonies of the power of the Spirit in evangelism. As the majority of WOL evangelistic teams, these women are filled with the Spirit in preaching the Word of God to believers and nonbelievers alike. After the initial preparatory work was done in frontier evangelistic ministry as MGs, these young women would then lead evangelistic meetings, life meetings, and truth meetings, in which they faced intimidating crowds of men and women they did not know well, but trusted their preaching to the power of the Spirit to bring change in the hearers; the result was often unbelievable. Amazed by the power of the Spirit dwelling in these young evangelists, people were convicted and repented of their sin, receiving God's salvation.

The experience of the Chinese house church movement evidenced the Pentecostal coming of the Holy Spirit to empower believers in evangelistic witnessing, to convict, convert, and give life. Their faith, theology, structure, and fruit say it all. As the three thousand were "added to their number that day" (Acts 2:41, NIV), so were the millions added to the WOL movement, part of the body of Christ.

CONCLUSION

Thanks to Howard Snyder's five-dimensional model of Pentecost, this study was able to view the WOL movement from a unique angle, yielding something otherwise uncovered in studies of Chinese Christian movements. This model has a wide-range zoom effect that provides both a great scope of concepts and deep-rooted biblical and historical details foundational to and part of the whole picture.

Believers can see how the Spirit of God works in this case through the human responses in faith, in theological reflection, and in structuring themselves in ways that contributed to the growth of the WOL movement. This chapter tried to go beyond the surface of the WOL phenomenon to reveal the dynamic within and address the "what" and "why" questions. From a theological perspective, the success of the movement can be attributed to the WOL believers' sensitivity and faithful response to the leading of the Holy Spirit. This is the Pentecostal coming of the Spirit as it played out in Acts 2 and subsequently in the history of the church. Tens of thousands of house churches exist today in the great expanse of rural China, and millions of Chinese have embraced the Christian faith because of this Spirit-led movement. All these bear witness to the dynamic synergy of Pentecostal renewal.

As Snyder concludes in his study of the Pentecostal renewal of the church, "Perhaps all the genuine revitalization movements of history are mere pointers and signposts, firstfruits of an eventual great Pentecostal renewal that fulfills and embodies all that has been promised—much as, in C. S. Lewis's vision, all genuine myths point to the one great and true Myth."[45] The experience of the WOL movement in China offers yet another "signpost" of how the Spirit of God works in context and uncovers a slightly nuanced synergetic dynamic out of their experience, which becomes part of the shared story of the universal body of Christ. The hermeneutical community grows because of the WOL experience, which is the point.

Chapter 7

Pentecostal and Charismatic Christianity in Protestant Taiwan

Iap Sian-Chin and Maurie Sween

ADECADE AGO PENTECOSTAL and Charismatic churches were described as being "in a state of tension with the other Protestant churches on Taiwan and with the larger Taiwanese society."[1] Since then relations with other Protestants have improved. The same cannot be said about society. This introduction to the historical developments and theological trends of those elements of classical Pentecostalism, the Charismatic movement, and the neo-Charismatic movement that have been influential will highlight some of the reasons. It will conclude with a discussion of the challenges and opportunities for the movement.

CLASSICAL PENTECOSTAL CHRISTIANS: STRUGGLING FOR SURVIVAL

The Assemblies of God

The Assemblies of God (AG) began ministering in Taiwan in 1948, just before the Kuomingtang (KMT) party relocated its government from China to the island. By this time two other Pentecostal-style churches had ministered in the territory. The Japan Apostolic Mission and the True Jesus Church had been established during the

Japanese colonial era. No detailed records remain about the Japan Apostolic Mission.[2] The True Jesus Church will be discussed below.

The story of AG beginnings is complex. Only few know that there are now five different AG groups on this island. The China Assemblies of God Taiwan District Council (CAG, 中國神召會台灣區議會) was the first to be established. This group is the successor of the China Assemblies of God General Council, a constellation of Pentecostal churches that were planted by missionaries from different countries who had scattered throughout China.[3]

The historian Murray Rubinstein has referred to the decline of the CAG's work in Taiwan as due to over-dependence on American missionaries.[4] However, the situation changed when the CAG became a self-propagating group. In recent years relationships have been established with AG churches in other East and Southeast Asian countries, particularly with Chinese-speaking communities in Singapore, Malaysia, and Hong Kong. Since 2011 Hetai Machi (Yen Chin Long, 顏金龍),[5] an aboriginal pastor from the Atayal tribe, has served as general superintendent of the CAG, which demonstrates a degree of indigenization.[6]

Another AG group is the Taiwan Assemblies of God (TAG, 台灣神召會), an assembly established in 1949 by the Finnish Free Foreign Mission (FFFM, 芬蘭自由海外宣道差會), which was an association of independent Pentecostal missionaries serving in Manchuria who eschewed forming a denomination.[7] Unlike the CAG, which since its beginning has concentrated on ministry in urban areas, TAG mission efforts have focused on rural locales. However, growth in the Taiwanese economy since the late 1960s has led to massive urbanization. This social change severely damaged TAG development. At present most of their churches appear to be weak and small. Lack of a younger generation of ministers is also a factor that has resulted in decline. Moreover, due to the Finnish Pentecostal preference for being autonomous, it was only in 1995 that the TAG churches formed an association. Not all churches planted by, or connected with, the TAG have joined. Yet in recent years the TAG and the CAG have started to hold annual joint meetings, reestablishing old connections.

In the 1960s CAG missionaries started to preach among aboriginal people.[8] This work resulted in the formation of the Assemblies of God Mountain District Council (神召會山地區議會), a body that in 1972 became independent from the CAG.[9] Unfortunately most of the churches, suffering from ineffective self-government and problems related to property ownership, have closed.

In 1954 the Pentecostal Assemblies of Canada came to Taiwan and named itself the Pentecostal Assemblies of China (PAOC, 中華聖召會). The PAOC churches cooperated with the FFFM and TAG in training ministers, providing both faculty and financial support. However, in 1985 the headquarters decided to discontinue PAOC work in Taiwan.[10] The local association was disbanded, with churches either closing or becoming independent. The remaining PAOC churches appear to be inconsequential to the Taiwan Pentecostal community, as many have lost their historical Pentecostal identity. The Taiwan Full Gospel Church (TFGC, 台灣純福音教會), planted by the Yoido Full Gospel Church in Korea, might be the most well-known AG denomination on the island. This church has benefited more than other AG churches from the reputation of its mother church. TFGC influence has been enhanced by the annual "Asian Christian Conference in Korea" (organized by its Korean mother church) and through publishing translated works by famous Korean Christian leaders. The Taipei church, under the TFGC, was affiliated with the CAG at their founding. However, in the late 2000s the relationship was severed.[11]

Other classical Pentecostal churches

Besides AG groups, the Foursquare Church (四方教會) and the United Pentecostal Church (聯合五旬節教會) have also developed mission enterprises in Taiwan. Both are of marginal importance to Pentecostalism (especially the latter, whose heterodox Oneness teaching has largely been rejected). In addition, the Church of God (Cleveland, Tennessee) (神的教會), has one church, located in Taichung, that remains in relationship with its mother church.

The Zion Church (錫安堂), a local group with classical Pentecostal origins, is worth noting. One of the founders in Taiwan, Pearl G. Young (榮耀秀), was connected with Ridgewood Pentecostal Church in New York. The leader of this congregation was Hans Waldvogel, who was associated with the Zion Faith Home in Zion City, Illinois, and influenced by Charles Parham's Pentecostal message.[12] However, this stream of Pentecostalism is different from other classical Pentecostals in several ways. They do not emphasize the doctrine of initial evidence, and German/Swiss Pietism is essential to their spirituality. Speaking in tongues and healing rituals are not usually as demonstrative as in typical Pentecostal services. "Waiting upon the Lord" and "inner life" are more essential. Their practices appear to be inward and quiet, involving meditation. Indeed, they trace their spiritual heritage to Pietists and also to some Catholic mystics such as Jeanne Guyon and Brother Lawrence. For them Pentecostalism is a type of mysticism, with Spirit baptism often interpreted inwardly. One can say that Ridgewood is a synthesis of Pentecostalism and Pietism.[13]

The Taiwan Zion Church has inherited this tradition and become distinctive for its devotional methods. One of its influential leaders, Grace Chiang (Jiang Xiuqin, 江秀琴), who traveled from Taiwan to Fremont, California, and in 1995 founded the Forerunner Christian Church (慕主先鋒教會), has, through her publications and rallies, made the spirituality of Zion Church (rooted in Ridgewood Pentecostal Church) well known and welcomed among Chinese Christians. However, in recent years some branches of the

Zion Church have begun to abandon their tradition and follow a Christian culture influenced by foreign neo-Charismatic and prosperity gospel preachers. Indeed, teachings popular among North American Protestants commonly find their way to Taiwan, where their impact can be significant. With regards to the Zion Church and Ridgewood Pentecostal Church, this can be seen in the widespread adoption of a dispensational premillennialism that was never part of their history, and also in some members becoming involved in a Christian Zionism campaign (e.g., praying for the peace of Jerusalem and unconditional support for a Jewish nation).

Identity

In Mandarin the term "Pentecostal" (五旬節派, *Wuxunjie pai*) is only known by few Taiwanese Christians. Most Christians in Taiwan use the term "Charismatic" (靈恩派, *Lingen pai*) in an inclusive manner, referring to various renewal movements. Interestingly, leaders from the classical Pentecostal wing (most notably AG groups) often discuss the difference between *Wuxunjie pai* and *Lingen pai*, and insist on distinguishing themselves from the *Lingen pai.*

The TFGC also takes the position that their group is *Wuxunjie pai* and in strong connection with the Korean Full Gospel Church. The main reason the CAG and TFGC maintain their distinctive Pentecostal identity might be because of the importance of relationships with overseas Pentecostal groups. The CAG not only relates with its mother church, the US Assemblies of God, but also has interaction with AG groups throughout East Asia. The TFGC is, through its mother church, part of an influential global network.

The TAG, owing to its relative anti-institution tendency, has less of a Pentecostal identity. Nevertheless, the TAG has not cut off relations with the FFFM. Leaders continue to identify themselves as rooted in classical Pentecostalism. By contrast, the Foursquare

Church has a rather weak Pentecostal identity, even among ministers. Some are not even Pentecostal in practice. Others have derived teachings about spiritual gifts from neo-Charismatic groups, described below. The Taiwan Foursquare Church has no official training institute, and some of its ministers have never undertaken any type of theological education. There is therefore no strong sense of Pentecostal identity in the Foursquare Church, and in Taiwan their churches do not commonly cooperate with other classical Pentecostal counterparts.

Classical Pentecostalism in Taiwan, contrary to the movement elsewhere, can be described as weak, particularly in terms of numbers of adherents and sizes of churches. The reasons are complex and various. Distancing themselves from several tendencies popular among contemporary evangelical Protestants, such as a bourgeoisie-oriented prosperity gospel (TFGC is an exception) and a purpose-driven concept of church growth, can provide some explanation. If the Religious Market Theory proposed by sociologists like Rodney Stark is reasonable,[14] Taiwanese classical Pentecostals may not be offering the religious goods that people demand. However, further study is needed to delineate the reasons why classical Pentecostalism in Taiwan has not developed as successfully as other renewal groups.

CHARISMATIC CHRISTIANS AND OLDER INDEPENDENT AND SPIRIT CHURCHES

With respect to the Charismatic movement, the current and popular threefold model of classification does not seem to be appropriate in the context of Taiwan. The island's mainline denominations did not experience a mass renewal during the 1960s. Most of the churches only started to accept renewal from the 1990s, when they were influenced by neo-Charismatic groups. Many of those that can be described as Charismatic are independent and indigenous churches that were established while the North American classical and Charismatic movements were flourishing. However, the boundaries between these and other groups are not clear-cut. It is thus helpful, when describing these churches, to relate Charismatic churches to older independent and Spirit churches.[15]

Among the churches that can be defined as older independent and spirit churches, the True Jesus Church (TJC, 真耶穌教會), with its Oneness theology, is noteworthy. In 1926 Barnabas Chang (Zhang Dianju, 張殿舉), a TJC leader from Fujian, China, visited Taiwan.[16] He was accompanied by Taiwanese Elisha Huang (Huang Chengcong, 黃呈聰) and some others. The first church was started in March of that year in Huang's hometown of Xianxi, Changhua. Elders and deacons were ordained. This church and two others were planted within only forty days of this first mission trip. Hundreds of people were baptized.

After learning about mission achievements in Taiwan, other preachers in Fujian (some of whom were Taiwanese) also crossed the strait to Taiwan in order to help with the newly established mission enterprise. They traveled widely, zealously working to convert the Taiwanese. However, their earliest work concentrated on Christians, most of whom were Presbyterians. As the Communist Party won control of China, TJC leaders began departing for the island. In 1945 a general assembly was formed in the central city of Taichung.[17] The denomination grew and by 2012 had 52,500 members and 244 churches, making the TJC the fourth largest denomination in Taiwan.[18]

The New Testament Church (NTC, 新約教會) could be one of the most controversial Protestant sects in Taiwan. Founded in Hong Kong in 1963 by an actress named Mui Yee (梅綺, aka Kong Duen Yee, 江端儀), the church holds many of the doctrines of classical

Pentecostalism, including that the baptism in the Spirit is evidenced by tongues. However, the NTC's Taiwan branch is not only concerned with spirituality but also has taken a political stand that is different from the apolitical attitude of the NTC elsewhere. A radical millenarian theology led Kong's coworker, Elijah Hong (洪以利亞), to establish a "Mount Zion," a new center of Christianity deep within Taiwan's southern mountains.

This action resulted in conflict with the KMT government. It is reported that many members were persecuted, detained, and beaten.[19] This is entirely possible, given that the troubles between the NTC and the government occurred during the era the KMT was implementing martial law. At present those who live at "Mount Zion" are committed to a kibbutz style of life. Inhabitants grow fruit and vegetables. Tourists often visit. The enmity between the NTC and the state is no longer extreme, though the museum on this Mount Zion continues to denounce the KMT regime as unjust.

During the era when the Charismatic movement was dividing churches, the Chinese Christian Prayer Mountain (CCPM, 中華基督徒祈禱院) in the town of Miaoli, directed by Daniel Dai (戴義勳), served as a bridge between Pentecostal/Charismatic and non-Pentecostal/Charismatic churches. The CCPM was related to prayer mountain movements in Korea. Taiwanese Christians, regardless of denominational background, traveled there to renew and strengthen their faith. Prayer Mountain is no longer generating as much interest as before, but it was a key factor in the establishment of the Pentecostal/Charismatic movement in Taiwan.

Other Charismatic groups, such as the Taipei Truth Church from Hong Kong (真道教會), which was planted in 1969, the Worship Center (敬拜中心) established by Chen Gongliang (陳公亮), and the Elim Christian Center (以琳基督徒中心) and Elim bookstore (which were indirectly connected with the Canadian Latter Rain movement), were to some extent pioneers in promoting renewal movements.[20] It is worth mentioning that by translating and publishing select Pentecostal/Charismatic writings, the Elim bookstore made Charismatic Christianity more acceptable among Taiwanese Christians.

Independent Charismatic ministries, with the exception of the TJC and NTC (which other Protestants see as exclusivist), have had a greater influence on Christianity in Taiwan than classical Pentecostals. They served as a transition to the subsequent emergence of neo-Charismatic Christianity in Taiwan.

NEO-CHARISMATIC CHRISTIANS

The Bread of Life

One of the first, and most influential, of the distinctly neo-Charismatic churches in Taiwan is the Bread of Life Church (BOL, 台北靈糧堂). The church originated from a network of churches founded in relation to the ministry of Timothy S. K. Dzao (趙世光, 1908–1973), an independent evangelist who established the first BOL in Shanghai, China, in 1943. The Taipei branch began in 1954. Until the early 1980s the BOL was, by all accounts, a typical evangelical church, with a congregation numbering about two hundred.

Though the church continues to define itself as evangelical, an emphasis on the Holy Spirit began shortly after Nathaniel Chow (周神助) became the senior pastor in 1977. Early in his tenure women in the church began praying for an infilling. Chow, who encouraged empirical faith, began to invite teachers from the United States and Asia to explain this aspect of Christian life. Speakers have included John Wimber, C. Peter Wagner, representatives from the Bethel Church in Redding, California, the International House of Prayer in Kansas City, Missouri, and the Agape Renewal Ministry (additional information to follow). The

teachings of Pentecostals in Asia, including South Korea's Yoido
Full Gospel Church, Singapore's Faith Community Baptist and
City Harvest churches, and Indonesia's Bethany Church of God
have also been endorsed.

Slowly practices such as speaking in tongues and prophecy, services that focused on inner healing and spiritual power encounter,
and organization into offices of apostle, prophet, evangelist, pastor,
and teacher were embraced. In 1996 the BOL adopted a cell model
of ministry. Remarkable growth followed. Over ten thousand currently worship in the central sanctuary. Church members in thirty
satellite stations participate in these services via video feed. One
hundred forty-five branch churches have been planted in Taiwan,
and two hundred twenty-one affiliated congregations have been
established on every populated continent, mostly in Asia.

Success in church growth has caught the attention of other
churches. Relationships with other churches are important to the
BOL, and the church actively promotes its experiences. Efforts
include organizing conferences and paying for speakers to attend
events organized by interested parties.[21]

The Agape Renewal Ministry

Another proponent of the movement in Taiwan is the Agape
Renewal Ministry (愛修更新會, ARM). The ARM was founded by
Ernest Chan (陳仲輝), a Hong Kong Chinese man who in 1965,
after graduating from Fuller Theological Seminary, pastored San
Francisco's Cumberland Presbyterian Church. During his twenty-
two-year tenure Chan promoted church growth by means of cell
groups, leading his congregation to become the first Chinese church
in the United States to reach over one thousand members.

In 1983, at a Full Gospel Businessmen's Fellowship, Chan prayed
in tongues. The experience led to close relationships with C. Peter
Wagner and John Wimber, both of whom offered Chan "napkin

contracts," permitting him to establish ministries in conjunction with their own. In 1987 Chan founded the ARM, which organized conferences to help Chinese realize the power of the Spirit in daily life.

After its tenth anniversary the ARM began to focus on training, founding the Agape International Leadership Institute (AILI), a school affiliated with the Wagner Leadership Institute. The AILI educates Chinese Christians in practical ministry, often translating and promoting practices staff believe will be helpful among the Chinese. Integral are the deliverance ministry designed by Cleansing Stream Ministries, Harp and Bowl prayer and worship, and the seven mountains dominion mandate for social transformation espoused by C. Peter Wagner's New Apostolic Reformation.

In the year 2000 the ARM began to establish training centers in Taiwan. The ARM currently has eighty full-time staff operating out of six branch offices. Stories of gold dust and diamonds falling during meetings, similar to incidents reportedly occurring in the Bethel Church of Redding, California, have caught the attention of the press.[22]

Notable individuals

Certain well-thought-of individuals have had a role in winning respect for the neo-Charismatic movement. One of the most important of these is James Shia (夏忠堅). This former BOL pastor became a prominent Protestant leader as a result of directing the Year 2000 Gospel Movement, a decade-long program that successfully united Taiwan's Protestant denominations in evangelism and mission. Shia extended this ministry through two organizations that continue to be at the forefront of ecumenical activities in Taiwan, the Chinese Christian Relief Association and the Chinese Christian Evangelistic Association.[23]

Felix Liu, a founder of the Evangelical Formosan Church (EFC,

台福教會) and recently retired president of their flagship seminary in California, also lends credence to the movement. The EFC is an increasingly influential evangelical denomination that was brought to Taiwan in the 1990s by Taiwanese immigrants from the United States. Liu did graduate studies at the Fuller Theological Seminary School of World Mission, where C. Peter Wagner mentored him. His PhD thesis was a study of the efficacy of prayers for healing.[24] Liu, who travels regularly to Taiwan to teach in the Taiwan branch of his denomination's seminary, urges pastors to end each sermon with an altar call that includes an invitation to come forward to receive prayer for spiritual, emotional, and physical healing.[25]

The majority of Christians in Taiwan are evangelical. In the 1960s theories on church growth developed at Fuller Theological Seminary became popular. In the 1970s, when Fuller's C. Peter Wagner began to teach that churches stressing signs and wonders were growing, many American evangelicals began to embrace practices common among Pentecostal and Charismatic Christians. Evangelicals in Taiwan were aware of the movement but slow to warm to the new "wave."[26] Over the past decade, however, led by the BOL and the ARM, and made more palatable by individuals like James Shia and Felix Liu, the practices of neo-Charismatic groups have been accepted and indeed have become influential among Taiwan Protestants.

CHALLENGES AND OPPORTUNITIES

In 1949 advancing Communist forces compelled the KMT party to move to Taiwan. With hopes of returning to the mainland, the KMT identified itself as the bastion of Chinese culture, promoting Confucian philosophy. However, to advance military and economic objectives, the party also developed relationships with Western powers. To this end the KMT welcomed foreign missionaries, treating them with more respect than the leaders of other religions. From the time the KMT arrived until 1987, order was maintained through imposing martial law, which restricted the activities of local civic and religious assemblies. The social changes that followed caused considerable anxiety.[27]

For the past fifty years Christians have made up about 5 percent of the population, leading researchers to describe their faith as "stagnant." Most consider Christianity a modern, Western, implant. The people of Taiwan are religious, however, and when martial law lifted, there was an increase in the activities of the more established religions. Approximately 78 percent of the Taiwan populace now belongs to a faith that is related to a major Chinese tradition, and even the 15.4 percent who claim no religious affiliation regularly pray to the ancestors and neighborhood gods. At present the largest religious group (38.8 percent) is made up of those who practice folk religion, an eclectic faith with no clergy, scriptures, or uniform rites, that has long mixed Buddhist, Taoist, and Confucian practices in efforts to appease gods, ghosts, and ancestors. Buddhists (18.6 percent) and Taoists (13.2 percent) follow in second and third place. Yet exclusivity is atypical, and even in temples syncretic practices are common.[28]

This is not the place to describe religious practices in detail. However, it should be noted that the religions of the ancestors meet many needs, among the most important of which is conveying an identity that connects the people of Taiwan to their past. They also provide a sense of security in the present, so much so that participating in ceremonies to procure blessings from ethereal powers is seen as a public duty. Rituals that seek to influence the spiritual realm on behalf of individuals, both living and dead, are ubiquitous. Yet the social benefits of religious practice are also palpable. Traditional religions offer fellowship and give direction and purpose. In Taiwan religious organizations commonly undertake charitable endeavors, with many building hospitals, schools, and homes for the elderly, and offering timely responses to other social needs.[29]

One should not disparage the motives that accompany these services. Though Buddhists, who have been especially active in helping the vulnerable, have a faith that includes building merit for salvation, leaders insist that good deeds not be done for personal benefit but with an attitude of selfless compassion. Indeed, religious observances of even the most raucous nature are marked by feelings of devotion and awe-inspired sincerity. The goal of the religious is harmony and human flourishing.[30]

Harmony and human flourishing: herein lies the opportunity for Pentecostal and Charismatic mission. A political agenda that, in conscious opposition to China, defends religious freedom, upholding a Confucian philosophy that stresses social harmony, has produced an environment where relationships between people of different religions are easily formed and discussions about matters of faith are accepted. Indeed, the convictions and activities of Christians are both respected and welcomed. In Taiwan Pentecostal and Charismatic Christians have ample opportunity to demonstrate the power of the Holy Spirit for human flourishing.[31]

This, however, has not been easy. On Taiwan the religions of the forebears conserve traditions that, in a time of rapid of social change, have advanced well-organized and thought-out solutions to modern dilemmas. Their vibrant practices and vivid testimonies of supernatural assistance are impressive.[32] When Pentecostal and Charismatic Christians have applied what works in other contexts to Taiwan, their ministries have not been particularly relevant to people longing for "that old-time religion," the worldview and stories of the past.

Relevance, the celebrated Taiwanese theologian Shoki Coe (黃彰輝) argued, can only come with a continual "double wrestle," wrestling with both the text and the changing context.[33] This chapter has shown that Pentecostals and Charismatic churches in Taiwan are self-governing, supporting, and propagating, yet not self-theologizing. The challenge is to better discern the message that should be shared and the form that message should take.

CONCLUSION

Though Pentecostal and Charismatic ministries have not greatly affected the general populace, the past decade has seen relations with Protestants improve. Indeed, several neo-Charismatic mega-churches have begun to exert considerable influence, especially within Mandarin-speaking churches.

The Pentecostal meta-culture produced by these neo-Charismatic churches is a matter of concern, however. Although they work ecumenically, the kind of unity they envision is what theologian Miroslav Volf has called the "centralized homogeneity" of Babel,[34] a unity that neglects diversity. Though they network, they hope all the churches in Taiwan will follow their spiritual approach. As a result, Taiwan Protestant denominations have been losing their identities and traditions. Aware of this, many in the renewal movement, we have noted, distinguish themselves as Pentecostal rather than Charismatic.

The unity that the Day of Pentecost disclosed was in variety and diversity. Allowing for differences can be helpful as churches face the challenge of wrestling with both the text and context. To end on a positive note, Pentecostal/Charismatic Christians in Taiwan, whom Rubinstein described as having "congruence"[35] with local religious sensibilities, are now well placed to help Protestants as they struggle to produce ministries that are appropriately relevant.[36]

Chapter 8

The Kingdom of God in Korean Pentecostal Perspective

Sang Yun Lee

WHEN CHRISTIANITY ARRIVED in Korea, the major concern of the missionaries and Christians was salvation in terms of what people could be saved "from" rather than what they could be saved "for."[1] With a future-oriented eschatological emphasis, they focused on salvation from sins. Over the course of the next century, however, the scope of salvation broadened to include salvation "for" other theological and sociopolitical aspects such as human rights, sexual and social equality, and dissolution of racial tension.

After the Korean War (June 25, 1950–July 27, 1953) the Korean people suffered from its aftereffects. They experienced the tragedy of fratricidal war, and most of them lost family members and living resources. Many experienced extreme poverty, illnesses, and despair. Since the 1960s, if salvation for many in the established Protestant churches meant liberation for social justice and human rights, for Korean Pentecostals it was *from* sins, illness, and poverty and *for* spiritual blessing, well-being, and prosperity. Some scholars think that the rapid growth of Korean Pentecostalism is due to its parallels with Korean shamanism.[2] However, contemporary Korean Pentecostalism is better understood in relationship to

the movement's rediscovery of the kingdom of God in both not-yet
and present aspects.

This essay will show that as the movement grew in Korea,
Pentecostals came to understand the kingdom of God not only as
"already but not yet" but also as present "here and now." In the
post-Korean War context, Korean Pentecostals have hoped for both
the kingdom to come and the kingdom "here and now" with the
doctrine of the threefold blessing based on the biblical text 3 John
2: salvation, divine healing, and prosperity.[3] The following analyzes
the kingdom of God in Korean Pentecostal perspective, especially
in terms of the people of the kingdom, the kingdom of God in
"here and now," and the good God (*Joeushin Hananim*) of Korean
Pentecostals.

THE PEOPLE OF THE KINGDOM

Who are the "people of the kingdom"? In order to appreciate what
is contested about this question, we will need to understand first
some debates about how some contemporary Korean theologians
have interpreted certain New Testament words.

λαός (*laos*) and ὄχλος (*ochlos*)

There is a Korean word composed of two Chinese characters, *Min*
and *Jung*. *Min* can be translated as "people," and *Jung* as "the mass"
in English. Literally the meaning of *Minjung* is "the mass of people"
or "a group of ordinary people" or "the masses."[4] However, Korean
socialists, nationalists, and even liberal theologians and progressive
Christians have used *Minjung* in other ways. For instance, *Minjung*
theologians do not want to translate the word simply as "the mass
of people" because "the mass of people" or "a group of ordinary
people" are inadequate for their intentions. Their theological concern is not about ordinary people but those who are marginalized
economically, politically, and socially in the society. In addition,

during the Cold War they avoided using the term "the people" for security reasons because it had political connotations and implications. Instead they translated the word *Minjung* as "the people of God."[5]

However, "the people of God" does not mean "the children of God" to *Minjung* theologians. They see *Minjung* (the people of God) as referring to those who are suffering from political oppression, exploitation, injustice, human rights violations, poverty, and so on. They distinguish the Greek term ὄχλος (*ochlos*) from λαός (*laos*) in the Bible in order to differentiate "the people of God" from ordinary people. According to Byung Mu Ahn (1922–1996), the founder of *Minjung* theology, Mark uses the term λαός (*laos*) only twice to quote scriptures from the Old Testament (Mark 7:6; 14:2).[6] Except for these two cases, Mark uses ὄχλος (*ochlos*) thirty-six times to describe "a group of people."[7] Ahn insists that Jesus of Galilee cannot be found without ὄχλος (*ochlos*) and the ὄχλος (*ochlos*) cannot be considered without Jesus in the synoptic Gospels, especially Mark.[8] In other words, Ahn understands that Mark used ὄχλος (*ochlos*) in relationship to the people surrounding Jesus and that for the second evangelist, Jesus was the Lord of ὄχλος (*ochlos*). More precisely, Ahn understands the ὄχλος (*ochlos*) as the socioeconomically and politically marginalized,[9] because the ὄχλος (*ochlos*) with Jesus were the poor, the sick, and the powerless. For *Minjung* theologians, Korean ordinary people who had neither power nor wealth are ὄχλος (*ochlos*).

In fact, *Minjung* theology is more than a political theology because it is deeply rooted in Korean history, traditions, culture, religion, and social matters.[10] During the transition period of rapid economic growth (1960s–1980s), Ahn and other *Minjung* theologians understood the *Minjung* as those who were exploited by capitalists and oppressed by political dictatorship. Students, workers, intellectuals, journalists, and even pastors fought for human rights, freedom of speech, and freedom of the press, as well as for laborers' rights and interests. Many were arrested and tortured in prison. In these circumstances *Minjung* theologians and churches recognized that their mission was to emancipate the people and Korean society from military dictatorship through Christ.[11] Based on the perspectives of liberation theology, Ahn identifies the people of Korea under dictatorship and suffering from poverty as the ὄχλος (*ochlos*).[12] Thus, the urban poor, factory workers working monotonously with machines every day, and women segregated as second-class citizens become the *Minjung* of *Minjung* theology.

However, Korean evangelical theologian Se Yoon Kim argues that "Ahn's identification of the ὄχλος (*ochlos*) as the *Minjung* is quite arbitrary"[13] because tax collectors, "the wrongdoers" in the Jewish society, were also welcomed by Christ. The dualisms presupposed in *Minjung* theology between "the oppressed" and "the oppressor" and "the wronged" and "the wrongdoer," the "oppressed" and the "wronged" limit the people of God to being the victimized social group. This reductionist view perhaps excludes even those who accept Christ as the Savior. In comparison with *Minjung* theology, the *Minjung* of Korean Pentecostalism are not only the "oppressed" and the "wronged" but also "the wrongdoer" and "the oppressor" who seek salvation.

In fairness to Ahn and other *Minjung* theologians, their efforts may be understood in part as attempts in contextualized mainline Protestant Korean theology. Note that many of the *Minjung* theologians derived from what may be understood as the postwar Korean "middle classes," and hence they were reacting in part out to the felt injustices suffered by the Korean masses. Even if their use of Marxist ideology is questionable, their motivations were to urge the established Korean Protestant churches to take up the cause of the marginalized and exploited masses of those in the lower classes of Korean society. Even if contemporary Korean Pentecostals might disagree with much of the *Minjung* theological claims, they ought to respect the fact that the more upwardly mobile Christians have a responsibility to speak and act on behalf of those less fortunate. We will return to this issue later in our discussion of Korean Pentecostal blessing theology.

Scripturally speaking, of course, the question is: Who were the *Minjung* of Jesus in the Bible? Did Jesus welcome and bless only the poor and the marginalized in society? Did He discriminate against the rich and those in power against ordinary people? Arguably, the *Minjung* were the people Jesus fed at the Sea of Galilee (Matthew 14:13–21; Mark 6:30–44; Luke 9:10–17; John. 6:1–14); the sick He healed; the people who cheered when He came to Jerusalem, saying "Hosanna! 'Blessed is He who comes in the name of the Lord'" (Mark 11:9; John 12:13, MEV; see also Matt. 21:9; Luke 19:39; although a few days later they cried out "Crucify Him!"—Mark 15:13; Luke 23:21; John 19:15, MEV; see also Matt. 27:23); and the sinners for whom He was crucified. Jairus, one of the rulers of the synagogue (Matt. 9:18–26; Mark 5:21–24; Luke 8:40–56), and the centurion who asked Jesus to heal his servant (Matt. 8:5–13; Luke 7:1–10; John 4:43–54) were also His people. For Jesus, the people of God are not only the poor, the sick, and the sociopolitically disadvantaged, but they are also those seeking His kingdom and salvation.

The Weary and Burdened

In the post-Korean war context, the *Minjung* of Korean Pentecostalism was not limited to a certain socioeconomical class but included ordinary Koreans spiritually lost, without much hope, and burdened and suffering from severe poverty and many different kinds of illnesses. Certainly the majority of Korean Christians remained politically quiescent.[14] Like most conservative Korean

Christians who adopted passive attitudes and stances toward political issues, Korean Pentecostals were also politically inactive. Nevertheless, Korean Pentecostalism was able to offer hope to its *Minjung* not through a vision of social reformation but with the threefold blessing.

The message of the threefold blessing was popularized by the Yoido Full Gospel Church (hereafter YFGC), which grew to become the largest church in the world by the mid-1990s. I propose that the YFGC's success can be attributed at least in part to how its message responded to the demands and needs of Korean people in the postwar context. The threefold blessing was received by Koreans because they understood it as deeply related to their ordinary lives. Well-known theologian Jürgen Moltmann does not hesitate to define the threefold blessing as a theology of hope in the Korean context.[15]

Some historical and demographic perspective might be helpful to appreciate the impact of the threefold blessing message. Since the 1970s the Pentecostal movement in Korea has spread nationwide and developed interdenominationally.[16] The Billy Graham Crusade held in 1973 and the EXPLO '74, a training conference for three hundred thousand Christians, was held in the Yoido Plaza. Seventy percent of attendees were saved.[17] In 1974 there were about three million Christians in Korea, but four years later the Christian population had reached up to seven million. In 1978 six new churches were started every day.[18] Against this backdrop, note also that there were only eight Pentecostal churches in 1952.[19] Although founded by Yonggi Cho with five members in the slum area of Korea in 1958, by 1993 the YFGC had become the largest Christian church in the world with seven hundred thousand members.[20]

This remarkable church growth raises some questions: (1) Why did people come to the church? (2) What type of people came to church? (3) Why were they enthusiastic about Pentecostalism?

Most Koreans were overwhelmed by heavy burdens of life after the Korean War. All national functions and systems were paralyzed. The infrastructure and resources for the nation's economy were destroyed. Although most people suffered from the aftereffects of war, at that time they could not receive even simple medical treatment since there were not many hospitals and doctors in Korea. After the Korean War the May 16 coup d'état broke out in 1961. During the military dictatorship the government imprisoned dissidents and restricted the press. Human rights and freedom of speech were frequently violated during rapid urbanization and industrialization. It seemed that there was no hope for Koreans at that time. However, Korean Pentecostalism grew within that seemingly hopeless context.

Like the YFGC, other Pentecostal churches were founded in urban and impoverished areas. At that time the mainstream of Korean Christianity had already settled in the center of cities and reached out to the middle to upper middle classes of society. As a result, the weary and the spiritually, physically, and financially burdened became the people of Korean Pentecostalism. The message of Pentecostalism was very simple. Korean Pentecostal preachers proclaimed the gospel of healing to the sick and blessings to the poor. Koreans had not heard this message of healing and prosperity from mainstream Christian churches before. In fact, these established churches taught them that prosperity was nonbiblical and of shamanist origins. The Pentecostal messages were very effective in reaching the poor and the sick and were welcomed by them. Korean Pentecostal churches started on the outskirt of cities and gave hope to Koreans under desperate situations.

According to Confucianism, traditionally Korean women had to obey their husbands and used to be mistreated unless they produced a son for the family. The childless had to let their husbands have other women to carry on the family line. The disabled also were often treated as social outcasts. Many who labored under the heavy burdens of life were attracted to Korean Pentecostal churches and were given hope by the threefold blessing. As a result, the weary and burdened became the people of the kingdom and experienced salvation, healing, and prosperity. Indeed, the poor were inspired to hope for prosperity and the sick encouraged to expect divine healing through the message of the threefold blessing.

THE KINGDOM OF GOD HERE AND NOW

Traditionally, Korean Christians have emphasized the kingdom of God as a future reality as they did not place their hope in this world. Through much of the twentieth century they underwent the hardship of the Japanese colonial rule, the Korean War, and the military dictatorship. Korean Christians were used to hearing messages about a future-oriented hope for the church. For them this world was temporary, but the kingdom of God was coming.

However, there is a question that if the kingdom is "already" within believers (Luke 17:21), how can the eschatological kingdom also be only "there and then"? American Pentecostal theologian Steve Land insists that there is both continuity and discontinuity between the present and the future kingdoms.[21] If the kingdom is disconnected from the present world, it would be transcendental and without relevance.[22] With regard to the continuity of the kingdoms, Land says that the eschatological kingdom will break into the present world in part through the history of humanity.[23] In addition to this, Canadian Pentecostal theologian Peter Althouse argues that creating anticipatory hope transforms the future into the present.[24]

Korean Pentecostalism's threefold blessing can be seen as establishing a connection between the disastrous present and the prosperous coming kingdom. Althouse says, "God's Kingdom is 'already' present through the inauguration of Jesus Christ and the activity of the Spirit, but 'not yet' fulfilled, as when the presence of God will be fully revealed. As such, the vision of the future Kingdom has transformative power in the present world."[25] For Moltmann, the kingdom is "an interaction between God and the world, God and human beings or between the Trinitarian divine Persons."[26]

According to Yonggi Cho, there are two aspects of the kingdom: "the future aspect of kingdom" and "the present reality of the kingdom of God."[27] Cho understands that the present kingdom can be experienced "here and now" through God's sovereignty even as the coming kingdom represents hope for the eternal life.[28] Yet the eschatological kingdom is also immersed in the present through Christ and the indwelling of the Spirit.[29] Cho says that "The Gospel deals not only with the hope for eternal life and the salvation of spirit and soul but also with prosperity in life and physical health and wellness that would keep the balance between spirituality and reality."[30]

Using 1 Corinthians 4:20 as a basis, Cho says that the kingdom is not "a matter of talk but of power." He understands that the miracle of healing is a sign of God's sovereignty in this present life.[31] Healing is therefore "a sign of the coming of the kingdom of God to the earth."[32] This means the experience of healing can be a means to experiencing the kingdom in this life.

Under Cho's influence, Korean Pentecostals expect that the kingdom can be realized in their lives. The kingdom is not merely to come but relates to matters of the present life as well. Anderson points out that the "full gospel" of Pentecostals and Charismatics contains "good news for all life's problems."[33] The message of the threefold blessing was the gospel and hope that Korean Pentecostals had in the post-Korean War context. After the Korean War, healing and prosperity became prominent parts of the gospel along with salvation.[34] The threefold blessing was welcomed by Koreans under those severe circumstances. They sought to experience the eschatological kingdom in this world by receiving the threefold blessing.

Yet Korean Pentecostals have to realize that as their contemporary context has changed, hope for the kingdom "here and now" also has to be transformed. The current political and socioeconomical situation in Korea is incomparable to its conditions after the Korean War. Moltmann says that the gospel brings "hope into an otherwise hopeless present, hope for justice and freedom and peace where injustice, oppression and conflict presently reign."[35] Yet hope cannot be hope unless it transcends present realities. After the Korean War, Koreans desired and needed a kingdom that alleviated their poverty and sickness. It seems that their hope now has been realized. National poverty no longer persists in South Korea, and the nation's health care has been developed as much as in some European countries. Contemporary Korean Pentecostals have already experienced plenty of material blessings and health care.

Thus, it is important for Korean Pentecostals to reconsider what the kingdom means in today's context. In the present situation, there are at least two aspects of the kingdom "here and now" that need to be accentuated. First, Korean Pentecostals have to ask how they can or ought to participate in the present kingdom. Surely, they should be discouraged from pursuing egoistic blessings. Rather, now is the time to emphasize that the kingdom of God is a matter of righteousness, peace, and joy in the Holy Spirit (Rom. 14:16). Yet there will be no righteousness, peace, and joy among people without wealth equity, sociopolitical justice, and social harmony.

Although Korean Pentecostals are conservative and have not

generally been sociopolitically active, they can participate in the present kingdom through sharing the burden of others. As we saw earlier in our discussion of Korean *Minjung* theology, even if one were to disagree with their overall proposals, it is essential to recognize that the present church of the middle and upper middle classes—out of which emerged *Minjung* theology in the 1970s and from which the threefold blessing message is disseminated today—has both theological and social responsibility to speak and act on behalf of the oppressed and marginalized of society. Hence Korean Pentecostals today can and ought to realize God's kingdom on earth by sharing their blessings received from God with others and caring for those who now live under desperate conditions.

Second is that the more Korean Pentecostals focus on the present kingdom, the less they emphasize the kingdom that is not yet. Christian hope and expectation of the coming kingdom of God is not a matter of realizing through human actions a utopian ideal on earth.[36] Hope for the kingdom must exceed a prosperous earthly life because the kingdom is not a matter of eating and drinking (Rom. 14:17). In other words, Christian faith cannot be reduced to being equivalent with a secularized desire or a selfish wish for a prosperous present life since there is also the kingdom to come with the second advent of Christ. With hope for the coming kingdom, Korean Pentecostals should not neglect storing up their treasures in heaven through serving others and sharing their blessings with those who are in need.

JOEUSHIN HANANIM (GOOD GOD), THE GOD OF KOREAN PENTECOSTALS

After the Korean revivals in Wonsan (1903) and Pyongyang (1907), repentance of sins was a central theme of Pentecostal preachers. For their sermons, the scriptures of the Old Testament were used more

often than the New Testament. To them, Christians needed to sacrifice everything for eternal life, and the kingdom was absolutely
other-wordly. Their sermons focused on the judgment of God and
keeping the Ten Commandments. As a result, instead of the God of
love, *Hananim* (the name of God in Korean language) became the
fearful One who will punish them unless He was obeyed. At that
time, due to their eschatological perspective, Korean Pentecostals
did not believe God would bless them in the present life. Their
dualistic eschatology emphasized either judgment or redemption.
Within this classical soteriology, redemption did not extend to
other dimensions such as freedom from political oppression and
liberation from poverty or illness.

Traditionally, Korean Christians accepted all misfortunes, natural disasters, sickness, and sufferings as God's punishments due
to their sins or unbelief. They even believed that good Christians
should not be prosperous, and that "if one desires spiritual comfort, one has to suffer in the flesh."[37] Perhaps they did not realize
how influenced they were toward this ascetic lifestyle by indigenous
religions, Confucianism, and Buddhism. Buddhist monks practiced a monastic life, and honorable poverty was preferred rather
than egoistic prosperity because of the Confucian influence. This
ideal was consistent with what converts learned from the early missionaries to Korea who held forth hope for eternal life because the
world will perish on the Last Day. Although the missionaries who
were influenced by the holiness movement were not directly against
prosperity, they had no interest in it. As a result, early Korean
Christians, including Pentecostals, did not pursue a prosperous life.

In the post-Korean War context, however, there was a promi-
nent change in Pentecostal understandings of God and redemption.
After the Korean War they added an adjective *Joeushin* ("good" in
Korean) in front of *Hananim*. Literally, *Joeushin Hananim* means

"the good God." This change reflects a transition in their under-standing of God's nature and character from the fearful God to the good God. To them, God is no longer the One who takes their belongings away due to their sins but the God who takes care of their hardships and willingly blesses them.

Harvey Cox, a religious scholar and attentive observer of global Pentecostalism, says that the "Pentecostals' God is more lover than judge, more concerned with human affection than with commanding obedience."[38] With *Joeushin Hananim*, Korean Pentecostals are also able to discover God's goodness and love. They believe in God who wants to give unlimited blessings to His people instead of the God who rebukes and punishes them.[39] Theologically, *Joeushin Hananim* is related to the goodness of God. *Joeushin Hananim* also illustrates the change of Korean Pentecostals' understanding of prosperity. They expect to be blessed by the generosity of God. To Korean Pentecostals today, having a prosperous life in God is as important as eternal life for the soul.[40]

Contemporary Korean Pentecostals thus have a holistic view about life. They do not dualistically separate eternal life and con-temporary life. Compared to the traditional understanding of wealth, they understand that prosperity is not secularistic but can be embraced as a divine blessing. To them, as contemporary life is considered an anticipation of eternal life, prayers for the prosperous and healthy life are prominent.[41]

If early Korean Pentecostals accepted poverty and illness as a destiny and thought that their lives on the earth needed to be sacrificed for the sake of eternal life, Cho believes that poverty and illness are caused by the devil, sin, and the curse. Thus, pov-erty and sickness need to be removed by the blessings of *Joeushin Hananim*.[42] This means that Cho understands poverty and disease not only in material terms but also as spiritual matters. He insists

that the work of Christ is both to break down the curses of sickness
and poverty and to save souls. Cho often says that Christians can
be rich because Jesus became poor on the cross to make His people
prosperous (2 Cor. 8:9); furthermore, believers can be healed by
Jesus's wounds (Isa. 53:4–5).[43] The theological foundations of Cho's
threefold blessing and fivefold gospel are *Joeushin Hananim*, and
hope that *Joeushin Hananim* will bless His people according to His
promises.[44] Rodrigo Tano says that the "message of the threefold
blessing and the fivefold Gospel is nothing less than an exposition
and practical application of the biblical truth that God is good and
his goodness meets the needs of human beings and fulfills their
aspiration for the good, successful, and abundant life."[45] However,
Joeushin Hananim has to be understood differently from the sha-
manistic quest for material blessings.

To Korean Pentecostals, *Joeushin Hananim* is the God who
intervenes in the hardships of His people. *Joeushin Hananim* is not
only the judge for the Day of Judgment but also the provider who
cares their daily needs (Exod. 13:13–14) and who heals them (Ps.
103:1–3; Exod. 15:26).[46] However, Korean Pentecostals have to recognize also that *Joeushin Hananim* is not a magic wand that gives
whatever they ask. They need to acknowledge that, as the suffering
of Christians for faith has to be understood in the goodness of
God, *Joeushin Hananim* often lets His people pass through trials
of faith and shows His goodness in the midst of their suffering and
hardship.

CONCLUSION

In the post-Korean War context, the futuristic kingdom was not
attractive to Koreans who were suffering from sickness and poverty.
To these Pentecostals, the kingdom is more that can be realized in
"here and now" through experiencing the healthy and prosperous

life in God. In this context, λαός (*laos*), the ordinary people who are the weary, the burdened, the poor, the sick, and the lost, became the people of Korean Pentecostalism. Korean Pentecostalism grew at least in part because of the message about *Joeushin Hananim* who cares about their spiritual, physical, and financial needs.

However, it is necessary to resist the idea that the kingdom and God can be reduced to prosperity theology and what humans need or want. Certainly the resurrection of Christ and the promise of His second coming are essential to the message about the kingdom. Korean Pentecostals have to maintain a balance between the kingdom here and now and the kingdom to come. Thus, Korean Pentecostals have to consider three theological matters more deeply. First, the kingdom is not intended solely to fulfill personal desires for a prosperous life in the "here and now." Second, suffering, as evil as it might be, can be and is often used by God to grow faith in His people. Finally, in the contemporary Korean context, Korean Pentecostals need to think more about how to participate in the kingdom "here and now" rather than merely claim the promises for health and prosperity in the present life.

Chapter 9

Toward a History and Theology
of Japanese Pentecostalism

David Hymes

"HE KNEW HOW to shout."[1] These are the words that John
Juergensen used in 1927 to describe Kiyoma Yumiyama, the man who would become the mainstay of
the largest Pentecostal denomination in Japan. Not that he was a
medical student. Not that he was proficient in German and English.
But that he could "shout." Pentecostalism in Japan carries a similar
DNA to that which evolved in North America, with a propensity
for less thought and more shout. This in no wise diminishes the fact
that the movement had a unique theological enterprise that separated itself from the more traditional forms of the Christian faith.

A preliminary foray into the topic of a Japanese Pentecostal theology is fraught with difficulties. First, although Paul Tsuchido
Shew[2] and Masakazu Suzuki[3] have contributed much to a renewed
understanding of the early Pentecostals in Japan, more work
remains to be done in the post-World War II era, leading up to the
present. Their investigations have overturned prior histories that
were centered on the victors of history,[4] while erasing the memory
of crucial players that strayed from the mainstream positions. The
era beginning in the mid- to late 1970s saw a strong Korean presence, which influenced the already established Pentecostal churches

along with the direct impact from the mission work by the Korean Full Gospel Church. Presently the horizon has broadened further with diverse missionaries representing their countries and differing traditions along with specific Charismatic ministries. These have combined to alter the Pentecostal state of the union. Historical studies in these most recent times need to be combined with the next stage of inquiry, which should include sociological and theological analysis being added to Shew and Suzuki's most excellent historical spadework.

Second, although Christianity in Japan has a long history reaching back to at least the sixteenth century, its growth has been minimal. In fact, "the combined membership of all Christian denominations and churches in the modern period has never reached 1% of the population."[5] The number of Christians presently is actually three times that of the early postwar period, indicating the intensity of the evangelistic efforts of both Pentecostal and non-Pentecostal churches.[6] Naturally this means that the churches in Japan placed much of their energy into evangelization and just plain survival, with very little time for theological reflection. Reflection, if any, is geared toward the mission task and therefore tends to be programmatic or project/task oriented.[7]

The growth of churches in Japan has been further hampered by a high defection rate.[8] One study by Kikuo Matsunaga indicates that the average Japanese Christian convert continues in his or her church for only 2.8 years after water baptism.[9] Early Pentecostal missionary efforts were no less troubled by this phenomenon. The aforementioned John Juergensen noted that people would leave "after two years, sometimes more and sometimes less."[10] He pondered, "There must be something wrong with the method we are using to bring salvation to the people."[11] Blame was at times placed on the interpreters and their lack of Pentecostal experience, or on the collective culture that caused many to leave the churches.

Needless to say, contextualizing the Christian message and especially Pentecostalism was and is a concern that "shouts out" to be heard in terms of evangelism and the pastoral efforts to enable long-term Christian commitment. However, little has been accomplished in this sphere by the Western transplant mission churches beside superficial adaptations to the Japanese culture.

The bottom line is that the Pentecostal churches along with the non-Pentecostal churches have not shown significant growth in Japan. Suzuki has calculated that there are about 64,700 Pentecostal church members in Japan. Based on his analysis of the *Christian Yearbook* of 2009, he notes that:

> Today, there are about 40 Pentecostal and Charismatic Protestant denominations, about 130 independent Pentecostal Charismatic churches and about 10 indigenous Pentecostal churches in Japan. Estimates for the numbers of churches/ adherents are 700/47,000 for Classical Pentecostal denominations, 220/7,500 for the Charismatic Churches, 120/6,500 for Independent Pentecostal and Charismatic Churches and 230/3700+ for Indigenous Pentecostals.[12]

The combined Christian church membership of Roman Catholics, Protestants, and Orthodox churches is about 1,126,000, which works out to 0.891 percent of the total population of Japan. This suggests that Pentecostals represent only 5.8 percent of the Christians in Japan.

Third, although Christianity in general and the Pentecostal tradition specifically is relatively small, there is a great diversity in both theological distinctives and ecclesiastical polities that are represented. Mark Mullins recently observed that, "in spite of the popular myth of the homogeneous Japanese and the small number of

Christians, one of the defining characteristics of this minority faith in Japan is the remarkable degree of cultural diversity."[13] When it comes to Pentecostals, the spontaneous growth of indigenous Pentecostal movements has been the catalyst in this sphere, while the churches that have been transplanted by Western missionaries adhere to their specific traditions. This does not mean that the Western missionaries were not cognizant of the need to adopt principles of indigenization like self-government, self-support, and self-propagation. However, most have not been able to shake off the appearance of being a foreign-born religion.[14]

In this chapter I will attempt to summarize recent developments in the history of the Pentecostal movement in Japan and further sketch some of the theological trajectories that have developed. I will conclude by proposing areas of theological reflection that may be crucial to the future of Pentecostalism in Japan.

HISTORICAL DEVELOPMENT

The Pentecostal era in Japan began in September 1907 with the arrival of Martin L. Ryan and his team from Spokane, Washington, who were known as the Apostolic Light or Apostolic Faith Movement. These fourteen adults and seven children[15] were motivated by the belief that the Second Coming was approaching and that they had received the gift of speaking in foreign known languages, xenolalia, specifically Japanese and Chinese. However, upon their arrival at Yokohama it was quite evident that this was not the case.[16] The Apostolic Faith Movement was not only hampered by the lack of language skills, but their finances were also just as wanting. The Ryan-led Apostolic Faith Movement ended when he, as the last member, left Japan in December of 1910, but their legacy did not end there. Coral Fritsch, a member of the Apostolic Faith Movement, had come in contact with the British missionaries to Japan, William and Mary Taylor, in 1908 and exposed them to the Pentecostal faith. Later, the Taylors experienced the Pentecostal Spirit baptism in the United Kingdom and returned to missionary work in Japan by 1911 as Pentecostals.[17]

The Taylors ministered as missionaries of the Pentecostal Missionary Union, first in Nagasaki and then in Kobe. William Taylor was endorsed as an Assemblies of God, USA missionary in 1917 working in the Kansai area. They were integrally involved in the founding of the early Assemblies of God mission work, and most significantly they ministered to Suwa, the future wife of Jun Murai, who would play a crucial role in the Japan Bible Church, which was an early union of Pentecostal ministries in Japan. He later established an indigenous Pentecostal movement known as the Spirit of Jesus Church.

Estella Bernauer arrived in Japan from Indianapolis for the first time in April of 1910. She was inspired to missionary work when Yoshio Tanimoto had come to her church and received the Spirit baptism so that he himself could minister back in Japan. Bernauer ministered in the Kanda area of Tokyo. Her ministry focused on university students who wanted to learn English because she was not able to master the Japanese language sufficiently to preach or teach. Her daughter, Beatrice, however was able to learn the language, and their ministry thrived. Estella Bernauer fellowshipped with the Moores, Grays, Juergensens, and Leonard Coote, showing that the early Pentecostal missionaries were not only in communication with each other, but also they assisted each other in their respective ministries.

Carl F. Juergensen and family arrived in 1913 as independent Pentecostal missionaries. Carl was later appointed as an Assemblies of God, USA missionary in 1918, following Estella Bernauer and William Taylor. All in all, seven Juergensen family members worked as Assemblies of God missionaries. Suzuki notes that the combined years of service by this family numbers up to 130 years.[18] Their work has lasted through the years represented by churches in Takinogawa, Jyujo, and Hamamatsu that still exist today.

Other pre-World War II Pentecostal missionaries of note include Robert Atchison, Frank Gray, Leonard Coote, Jessie Wengler, Alex Munroe, Gordon Bender, Mae Straub, Florence Byers, Harriett Dithridge, and Norman Barth. Among these Leonard Coote stands out. Coote was a British layman who came to Japan in 1913 to work in the Japan office of the British company Lever Brothers. Although brought up as a Methodist, he had a "born-again" experience in early 1914 in light of his association with the holiness mission organization the Japan Evangelical Band. J. B. Thornton, an American missionary, was critical here. He did not think too highly of theology, and it is likely that Coote assimilated this perspective. In fact, Thornton promoted a highly literalistic understanding of the Bible, which would influence Coote in the years to come. It was Mary Taylor, however, who ministered to Coote concerning the Spirit baptism, and he received the Pentecostal experience in late 1917. From here Coote becomes a most effective Pentecostal evangelist, threading together the different ministries throughout the Kanto and Kansai regions. Beginning in Kobe with the Taylors, he ministered in Yokohama with the Grays, then with the Juergensens in Tokyo, and later he is once again in Tokyo working with Bernauer. The year 1919 was one in which Coote's ministry reached a certain peak where powerful Pentecostal manifestations were occurring with consistency. It was the Yokohama earthquake in 1923 that cooled the flames for a while. He then moved to the Kansai region continuing to minister there until 1940, going to the United States during the war and returning in 1949. He completed his service in

1967, having established multiple churches and a thriving ministerial training institution, the Ikoma Bible College.

In 1920 for the first time a Pentecostal association was formed in Japan under the name of the "Japan District of the American Assemblies of God."[19] This association led to a financial cooperation coordinated by the Assemblies of God, USA that assisted in the purchase of the first property and building of a Pentecostal church, the Takinogawa church. This church and the Otsuka Church, also called the Nishi-Sugamo or Sugamo church, would become the two foci of the fledging Pentecostal movement in the Tokyo area. Furthermore, desires to establish Bible schools to train Japanese coworkers were envisioned.

By 1927 the association was known as "The Japan Pentecostal Church," with ministries in both the greater Kanto and Kansai regions; however, membership was limited to missionaries. Finally in 1929 it was reorganized as the Japan Bible Church with Japanese ministers having equal voice and voting rights. This did not mean that Pentecostalism in Japan had attained a paradise-like bliss. Earlier rifts concerning the so-called "new issue" or the Oneness doctrine had disenfranchised the Grays and the Cootes, leading to separate ministries in the Kansai region with a Oneness Pentecostal leaning. Internally, Harriett Dithridge had removed herself from the missionary fellowship in 1929 when it had been decided that her Bible school for women was to be closed and merged with a men's school. In spite of these disruptions, a strong revival period was developing with intense "tarrying services" beginning in 1936. Needless to say, concurrent storm clouds were starting to reappear, as the Takinogawa Church renamed itself the Assemblies of God Takinogawa Mission and began to pull away from the Japan Bible Church. Marie Juergensen and Kiyoma Yumiyama led a cluster of ministries under the banner of the now independent Takinogawa

Mission, while the majority of the missionaries and remaining Japanese ministers were coming together under the leadership of the Otsuka Church with Norman Barth and Jun Murai leading the way.

It was in this divided state that the eye of the typhoon approached the Pentecostal ministries with the upcoming war looming ahead. The Japanese government established a new Religious Organizations Law in 1939 that would be enacted in the following year. This law meant that the Pentecostal churches had to join the United Church of Christ in Japan and that foreign ties must be severed. In 1940 the Japan Bible Church officially broke ties with all foreign organizations to satisfy this new government regulation, with Murai as the superintendent and adding the word "Denomination" to its name. In 1941, however, Murai dissolved the Japan Bible Church Denomination without providing an organizational entry into the United Church of Christ in Japan, a measure to preserve the association through World War II. He instead formed the Spirit of Jesus Church. While some of the Japan Bible Church ministries were able to join as independent churches, the Takinogawa Mission joined as a unit. Coote's work, the Japan Pentecostal Church, ended up disbanded for the duration of the war.[20]

When the war ended in 1945, a new era dawned for Pentecostalism in Japan. First the postwar Constitution of Japan (1947) allowed for freedom of religion and a principle of the separation of religion and state. The war era combinations of Christian churches and organizations under the United Church of Christ in Japan was no longer necessary, and the Takinogawa Mission could now stand on its own. Furthermore, General MacArthur's call for missionaries to once again begin their activities in Japan brought Pentecostal missionaries from throughout the world.

Through the efforts of Kenko Ohchi and Tsuru Nagashima, the

Kansai-based Hajime Kawasaki and Kiyoma Yumiyama from the Takinogawa Mission began talks that would lead to the founding of the Japan Assemblies of God in March of 1949. The seven missionaries and twelve Japanese ministers who gathered for the meeting agreed to found both a religious organization and a Bible school. Yumiyama was elected as the first general superintendent, and he continued to minister in this capacity for twenty-five years, while leading the Bible school for many more years.

The period beginning in the 1950s through the middle of the 1960s brought a flood of Pentecostal groups. Shew notes that:

> Some of the significant arrivals include International Church of the [Foursquare Gospel] (1950), Open Bible Standard Churches (1950), Church of God (Cleveland, TN, 1952) and Pentecostal Church of God (1954). Oneness groups also started mission work in Japan, including the United Pentecostal Church International (1963). And a number of Scandinavian organizations pioneered missions during this period including Fellowship of Christian Assemblies (1948), Swedish Free Missionaries (1950), Finland Free Foreign Mission (1950), and Free Christian Mission Group (1950, from Norway and Denmark). These Scandinavian groups later merged into the Independent Pentecostal Church Fellowship.[21]

During this same period the Spirit of Jesus Church showed phenomenal growth; however, since their statistics include baptism for the dead, an accurate account is not possible. The *Makuya* or Original Gospel Movement's beginnings can be traced back to 1948 when the founder Ikuro Teshima had a Pentecostal-style experience, but it was in 1950 that a "Makuya Pentecost" broke out during a prayer conference and "many fell to the floor and spoke in tongues."[22] This indigenous Pentecostal movement grew to about sixty thousand members by 1979, according to Carlo Caldarola.[23]

In 1976 Paul Yonggi Cho began his mission venture in Japan with the establishment of a church in Osaka. A Tokyo church with many branches followed in 1978. Mullins notes that "by 1989, the Full Gospel Mission in Japan had grown to nine churches and a membership of some five thousand guided by twenty missionary pastors."[24] Characteristic of this Full Gospel work in Japan is that the majority of the membership is from the Korean expat community. The initial growth seems to have slowed down. As Mullins indicates:

> The most recent data on the Full Gospel Church mission indicates that there has been a steady investment in resources and new church development over the past two decades. There are now 105 missionaries working with 74 churches in Japan, but the membership has only increased to 5,703. These churches continue to primarily attract Koreans and have made little headway within the larger Japanese population. In the Tokyo Church, for example, which is the largest Full Gospel Church in Japan, only 100 of the 1,200 members are Japanese. It is safe to conclude that more that [sic] 90 percent of the membership is still Korean in these churches across Japan.[25]

Along with the Korean mission, the 1980s and 1990s brought to center stage a series of international ministries. The influence of such Third Wave Charismatics as John Wimber, Peter Wagner, and Cindy Jacobs was combined with evangelists such as Carlos Annacondia and Benny Hinn. These ministries and others had several effects.

First, as Pentecostal groups such as the Japan Assemblies of God attempted to gain recognition from fellow evangelicals, they were confronted with what traditional evangelicals considered extreme behavior and false teaching. When Japan Assemblies of God applied for membership in the Japan Evangelical Association, they were initially rejected. The point of contention was a "Provision on Charisma," which ultimately contended over the possibility of "personal revelation." The "misunderstandings" were clarified and the Japan Assemblies of God were admitted in 1988.[26]

Second, in 1994 another contention developed within the Japan Evangelical Association in which the Theological Committee contested "power evangelism" and other Third Wave activities, causing a division among Pentecostals and the establishment of the Nippon Revival Association, a Charismatic organization, in 1996.

A renewed Pentecostal association called the Japan Pentecostal Council was formed in 1998 with the purpose "to promote the sound growth of the Pentecostal faith in Japan."[27] Ten initial Pentecostal groups were represented. The future of Pentecostalism in Japan is now coordinated with a means of communication and solidarity.

THEOLOGICAL TRAJECTORIES

J. Nelson Jennings has observed that "Christian theology in Japan has more than enough variety to persuade one to abandon any effort to encapsulate within a single description all of its hues, shades and accents."[28] Pentecostalism is no different. On one hand there are many varieties of transplanted Pentecostal churches, whether from the West or East, that maintain a strong solidarity with their respective sending organizations in terms of doctrine and liturgical practices. The Japan Assemblies of God, for example, follows the US Assemblies of God's Statement of Fundamental Truths. Former superintendent Akie Ito has authored a commentary on each of the sixteen articles that adheres to the USA document.[29] The Korean Full Gospel churches in Japan have rigidly followed the cell structures, prayer intensity, and even the shout of "hallelujah" when a speaker takes to the pulpit. On the other hand there are several indigenous Pentecostal associations that provide a greater scale of diversity and contextual innovations, such as the Spirit of Jesus Church and the *Makuya* or Original Gospel Movement.

The first significant theological issue, however, was the so-called "new issue," which was imported from the United States. Frank Gray was the earliest missionary that records clearly indicate that he was convinced by the doctrine. Leonard Coote, who was the most important figure when it comes to postwar expansion of the Oneness movement, paradoxically does not seem to have committed himself to the doctrine in the prewar era. Paul Shew has subjected the question to a thorough analysis.[30] His conclusion is that Coote "tended towards a Trinitarian nature of the Godhead as opposed to a modalist theology,"[31] but he consistently baptized in the name of Jesus following a literalistic interpretation of the formula in the Book of Acts. In the postwar era Coote was associated with two larger Oneness organizations: the United Pentecostal Church in Japan and the Next Towns Crusade. Both of these groups have been concentrated in the Kansai region and have not shown exceptional growth. Yasunori Aoki has recently indicated that Japanese pastors in both of these groups tend to not promote the modalistic theology.[32] Fellowship is valued more than this doctrine. From a Western perspective Trinitarian versus modalism is considered an important theological difference. In contrast, in recent times, the Japanese Pentecostals have not found such theological differences as a deal breaker. In fact, Miyake has proposed that "Japanese religious thinking is closely related to the sense of social belonging."[33]

The second significant theological issue deals with Jun Murai and the Spirit of Jesus Church. Here the breach between other Pentecostals was definitive, and the interpersonal ties were severed. The precursor to the shift in Murai's theology may have begun even before his crucial trip to Taiwan where he visited the True Jesus Church. First, as most prewar Japanese Pentecostals, Murai's theology was based on a modified dispensational theology that believed the Holy Spirit was working in the church today as in the New Testament era with signs, miracles, and tongues.[34] Murai combined this with the developing nationalism of his time and began to conceive of Japan as eschatologically significant. In 1940 he wrote, "God chose Japan for the last days. In Japan, God brought a true Christianity. God brings the light from the East, from Japan, to Asia to the World. This is God's plan and also our mission."[35]

A note of concern must be raised in terms of a proclivity toward ultra-nationalism and what some have called "Japanese Christianity," in both Murai and other prewar Japanese Pentecostals. Suzuki points out that "the Japanese Pentecostal Christians did not oppose the war but, on the contrary, supported both it and the government."[36] To back up this claim, he notes that on the occasion of the emperor's birthday in 1939, Hajime Kawasaki had invited another pastor to his church so that the church may "raise the authority of our home country Japan and to pray for the good luck and safety of our emperor's army."[37] Murai seemed to understand the militarism of Japan as another sign of the end times when he wrote, "without the pond of fire there will not be the New Heaven and New Earth."[38] These statements and general attitude are far from the approach of the Barmen Declaration in 1934, where the Confessional Church in Germany with strong theological leadership by Karl Barth stood adamantly against the Nazi-inspired "German Christian" movement. Granted, the Confessional Church was much stronger numerically than the small group of Christians in Japan. Toshio Sato astutely queries and answers his own question:

> What kind of people were likely to turn to Japanese Christianity? The first group were those who had adopted liberal Christianity....The second group were those associated with pietism. More concerned with the Bible and piety than

with orthodox doctrine, they were sincere Christians. They believed that the Japanese should embrace the Japanese spirit, but that sinners are unable to do so. Only when one is justified by faith and sanctified can one become a master of the true Japanese spirit. In this way, they combined Christianity and the spirit of Japan.[39]

The enculturation of the Pentecostal message with little interest in theological reflection now began to show itself as the Achilles heel to Japanese Pentecostalism and Jun Murai.

Ironically Murai is attracted to practices and teachings of foreign origin.[40] This in spite of the fact that he wrote:

> The one who holds God's seal is appearing from the land of the rising sun. Holding God's seal indicates a true church, and the church actually appeared. It is impossible to seal or to make the salvation of the one who needs to be sealed complete unless by a true church. Therefore, God did not choose the Western countries but chose Asia. And the true church will come from the East and will spread to all the earth.[41]

Under the influence of the True Jesus Church of Taiwan, Murai adopted several of their practices, such as: baptism in the name of Jesus, a renewed emphasis on glossolalia, foot washing as a sacrament, and keeping the Sabbath. It seems that Murai even joined the ranks of Oneness when he was re-baptized in the name of Jesus.

Most intriguing is how Murai dealt with issues regarding death, ancestors, and the spirit world. Murai instituted a rite of baptism for dead ancestors that he called *senzo no migawari senrei* (vicarious baptism for ancestors). Murai believed that salvation of the dead was a lost biblical doctrine that in the last days was being restored by the Spirit of Jesus Church. Mullins explains Murai's theology of ancestor salvation in the following way:

...the spirits of all those who died without salvation and
without receiving water and spirit baptism are presently in
Hades. Although their bodies decay in the grave, their spirits
can be saved through the forgiveness of sins. The authority
to forgive sins, Murai maintains, has been forgotten by the
modern church along with all the signs, miracles, and wonders that characterized the early church. Through the ritual
of vicarious baptism, the good news of the forgiveness of sins
is communicated to the dead and their spirits are transported
from Hades to Heaven. Believers are assured that all their
doubts and misgivings regarding the state of their ancestors
can be resolved through their ritual of baptism. This ministry
to the dead is simply carrying on the work begun by Jesus
Christ when he descended into Hades and preached to the
imprisoned spirits (see 1 Peter 3.18–22).[42]

Murai should be credited with identifying a significant area of
contextual concern, that of death and ancestors; however, his biblical and theological solutions are far from acceptable within most
Pentecostal circles.

The third significant theological issue continues to deal with
that of contextualization, but this time in terms of the indigenous
Pentecostal association, the *Makuya* or Original Gospel Movement.
Teshima, the founder, was originally part of the Nonchurch movement until his Pentecostal experience. This aspect of his background
may account, in part, for his antagonism to Western Christianity.[43]
Mullins lists several other areas in which the Nonchurch movement
influenced Teshima: "independence from Western church traditions
and rejection of the sacramental system and denominational polities, an emphasis on studying the Bible in the original languages,
and the practice of meeting primarily in rented halls and members'
homes, rather than investing in church buildings."[44]

Also the Makuya movement was sensitive to many of the concerns
of Japanese folk religions, allowing for greater contextualization

and appeal. Teshima insisted that the early Japanese tales such as those recorded in the *Kojiki, Nihon Shoki,* and the *Manyoshu* be understood as a non-canonical "Old Testament" for Japanese spirituality. This led Teshima to include several ascetic practices as a means of spiritual training. The Makuya movement therefore utilized the "*misogi* water purification rituals, including *takiabi* or standing under a waterfall, and *hiwatari* or walking across a bed of hot coals."[45] Whether one agrees or disagrees with these practices, the effort to contextualize the gospel within Japanese culture is noteworthy.

The fourth issue arises from outside groups such as the Korean churches and differing Third Wave and Charismatic ministries. Topics include cross-generational retribution or bloodline curses from the Koreans; power evangelism with healing and exorcisms from the Third Wave; teaching and missional practices involving so-called territorial spirits and prayer walks; and last but not least the Charismatic ministries that have centered on prophecy. These, as indicated above, have impacted the struggle for the evangelical recognition of the Japanese Pentecostal organizations. These various teachings have been generally accepted at face value in their initial propagation. Little theological reflection has been paid to these topics.

Pentecostal theology in Japan has had both foreign and indigenous sources. The "less thought" sequence in the Pentecostal DNA has hampered a more serious interaction with many topics that have been themselves "shouting" to be heard.

THEOLOGICAL REFLECTIONS

The future is difficult to predict, and it is especially precarious to speculate as to what theological issues will be the talk of the Pentecostal town. One area of concern that we can be sure of will be pastoral theology and the crucial issue of evangelism. With a declining birth rate and an aging population, Christianity in Japan is showing signs of a steady decline. Most crucial is the aging of the clergy and lack of candidates for ministerial training. This phenomenon can be noted widely across all church groups. Mullins notes that:

> A recent study of the Catholic Church projects that the number of priests will decrease by one-third or one-half within the next 15 years.... The largest Protestant denomination, the United Church of Christ in Japan, reported that 228 churches (13%) were "pastorless" in 2003, and that number is expected to more than double in the next decade.[46]

The Japanese Pentecostal churches are no different. Suzuki writes that:

> The average age of the JAG ministers keeps rising, with the result that in 2011 close to 100 ministers and wives are over 70 years old. Since there are only sixteen full-time CBC students in the 2011 school year, the expected graduates will be insufficient to fill the vacancies created by the retiring ministers in coming years.[47]

It is highly probable that theological reflection will decline as organizations become desperate to find new ministerial recruits. Pastors will have little time to study, some being required to pastor multiple churches. The historical tendency of the Pentecostal churches in Japan to grasp for new techniques without philosophical and theological integration will continue.

Another concern in the area of pastoral theology is the churches' ability to theologically interact with current events that affect evangelism and Christianity, or for that matter, Pentecostalism. The so-called Aum Affair is a case in point. In 1995 this religious group,

Aum Shinrikyo, released sarin gas on several subways in Tokyo, killing thirteen and injuring fifty-four people. The aftermath for religions in general was that laws governing religious organizations were altered to protect the public, more than the freedom of religion.[48] A deep distrust of religions in general also arose[49] with some groups being considered "cults." The Pentecostal churches never really addressed this issue. In fact, ministries that specialized in dealing with people coming out of Christian cults exacerbated the problem, casting suspicions on any ministry that was different.

A final component that intersects with pastoral theology is that of contextualization of the Pentecostal message. As indicated in the case of Jun Murai and the Spirit of Jesus Church, dealing with death and ancestors is crucial for a richer integration into the Japanese culture. Pentecostal theology from the transplanted mission groups has not been able to make significant contextual adaptations in any other area. This needs to be a priority.

Second, in a more general way, Pentecostalism has great theological potential in dealing with many deep-rooted folk religious issues such as the world of the spirits, curses, and blessings. Taking one example, Mullins notes that, "while many Japanese Christians are deeply concerned about the salvation of their ancestors, they also harbor fears about the possible misfortune (*tatari*) they may suffer at the hands of malevolent spirits of the dead known as *onryo*."[50] This sphere is one that has traditionally been occupied by Japanese folk religions and in the postwar era dominated by the New Religious Movements. As Mullins notes, "scholars estimate that between 10-20% of the population belongs to one of these new religious movements."[51] Both the Spirit of Jesus Church and the Original Gospel Movement aggressively dealt with issues that were in this category.

A theological issue that may be parallel here is that of the doctrine of revelation. This topic became an issue when the Japan Assemblies of God was seeking recognition from the Japan Evangelical Association. At that time it was argued that Pentecostals do not believe in "personal revelation," an idea that some Charismatics have understood as tantamount to a betrayal of a Pentecostal distinctive, that God still speaks today. The leadership of the Japan Assemblies of God was approaching the topic from a more rigid "general" and "special" revelation categories found in many evangelical systematic theologies.

This topic has two components that have not been dealt with to date. First, the early postwar era was dominated by a Barthian understanding of revelation within the mainline churches. This may well have been a reaction against those prewar theologies that have been labeled "Japanese Christianity." Both apologetics and enculturation of theology were discouraged. This even led to the poor reception that Kazoh Kitamori received from his *Theology of the Pain of God* in Japan.[52] In others words, a narrow view of revelation has tended to discourage the contextualization process in Japan.

Second, Mullins has observed that the indigenous movements in Japan have tended to have a broader conception of revelation. Mullins notes that:

> The traditional Protestant understanding of revelation has been that God spoke through the prophets, Jesus, and the apostles, and that this process of revelation ended with the canonization of the Old and New Testament Scriptures. Most Protestant denominations maintain that the charismatic gifts also ended with the early church, since their primary purpose was to confirm the truth of the Gospel for the first Christian communities. Indigenous movements, for the most part, maintain that God's self-revelation did not end with the canon of the Christian Scriptures, and that God continues to reveal

deeper truths to those who are open to the ongoing work of the Holy Spirit. While most of these movements operate with the closed canon, many share a common belief that God continues to reveal new truths hidden from or as yet ungrasped by Western churches.[53]

Further theological reflection is necessary in dealing with this topic from a Pentecostal perspective, one that may be fruitful not only for Pentecostals themselves but also for evangelicalism and evangelism in Japan.

Third and finally, Pentecostalism in Japan has suffered a grave malady that might be called anti-intellectualism or a general disinterest in the cognitive aspects of Christianity and Pentecostalism. One may brush off this observation as being synonymous to the DNA of Pentecostalism itself, more "shout" and less "thought"; however, I would argue that there is a uniqueness to this development in Japanese Pentecostalism that has been negatively impacting its growth.

Two Japanese Pentecostal scholars, for example, have cogently argued that there is resistance on the part of Japanese toward Christianity because they consider it "a knowledge-centered religion." As Miyake notes, "if we present the gospel as no more than knowledge, we notice that many of the Japanese do not have an interest in the gospel."[54] Makito Nagasawa, whom Miyake quotes approvingly, states that, "in the Japanese context, truth is experiential and personal. Truth as philosophical or conceptual, separated from feeling, is almost meaningless to the Japanese."[55] The solution then is to promote experience first, then knowledge can be acquired. This approach is probably not that unique to Japan, as others such as Rick Richardson quip, "Experience comes before explanation."[56] The problem is that this is not always the case. At times knowledge comes first. At times experience comes first. In fact, artificially dividing knowledge from experience and vice versa may be the real problem, a classic "either-or" fallacy, which should be answered "both-and."

Furthermore, it is possible that the understanding that Christianity is for intellectuals may be viewed also from another perspective. Mullins notes that it is because "both missionaries and Japanese Christian leaders have been pioneers in a number of fields, including social welfare, medical work, and education"[57] that Christianity is recognized as having a positive impact on Japan. Mullins further postulates that, "the problematic image and reputation of Christianity as a religion 'for intellectuals,' however, has been created in part by this emphasis on education."[58]

CONCLUSION

Pentecostalism, beginning in 1907, evolved from a small cluster of independent-minded foreign missionaries to over forty Pentecostal and Charismatic denominations. There are both transplanted mission churches and indigenous works that believe, proclaim, and live a Pentecostal faith with signs and miracles for today. Yet the "shouts" of these ministries have not been able to convince the majority of Japanese today. A rethinking is necessary today, as was the case for John Juergensen, who queried, "There must be something wrong with the method we are using to bring salvation to the people."[59]

Part III: Southeast Asia

Chapter 10

The Pentecostal Movement in Vietnam

Vince Le

T HE SOCIALIST REPUBLIC of Vietnam is located on the eastern margin of mainland Southeast Asia, with China bordering on the north, and Laos and Cambodia bordering on the west. Vietnam possesses a long coastal line on the east and the south, bordering the Gulf of Tonkin, the Gulf of Thailand, and a body of water known to Vietnam as "the East Sea." The country nowadays boasts a multiethnic, multicultural identity perceived as a result of a few thousand years of interactions between the Việt people with the Chinese, the Cham, the Khmer, and many other people groups. The *2009 Vietnam Population and Housing Census* shows the Việt people account for 86 percent of the country's population of 86 million people. More than fifty other ethnic minority groups make up 14 percent of the population.

The same 2009 census also lists Roman Catholicism and Protestantism as two among six largest religions of Vietnam, comprising of about 6 percent and 1 percent of the national population respectively.[1] It is also noteworthy that the census renders the designation *Protestantism* into Vietnamese as *Tin Lành* (literally means Good News; in English, evangelicalism), a term widely used by both the Vietnamese public and believers to refer to Protestantism.

I shall follow the conventional practice of using the term *evangelicals* to refer to all Protestant Christians in Vietnam.

The Vietnamese Pentecostals are categorized as a subgroup of the Vietnamese evangelicals. It is believed that 30 percent of the evangelicals are Pentecostals. In sheer numbers, different sources suggest that the evangelical population of Vietnam ranges from 734,000 to 1,300,000 people, and the Pentecostal population from 220,000 to 400,000 people. Statistics suggest there are more than fifty Pentecostal groups in Vietnam, with the number of followers of each group varying from a few hundred to tens of thousands. According to a Vietnamese social researcher, evangelicalism is the fastest-growing religion in contemporary Vietnam. From the end of the Vietnam War in 1975 to the present time, the entire evangelical population multiplied sixfold, and the predominantly Pentecostal house church population grew from virtually 0 to 400,000 people.[2]

One notable demographic fact about the Vietnamese evangelicals and Pentecostals is that more than three quarters of them are ethnic minorities who live in the highlands and mountainous areas of the country. The Việt people, who comprise 86 percent of the population, make up less than a quarter of the evangelical and Pentecostal population of Vietnam. As a result, a typical Vietnamese Pentecostal is an ethnic minority who lives in the highlands, probably a woman, who speaks her native language. Many ethnic minority Pentecostals can also communicate in Vietnamese (the language of the Việt people).

Because the terms *evangelical* and *Pentecostal* may mean different things to different people, I will begin this chapter with an attempt to define these terms as they are used in the Vietnamese context. After that, the chapter will focus on the beginning, the current situation (in terms of organization, spirituality, and activities), and then conclude with prospects of the Vietnamese Pentecostal movement.

The Vietnamese Evangelicals and Pentecostals

Vietnamese evangelicals possess a high view of Scripture, a strong commitment to evangelism, a devotion to holiness as a way of life, and an understanding that the church is living in the last days of history.[3] Vietnamese Pentecostals believe the same thing, but building upon the evangelical foundation, they emphasize the personal, direct, and miraculous encounter with God, which they believe can be mediated through practices such as participatory worship, speaking in tongues, fasting, and prayer for healing and deliverance.

In the following I attempt to describe the organizational relationship between the Vietnamese evangelicals and Pentecostals, but at the end will suggest that it is better to use the definitions that I proposed in the previous paragraph. From an organizational perspective, the Vietnamese evangelicals are either those who belong to the Evangelical Church of Vietnam (ECVN) and the Vietnam Christian Mission, the two older and larger evangelical establishments in the country, or those who belong to other smaller evangelical groups.[4] These smaller evangelical groups, which are often called the house churches, were formed by:

1. Those who could trace their Christian affiliations to the missionary efforts of various Christian foreign missionaries in South Vietnam before 1975. Among them were the Mennonites, the Baptists, and the members of the Assemblies of God (AG), to name a few.[5]

2. Those who were expelled from the ECVN in the
   1980s due to conflicts in doctrines or polity

3. Those who left Vietnam as boat people since 1975 to
   as late as the 1990s, were converted to Christianity in
   refugee camps, but had to return to Vietnam because
   they were denied permanent resettlement to a third
   country

4. Those who converted to the evangelical and
   Pentecostal faiths while working or studying in
   Eastern Europe and the former Soviet Union during
   the dramatic political changes in 1989 and after, and
   subsequently returned to Vietnam

5. Those who disassociated with any of the above groups
   and formed new affiliations with other church traditions and/or denominations that in the last decade
   showed interests in planting churches in Vietnam,
   among which were the Methodists and the Anglicans

6. Those who converted while temporarily migrating for
   work, either from rural areas to big cities in Vietnam,
   or from Vietnam to Malaysia, South Korea, Taiwan,
   and as far as the Middle East as part of the state's
   labor export program

The designation *house church* derives from the fact that smaller
evangelical groups gather and worship in private houses or rented
facilities because they have not been granted legal status and/
or have not had enough financial resources to buy property and
open a church building. Additionally, in some mountainous areas
the already established ECVN and the Vietnam Christian Mission
also use private houses as worship venues in areas where they have

not had church facilities. Because the house churches often show interests in having their own worship buildings, the house church reality is an operational solution to respond to the challenges of opening a new church facility; it carries, however, little theological significance to the house church people.

In Vietnam many, but not all of the house church groups are Pentecostal. It is, however, problematic to define the Vietnamese Pentecostals from an organizational perspective by simply saying that the Pentecostals are confined within a clear segment of the house churches. The reason is the organized Pentecostal house churches do not represent all the Vietnamese Pentecostals. There are Pentecostal-oriented evangelicals well versed in Pentecostal spirituality who have stayed within their current evangelical groups rather than joined a Pentecostal group. With this in mind, it is more helpful to define the Vietnamese Pentecostals in terms of beliefs and practices rather than from an organizational perspective.[6]

THE BEGINNING OF POSTWAR VIETNAMESE PENTECOSTALISM

In this section I present some of the key elements of the Vietnamese Pentecostal collective memory from the beginning of the movement and identify some of the factors that contributed to the outbreak of Pentecostal phenomena among the Vietnamese evangelicals in the 1980s.

It is common to cite the incidents of speaking in tongues, which happened to a number of Vietnamese evangelicals in the 1980s, as inaugurating the movement. It is, however, difficult to pinpoint when, and to whom, the first Pentecostal experiences happened because different Pentecostal leaders and groups remember it differently. The following situates the outbreak of tongues among the Vietnamese evangelicals in the 1980s:

- The context was postwar (i.e., post-1975) socialist Vietnam, in which the evangelical practices, or any religious practice for that matter, were not encouraged. Local churches were allowed to open only two hours per week for a worship service on Sunday.

- The tongues-speaking phenomenon began as a cell group movement amidst fasting, prayer, and Bible studies. These gatherings in private houses emerged in response to the state's restriction of religious activities in 1981–1982.[7]

- The phenomenon of tongues happened to a number of evangelical pastors and believers around 1982–1983 and became more popular in 1984–1985.

- The first outbreaks of tongues in postwar Vietnam happened without foreign intervention.[8]

- The movement took shape when the ECVN (South) decided to excommunicate pastors who practiced tongues in 1989.[9] Tongues-speaking evangelical pastors and believers continued to use existing cell group systems as the movement structure.

Many stories of the early Pentecostal experience have similar elements. One typical story derives from 1982. The venue was the private house of an evangelical believer in Hồ Chí Minh City. The occasion was a small group prayer meeting. The purpose was to pray for church revival. The unexpected experience was the speaking of tongues. The result was a renewed passion for mission and church revival.

As of today, little is known about the early Pentecostal experience from the perspective of the ethnic minority peoples who make up the majority of the Vietnamese Pentecostal demographic. Most accounts of this period suggest the renewal first came to the Southern Việt evangelicals, who in turn missionized the Việt people who lived in the North and the ethnic minorities who lived in the highlands and the mountainous areas. This perspective adequately registers the agency of the Việt people but overlooks that of the ethnic minority Pentecostals.

Two converging streams fed the outbreak of the Pentecostal phenomenon among the Vietnamese evangelicals in the early 1980s: the evangelical focus on revival and the knowledge of the practice of tongues speaking. Revival, understood as an experience of mass conversion and a renewed commitment to evangelism and holiness from within an evangelical body, is a major theme in Vietnamese evangelicalism. Revivals often include emotional public expressions (such as crying, laughing, confession, reconciliation, and forgiveness) and miraculous experiences (predominantly bodily healing). Memories of two previous revivals continue to shape the Vietnamese evangelical and Pentecostal understanding of revival: the revival among the students of the ECVN's Bible Institute in Nha Trang in 1971 and the preaching tour of the Chinese revivalist/evangelist John Sung in 1938.[10]

Although knowledge of tongues as a spiritual practice is not mentioned much, R. A. Jaffray, field secretary of the South China Alliance Mission and the chief architect of the Christian and Missionary Alliance (C&MA) work in Vietnam in the 1910s and 1920s, was himself a tongues-speaker.[11] Additionally, most, if not all of the earliest C&MA missionaries had worked in South China before coming to Vietnam. They must at least have known of the manifestations of tongues among C&MA missionaries and native believers in South China in 1907.[12] Last but not least, the Pentecostal denomination the Assemblies of God (AG) had done considerable work in South Vietnam from 1972 to 1975.[13] As a result, knowledge of the practice of speaking in tongues survived among the Vietnamese evangelicals, and, together with the desire for revival, it contributed to the Pentecostal outbreak in postwar Vietnam.

THE ORGANIZATION OF VIETNAMESE PENTECOSTALS

It is best to understand the Pentecostal movement in Vietnam in terms of organizational networks, individual networks, and international connections. The most notable organizational networks are the two Vietnamese Christian Fellowships (two networks using the same name) in the South and the Hanoi Christian Fellowship in northern Vietnam. These networks include both Pentecostal and non-Pentecostal house church groups, but the Pentecostal groups make up a majority within these networks. Organizational networks mobilized resources for evangelistic campaigns and built coalitions for interacting and engaging with other social institutions, including the government.

Individual networks are more informal, referring to the transdenominational connections among the individual Pentecostals and the Pentecostal-oriented evangelicals who are not affiliated with the Pentecostal groups. These individual networks are often lay-initiated. They are effective in pulling resources and expertise among the urban Pentecostals for short-term evangelism, musical projects, and Bible training.

In terms of international connections, the Pentecostal groups, and other house church groups for that matter, often have extensive relationships with overseas Christian bodies, either through denominational or network affiliations, thus building up a sense of transnational identity. This transnational identity sometimes causes the public to perceive Pentecostal groups as foreign institutions.

This is an inaccurate perception, as it is normal for social and religious movements (such as the worker's movement) in Vietnam to cultivate and negotiate both a local and a global identity.

International denominational affiliations can range from being very Pentecostal to very non-Pentecostal. The name of a Pentecostal group can be very misleading in terms of its significance inside and outside the Vietnamese context. For example, the United Presbyterian Church of Vietnam, which is affiliated with the Presbyterian Church (USA), is in reality one of the larger Pentecostal churches in Vietnam, while its American counterpart is not a Pentecostal denomination. As a result, spiritual practices and emphasis on the miraculous are better indicators of whether a group is affiliated with the Pentecostal movement.

While international denominational affiliations may be less obviously Pentecostal, international network affiliations are often Pentecostal, albeit rather informally. These connections may include the Word of Faith network in North America, the Empower21 movement, or Pentecostal training schools such as Christ for the Nations Institute (Dallas, TX) and Rhema Bible Training College (Oklahoma City, OK). In recent years Vietnamese Pentecostals have begun to explore and attend conferences organized by other Latin American and Asian Pentecostals, thus consciously cultivating a Global South Pentecostal identity.

THE SPIRITUALITY OF VIETNAMESE PENTECOSTALS

By spirituality I mean the beliefs and practices that shape the Pentecostal experience of God and the way God works in individual believers and in the world through the Holy Spirit. In terms of beliefs, the Vietnamese Pentecostals adhere to a Pentecostal fourfold gospel, confessing Jesus, in the power of the Spirit, as Savior, Spirit baptizer, healer, and coming King. In Vietnamese Pentecostalism, the wide reception of the Pentecostal fourfold gospel is due to the following reasons:

- The C&MA missionaries introduced their own version of fourfold gospel to Vietnam as soon as they arrived to the country in 1911.[14] The C&MA's fourfold gospel, which expresses Jesus as Savior, sanctifier, healer, and coming King, has been chosen as the logo of the ECVN since 1927–1928. The only difference between the C&MA's fourfold gospel and the Pentecostal fourfold gospel is that one has Jesus as sanctifier and the other has Jesus as Spirit baptizer.[15]

- Two of the largest Vietnamese Pentecostal groups, which currently affiliate with the International Church of the Foursquare Gospel and the World Assemblies of God Fellowship, have familiarized Vietnamese Pentecostals with the Pentecostal fourfold gospel.

- The Pentecostal fivefold gospel, which comprises the Pentecostal fourfold gospel and the additional item of Jesus as sanctifier, is less well known in Vietnam because sanctification is understood as a lifelong process, rather than a definite moment that happens between the day a person converts and the day he or she first experiences speaking in tongues.

Vietnamese Pentecostals, in their interaction with other overseas Pentecostals, also developed a set of practices to mediate their experience of God and God's work in the world. Notable practices include Pentecostal worship, prayer for divine intervention, speaking in tongues, and fasting.

Pentecostal worship. In late 1990s the music of Don Moen and Darlene Zschech set a standard for Vietnamese Pentecostal worship. More recently the Internet has informed Vietnamese Pentecostals of new trends in global Pentecostal worship. In its current configuration, Vietnamese Pentecostal musical style is a mixture of the influences of the older evangelical tradition (coming from the early C&MA missionaries and other South China evangelical sources), the contemporary (mostly North American) Pentecostal way of worship, and Vietnamese pop music. It is one area where Pentecostals influence evangelicals and Charismatic Catholics, both of whom use Pentecostal songs in their worship services.

Prayer for divine intervention. Divine intervention can be for physical and psychological healing, exorcism, and deliverance from a bad situation. It is noteworthy that prayer for deliverance and belief in the reality of the demonic is not new among Vietnamese evangelicals and Pentecostals. Pioneer C&MA missionaries in Vietnam also practiced prayer for divine intervention in the early twentieth century.[16]

Speaking in tongues. Tongues speaking was a defining practice of Pentecostalism in the early days of the movement in Vietnam. In recent years the practice has become less prominent among the Vietnamese Pentecostals. Prayer for deliverance and healing, broadly understood as miraculous experiences of the divine, has become more central for the movement.

Fasting. The Vietnamese Pentecostals believe that ascetical fasting has the capacity to bring believers closer to God. However, they also fast to express the desire to be empowered by the Spirit for a more effective Christian ministry, to appeal to God's power and mercy in order to alter an undesirable life condition, or to plea for social transformation. Second Chronicles 7:14 shapes the Vietnamese Pentecostal belief that when they fast with humility and contrition,

God will forgive and heal the land of Vietnam. Fasting thus has a clear social dimension in Vietnamese Pentecostalism.

THE ACTIVITIES OF VIETNAMESE PENTECOSTALS

Training and evangelism are two major church activities among the Pentecostals. Training is closely connected to the translation of Pentecostal literature into Vietnamese and other ethnic languages, and social work (understood as relief and humanitarian aid) is often regarded as a preparation for evangelism.

Training. The training of church workers focuses on providing practical skills for effective church work and knowledge that aligns with existing beliefs and practices. Training content often come from two sources: (1) the teachings that many early Pentecostal leaders received when they were students at the ECVN's Bible Institute before 1975, and (2) Pentecostal teachings from the West that have been translated into Vietnamese since the 1980s.

In the late 1980s and early 1990s foreign Christians smuggled Bibles into Vietnam. Coming with them were books written by Yonggi Cho and Kenneth Hagin, among others, which introduced tongues-speaking Vietnamese evangelicals to other Pentecostal beliefs and practices. Ralph Mahoney's *The Shepherd's Staff* and the School of Workers series, developed by a Filipino Christian group, Christ, the Living Stone Fellowship, were two major manuals translated and widely used for the purposes of training church workers.

Since Vietnam and the United States normalized diplomatic relations in 1995, missionaries came to Vietnam more often and brought with them books written by Joyce Meyer, Benny Hinn, and other Pentecostal preachers associated with the Word of Faith movement. The International School of Ministry's curriculum (http://www .isom.org/), a Pentecostal-oriented video Bible training program featuring well-known preachers such as Jack Hayford, Reinhard

Bonnke, and Joyce Meyer, was translated and shared among the Vietnamese Pentecostals as another major training resource.

As the Vietnamese economy took off in the 2000s, the teaching of wealth and social influence gained wider attention among the Vietnamese Pentecostals. It reflected the desire for recognition of a group that had experienced social marginalization. The teaching about reclaiming different public spheres served as a framework for prayers for social transformation and fostered the Pentecostals' dream of having greater social influence.[17]

Claudio Freidzon's *Holy Spirit, I Hunger for You* was perhaps the first book by a Latin American Pentecostal translated into Vietnamese. This book and videos of Reinhard Bonnke's African crusades provided Vietnamese Pentecostals with new information about the Pentecostal movement from outside the more familiar North American and Korean settings.

Evangelism and social work. The Pentecostal faith grew more rapidly in the highlands than in the lowlands, in the rural than in the urban areas, and among migrant workers and manual laborers than among city dwellers. The 2000s saw Vietnamese Pentecostals embracing a transnational mission to evangelize migrant workers, who were working in Taiwan, South Korea, and Malaysia. They did so in collaboration with the Vietnamese in diaspora and other Christian groups in those host countries.

At home and abroad the Vietnamese Pentecostals borrowed the following evangelistic methods from the evangelicals: (1) an individualized approach using personal testimony and Bill Bright's *Four Spiritual Laws* and other tracts, (2) a local church approach that included evangelistic services, and (3) a mass approach using crusade evangelism during the Christmas season. True to their focus on the miraculous, Vietnamese Pentecostal evangelism emphasized deliverance from crises such as health problems, domestic and finance issues, and addictions.

Vietnamese Pentecostal provision for the needy, materially and emotionally, is often undertaken as a prelude to evangelism. Vietnamese Pentecostals have not yet developed their own ways of dealing with poverty and structural injustice.

There is an increasing awareness among Vietnamese Pentecostals that evangelism and social work are two inseparable aspects of a single Christian approach to the world. This is, however, a model of foreign missions that often leaves the public with an impression that a local Vietnamese church that engages in humanitarian aid (often with funds coming from overseas) is an agent of a foreign institution, rather than a local group sharing similar struggles with other local people. The model has to be used with caution.

One social ministry of the Vietnamese Pentecostals that has been recognized is the work among the drug addicts in the cities. The Vietnamese media have reported positively on some successful cases. Through engagement in long-term projects like working with drug addicts and former drug addicts, the Pentecostals have an opportunity to engage a single issue in its spiritual, psychological, economic, and social complexity. This helps the Vietnamese Pentecostals to think about how they can best interact with society and address injustices on their own terms.

PROSPECTS FOR THE FUTURE OF PENTECOSTALISM IN VIETNAM

The future of the Pentecostal movement in Vietnam will depend on how its members navigate the following issues:

Issue of leadership. By large a typical Pentecostal leader is a clergyman who belongs to the majority Việt ethnicity. Highlanders who are ethnic minorities but are a majority within Vietnamese

Pentecostal organizations deserve more space to exercise leadership. Additionally, women and urban lay professionals are two other groups that should be recognized more formally in church leadership. It is expected that church decision making and management will become more transparent to balance the current leadership practice that depends much on the personal charisma of individual leaders.

Issue of cultural engagement. Much effort has been invested in discussions on how Vietnamese Pentecostals can adapt their faith to Vietnamese culture. The more pressing question, however, is to ask who has the right to define Vietnamese cultural identities, and who benefits from a particular construction of culture and identity. This discussion will benefit Vietnamese Pentecostals in the long run as they develop their own sense of what it means to be Vietnamese and Pentecostal. Entailed in this issue of culture is the requirement to navigate the intersection of Vietnamese Pentecostal culture and Vietnamese pop culture, and between Vietnamese Pentecostal culture and the global Pentecostal movement, in the context of globalization and migration.

Issue of theological studies. Theological studies, understood as a critical discipline devoted to the Christian navigation of life and reality from biblical, historical, theological, practical, and interdisciplinary perspectives, is still a challenging concept to Vietnamese Pentecostals. In the Vietnamese Pentecostal imagination, theological education should be advanced training that powerfully reaffirms current beliefs and practices, rather than critically engages with contexts and traditions. However, far from debilitating Vietnamese Pentecostal spirituality, critical reflection on the everyday practices of leadership, cultural engagement, and theological studies can also inspire Pentecostal spirituality and thus will steady the growth and direction of the Pentecostal movement in Vietnam.[18]

Chapter 11

Pentecostalism in Thailand

James Hosack and Alan R. Johnson

P ENTECOSTAL CHRISTIANITY CAME to Thailand shortly after
World War II via the mission efforts of four classical Pentecostal groups from the West over a period of three decades.
By the 1980s independent Charismatic movements began to emerge
as well, with one, the Hope of Bangkok church, growing to some
fifteen thousand adherents at its peak.[1] Contrary to Pentecostal
rhetoric in the West, recent research shows that Pentecostal groups
have not grown significantly faster than their non-Pentecostal
counterparts. However, Charismatically inclined Christianity has
produced the most robust growth. This chapter overviews these
developments and explores the opportunities and challenges facing
Pentecostalism in Thailand. Pentecostals will need to wrestle with
the vitality of their own movements, issues of context in evangelism and discipleship in the Buddhist environment, challenges with
training as personal ties are more powerful than doctrinal distinctives, and the task of mobilizing people for ministry and mission.
The lack of Pentecostal writing and reflection and the fact that an
increasing number of ministers in Pentecostal groups are receiving
their theological education in non-Pentecostal seminaries is a trend
that could result in diluting Pentecostal distinctives in the future.

THE BEGINNINGS OF PENTECOSTALISM
IN THAILAND

Five different Protestant organizations arrived in Thailand between 1828 and 1850. By 1850 only the American Presbyterian Mission remained, and it stayed the dominant organization in the country until World War II. Although a time of significant growth took place between 1884 and 1914 in Northern Thailand, in general the Protestant church experienced little growth.[2] Prior to 1934 much of the church's work remained in the hands of missionaries. However, an attempt at indigenization took place in 1934 when believers connected to the Presbyterian and American Baptist works formed a national church organization called the Church of Christ in Thailand (CCT).

In an attempt to stem membership losses in CCT churches, Boonmak Kittisarn, then general secretary of the CCT, invited Chinese evangelist John Sung to hold meetings in Thailand. The Chinese Maitrichit Church in Bangkok hosted Sung's meetings in March and April 1938. Further meetings were held in Chiang Mai and Lampang in the North and Trang in the South in 1939.

Some CCT leaders did not want Sung to come to Thailand. Perhaps they feared his ministry would cause church splits, as had happened in some other countries. Others suggest that some reluctance was due to reports of demonstrations of *charismata* occurring in his meetings, particularly prayer for the sick.[3] There is some disagreement as to the impact that Sung's ministry had on the unchurched; yet there is agreement that his ministry significantly impacted the spiritual fervor of CCT church members who, previously, were at best nominal Christians. In 1939 Sook Pongsnoi, the pastor of the Trang CCT church, reported:

> I invited Dr. Sung to come to Trang and through him God has poured out a mighty blessing upon the people of this city. The Trang church is now on fire for God and has been packed with people every Sunday since Dr. Sung went away.... We are feeding on the Word of God as never before, and last Sunday sixteen women and five men were baptized and twenty baptized children confessed their faith in Jesus Christ and all united with the church. Two backsliders also came and confessed their sins.[4]

Sung's meetings likely helped strengthen God's people for the persecution to come during World War II. It is documented that many renounced their faith during those tumultuous times.[5] Yet several church leaders, including Kittisarn and Pongsnoi who were touched by God in Sung's meetings, boldly encouraged believers to hold firm to their faith and not turn away.[6] Some see this hunger for spiritual revival as laying the groundwork for the soon arrival of the Pentecostal Movement.[7]

THAILAND'S EARLY YEARS OF PENTECOST

After World War II a new surge of missionary activity took place, including the arrival of Thailand's first Pentecostal missionaries, Verner and Hanna Raassina, sent by the Finnish Free Foreign Mission (now FIDA International), in 1946. They initially planned to minister in Burma, but when denied visas they were rerouted to Bangkok arriving on November 17, 1946.[8]

While on their voyage they spent most of their cash treating Verner, who fell ill with typhoid. Upon arrival in Thailand they were informed that their home church could no longer support them as Finland's newly formed Communist government forbade finances being sent to support missions work.[9] When Boonmak Kittisarn heard about their plight, he invited them to stay at a school owned by his family. This marked the beginning of a blossoming friendship between him and early Pentecostal missionaries to Thailand.

Thailand's first Pentecostal church was probably in Petchabun. One day a man arrived at the Lomsak Preaching Center and told the Raassinas about an old man in the remote village of Huay Saw-ing with beliefs similar to theirs. The man was derogatively nicknamed "Old Father Nothing" because he refused to serve the old gods. In July 1949 the Raassinas set out to see if this story was true.

As they neared the village, the old man met them saying, "Teacher, you have finally come!" He explained how thirty years before, a Thai Christian had given him a Scripture portion. The village had only one person who could read, and that rather poorly, so little of what was read could be understood. The man explained that he had been asking God to send them someone to explain the book's meaning. Verner explained the gospel's meaning to an attentive audience. After three days twenty-two men decided to follow Christ. In a second visit another twenty people accepted Christ. Later, in 1956, Huay Sawang became the setting for the first major outpouring of the Holy Spirit upon Thai people.[10]

Around the same time that the Raassinas moved to Petchabun, due to the increasingly liberal leanings of the CCT, Kittisarn resigned from that organization and started an independent church in the capital called Bangkok Church.[11] During its early years it is unclear how Pentecostal the Bangkok Church was in practice and beliefs. However, between 1956 and 1958 the church took on a distinctive Pentecostal flavor.

Starting in 1951, Pentecostal missionaries from other countries began arriving, particularly from Scandinavia. Adolph and Karen Nilsen transferred from China to Thailand, becoming the first missionaries from the Swedish Free Mission. Later that year Esther Bastrup from the Norwegian Free Foreign Mission also transferred from China to Thailand. Then the Danish Pentecostal Mission and Orebro Mission from Sweden also sent missionaries to Thailand. Because of similar backgrounds and beliefs, in 1973 these groups merged their works organizationally under the name Scandinavian Pentecostal Mission and formed churches called the Foundation of the Full Gospel Churches in Thailand (FCT).[12]

THE IMPACT OF THE T. L. OSBORN EVANGELISTIC MEETINGS ON THE THAI PENTECOSTAL MOVEMENT

Greatly impacting the early expansion of the Pentecostal Movement in Thailand was the open-air meetings of T. L. Osborn in 1956 in Bangkok and Trang. Thousands attended the meetings, with several hundred converting to Christianity and many healed. Two of those healed were Saman Wannakiet, a Presbyterian pastor, and Chaiyong Wattanachan. Both men were subsequently filled with the Holy Spirit and then formed an evangelistic team to take the gospel message to the entire country.[13]

One member of the Osborn ministry team, Don Price, was asked to dedicate the church building recently constructed in Huay Saw-ing. Thailand's first Pentecostal revival began there as people were filled with the Holy Spirit in response to Price's preaching.[14]

Meanwhile Wannakiet and Wattanachan traveled to Chiang Rai to visit some Presbyterian churches. Numerous church members were baptized in the Holy Spirit in response to their preaching. When faced with opposition, some members broke away from their churches and formed separate congregations. Kittisan and some Finnish missionaries began visiting these congregations regularly. Eventually these churches, and other new church plants, became linked with the Finnish Free Foreign Mission (FFFM) network of churches.[15]

In 1957 Wannakiat and Wattanachan held evangelistic meetings in

Nakorn Pathom, where fifteen-year-old Wirachai Kowae responded to the gospel. Shortly thereafter, under the teaching of Wannakiat and Wattanachan, Kowae was baptized in the Holy Spirit and felt God calling him into full-time ministry. During school breaks Kowae traveled with Wannakiat and Wattanachan in their evangelistic meetings. After completing secondary school at the age of seventeen, Kowae began to minister on a full-time basis. He has played a significant role in the Pentecostal Movement in Thailand, starting the Thailand Assemblies of God, and served as the head of the Evangelical Fellowship of Thailand.

The trickle of Pentecostal ministries that had begun in Thailand in the 1940s became a flood by the end of the 1960s. Dr. Nithi Eowsriwongs writes: "By 1960 we see that the Pentecostal group was still quite small.[16] But after 1960 an increasing number of new Pentecostal organizations entered [Thailand] to join the task and expand the work to various provinces..."[17]

In 1961 William and Ellen Butcher, the first missionaries sent by the Pentecostal Assemblies of Canada (PAOC), arrived in Thailand. Churches associated with the PAOC are called Full Gospel Assemblies of Thailand (FGAT). Church growth was slow until 1972 when Jaisaman Church was started in Bangkok. Under the leadership of Nirut Chantakorn, Jaisaman this became one of Bangkok's largest churches. As of 2015 FGAT has ninety registered churches in Thailand,[18] three branch churches overseas, and missionaries serving in China, Germany, and Nepal.[19] In 1973 they started Thailand Pentecostal Seminary, the only Pentecostal school in Thailand offering an masters degree.

During the Vietnam War many American troops were stationed in Thailand. Several new organizations developed as a result of this American presence. In 1967 Charles Austin, an officer stationed near Udorn Thani with connections to the Church of God (Cleveland,

TN), started Plukjit Nonsung church. In 1978 Rod Richie, the first missionary sent to Thailand by Church of God World Missions (COGWM), planted a church in an apartment complex on Plukjit Street in Bangkok. The name *Plukjit* (meaning "an awakened heart") was adopted to refer to that church and denomination.[20] There are currently eleven Plukjit churches.

In 1968 an American Assemblies of God (AG) missionary, Ervin Shaffer, opened a Servicemen's Center in Bangkok for GIs serving in the Vietnam War. About the same time Wirachai Kowae, studying at the Bible Institute of Malaysia, learned about indigenous church principles followed by AG and fully embraced this methodology. Through Shaffer's influence, AG missionaries in serviceman's ministry began working alongside Kowae and other Thai ministers. Kowae founded the Thailand Assemblies of God (TAG) in 1969 and the first United States AG missionaries to work explicitly with the TAG came in the early 1970s. In 2015 there were 151 churches associated with the TAG. Kowae has had significant influence on both Pentecostal and non-Pentecostal Christianity. He is highly respected for his integrity, diplomacy, and generosity. In more recent years he has served on committees made up of all the religions in Thailand that advise the government on religious matters. On December 24, 2014, he was privileged to pray personally with General Prayuth Chan-ocha, Thailand's prime minister at the time.[21]

The Thailand Church of God of Prophecy also began through the efforts of an American serviceman, Thomas Filtman, who started a church in Korat in 1969. Gary Holcombe, their first missionary, arrived in 1977. As of 2015 they had eight registered churches with the work concentrating on Northeast Thailand.[22]

With the influx of many new Protestant evangelical organizations entering Thailand in the 1960s, a covering organization called the Evangelical Fellowship of Thailand (EFT) was started to represent these diverse groups to the government. The EFT became a legal entity in 1969 with most Pentecostal and other evangelical organizations coming under the umbrella of the EFT.

THE PRESENT SITUATION OF PENTECOSTALISM IN THAILAND

Thai Pentecostal Christianity from post-World War II through the 1960s was generally started by missionaries connected to Pentecostal movements in the West that trace their spiritual roots back to the turn-of-the-century Pentecostal revival at Azusa Street. The current shape of Pentecostal Christianity in Thailand is directly related to the waves of Charismatic organizations that came to Thailand in the 1970s and started various ministries and the rise of indigenous Pentecostal/Charismatic Thai church movements.

The first of several Charismatic training institutions began in 1975 when Duane Klepel started Christ for Thailand Institute in Chonburi. That institute has subsequently trained over 290 students, with 86 percent of the graduates involved in full-time ministry.[23] Christ to Thailand Mission, a short-term training center in Khon Kaen under the leadership of Sonny Largado and Pedro Belardo, trained people from a broad spectrum of Christian backgrounds. Christ to Thailand Mission has nineteen churches, mostly in Northeast Thailand. Other Charismatic training centers include Victory Bible College International in Chonburi, Living Word Ministries International in Chiang Mai, and Rhema Bible College in Bangkok.

In addition to T. L. Osborn's successful open-air evangelistic services, another well-known evangelist, Wayne Crooke, regularly held healing and evangelistic meetings throughout Thailand starting in 1979.[24] Crooke reports holding over one hundred meetings in which he prayed for over a million people.[25]

Other independent Charismatic churches and organizations also began in this period, including Bangkok Fellowship Church (1969) with a network of twenty-six daughter churches. A former Baptist minister, Wan Phetchsongkram, started Romklao Church (1979), now with thirty-two churches. Other significant independent Charismatic churches include Sahaphan Church Khon Kaen and Fa Muang Thai Church.

Thailand's most well-known Charismatic church is Hope of Bangkok, which was begun by Kriengsak Charoenwongsak in 1981. In 2009 Hope Church network estimated a membership of over ten thousand meeting in various Bangkok locations, and another fifteen thousand members in 430 locations outside of Bangkok. They also claimed 120 Hope churches in other parts of the world. Since that time the church splintered. Some churches dissolved and the members incorporated into other churches, and several streams of church movements remain as smaller networks of their own. As of 2015 there still remain 206 churches in the country identified as Hope churches.

Chantakorn resigned from Jaisaman Church and started Ruam Nimit in 1990. Today twenty-three churches are associated with Ruam Nimit. Other Pentecostal or Charismatic organizations entering Thailand since the 1970s include Church of the Foursquare Gospel and the Vineyard.

In recent years it has become difficult to designate which churches are Pentecostal and which are not. Mäkelä expresses the problem well when he says: "It is difficult to make classifications based on... backgrounds. One distinction could be the division into Pentecostal or Charismatic churches and others, but even this classification is problematic (as) practices like praying for the sick and exorcisms are practiced widely."[26] Clearly, in the seventy years that Pentecostals have been in this country, they have had a significant influence on the nature of Christianity as practiced in Thailand. It is anticipated that this trend will continue into the future as well.

In order to provide a sense of the scope of the major Pentecostal and Charismatic church movements that are known and tracked statistically in Thailand, we have presented the most current information available to us in the following chart:

INDIVIDUAL CHURCH STATISTICS BASED ON LAST KNOWN DATA

Organization	Year Started	Number of Churches[27]	Other Information
Full Gospel Churches in Thailand (FGCT)	1946	127	Associated with FIDA (FFFM) The Full Gospel Bible College (Thonburi)
Fellowship of the Full Gospel Churches in Thailand (FCT)	1951	65	Associated with the Scandinavian Pentecostal Mission *Way of Life* radio/TV broadcast Southern Theological Institute (Prachuab Khiri Kan)
Foundation of United Pentecostal Church Thailand	1959	5[28]	Associated with the United Pentecostal Church
The Full Gospel Assemblies of Thailand (FGAT)	1961	90	Associated with PAOC Thailand Pentecostal Seminary (Bangkok)
Church of God World Missions Association (Plukjit)	1967	11	Associated with the Church of God (Cleveland, TN)
Church of God Prophecy	1969	8	Associated with Church of God of Prophecy

Organization	Year Started	Number of Churches	Other Information
Thailand Assemblies of God (TAG)	1969	151	Associated with Assemblies of God Thailand Assemblies of God Bible Institute (Bangkok)
Bangkok Fellowship Church	1969	27	Indigenous
Thailand National Institute for Christ	1975	9	Initially a Bible school (Pakchong)
Christ to Thailand Mission (CTM)	1976	19	Associated with Christ to the Philippines Christ to Thailand Mission Training Center (Khon Kaen)
Romklao Church Association	1979	32	Indigenous
Hope Church	1981	206	Indigenous
Fah Muang Thai Ministries	1982	2	Indigenous
Living Word Ministries Organization	1987	1	Initially a Bible school (Chiang Mai)
The Vision Full Gospel Church Association (Ruamnimit)	1990	23	Indigenous
Christian Outreach Center (COC)	1995	2^{29}	Indigenous
Foursquare Gospel Church of Thailand	1998	14	Associated with the International Church of the Foursquare Gospel
Victory Churches International	1999	6	Initially a Bible school (Sriracha)

Organization	Year Started	Number of Churches	Other Information
Rhema Christian Organization	2000	2	Initially a Bible school (Thonburi)
Vineyard Church	ca. 2004	8[30]	

The organizations and statistics here are those that can be tracked. Yet within Thailand Protestant Christianity there are other groups with Pentecostal and Charismatic roots not so easily counted. In the Thailand Assemblies of God, for instance, a leader in the Hope Church movement left and connected with Wirachai Kowae in the 1990s. Wirachai sent him to plant a church on the Thonburi side of Bangkok. As his network grew, he moved out of the TAG and is now registered directly with the EFT.

PROSPECTS FOR THE FUTURE OF PENTECOSTALISM IN THAILAND

The brief overview above illustrates the complexity of attempting to capture Pentecostalism in the Thai context. The four major Thai Pentecostal organizations that are related to Pentecostal missions in the West with their roots in the Azusa revival continue to represent classical Pentecostal doctrine and practice. But the last four decades brought an influx of Pentecostal and Charismatic strains of faith that are truly global in nature and not simply based in the West. Thus the Protestant faith in Thailand is in many places Charismatically oriented. The fluidity of movement between organizational lines in Thai Protestant Christianity means that increased openness to the work of the Spirit has spread far beyond the boundaries of Thai classical Pentecostal organizations.

It is precisely the global influence of Pentecostal/Charismatic strains of belief and practice combined with the permeable boundaries of Thai Protestant Christian faith that pose distinct challenges to the explicitly Pentecostal Thai organizations. The importance of relationships and the seeking out of patrons for help means that organizational connections are often made not on the basis of doctrinal and theological understanding, but rather on interpersonal relations. The dilution of Pentecostal understanding among ministers and church members is a reality that will only increase as technology continues to bring the world closer.

The difficulty in getting ethnic Thai into Bible school ministerial training programs is another local context factor in the mix. Non-ethnic Thai tribal Christians are entering Thai Bible schools in large numbers while ethnic Thai Christians stay away. This is making it more difficult to find ways to engage the ethnic Thai church in reflection on the Scriptures and the work of the Spirit. The default then becomes their exposure to whatever current trends are entering via seminars, conferences, various church events, and what they can watch on the Internet. This tends to be focused on pragmatic practice and whatever is current in the global Charismatic scene. The power of the influence of these practices is based on the fact that they are seen as promoting church growth and ministry success since the overseas churches sponsoring such events are large and influential. The prosperity theology; extreme views on faith healing; deliverance ministry and casting out demons through vomiting; the promotion of new wineskins; seeking flakes of gold on people's hands; use of flags and dance in worship; bringing in Jewish elements such as blowing the shofar; the styles of Korean, Nigerian, Singaporean, and other groups who advocate their particular methods of worship; and prophetic words from well-known international figures—all are moving through Thai churches, both Pentecostal and non-Pentecostal.

While some of these things are not explicitly tied to a Pentecostal or Charismatic agenda, they are nonetheless connected to such groups outside of Thailand and are seen to represent the cutting edge of ministry. The lack of biblical reflection about the work of the Spirit among God's people means that when things do not work or problems arise, church members and pastors are left without any resources to think about what is happening and as often as not jettison something while hunting for the next big seminar event. In all of this, Thai culture is ignored and churches continue to reinforce the most common Thai objection against the Christian faith, that it is a foreign religion.

Pentecostal organizations find themselves behind in trying to train ministers who come into their movement and who may hold very diverse views from their own. The problem is compounded because of the dearth of theological writing in general and on Pentecostal theology, particularly by Thai scholars and leadership. The vast bulk of Christian material is still translated from Western writers. Our experience of teaching in our local Thai organization's Bible school shows how confused students are because they read popular pieces that have been translated that promote a wide range of practices and beliefs, and they have no grid upon which to make judgments from Scripture. The lack of Thai Pentecostal theological reflection is increased because so many who pursue advanced education and degrees do so in institutions that are not Pentecostal.

From our viewpoint as expatriates who have been involved with a Thai Pentecostal movement for thirty years each, here are some of the crucial arenas that we hope can be addressed by Pentecostal movements and Charismatically inclined Christianity in the future. While there are numerous issues that could be tackled, a critical nexus forms around the issues of a small church in a sea of Buddhist people that needs to wrestle with context sensitivity, the foreignness of the Christian faith, and moving past Jesus as patron to mobilizing believers for mission in their own culture and beyond.

Marten Visser's research on Thai Protestant conversion patterns revealed that while all Charismatic denominations grew at a much higher rate than the Presbyterian districts of the Christ Church of Thailand, they grew only slightly faster than all the other non-Charismatic denominations.[31] This runs counter to Pentecostal rhetoric in general about the role of signs and wonders and manifestations of Pentecostal power as being the primary key and accelerator in evangelism. Pentecostal and Charismatic organizations have no lack of works of power. Yet church growth among the ethnic Thai, while steady and robust, is still quite modest when compared with other parts of the world and among other people groups. This situation seems to beg theological reflection by Pentecostals to ascertain what other issues are present and to bring light from other areas of Scriptures to bear on this reality. If signs and wonders are not resulting in longed for growth, what else is happening? Pentecostals and Charismatics reflect the foreignness of the Christian faith that exists in the whole Thai Protestant church movement. Today the biggest barrier to the non-Christian Thai is that to be Thai is to be a Buddhist and the Christian faith is seen as the faith of the white Western world.

Does pneumatology have anything to say about context sensitivity in the way we share our faith and structure our life together as God's people? The Spirit's work in creation of humans with the capabilities of varying responses to their environments that results in the cultural variation of our world, along with the Spirit's speaking through a diversity of cultural forms to God's people through the ages, would indicate that local Christians are free to draw upon local culture in positive ways to help communicate the beauties of the gospel. Pentecostal reflection on evangelism and church planting in context would help to break down the assumption that their current models for "doing church" are the only way, rather than representing one version of the faith that appeals to some, while not touching the heart cords of millions of Buddhist people around them.

Pentecostal methods emphasizing the nearness of God and His power to answer prayer resonate with Thai Buddhists who seek help for daily needs through a variety of folk religious practices. When Jesus answers prayer, it opens eyes and hearts. The problem, however, is that posing Jesus as spiritual patron dispensing benefits also plays right into the Thai notion of switching allegiances when benefits cease to flow as expected. A second issue is that the "Jesus as patron" view creates problems in discipleship and derails mobilizing people for ministry because their new faith is about them and benefits received and not about sacrificing one's life in Christ's service. Will Pentecostals be able to develop a theology that can embrace God's dynamic presence and intervention with suffering and unanswered prayer? Can Pentecostals move people past the enjoyment of blessings to embrace their missional responsibility both among their own people and to the unreached in other cultures as well?

One hopeful development emerged recently at the World Assemblies of God Fellowship's (WAGF) World Mission Congress held in Bangkok in February 2015. A Thai language workshop was held for the 243 Thai participants with a focus on developing cross-cultural missions-sending structures to put laborers among unreached people groups. Pentecostal leaders are emerging who are prepared to work to see a missions-sending structure formed among the four Thai organizations that relate to the WAGF. If this happens, it carries great promise to help mobilize denominational and independent Pentecostals and Charismatics around global missions that will have an affect on raising awareness for local evangelism as well.

Pentecostal and Charismatic Christianity in Thailand is a vital and diverse movement that has had a deep influence on the Protestant movement. While some of the movements are connected to Western Pentecostal missions efforts, they have developed their own organizations, leadership, and vision and have moved beyond being the children of the West. Indigenous movements have sprung up as well. Challenges Pentecostals face in the future concern providing training for a fluid ministerium due to the permeable lines of the denominational environment, developing Pentecostal writers and theologians who can begin to publish local material on issues of importance to the Pentecostal church, and to start theological reflection on issues of culture and current Pentecostal approaches to evangelism and discipleship.

Chapter 12

Pentecostalism in Singapore and Malaysia: Past, Present, and Future

Timothy Lim T. N.

THIS ESSAY INVESTIGATES the origins, growth, and future of Pentecostal and Charismatic renewal in Singapore and Malaysia.[1] Historians trace the beginnings of the global Pentecostal movement to the Azusa Street Pentecostal Outpouring in 1906, even though discrepancies exist as to whether William Seymour or Charles Parham played more instrumental roles.[2] Revivals were reported in Pyongyang and at other locales between 1901 and 1910, and sometimes these are not traceable to the North American renewal movement.[3] Today's Pentecostalism represents a global cluster of movements that transform not just the unconverted but also Christians.[4] For this chapter, Pentecostalism includes various renewal streams (classical, neo-Pentecostals, Charismatic, neo-Charismatic, and third wavers) who share similar phenomenological experiences of the Spirit—Spirit baptism, *glossolalia*, operation of charismata, power encounters, healing, exorcism, and deliverance ministries—although each of these streams would nuance their history, theology, and practices. I will briefly introduce the history of Pentecostal and Charismatic renewal in Malaysia and Singapore. Similar to the global Pentecostal narratives, Pentecostal and Charismatic renewal in both countries have grown robustly amid experiences of plurality (ethnic, racial, and religious), intolerance, and sometimes, persecution. However, due to their respective sociopolitical contexts, Pentecostals and Charismatics in Singapore and Malaysia developed in distinct ways, compared to each other and the West. Finally, I will examine the prospects and challenges in theology, faith formation, outreach, interreligious engagement, and social witnessing.

MALAYSIA PENTECOSTALISM: BRIEF HISTORY TO PRESENT

From the 1930s the Spirit weaved His tapestry for Malaysian Pentecostalism in the Muslim Shari'ah law environment. The Malays in the peninsula encountered Nestorian settlements in the seventh century, Portuguese Catholicism and Dutch Reformed Presbyterianism between the fifteenth and seventeenth centuries, and centuries later, British Protestantism, Brethren, Evangelical Lutheran, and other missions.[5] From the 1970s, Pentecostalism grew rapidly, and by the mid-1980s more than two-thirds of the evangelicals and mainliners were Pentecostals.[6] The leaders gained sociopolitical credibility. However, like the rest of Malaysian Christianity, Pentecostals continued to receive threats for their faith.

Jin Huat Tan traced four distinct developments of Pentecostal renewal in Malaysia: Indian Pentecostal developments, Chinese-speaking and English-speaking Assemblies of God (AOG), Charismatic renewal among mainline churches, and indigenous renewals.[7] First, the Ceylon Pentecostal Mission (CPM) labored among migrant Indians and Sri Lankans at Ipoh in 1930. The ministry expanded to Port Dickson, Kuala Lumpur, Teluk Anson, Penang, and other parts of the peninsula. CPM was registered as the Pentecostal Church of Malaya (PCM) in 1952, and today it has about fifteen hundred members, mostly Indians.[8] A recent source included Indian immigrants among the largest Pentecostal groups in Malaysia.[9] Some CPM congregations left and became Tamil-speaking AOG churches under the initiative of Chris Thomas, the first dean of the Bible Institute of Malaya, in 1968.

Second, Chinese churches blossomed after John Sung's revival meetings in the peninsula and Eastern Malaysia among Methodists and Presbyterians between 1935 and 1940. Observable Spirit-filled evidences included weeping, conviction of sins, conversions, consecrations for full-time Christian service, signs and wonders, singing short gospel choruses, and loud prayers. Chinese-speaking Assemblies of God (AOG), which was started in the Peninsular Malaysia in 1934, subsequently moved to Ampang and Padu in 1935. They became affiliated with AOG in the United States in 1940 and registered officially with Malaysian authorities in 1953. The first church building was erected at Jalan Sayor in 1955. AOG missionaries serving formative churches in China between the 1950s and 1960s also helped churches in Penang. Hong Kong actress Kong Duen Yee, who visited Penang in 1963, started her affiliation of churches known as New Testament Church after she preached at a series of meetings. Some folks who experienced Spirit baptism renewal under Yee's itinerant preaching later formed their own assemblies or congregations after their Brethren and other congregations ousted them. For instance, Brethren Elder Teh Phai Lian of Burmah Road Gospel Hall started the Church of Penang, which was later renamed Charismatic Church of Penang.

The third phase of development identified by Tan begins when former CPM members organized the English-speaking Assemblies of God (AOG) before the 1960s. These churches grew under David Baker and Lula Ashmore Baird's parallel missionary efforts in China. They branched out from Penang to Ipoh, Taiping (Aulong villages), and Kuala Lumpur. Twenty youths attended a 1957 Youth

Camp at Port Dickson and were baptized in the Spirit. To cope with the Pentecostal growth in Malaysia and Southeast Asia, the Bible Institute of Malaysia (later renamed Bible College of Malaysia) was founded in 1960. The institute trained AOG pastors for church planting, evangelism, and pioneering work between 1960 and 1980.[10] By 1970 nearly every town in West Malaysia had an AOG church, and interestingly they used the Navigators' materials to disciple students, 80 percent of whom were Chinese.

Between the 1970s and mid-1980s AOG membership surged after three hundred youths were expelled from mainline churches in Klang Valley because of their Charismatic experience. As the Charismatic renewal was not supported by mainline denominations, many young enthusiasts left their churches to start either AOG churches or new independent Charismatic churches. Examples included the Tabernacle of Glory in 1974 and the Latter Rain Church in 1975, each becoming bridgeheads for church plants throughout Malaysia. Calvary Charismatic Centre gathered in 1978 for mainline members who were uncomfortable with attending AOG churches. Renewal Lutheran Church began Deeper Life Seminars in the 1980s, and organized other gatherings such as The Word Center and New Life Restoration Center. Various businessmen and leaders from various denominations (Brethren, Roman Catholic nuns) formed The Full Gospel Assembly, Kuala Lumpur in 1981, and it later became affiliated with the Full Gospel Businessmen Fellowship International.

Charismatic renewal varied in the 1980s and 1990s. In 1982 South Korean pastor Paul Yonggi Cho conducted a church growth seminar in Singapore.[11] Thereafter, Malaysian AOG leaders who attended the seminar began initiatives toward urban outreach and conceiving megachurches. Thousand-member churches emerged, such as Glad Tidings and Grace Assembly in Klang Valley. The prosperity theology became a mainstay with Abundant Life Center's invitation to American Charismatic faith healer T. L. Osborn. Emphases included faith healing and deliverance ministries, adding to teachings on the baptism of the Holy Spirit and speaking in tongues.

The prophetic movement emphasizing personal prophecies fell on older and newer Charismatic churches from the 1980s. The prophetic wave also entered some mainline churches. Leaders like Rev. Peter Young of St. Gabriel's (Anglican) Church (also leader of Scripture Union) experienced renewal despite reservations by mainline denominational leaders and reaction from cessationistic and dispensational evangelical Brethren churches.[12] St. Gabriel's Church became a point-church, organizing Charismatic renewal meetings and collaborating with All Saints' Church and Christ Lutheran Church, Setapark. Young's influence as an evangelical leader with Scripture Union's network of churches helped evangelical and mainline churches to receive Pentecostal and Charismatic renewal amid their critics. A series of joint seminars at Trinity Methodist Church, Petaling Jaya, featuring both Baptist Douglas McBain and Benedictine priest Ian Petit, was supported by the Anglican, Baptist, Brethren, Evangelical Free, Lutheran, Methodist, Pentecostal, and Roman Catholic churches.

A proliferation of prophetic ministries characterized Malaysian Pentecostal/Charismatic renewal in the 1980s and 1990s. Still, notable leaders, including Revs. Peter Tan (now known as Johann Melchizedek Peter), Paul Ang, and David Wong Kim, all delivered accurate prophetic words and became popular Bible teachers among churches in Malaysia, Singapore, and Indonesia.[13] These ministers formerly served together at the Tabernacle of Glory. However, moral scandals in Peter Tan's ministry led to his migration to Australia. Consequently, many "prophets" or "ministers who moved in the prophetic" left Tabernacle of Glory.[14] The prophetic movement renewed many churches until the wider prophetic movement (though not a result of Paul Ang or David Wong Kim's impeccable services) was questioned, especially after the demise of the Anglican bishop of West Malaysia Tan Sri John Gurubatham Savarimuthu in 1994; the Anglican bishop received a prophecy that he would have a long life and ministry amid his illness, but he died shortly afterward.

By 2000 there were 291 English-speaking AOG churches throughout Malaysia. Newer churches, such as Renewal Lutheran Church and Damansara Utama Methodist Church, experimented with music and performing arts in their outreach to youths (without the approval of AOG Leadership/Council in the late 1990s and 2000s): they mirrored Scripture Union's musical rallies around the country from 1975–1979.

Tan's final phase starts with the indigenous Pentecostal revival among the Kelabits in 1973, which led to several contextual expressions and Spirit outpouring among secondary school students in Sarawak. These expressions became the Sidang Injil Borneo, which was originally founded by Borneo Evangelical Mission.[15] Crusades with Indonesian evangelist Petrus Octavanius were instrumental in indigenization efforts. Prayer movements developed at Bario in 1979, and revival meetings were organized at Ba Kelalan in 1981–1985.[16] Other initiatives were the planting of indigenous Chinese Pentecostal congregations, such as MengfuJiaohui (Blessed Church, Kuching), and local worship or gospel song productions in Sarawak.[17] Pentecostal and Charismatic phenomena, altar calls, deliverance, and healing ministries were reported in the Anglican Church of Sabah.[18]

Pentecostals and Charismatics have increased their influence with Malaysian Christianity and politics. I will mention an example. In the 2000s the National Evangelical Christian Fellowship Malaysia (NECF) was a critical mediatory agency among its network of churches. Pentecostals in NECF network included Assembly of God, Full Gospel Assembly, Full Gospel Tabernacle, and Latter Rain Church.[19] The then NECF Secretary General, Rev. Dr. David Wong Kim Kong, was a widely respected Pentecostal leader and had been instrumental in reconciling conflicts between Pentecostal and non-Pentecostal evangelical churches. One of his initiatives (Malaysian CARE) before he joined NECF became a primary collaborative project for churches to express social concern of the church.[20] He was conferred "The Most Distinguished Order of Chivalry" (Johan Mangku Negara) by the Malaysian prime minister and was regularly invited to advise interreligious affairs in states and in the political structures of the nation. Despite his critics,[21] he has been serving as principal consultant of the Leadership Training Academy since his retirement from NECF.[22]

Threats continue to affect Malaysian Christianity. The Pentecostal/ Charismatic movement is not spared. For instance, fringe groups bombed the Metro Tabernacle Church because its senior pastor, Rev. Ong Sek Leong (also, general superintendent of AOG of Malaysia), was the chairman of the 23rd Pentecostal World Conference, Kuala Lumpur, held in June 2013.[23] Churches in Malaysia face persecution periodically due to non-Christian religious pressures. A church retreat center near Tapah was raided in January 2001, and the Bible Society of Malaysia was raided by Selangor Islamic authorities, JAIS (Jabatan Agama Islam Selangor).[24]

SINGAPORE PENTECOSTALISM: BRIEF HISTORY TO PRESENT

From the beginning, Singapore Pentecostalism and Charismaticism contended with the largely evangelical Protestant presence, along with the near century-old Catholic and Anglican missions in the land.[25] It attracted Christians seeking renewal. The robustness appealed to younger generations who were seeking self-identity and success in an affluent society. Creative ways of harbingering for plurality, prosperity, and outreach have characterized the LoveSingapore network of churches.[26]

Singapore Pentecostal/Charismatic renewal historiography developed in several phases.[27] First is Western influences traced to Assemblies of God missionary efforts and Finnish Pentecostal mission. After AG missionaries Rev. Cecil and Edith Jackson were expelled from Mainland China in 1928, they labored with the Cantonese community in Singapore and started a school for children in Balestier in 1929. Missionaries, including Rev. Lawrence McKinney, joined them to reach English-speaking Singaporeans in 1932. The newly formed group spilt, with McKinney starting Elim Church and the rest becoming independent Pentecostal gatherings before the Japanese occupation (1942–1945). Between 1947 and 1960 other missionaries established five other AG churches.[28] In 1958 seven Pentecostal churches and an independent church collaborated to organize a two-week salvation-healing crusade, which extended for another three weeks. Finnish Free Foreign Mission of the Pentecostal Churches of Finland planted several churches: Zion Centre (renamed, Zion Full Gospel Church) in 1949, Glad Tidings Church in 1957, and two other independent congregations.

Second are Asian influences traced to the positive reception of John Sung's revival meetings, and especially Hong Kong actress Kong Duen Yee's itinerant ministry in 1963. Christians from the Brethren tradition who received the renewal experience were not allowed back in their churches. These newly Spirit-baptized believers, including the late Elder Goh Ewe Kheng of the Brethren Assembly, formed a nucleus of churches, which became the Church of Singapore.[29] Elder Goh chaired the Evangelical Fellowship of Singapore (EFS) in the mid-1990s and led a number of evangelicals into the Pentecostal renewal. He was chairman emeritus of Ting Ling Bible School and an elder of the Church of Singapore.[30]

Third, the late 1970s to mid-1980s saw signs of vibrant Charismatic renewal among some mainline Protestants (Anglicans, Lutherans, Methodists, and Presbyterians), free-church believers and evangelicals (e.g., Baptists, Evangelical Free, and Brethren churches), and Roman Catholics.[31] The Full Gospel Businessmen Fellowship in Singapore was formed in 1972; they organized the Spiritual Renewal Fellowship in 1974 for Pentecostals and Charismatics who had experienced the renewal, and was reorganized in 1975 to welcome other professionals.[32] In 1985 Emeritus Bishop Doraisamy of The Methodist Church in Singapore attributed its decade of church growth and membership to the influence of the Charismatic renewal.[33] Pentecostal significance for the Methodism was affirmed recently by one of its theologians, Dr. Roland Chia.[34]

A fourth phase was initiated in the late 1970s when Rev. Chiu Ban It, the sixth Anglican Bishop of Singapore cum Chair of Scripture Union, Singapore, became a Charismatic after reading American Anglican clergy Dennis Bennett's *Nine O'Clock in the Morning*.[35] The renewal movement received impetus for growth under Bishop Chiu and Bishop Moses Tay (who became archbishop of the province of Anglican Church in Southeast Asia).[36] The unparalleled Pentecostal and Charismatic deliverance ministry of the Church of Our Saviour, under the leadership of Senior Pastor Rev. Derek Hong, was and is still a shining example of renewal in an Anglican congregation.[37] With his bishops' blessings, Rev. Canon Dr. James Wong played an instrumental role as founder-president of the annual Festival of Praise, which gathered churches from various denominations, including the Charismatic LoveSingapore movement since 1986.[38] However, the Anglican embrace of Spirit-filled renewal cooled off during immediate past Bishop John Chew's

time.[39] Prospects for Pentecostal/Charismatic renewal in Singapore
Anglicanism have yet to be a significant statement since the present
bishopric of the Rt. Rev. Rennis Ponniah.

Among the fifteen Brethren churches in Singapore, Living
Sanctuary Brethren Church (LSBC) and Bethesda Bedok-Tampines
Church (BBTC) are shining examples of the Charismatic renewal.[40]
The two churches not only maintained fellowship with other
Brethren churches, but they have also brought the autonomously
run Brethren or Bethesda churches together under the Brethren
Network Fellowship, Singapore. LSBC stood out as a community
outreach church with its community penetration (CP) program.

In the Catholic Church, the Charismatic renewal began with a
prayer meeting led by Edmund Ang in the Church of the Nativity
of the Blessed Virgin Mary (abbreviated, Nativity Church) in
1979.[41] Nativity Church members founded the Chinese Charismatic
Renewal in 1995 and introduced the renewal to the Church of
St. Anne in 2006; renewal in St. Anne is now called the Burning
Bush Charismatic Prayer Group.[42] There are perhaps other
Catholic renewal developments in Singapore that are not reported.
Ambivalence between Catholics and evangelical Protestants
remains in the churches' consciousness despite the Roman Catholic
Archdiocese of Singapore's membership with the National Council
of Churches of Singapore and the presence of the Archdiocesan
Catholic Council for Ecumenical Dialogue (ACCED), which is led
by Rev. Msgr. Philip Heng, SJ.[43] The first joint healing service was
attended by five hundred Catholics and Protestants at Aldersgate
Methodist Church on October 6, 2014, and was graced by Catholic
Archbishop William Goh, Methodist Bishop Dr. Wee Boon Hup,
and Lutheran Bishop Terry Kee.[44]

A further, fifth phase might include when some independent
Charismatic churches that emerged from the Charismatic renewal

in the mid- to late 1980s grew to become megachurches, especially since the 2000s. New Creation Church, which started under Rev. Henry Yeo, transited its leadership to Senior Pastor Joseph Prince and reported twenty-four thousand members in 2014.[45] It owns a state-of-the-art theater-seating worship auditorium and several businesses—Daystar Child Development Centre, Rock Productions (including their now expired acquisition, Marine Cove, previously East Coast Park Recreation Centre), and Omega Tours and Travel.[46] A few years before New Creation Church more than doubled its membership, Faith Community Baptist Church (FCBC) was the largest church in Singapore. FCBC's senior pastor Rev. Lawrence Khong's illusions-magic ministry for outreach (since 2001 and MagicBox production in 2008),[47] sociopolitical statements supporting Singapore's penal code on criminalizing queer lifestyle (in 2013),[48] among other nonconventional initiatives, resulted in some three thousand members leaving the church; nonetheless, FCBC remained ten thousand strong.[49] Khong remains seen as the Singapore coordinator for the Spiritual Warfare Network, first appointed by C. Peter Wagner at the International Spiritual Warfare Network Consultation in Seoul, Korea, in 1993.[50] City Harvest Church (CHC)'s former senior pastor Rev. Kong Hee, along with five church leaders, still faces allegations for redirecting church funds meant for a new church building to support their co-pastor Sun Ho's music career as their outreach in the performing arts industry; CHC had nearly twenty thousand members in 2012 before the controversy.[51] Other congregations such as the seven-thousand-member Trinity Christian Centre, the one-thousand-member Cornerstone Church (which sought accountability with Zion Fellowship International from Waverly, New York), and the year-2000-inaugurated RiverLife Church of two thousand members add to the local renewal expressions.

Finally, more recently, some Malaysian Pentecostals have crossed the border of the peninsula to start a College of Prophets for River of Life Ministries (distinguished from RiverLife Church, Singapore).[52] They joined the prophetic call of Singapore Christianity's "Antioch of Asia" status, which has been affected for decades by many evangelical missional para-church organizations, and the annual trans-denominational GoForth Conference among the churches and para-church organizations, coordinated by Singapore Centre for Global Missions (SCGM, previously known as Singapore Centre for Evangelism and Missions, SCEM).[53]

The interreligious and intra-religious engagement in Singapore, unlike the Malaysian Shari'ah Law arrangement, is governed by a statute, Maintenance of Religious Harmony Act (approved March 31, 1992, and revised July 31, 2011).[54] Together with the Interreligious Confidence Circle (IRCC) operating in the country's electoral constituencies, "the government plays an active but limited role in religious affairs, including efforts to promote religious harmony and toleration."[55] With this backdrop, Pentecostal and Charismatic churches negotiate in the public spaces and creatively express their faith, thereby transforming religious discourses and practices and generating new forms of identification with global renewal movements.[56] Pentecostal/Charismatic public engagement, however, did not lead the Singapore churches' public witness; the burden fell on the National Council of Churches, Singapore, and its collaboration with Trinity Theological College, Singapore.[57] One author calls these ranges of development "filling the moral void."[58] Megachurches operate unique social and community outreach programs, some of which are on a national scale, and in collaboration with non-Pentecostal non-Charismatic Protestant churches in and across various constituencies. Other events are more spiritually geared, such as the multi-tiered events of the nearly two-and-a-half-decade-old

LoveSingapore movement, which included the iconic year 2000 annual prayer walks that at its peak drew more than sixty thousand believers from hundreds of churches, not forgetting that the LoveSingapore also brought together 120 churches and leaders— Pentecostal, Charismatic, Evangelical Free, and other Protestant— that was unprecedented before the recent decade of GoForth efforts.[59]

Few can disregard the Spirit-empowered mission of renewal in Singapore even though its critics remain vocal, and these critics indirectly ensured the accountability of the churches in the secular, civil, and public square. Dominant critics in recent years include challenges to the prosperity theology teachings.[60] Controversies arose from City Harvest Church and Faith Community Baptist Church, and to a lesser extent, the "extreme-grace" and highly remunerated pastors of New Creation Church or the intended "takeover" of Association of Women Action and Research (AWARE) by Church of Our Saviour. Proselytization and scandals among churches in Singapore that caught the attention of the public and media seem to stem mostly from independent Charismatic churches.[61] Some critics include fundamental churches that continue to decry the "apostasy" of Charismatic renewal.[62] Even AG theologian Simon Chan critiqued Pentecostal/Charismatic expressions, especially LoveSingapore, as "not deeply rooted in scripture or the Christian tradition, but in pragmatism," being one "very much conditioned by the prevailing culture."[63] And in addition to the handful of more established interdenominational or union seminaries, Pentecostals have few Bible colleges, seminaries, and nonconventional colleges that support the development of its leaders: Asia Theological Center (formerly, Asia Theological Centre for Evangelism and Missions), Assemblies of God Bible College (formerly, Bible Institute of Singapore), TCA College (formerly, Theological College of Asia), and Tung Ling Bible School. These are among the vibrant claims to Holy Spirit movements in Singapore.[64] The pneumatological vibrancy led Baptist scholar Johnson T. K. Lim to initiate a multidisciplinary conversation among sixty-six international scholars on the Holy Spirit (2015) in relation to hermeneutics, the Bible, the church, Christian living, Christian witness, ministry, preachers, theologians of the Spirit, and a range of pneumatological issues, intended for a trans-denominational lay-readership.[65]

PROSPECTS AMID CHALLENGES

Exciting prospects await Singaporean and Malaysian churches amid challenges in theology, faith formation, outreach, interreligious engagement, and social witnessing. The unknown is whether churches can renegotiate "spaces" for the future. Like the rest of the religions in Asia, Pentecostalism has to construct and negotiate its platform, reform its movement to adjust to shifting sociocultural dimensions and values, and contextualize sensitively in a land of religious, cultural, ethnic, and socioeconomic pluralities.[66]

Theology

In the transmission of faith from the Western Hemisphere, theology and praxis interacted uneasily. Church leaders often relegated contextual theologization as missiology even as theological taxonomy of the Western world had caricatured non-Western, indigenous contextual theological endeavors as too missiological.[67] Asian voices found themselves submerged under Western ways of expressing the faith. Contextualization is especially challenging among Malaysian Pentecostals, as it is in the rest of Southeast Asia.[68] Malaysian Catholic Pentecostals' use of the language of possession, exorcism, and the name of "Allah" have raised questions of its contradistinction from similar terms used in other religious faiths. These are examples of the challenge of contextualization and inculturation that cuts across renewal movements in Asia.[69] How may local leaders and Western observers receive local theological thought and practice in promising directions started by the Centre for the Study of Christianity in Asia, Trinity Christian College, Singapore's commissioned theological and ecclesiological monographs?[70]

The challenge of theology amid enculturation did not help when local megachurches in Singapore either disregarded theological education (such as is evident in New Creation Church, Singapore) or started their own non-locally-accredited, though international-affiliated, Bible institutes or schools (e.g., City Harvest Church and FCBC's respective program offerings) that maintained differentiated hermeneutics and reading from historic seminary education. Would this proliferation amid currently recognized Pentecostal offerings (e.g., ACTS College, formerly AG Seminary Singapore, TCA College, Tung Ling Bible College) widen the already polarized, local renewal developments, thereby diluting its witness among mainstream evangelical Christianity, whose colleagues are trained in established and newer institutions (e.g., Trinity Theological College, Singapore Bible College, Discipleship Training Centre, Biblical Graduate School of Theology, and Baptist Theological Seminary)? In regards to the place of theological education, the Malaysian Pentecostal movement may experience less fragmentation than what is happening in the much smaller Singaporean island context.

Faith formation, seminary, and ecclesial unity

The reality of splintering or lack of active efforts toward legitimate unity at both fronts is a concern among Pentecostals and Charismatics, and between renewal and other Christian traditions, including historic Orthodoxy and the Roman Catholic Church, especially in Singapore. While churches do not live in a bubble, it appears that denominations in Singapore have been slow to keep up with official dialogues and developments between churches at the world and international levels. Denominations in Singapore do not yet have ecumenical officers, and apart from the rare joint commemorations, churches do not actively demonstrate efforts to heal memories or reconcile doctrinal differences. Across the border, interdenominational collaborations among Malaysian churches as well as insights at world Christian levels have much to offer for the ecumenical trajectory of churches in these two countries.

A related issue is that the proliferation of Bible colleges and seminaries in Singaporean churches celebrate diversity and vibrancy of many educational settings for theological learning. Yet the innumerable institutional setups only speak to the reality of the disunity among churches. Unlike the reality of geographical distance between states in Malaysia, which perhaps warrants the existence of many schools,[71] I wonder how seminary education could more ecumenically and wholistically pull the churches' resources together in equipping leaders and training disciples, instead of the unspoken competition that exists among them in Singapore. I do not denigrate the actuality of target audience service in denominational seminaries such as the Union College consortium of Trinity Theological College, and the other laity-directed program offerings such as Biblical Graduate School of Theology and Discipleship Training Centre. Also, how would seminaries in Malaysia (no doubt spread thinly by its wide geographical states) speak to the many issues of faith formation and relational development between churches of various denominations and traditions: would the Pentecostal/Charismatic ethos promote unity and leadership with mainline churches and other non-renewal evangelical and indigenous churches? It appears that seminaries still keep their turf amid observable collaborations inter-ecclesiastically, claims Catholic Archbishop-elect, Julian Leow.[72]

Outreach: evangelism, interreligious engagement, social witness, and the civil space

Perhaps the most difficult to envision is whether Pentecostals/ Charismatics can advance the Spirit-empowered mission for evangelism and outreach. After all, many megachurches (planted and blossomed in renewal traditions) are already engaging in state-of-the-art evangelism, mass missional consecration, and mobilization. Church growth in megachurches in Singapore and Malaysia are not merely attributed to transfer growth from other churches (also known as "stealing sheep") but also due to the robust and creative evangelism to the unchurched and younger generations.[73] Churches have also seen phenomenal increases of support for missions and missionaries. Literally, to a large extent, with the successes of the GoForth Mission Conference the aspiration for "Antioch" has already become a reality well beyond an originally Lausanne-initiated vision for an accelerated outreach in the AD2000 movement (commonly associated with Bill Bright, Billy Graham, Philip Teng, and others).[74] Still, other religions in Asia (including Malaysia and Singapore) continue to regard Christianity as a foreign religion, whose church architecture, beliefs, and liturgy appear to be patterned or expressed consistently with the Christianities of the European traditions.[75]

Apart from evangelism, outreach may also be considered in various aspects: interreligious engagement, social witnessing, and Christian presence in the civil sphere, though the trajectories for Singapore and Malaysia will be different in many respects. Apart from the active Islam dialogue with Christianity in Malaysia, it is perhaps reasonable to acknowledge that there is limited interreligious engagement between Pentecostals and other religions in

Singapore.[76] It is not that Christianity or Pentecostalism is not interested in interreligious understanding. Many seminars have been conducted on formulating clear positions of harmonious engagements.[77] What remains unpublicized are official engagements, if any, in light of the various sociopolitical states and realities (briefly described above). For instance, the reality of Islamization in Malaysia remains a challenge.[78] Would interreligious sociality be forged any differently if more of the "closed-doors" sessions between religious groups in both countries were open to public observation?

Further, is religion merely an arena for private practice, and what is the extent of Christianity and discipleship's social and public witness? And is it really possible to separate or even delineate between the belief and practice of one's faith in the private and public spheres such as is evident in the differentiated practices in Singapore and Malaysia? In Singapore's "state communitarian multiculturalism," Singapore sociologist Goh reminds that, "the state acts as both the guarantor and cultivator of a secular public morality crafted from the wellsprings of the citizens' religious beliefs and values"; consequently, "religious pluralism is not only to be arbitrated, but has to be protected as the very source of the nation's secularity."[79] Yet, in Malaysia, the Islamic statehood, no doubt with a promise for freedom of practice of religion, has been a particular challenge for Islamic-Christian relations, so much so that 2015 World Watch List ranks Malaysian Christianity thirty-seventh on the global persecution index.[80] While both nations vary in their approaches to major and minority religions, the sociopolitical implications of negotiating religious space in the public and private dimensions of life appear similar. Religion not only occurs in the private sphere, but it also carries ramifications for the public sphere.[81] In that sense, Pentecostalism and Charismaticism do not operate any differently from the practice of the wider Christian traditions in both countries.

The question is: Does the "many tongues of the Spirit" allow more innovative approaches than have yet been seen in the sociopolitical sphere? And how may Christianity, and especially the Pentecostal/Charismatic movement, avoid the pitfalls of a prosperity and success-driven spirituality in its witness, which a prominent social theologian, Mark Chan, calls, a "narcissistic spirituality"?[82]

Singaporean and Malaysian Christianity appear to have thrived in social witness, e.g., the realm of non-evangelistic social engagements. The governments have welcomed social contributions of religions, and various Christian groups in Singapore, for instance, have been lauded by the state leaders.[83] One wonders if the public recognition subtly pushes Singaporean Christianity's continual social engagement in ways that unwittingly moderates the evangelistic thrust of the gospel and encourages the emergence of Christianity as a religion in the civil sphere that has to carefully negotiate its presence without expressing any hint of civil disobedience, even if occasionally needed? I am not disregarding the complexity of such public witness and social responsibility, and Christianity's contribution to the ongoing construction and development of public policy, which have been duly pointed out by social scientists, theologians, and pastors.[84] I am merely asking if Singaporean Christianity, as well as Malaysian Christianity in this regard, is more or less limited to the roles prescribed to them, or if such is even necessary for the social harmony and interreligious cohesion that are so badly needed in this region? It is against this larger backdrop that we will need to keep watching how LoveSingapore's ongoing social contributions and attempts to sound out conservative conscience of the public navigates the entrenched secular position of a pluralistic context.

CONCLUSION

From the early beginnings of renewal Christianity to the present
in Malaysia and Singapore, the movement has found pathways for
growing the faith amid challenges. While it may be too much to
claim that prospects are bright or promising, it would be fair to recognize that the renewal movement stands at a crossroad as it moves
into a new era: Will it continue to shine and open up new frontiers
as it has, or will it be become submerged into mainstream evangelical Christianities of Singapore and Malaysia, amid the complexities
of private and public spheres of intra-Christian development, interreligious engagement, and religious-sociopolitical involvement?
While this essay does not answer the question definitively, it pulls
together some past and present trajectories toward a reimagining
of the multidimensionality of Pentecostalism and Charismaticism
in both lands.[85]

Chapter 13

American Missionaries and Pentecostal Theological Education in Indonesia

Ekaputra Tupamahu

WITH MORE THAN 237 million people living throughout some eighteen thousand islands, and about 207 million Muslims, Indonesia has the largest Muslim population in the world.[1] Even though there is a great cultural, ethnic, and religious diversity, Islam is still the dominant religion with Christianity making up about 10 percent of the total population. In recent decades, however, the Pentecostal movement has become a growing segment within Indonesian Christianity. Among roughly 16 million Protestants, there are about 6 million Pentecostals in Indonesia today.[2] This chapter reflects on what has happened in this religious movement. It focuses on the birth and development of Pentecostal Bible schools led by foreign missionaries. Basing this discussion mainly on missionaries' reports and newsletters, I will utilize Mary Louise Pratt's work on travel writings to help frame the discussion.

I hope to show that Indonesians have not been passive recipients of what American missionaries brought. Rather, they have consciously selected, adjusted, and reformulated the legacy they received from missionaries. In the first part of this chapter I will discuss the conceptual framework derived from Pratt's book *Imperial*

Eyes. After that I will examine closely the works of American missionaries, especially in the Indonesian Assemblies of God,[3] and the birth of Pentecostal Bible schools in Indonesia. This chapter documents how Indonesian Pentecostals have received and adapted the model of Bible college that Western missionaries brought them in the early stages of Pentecostal history.

A THEORETICAL FRAMEWORK

Mary Louise Pratt, professor of Spanish and Portuguese at New York University, published *Imperial Eyes: Travel Writing and Transculturation* in 1992. It analyzes the writings that European travelers produced from the 1750s to 1980s. This essay is conceptually indebted to Pratt in various ways. First is her idea of contact zone. Pratt defines "contact zones" as "social spaces where disparate cultures meet, clash, and grapple with each other, often in highly asymmetrical relations of domination and subordination—like colonialism, slavery, or their aftermaths as they are lived out across the globe today."[4] Moreover, Pratt identifies it as the "space of colonial encounters... in which peoples geographically and historically separated come into contact with each other and establish ongoing relations, usually involving conditions of coercion, radical inequality, and intractable conflict."[5] This is basically the space where the power struggle and the struggle for power takes place.[6] This concept of contact zone is essential for our purposes as it helpfully illuminates the space where the Bible schools were built. In other words, it is within this kind of interaction between both missionaries and Indonesians that brought about the establishment of Bible schools.

A second helpful notion from Pratt is that of transculturation. Pratt, borrowing from the works of other ethnographers, explains that the term *transculturation* is used "to describe how subordinated and marginal groups select and invent from materials transmitted to them by a dominant or metropolitan culture."[7] She sees a close connection between contact zone and transculturation, because the latter is "a phenomenon of contact zone."[8] In addition, Pratt points to the reciprocity of determination and domination relations between the colonies and the metropolis:

> In the context of this book, the concept serves to raise several sets of questions. How are metropolitan modes of representation received and appropriated on the periphery? That question engenders another perhaps more heretical one: with respect to representation, how does one speak of transculturation from the colonies to the metropolis? The fruits of empire, we know, were pervasive in shaping European domestic society, culture, and history. How have Europe's constructions of subordinated others been shaped by those others, by the constructions of themselves and their habitats that they presented to the Europeans? Borders and all, the entity called Europe was constructed from the outside in as much as from the inside out. Can this be said of its modes of representation? While the imperial metropolis tends to understand itself as determining the periphery (in the emanating glow of the civilizing mission or the cash flow of development, for example), it habitually blinds itself to the ways in which the periphery determines the metropolis—beginning, perhaps, with the latter's obsessive need to present and re-present its peripheries and its others continually to itself.[9]

Pratt's questions go in both directions: to the metropolis and to the colonies. The modes of representation created by the metropolis as a result of the encounter in the contact zone affect not only people in the periphery, but those in the metropolis as well. Due to space constraints, however, I will only discuss the effects of the interactions in the contact zone on the people in the periphery (transculturation) and leave for future exploration the aspect of the influence of the interaction in the contact zone to the metropolis. Thus, I aim to show that Indonesians are not passive recipients of "materials transmitted to them" by foreign missionaries. In the case of Bible schools, Indonesian Pentecostals select and invent from the educational model they received from missionaries.

AMERICAN PENTECOSTAL MISSIONARIES IN INDONESIA

The Pentecostal movement began its life in Indonesia prior to the latter's independence in 1945. Even though Indonesia was a Dutch colony (*Nederlands-Oost-Indië*)[10] for around three centuries, Pentecostalism came to Indonesia with a very strong American influence. Yet the early contacts were made by missionaries of Dutch descent in 1921: Dirk and Stien van Klaveren and Cornelis and Mies Goesbeek, of Bethel Temple, a church located in Seattle, Washington, in the United States.[11] They originally went to work in Bali but then moved to Java due to a governmental restriction of missionary work in Bali.

Generally speaking, when missionaries left the United States, they felt called by God to accomplish a divine mission. To them the world was dark, evil, and lost, so missionaries were the bearers of God's salvation and light to the world. Christianity, in one sense, became the answer for the darkness of the world. Leaving their home country was not easy. Kenneth McComber, a missionary from Michigan and a Central Bible College graduate,[12] for example, reported on his challenging missionary journey to Indonesia in 1954. His writings will reveal more clearly the experience in the contact zone from a Western perspective. He divides his story according to the five senses: smell, sight, taste, hearing, and feeling. First, the smell in Indonesia was quite different. About a return trip to Jakarta, he recalled, "Through delicate memory I 'smell' again the stench of the dirty canal that runs through the heart of the city. The canal where people wash their clothes, take their baths, and brush their teeth. Memories of their native foods cooking, giving off their peculiar odor that one does not smell in America."[13] For him, missionaries had to adjust to this strange smell, otherwise they would "live in misery."[14] Second, visually things were different. In the winter he missed not only hearing Christmas carols but also seeing snow. Third, the sounds are "very different" from the United States, especially the sounds from food vendors. Not only that, also dissonant were the "squealing of pigs, the barking of dogs, and strange music...in a language hard to understand."[15] Fourth, the food tasted different also. "It not only smells different but it tastes different, and pardon my redundance if I infer that it *is* different."[16] Fourth, the feelings of "loneliness, uncertainty, the loss of fellowship" with other Americans were very challenging for him. He further recalls the uneasy feeling of the "watchful eyes upon you, watching to see if you are friend or foe."[17] He then concludes the report by saying:

> As for me, after one term on the field, I want to go back again and in going back I must make adjustment all over again. Strange that I should want to go back to Indonesia to those sights, and sounds, smells and tastes—and feelings that we know so little about here in these United States. I suppose it is because I *feel* the call of God to go back to those poor lost souls. But if every missionary is honest he will have to agree, when all is said and done that there is *no place like home*. That certainly is ironical, for most missionaries really have no home at all.[18]

It is remarkable that after describing Indonesians as almost complete "others" (read: strangers) on many levels, he still wanted to go back and live with "those poor lost souls." McComber is one of many missionaries whose reports reflect the "othering" (or alienating) of Indonesians.[19] One might infer that the othering project was necessary in order to maintain the need for mission and conversion. The other is integral to the identity and the calling of the missionaries, as without the other there will not be the need for mission and conversion.

The darkness of the world was not only perceived from a "spiritual" perspective but also at the cultural and racial levels as well. When Harold Skoog and R. B. Caveness went to Ambon, Maluku, in the eastern part of Indonesia, they wrote: "After being in a few [church] services with these dark-skinned people, we realize how great the need is to bring them light. They are steeped in superstitions and customs and have a great fear of their own people, which keeps them from accepting the gospel readily."[20] The association of skin color with evil and sin may be astonishing for contemporary sensibilities. But recall that the audience of this report was mainly people in the United States, and like other such documents of its time, it participated in a discourse of colonial representation. It echoes what Frantz Fanon says: "In the collective unconscious of *homo occidentalis,* the Negro—or, if one prefers, the color black—symbolizes evil, sin, wretchedness, death, war, famine."[21]

Pratt shows further that in the contact zone, there exists the phenomenon of "anti-conquest," a term that she defines as "the strategies of representation whereby European bourgeois subjects seek to secure their innocence in the same moment they assert European hegemony."[22] Skoog and Caveness's statement is precisely a manifestation of anti-conquest. They secure their colonial innocence by arguing that the mission is to bring the "light of salvation" and not to colonize, but at the same moment they posit a white American hegemony. They wrote further:

> If you were to visit our mission field here in the Netherlands East Indies, you would observe many new sights even as we did. Upon alighting from the plane, you would be met by a dilapidated truck which would take you for an uncomfortable ride to the pier where the scow, sued as a ferry boat, would be waiting to take its load of passengers across the bay to Amboina village. If the day happened to be clear we would get a glimpse of the beautiful coral sea gardens, reputed to be among the finest of this type in the world. As we near Amboina we scan the horizon for a glimpse of a neat little city, but a panorama of sprawling, hastily constructed *atap* (thatch) houses standing upon and between the ruins of the former dwelling greets our eye. The whole appearance is one of disorder, and among all of this disorder are people for whom Christ died: upon whose faces have been so indelibly written the marks of sin and sadness.[23]

After speaking about the darkness of skin as the representation of evil and lostness, Skoog and Caveness now invite American readers to cast a hegemonic gaze upon the Ambonese. The contrasting description of nature and human beings is quite disturbing. The natural world is beautiful, but in contrast, the disorder of the town reflects the disorder of its inhabitants. Set in broader context, it is worth noting that the majority of the population in Ambon was Christian when this report was written. Christianity is still the dominant religion in Ambon today. This said, it is apparent that the mission is not only a "spiritual" mission of converting non-Christians to Christianity, but also the mission of bringing orderly Western civilization to the disorder of Indonesia.

The Opening of Bible Schools

This mission of saving and civilizing Indonesians was at the center of Pentecostal American missionary efforts. The idea of starting Bible schools was born out of the desire to expand and increase the number of workers to carry on the same mission. So, the original goal of building the theological education system was to transfer the same passion for evangelistic work from missionaries to the local Indonesians. It needs to be pointed out that missions is understood in a narrow sense as winning souls or converting people to Christianity. Paul Lewis points out correctly that "The early Pentecostals were quick to realize the need for some method of disciplining new converts and training workers for the harvest."[24]

One of the earliest Pentecostal Bible schools was opened in Surabaya by W. W. Patterson, a missionary from Bethel Temple in 1932. Lewis explains that "from its inception the emphasis of the school was basic understanding of doctrine and a practical application of biblical truth. The course lasted less than a year, and then graduates were quickly thrust into full-time ministry."[25] The short-term program is still maintained by *Gereja Pantekosta di Indonesia* as the model for ministerial training program until now. The school was later moved from Surabaya to Lawang and eventually to Beji.

The first Assemblies of God missionary, Kenneth G. Short, arrived in Kalimantan (then Borneo) in 1936. After several months working in a village called *Poelang Pisau,* he reported that: "something was lacking. There needed somehow to be a demonstration of the power of God to awaken these darkened hearts to the reality of the power of God. One day it happened!"[26] According to his report, a little girl then was healed from total blindness. Short wrote, "The force of it [healing] shook the whole village. Saridjan, the little girl's brother, gave his heart to God because of it, and not only Saridjan, but the whole family and all the relatives living under the same roof."[27] Apparently for Short, healing is not the end in itself. Healing is always for confirmation of the Pentecostal message. Moreover, Short began to feel the importance of starting a training center for

Christian workers. Here is what he had to say about a theological education model that would work in an Indonesian context:

> We feel that often a zeal without knowledge is more destructive than constructive, especially in the matter of native men stirred to minister to their own people. So we very definitely felt the need of a Bible School. Our plan was to erect a thatched building exactly after the pattern to which they are accustomed. They would eat their native food, live a normal Dayak life while in training. During the time outside of the classroom, these young men would be given work to do around the station which would help pay for their food. On weekends it had been our plan to take these students to different villages—one village a week. We would first have a general mass meeting for the entire village, ministering to such a large group by aid of a public address system mounted on the motor boat. Immediately following, the students would enter every hut in the village, two by two, leaving a personal word of testimony and a printed portion of God's word.[28]

This is a typical project of many Pentecostal missionaries. When they came, after living and ministering to the people for a short period of time, the first thing they did was to establish a Bible school.

In the subsequent years many Bible colleges were established throughout Indonesia. In his 1949 report missionary John C. Tinsman from the Netherlands East Indies wrote:

> On the island of Ambon God has blessed establishing two good workers. At Kate-Kate, where Mr. and Mrs. R. M. Devin live, there has been a gracious moving of the Holy Spirit among the near-by *Kampoengs* [villages]. There have been a number saved and filled with the Spirit, and in spite of continued persecution these converts are building their own church. We are amazed at the zeal of these people and rejoice in their work of grace which is operating in their lives. Along with the Devins

we hope to open the Bethel Moluccan Bible Institute at Kate-
Kate on January 15, for training of native workers. We are
trusting the Lord for potential spiritual leaders among the
young men, so that when properly trained we can use them to
thoroughly evangelize the Moluccas.[29]

This statement shows that one of the sole purposes of theological
education was evangelism. It is apparent that after the native people
are trained, missionaries intended to "use them to thoroughly
evangelize the Moluccas." Furthermore, in his 1947 report to Noel
Perkin in Springfield, R. M. Devin wrote:

We are building a temporary *atap* building from our funds
on hand, that figure will handle about 25 students, then
later, when it is possible to make an arrangement to buy or
lease Kate-Kate, we will plan on something permanent. Our
thought is to take 25 students the first year, 25 the second,
25 the third—this will mean altogether, facilities for 75–100
students....Now as to the expense, it is our idea that it will
require about $10.00 per month per student....We will charge
each student for this each month and he will be required to
perform an equivalent amount of work, or on a contract basis
with the plantation, bring in harvests, of which they will give
him ½, which can be credited against him.[30]

One can see in this report a very detailed plan to build and run
the Bible school in Maluku. It was clear that students did not receive
a free education. They had to work to pay for their tuition and
daily expenses. American missionaries typically did not create an
environment in which Indonesians depended on them financially.
This is still true today. Bible schools in Indonesia, especially in the
Assemblies of God, do not depend on foreign money for their daily
operation. So, the Bethel Bible Institute in Maluku was established
in 1949 and remains in operation today. Almost all Assemblies of
God ministers in Maluku are graduates of this Bible school. The

name of the school now is *Sekolah Tinggi Teologi Maluku* in Kate-Kate, Ambon.

Another American Pentecostal missionary, Leonard Lanphear, wrote in a 1953 report about his work in Minahasa:

> After fourteen months of labor we now have a great joy of seeing seven churches standing as lighthouses in Northern Sulawesi. Four of the seven have their own national pastors, Spirit-filled and longing to see God do a mighty work among this people. The care of the other three churches has been undertaken by two fine young men who are graduates of Bethel Bible Institute, Ambon, where the Devin family have labored long and faithfully....A further development in the work was the opening of the Minahasa Bible School. We had had many inquiries as to what opportunities for Bible School training there might be, and the more we saw of the need, the more we realized we must have a school in our area. Already there was a good nucleus of students with which to begin. So, with God's help, we were able to erect some very inexpensive, native-style buildings in which to establish our Bible School. We opened with 14 students. It was thrilling on that first day of school to stand before those expectant men. We know the lives of sin and darkness from which they had been snatched. Now we saw the light of heaven on their faces and their longing to be fitted for the Master's service.[31]

This is the beginning of the establishment of *Sekolah Alkitab Minahasa* (now *Sekolah Tinggi Teologi Parakletos*) in North Sulawesi. Again, the desire to change people who live in "sin and darkness" became the driving motivation behind the building of this Bible School.

The Busby family's and Margaret J. Brown's work in Jakarta in 1946 resulted in a church that had about one thousand children every Sunday. A magazine in the United States, *The Missionary*

Challenge, reported this about the explosion of this children's ministry:

> You may wonder how it would be possible to get Sunday school work in a foreign land to advance it as it does in the States; and how Sunday school classes abroad can be graded according to Sunday school organizational standard? Mr. and Mrs. Busby point out that much of their success along this line may be attributed to the fact that the Djakarta Bible Institute was started three months after the church and Sunday school we began.[32]

One of the classes they offered in the Djakarta Bible Institute "taught the students to use most of the available visual aid material known in the States."[33] Hence, the model and method of doing church in Indonesia was transplanted from the United States through a Bible school. These Indonesian students were taught to imitate the American Sunday school model. They reported in 1950, "Teaching classes is not all there is to conducting Bible school in Java. Lessons must be translated, then stencils cut, copies run off for the student's use for there are few textbooks in their languages. It means hours of work each day for every member of faculty."[34] By 1953 the school had produced seven pastors, five assistant pastors, three deacons, four deaconesses, twelve Sunday school leaders, and four Bible school teachers.[35] In 1957 the same magazine reported that the Busby family was in a great financial need of about $40,000 to purchase a property for the so-called "Revival Center" that "must include an auditorium for regular worship service, headquarter, Bible School and dormitories.... There were about sixty students at the school now [1957]."[36] This Bible school is the seed of *Sekolah Tinggi Teologi Ekklesia* today.

In 1954 it was reported that the Assemblies of God missionaries had built four Bible schools in Indonesia (Sumatera, Jakarta,

Maluku, and North Sulawesi) with about eighty-eight students. As early as 1959 a great number of missionaries were fully concentrated on the work of building and maintaining Bible schools.[37] Missionaries held the leadership positions in all these schools. Harold R. Carlblom, in his 1959 report to the field secretary of the Far East of the Assemblies of God, Maynard L. Ketcham, wrote: "All other missionaries are occupied in Bible Schools. We are the only ones available for evangelistic work."[38] Bible schools were the front line of Pentecostal missionary works in Indonesia.

Pratt, interestingly, shows a parallel between scientific travel writings and Christian missionary movement. She writes about how Linneaus was very proud of his disciples who had gone around the globe to map the world according to his taxonomic system:

> It is as if he [Linneaus] were speaking of ambassadors and empire. What I want to argue is, of course, that in quite a significant way, he was. As Christianity had set in motion a global labor of religious conversion that asserted itself at every point of contact with other societies, so natural history set in motion a secular, global labor that, among other things, made contact zones a site of intellectual as well as manual labor, and installed there the distinction between the two.[39]

The same is true also of Bible schools in Indonesia. It is in a way an American project of creating "a global labor of religious conversion." In a similar vein, Edna M. Devin wrote in 1956: "Our five Bible schools are trying to train enough workers to reach the eighty million souls in Indonesia."[40] Producing workers/laborers was at the heart of the Bible schools' project in Indonesia.

The Bible school (or Bible institute) model of theological education was thoroughly dominant among American Pentecostals. Phillip Douglas Chapman explained that the Bible school movement in the United States in the late nineteenth century through early twentieth century was prevalent across three different segments: (1) holiness schools, (2) Pentecostal schools, and (3) fundamentalist schools.[41] Pentecostalism's participation in the Bible school movement in America influenced the work of missionaries abroad as well. Thus, it is not a surprise that when missionaries left the United States, the idea of starting Bible schools became their foremost goal. They followed the model of theological education that they saw in their homeland. In fact, most American missionaries who went to Indonesia were products of Bible schools.

SOME REFLECTIONS ON INDONESIAN TRANSCULTURATION

It needs to be acknowledged that Bible schools have played an instrumental role in the process of building the foundation and expanding the Pentecostal movement in Indonesia. Yet they are not only factories of the national church workers but also producers of Bible teachers and missionaries. Almost all national leaders in the Indonesian Assemblies of God, for example, are the products of Bible schools. Gatut Budiyono, the current president of *Sekolah Tinggi Teologi Satyabhakti* and the general treasurer of Indonesian Assemblies of God, reported in a recent interview with a local newspaper that 95 percent of its graduates are still active in one form or another of church ministries.[42] The story of the Indonesian Pentecostal movement would have been different if the missionaries did not open these Bible schools.

The existence of the Bible schools in Indonesia is the creative work of American missionaries. Since most of the missionaries work at the Bible schools, it is not an exaggeration to conclude that Bible schools became a sort of main "contact zone" between Western American Pentecostalism and Indonesian Pentecostalism. They were the primary spaces where American Pentecostals interacted with Indonesians. Indonesian students are basically isolated on the campus for almost the entire week. They are allowed to leave campus only during the weekend for ministries, and one day off during the week. The rest of the week they live with a very strict regimented system in the campus dorm.[43] Every activity (e.g., classes, chapel service, meal time, etc.) is signaled by the bell ringing. In chapel, males and females sit separately. These regulations are primarily designed by American missionaries.[44] Such practice ensured, intentionally or not, the Western hegemony among Indonesian Pentecostals. Nevertheless, as I have noted in the beginning of this essay, Indonesian Pentecostals have also consciously selected, adjusted, and reformulated the American legacy they received. Their achievements can be appreciated theologically, administratively, ecumenically, and academically.

Theologically, Indonesian Pentecostals have seen fit to adapt the curriculum they inherited from the missionaries. In general, missionaries who came to Indonesia believed strongly in the distinctive Pentecostal convictions, such as the manifestations of power of the Holy Spirit (e.g., healing, gifts of the Spirit, etc.) and speaking in tongues as the initial physical evidence of the baptism in the Holy Spirit. Bible schools would offer *Doktrin-Doktrin Alkitab* (Bible doctrines) class for all incoming students with P. C. Nelson's *Bible Doctrines* as its main textbook. In addition, Pentecostal theological distinctiveness is also emphasized strongly in the pneumatology class. Consequently, those who have gone through Bible school training in Indonesia will very likely affirm these basic Pentecostal convictions.

However, American missionaries came not only with Pentecostal convictions but also with a deeply held dispensationalist eschatology. The "Daniel–Revelation" class had been part of Indonesian Bible college curriculum to ensure that students will be able to know

and teach this doctrine. Students are required to draw and memo-
rize the long and detailed chart of dispensations from Adam and
Eve to the coming of new heaven and new earth. Books from Dallas
Seminary professors, such as John Walvoord and Charles Ryrie, are
translated into Indonesian by *Gandum Mas*,[45] a publishing house
run by Indonesian Assemblies of God. However, in 1996 a change
began to take place in the Bible school curriculum. Some younger
Indonesian Bible school professors begin to realize that putting the
books of Daniel and Revelation together in one course might serve
the dispensationalist theological purposes well, but could not be
sustained from the historical critical perspective. They then pushed
to separate the study of these books and approached both from
a strictly historical point of view. Consequently one can see the
weakening of the influence of dispensationalist theology, especially
among younger generation Indonesian Assemblies of God pastors
and teachers.

Beyond the doctrine of eschatology, some young Indonesian
Pentecostal thinkers who have been educated in a Bible school
system have begun to reflect and reformulate theological concepts
from their Indonesian context. They do this most of the time as a
sort of reaction or response to the theology that they have received
from missionaries. An example is Gani Wiyono's article on the
Christology from an Indonesian context. He expresses a concern
that Indonesians received a Western image Christ and "by and
large that Christology reflects the thought patterns, general orientation, and the contextual need of the West."[46] The Western Christ
that Wiyono responds to is apparently the Christ he learned from
missionaries in the Bible school. Wiyono argues that "the time has
come for Asians to begin to seek 'the biblical images of Jesus' which
arise out of their particular contextual need."[47] The figure of *Ratu
Adil*, a "mysterious and popular messianic-eschatological figure

among Javanese,"[48] he proposes, should be an image suitable to the Indonesian context, especially in Java. It is the Christ who brings liberation, harmony, and hope to the Indonesian people.[49]

A second instance is Agustinus Dermawan. His article on the Spirit in creation argues for a more environmental-friendly Pentecostal theology.[50] Dermawan contends that the Pentecostal view toward the world or the environment has been deeply affected by the other-worldly pessimistic attitude rooted in their premillennialism [dispensationalist] eschatology So, he thinks that Pentecostals need to look into the biblical vision of the Spirit in creation in order to build a more responsible environmental theology. Dermawan further proposes an Indonesian model of *Ibu Pertiwi* (Mother Earth) as a theological paradigm to understand Pentecostals' relation to nature. The idea is that nature is the mother of human beings.

> The symbol of *Ibu Pertiwi* is a relational symbol. The figure of a mother is also very concrete and familiar to us. Everyone knows what a mother is, so whose heart would not be moved when he/she sees his/her mother grieving? It is also apparent that the relationship between *Ibu Pertiwi* and Indonesian people is based mainly on intuitive and mystical relational. We cannot see when *Ibu Pertiwi* is sad with our bare eyes, but we can only feel. Moreover, the beauty, peace and prosperity of the nation represent the happiness of *Ibu Pertiwi*. Its beauty represents esthetical values.[51]

These examples show that Indonesian Pentecostals are not just passive recipients of American missionaries' theologies. They have selected, adjusted, and reformulated theological reflection from within their Indonesian cultural and social location.

Second, on the administrative level, within the process of negotiation of power relations between Indonesian faculty members and missionaries, the Indonesian government has played a significant role in Indonesia. The leadership of *Sekolah Tinggi Teologi Satyabhakti*, for instance, had been missionaries since establishment of this school in 1961, and only in 1974 was the leadership transferred to Indonesians due to the government banning foreigners from leading any formal institution.[52] However, even though missionaries are not on the top of leadership, they are always in the membership of *Badan Pengurus Harian* of the school. The negotiation of power between American missionaries and Indonesians is an ongoing process.

Ecumenically, relationship between Pentecostals and other Christians in Indonesia reflects the transculturation process. The mission of conversion that missionaries brought from America and taught in Bible schools nurtured a reluctant attitude toward engagement in ecumenical relationship. Some missionaries even created negative and somewhat insulting jokes about other non-Pentecostal denominations in Indonesia. For example, GPM, the abbreviation of *Gereja Protestan Maluku* (Moluccan Protestant Church), is jokingly changed into *Gereja Pasti Mati* (Church that will surely die), or GMIM (*Gereja Masehi Injili Indonesia*) in North Sulawesi into *Gereja Mati Iblis Menang* (Church dies, the Devil wins). Jokes are not a play on words but reflect instinctive reactions to tensions between Pentecostals and other Christians.

Indonesian Pentecostals, however, have begun to depart from this denominational exclusivism. One factor that motivates this departure is the fact that local virtues of *rukun* (harmony) and *gotong royong* (communal work) are rooted deeply in the psyche of Indonesians.[53] At the lowest level of Indonesian society, people are organized by the so-called *rukun tetangga* (neighborhood harmony) and *rukun warga* (harmony of people). Gatut Budiyono, for instance, is actively involved in the ecumenical movement in the city of Malang, East Java. *Sekolah Tinggi Teologi Satyabhakti* that he leads has many times been the venue for ecumenical events (e.g., ecumenical Christmas celebration, ecumenical worship gathering, etc.). *Gereja Kristen Indonesia* (Indonesian Christian Church), one of the leading mainline non-Pentecostal denominations, after being expelled from their place of worship in 2003, have used the chapel of *Sekolah Tinggi Teologi Satyabhakti* for their weekly worship gathering until today. Maria Taihutu, a female president of *Sekolah Tinggi Teologi Maluku*, is a respected ecumenical figure in Maluku. She invites non-Pentecostals to teach courses as adjunct professors at the school and speaks/preaches widely outside Pentecostal circles. It is important to note that their openness to ecumenical relationship does not weaken their Pentecostal conviction. Instead, they become a sort of representation of Pentecostal movement within the larger Christian context in Indonesia.

Finally, the process of transculturation takes place within the context of degree-granting programs. As mentioned above, the original mission of the Bible schools was to produce workers/ ministers for missionary projects as quickly as possible. Offering a higher theological degree was not their focus. In fact, when missionaries were in the top leadership position (i.e., presidents) of Bible schools, most of these schools only offered a three-year diploma program. Indonesian Bible schools nowadays, however, have begun to concentrate on offering higher degrees of education. Many of these schools have developed master's degree programs, and some now even offer doctorate programs. Gani Wiyono points out that:

> In the last few years Pentecostals have realized that a decent theological training is very important for having a successful ministry in the present context of Indonesia. Therefore in addition to continuing a practical, short-term approach to ministerial training, they also have begun to develop Bible colleges and seminaries. Some Pentecostal denominations, such as Indonesian Bethel Church (*GBI* or *Gereja Bethel*

Indonesia) and the Assemblies of God in Indonesia (*GSJA* or
Gereja Sidang Jemaat Allah), offer a graduate program. The
Full Gospel Church (GISI or *Gereja Injil Seutuh Indonesia*)
has even started a Doctor of Ministry program.[54]

Wiyono is right in the idea that Pentecostals recently began
to realize the need for a decent theological education. Since he
wrote this piece in 2005, there have been further developments.
For example, in 2011 *Sekolah Tinggi Teologi Bethel,* a school run
by Gereja Bethel Indonesia (Indonesian Bethel Church), in Jakarta
started their own ThD program in theology, counseling, and
Christian education. The program is accredited by the Indonesian
Department of Religious Affairs. But if there has been over the last
generation a tendency among Pentecostals in America to expand
their Bible schools into comprehensive universities, Indonesians
are not quite there yet. There is not one Pentecostal university in
Indonesia. There has been an ongoing discussion among Assemblies
of God leadership to expand *Sekolah Tinggi Teologi Satyabhakti* to
a full-fledged university, but its implementation is still a long-term
agenda.

Furthermore, in more recent years the Indonesian government through *Badan Akreditasi Nasional Perguruan Tinggi* (The
National Accrediting Board) has been pushing every accredited
college and university to do more research and publication. The
accreditation is extremely crucial for the existence of Bible schools
because without it their degrees will not be acknowledged by the
government. Pentecostalism has been known in Indonesia for easy
degree programs. Jan Aritonang observes:

> There are even some Evangelical and Pentecostal schools
> that offer higher degrees, like Master of Divinity, Master of
> Theology, and even Doctor (including Doctor honoris causa),
> in only a few days, weeks, or months of quasi-study, without

a thesis or dissertation, or by faking it. These degrees usually were awarded to or bought by businessmen, church leaders, or officials in certain government departments. This phenomenon can create the impression that theological schools in Indonesia, as some pseudo-theological education abroad, fall victim to commercialization, which actually insults the quality of education and jeopardizes the future of the nation.[55]

However, with this new government regulation, if a school cannot meet the academic standard set by the government, it will be demoted from a degree-granting institution to a mere training center. Pentecostal schools cannot continue this practice.

Consequently this will affect the way Bible school professors/ teachers conduct themselves academically. Publishing research has not been a priority in Indonesian Bible schools because they tend to focus more on spiritual formation and basic biblical and theological training. Whether they like it or not, the academic demand from the government has pushed them to alter and modify their academic practices and commitments. To put it differently, the model of theological education brought by missionaries that focuses merely on producing workers quickly may have worked in the past, but in order to fit the current Indonesian context, it needs to be adapted and adjusted.

After about eighty years in the country, Pentecostalism unfortunately has not been able to develop serious scholars and thinkers who actively produce literature and contribute to the larger theological discourse in Indonesia. Two examples that I have discussed above, Gani Wiyono and Agustinus Dermawan, represent an emerging group of Indonesian Pentecostal scholars who are taking up this challenge. Most Indonesian Bible school professors concentrate mainly on teaching and not on research. The lack of rigorous scholarship can be seen not only in the Assemblies of God but also in the Indonesian Pentecostal movement as a whole.

CONCLUSION

There is a need for Indonesian Pentecostal scholarship to reflect on the history of the movement, react to the dominant American mentality, and rebuild a new narrative from their social location. The narrative of Indonesian Pentecostalism has been largely dominated by the voices of missionaries. In order to go beyond that set of perspectives and perhaps develop an authentic indigenous form of Pentecostal spirituality, Bible schools need to focus not only on creating church workers but also on nurturing critical scholars. Nevertheless, the truth can be discerned in what sociologist Margaret Poloma says: "Pentecostalism is not simply another example of an American export. In many countries the most rapidly growing Pentecostal churches have developed a form of Christianity quite different from its American cousins."[56] The challenge still remaining for the future is for Indonesians to rearticulate and reformulate their Pentecostal narrative both historically and theologically.

Chapter 14

The Demise of Pentecostalism in the Philippines: Naming and Claiming the Impossible Object and the Politics of Empowerment in Pentecostal Studies

Giovanni Maltese and Sarah Eßel

SPECTER IS HAUNTING the Philippines—the specter of Pentecostalism. While David Barrett's *World Christian Encyclopedia* published in 1982 listed only a few "Catholic Pentecostals (or, Catholic Charismatics),"[1] its second edition published in 2001 lists Pentecostal/Charismatics (hereafter PC) as a "trans-megablock" with an estimated adherence of 20,050,000, equivalent to 26.4 percent of the total Philippine population.[2] According to a nationwide survey conducted by the *PEW Forum on Religion and Public Life* in 2006, the PC movement in the Philippines is even said to comprise up to 44 percent of the Philippine population.[3]

Data from field research conducted between 2009 and 2014 by Giovanni Maltese in Negros, Cebu, Manila and Mindanao,[4] however, seems to present a different reality. On the ground, leaders and members of the churches both typically and explicitly subsumed under the nomenclature PC in the mentioned surveys reject this name—they refuse to form a "trans-mega bloc." Whereas most Catholic groups would identify as "Charismatic" (yet not

Pentecostal), Protestant and evangelical churches again distance themselves from the term that to them is reserved for the afore-mentioned Catholic groups. The name Pentecostal, in turn, is vehemently repudiated by nearly all respondents, regardless of their spirituality, beliefs, affiliation, or organizational background. Even pastors and members of denominations such as the Church of the Foursquare Gospel or the Assemblies of God, usually referred to as classical Pentecostals by researchers, refused to be called by this name. A quick full-text search of the latter's official websites gives remarkably few hits for the term *Pentecostal*.[5] In an interview with Giovanni Maltese, Eddie Villanueva, the founder of Jesus Is Lord Worldwide (JIL), who is regarded by nearly all publications on Christianity in the Philippines as the PC movement's poster child (next to Catholic El Shaddai leader Mike Velarde), made strong objections to being identified as Pentecostal (Villanueva, personal interview March 10, 2013). He also distanced himself from the name "Charismatic," albeit compared to "Pentecostal" in a less aggressive manner (Interview, Dumaguete, May 2013). Likewise, leaders and members of local churches whose denomination's official name reads "Pentecostal," such as the Oneness United Pentecostal Church or the Pentecostal Church of God Asian Missions, make big efforts to mark a difference between themselves and "the Pentecostals." Yet whereas one would expect at least those whose name includes the very word *Pentecostal* to engage in discussions about what proper Pentecostalism should entail and define it accordingly, thereby claiming the term for themselves, the contrary is the case. Members and leaders of these groups were found to refrain from defining the term positively—despite their own use of the very term "Pentecostal" in the names of their organizations. Instead, they limited themselves to describing what the others, "the Pentecostals," are like and why they themselves should not be considered "Pentecostal" at all. The name "Pentecostal" appeared to be an almost derogatory term. When asked to locate their churches within the Christian landscape, the interviewees would sometimes say "full gospel," "Bible believing," and other times refer to themselves as "born again" or evangelical[6]—notably, as opposed to Catholic—but not as "Pentecostal."[7] Are we thus witnessing the demise of Pentecostalism or of the PC movement in the Philippines? Given that studies on the PC movement in the Philippines usually describe the movement as one that empowers its participants (in some way or the other),[8] at first glance it appears bizarre that hardly anybody wants to be part of it, begging the question how to understand this gap between scholarly representation and self-description.

We propose to read this gap as a political gesture. Accordingly, the discrepancy between scholarly representation and self-description may be understood as a form of protest against being co-opted for an ideological, political, or denominational agenda.[9] Against the ubiquitous image of the Philippines as a poverty-stricken country governed by a corrupt leadership and dependent on foreign aid (such as US aid, World Bank, Asian Development Bank, etc.), the media like to characterize "the Charismatics" as "numb mass." They are depicted as a crowd of insecure people who lack proper self-consciousness and do everything their money-grubbing dem-agogues command them—even if this means turning umbrellas upside down and waiting for God to fill them with peso bills, rather than acquiring a proper self-consciousness and change their own and their fellow people's fate.[10] Likewise, although in a more sophisticated manner, researchers have been using the PC move-ment as a projection screen for promoting various approaches to understanding the disease of the "sick man of Asia"[11] and its cure. The self-given task to explain the "explosive growth"[12] of a move-ment that cannot be clearly defined and is yet assumed to be a "trans-mega bloc" offers the possibility to formulate both a problem and its solution. The latter is then evidenced with examples, drawn from the variety of groups subsumed rather arbitrarily under the name PC. The study of Christl Kessler and Jürgen Rüland, scholars of political and social science, see the PC movement as a hindrance to a solution for the county's disastrous situation. The success of what Kessler and Rüland name the PC movement, according to the authors, is due to a populist character, which promotes an "enchanted worldview" and retreat from society[13] and effectively hinders political, economic, and social reforms. The latter can only be achieved through what the authors call "structural change," yet without defining it.[14] The study does not engage in a discussion about if and how structural change is debated among the various groups interviewed. Rather, the authors use data from interviews conducted in Metro Manila (mostly with Charismatic Catholics), which lack a proper contextualization, and apply their observation to PCs in the Philippines as such. The conclusion, thus, sees the movement as a potential threat to democracy and unable to address issues of social justice, albeit they concede it some empowering features.[15] Other studies portray the PC movement as the new face of social engagement, which draws on spiritual resources and is thus best fit to improve the country's situation.[16] In both cases, it is the assumed statistical significance of the PC movement in relation to the Philippine population as a whole, which lends each argument strength in making claims about the state of the Philippine society as a whole (and even beyond, given the presumed global expansion of the PC movement).

This chapter analyzes one example of such a way of making claims about the current conditions of the Philippines by drawing on Pentecostalism as a coherent movement and offering a solution for the development and betterment of the country, which does not necessary meet the (self-)perception of what is claimed to be Pentecostal. Our discussion of a recent study conducted by Philippine Assemblies of God theologian Joseph Suico will show how PC-ness is constructed in order to support the researcher's claim concerning the country's status quo and enabling him to make suggestions with regard to the country's future. Most studies on the PC movement in the Philippines[17] center around the statement of a national crisis and the boom of churches subsumed under the name Pentecostal or PC, and then proceed to explain the causality between crisis, the PC's success, and possible betterment of the Philippines. In line with these studies, Suico too suggests possible betterment along the rhetorics of empowerment and change, while the latter is characterized in more detail through notions such as liberation, progress, transformation, and development. Our discussion shows how this work converts differences, found among the people(-groups) studied, into equivalences by means of selection and exclusion, which in turn create relations between the object of research and the researcher's concept of empowerment and change. It is this conversion of difference into equivalences that makes possible to conceive of these (diverse) groups as a coherent movement, which, according to Suico, lacks proper self-consciousness and empowerment and is in need of a proper agenda in order to contribute to the betterment of its participants and the Philippine society as a whole. On the other hand, the very act of converting difference into equivalence also poses a dilemma about how such an empowerment and change at the heart of the PC movement should look like. This dilemma in turn creates a "free space"[18] for the researcher himself, an empty space that needs to be filled by academic research and its subsequent suggestions on how such empowerment and change should look like.

In contrast to the just presented study, the authors of this paper propose a different agenda for academic research. Instead of making claims concerning the current state of the PC movement in the Philippines and the future development it should take alongside the movement's possible contribution to the betterment of the Philippine society, the authors suggest to show how the research itself produces such claims, and to disclose the contingency of such claims by working out where the research in question works to effectively silence differing voices and exclude alternative readings. It is the authors' hope that this may lead scholars of the PC movement, as well as members of the intelligentsia and leadership of denominations, (mega-)churches, and parachurch ministries, to rethink the way in which numbers and statistics have been used to make certain claims, and at whose costs such claims have been made. As such, the authors wish to offer a fresh reading of the material at hand, which will hopefully again become contested and criticized by future scholarship. With this, the authors seek to raise awareness for the changing interests and concerns at stake in studies of the PC movement.

ON THE POLITICS OF HISTORIOGRAPHY

The work discussed in this chapter is the PhD thesis "Institutional and Individualistic Dimension of Transformational Development: The Case of Pentecostal Churches in the Philippines" (2003) by Joseph Suico,[19] whose results have been published in article form in a journal linked to Assemblies of God theologians in the United States.[20] Suico's starting point is twofold: on the one hand he assumes a national crisis that calls for engagement toward national transformation and development; on the other, he adheres to the common perception that Pentecostals are reproducing neo-colonial relations with the United States, due to their closeness to North American missionaries and that they are seductive of the poor and indifferent to social change (iii, 1, 9). Drawing from qualitative and quantitative data, Suico then seeks to compare the relation toward social and political involvement between two Assemblies of God (hereafter AG) congregations and two Catholic parishes. Himself a member of the AG who held different positions in the denominational leadership as well as in its flagship school Asia Pacific Theological Seminary (7), he comes to a twofold conclusion. On the one hand, there are no official statements by the AG as an institution regarding active sociopolitical involvement, besides charity projects. Yet on the other hand, the practice of Pentecostal churches on the ground is inherently empowering and transformative. According to Suico, this transformative thrust results from a specific spirituality and experience, i.e., Spirit baptism, that empowers all believers to advance the kingdom of God.

As such, Suico considers this spirituality to be an element of radical equality (67), which displays in an effective evangelization and individual healing ministry and which is causative for the numerical growth and success of Pentecostal churches, like the AG (4). Yet a "lack of knowledge and understanding of the significance of the Pentecostal experience" (2), and a dependency on US missionaries with "roots [...] in Fundamentalism" (1), have hindered Pentecostals from formulating a transformational theology of social action needed for a more effective ministry to the society and for the development of the Philippine nation as a whole. Hence, besides what he calls microlevel engagement, there has been no official engagement in social and political issues. Thus, Suico's work aims at reflecting on this experience in a way that allows Pentecostals to become aware of their (yet to be unleashed) sociopolitical potential for the transformation and development of society at large. Drawing from theologians linked to the US-based Society of Pentecostal Studies, he thus continues to lay out a theological sketch intended to lead Pentecostals to see and maximize their transformative potential. For Pentecostals this means to regard themselves not merely as agents who help change peoples' private lives, but to develop an awareness of their potential as institutional and collective agents for social change in the Philippines. Thus, rather than playing out political and social action against evangelization, individual healing, and church growth—as is usually done, according to Suico—he argues for a theology that sees these two positions as complementary.

This theological approach therefore not only frees Pentecostals from the stigma of "fundamentalism," but given its holistic approach—i.e., the integration of social action based on structural change and evangelization based on individual change—it is the best sociopolitical approach for an effective transformation and development of the crisis-ridden nation. His work hence pursues a threefold goal. First, it tries to disprove that Pentecostalism is necessarily and inherently opposed to national development or structural change, a position widespread among Philippine intellectuals. Secondly, Suico accuses fundamentalists in his own camp of misunderstanding their own Pentecostal experience. And thirdly, Suico offers the latter and others, who according to him are Pentecostals, a solution to both the allegation waged by outsiders, as well as the lack of proper knowledge about themselves and their experience, by offering them a theology and an agenda for social and political action (albeit without proper content) intended to enhance both their nation's conditions as well as their own.

CONSTRUCTING PHILIPPINE PENTECOSTALISM

Suico's work begins by placing Pentecostals in the position of needing to justify why they did not actively participate in the People Power rallies that ousted Ferdinand Marcos (1986) and forced Joseph Estrada out of office (2001). He thus begins with the accusation that Pentecostals would have betrayed their country in its fight against dictatorship and other national crises as the main reference point of his study. Yet, rather than contextualizing this criticism and showing who the detractors are and which people (or people groups) were targeted by this allegation, Suico proceeds to discuss similar criticism found in literature on worldwide Pentecostalism, and especially in Latin America. All the while the existence of Pentecostalism as a homogenous impressive global phenomenon is taken for granted, albeit remaining vaguely undefined, oscillating between the inclusive characterization used in the literature he refers to (which coincides with the definition adapted by Pew and other studies) and a less inclusive definition modeled after his own denomination, the AG. Even when Suico mentions scholars who define Pentecostalism as "a belief in the experience known as the baptism in the Holy Spirit subsequent to conversion," or as the belief in "salvation, healing, baptism in the Holy Spirit with the evidence of speaking in tongues, second coming of Jesus Christ," he does not side with either of the two (13). Rather he repeats that the "perceived indifference of Pentecostals toward socioeconomic and political issues has been attributed to various reasons," thus making this a distinctive element of what he names "Pentecostal" (13). Two chapters later he offers yet another definition, in which Pentecostal is said to include "classical Pentecostals" and "independent Pentecostals," but again refrains from explicitly defining anything. Again, the term "Pentecostal" remains effectively unexplained (67).

The context of this allegation is the fundamentalist/modernist controversy to which Suico refers in the beginning of his study (1). Emphasizing that Pentecostalism is perceived as belonging to the "fundamentalist camp," it is clear that the detractors he has in mind are to be found on the other side of the fundamentalism/ modernist divide. These would be, firstly, mainline Protestants close to the World Council of Churches, such as those organized in the National Council of Churches in the Philippines (NCCP), and, secondly, it would be intellectuals and Catholic theologians. Both are known for their nationalist and rather left-leaning approaches to development and change for the Philippines.[21]

In an argumentation that is both self-critical and apologetic, Suico thus tries to deconstruct the necessary relation between Pentecostalism and fundamentalism. He admits fundamentalist tendencies but attributes them to something that is foreign to Pentecostalism as such, being the product of "a North American culture" imported by missionaries along with the gospel (9–29). Fundamentalism, as understood by Suico, is an attitude that denies the holistic character of a person by privileging other-worldly needs at the expense of this-worldly, material needs and structural approaches to change. The root of such fundamentalism, according to Suico, is a dualist epistemology stemming from European enlightenment and imported by colonizers and missionaries. "The Filipino culture," in contrast, is characterized as "intuitive, integrative and wholistic [sic]," which includes the individual and the other-worldly dimension criticized by Pentecostals' detractors (27). Drawing from an essentialist discourse on "Filipinoness," prominent among said detractors, Suico hence indicts fundamentalists and Pentecostals who stick to fundamentalist tendencies of being a hindrance to the development and betterment of the country, which has to be achieved by Filipinos and on Filipino terms. Yet at the same time he accuses Pentecostals' very detractors of being fundamentalist too. In tacitly creating an equivalence between a focus (albeit not exclusive focus) on other-worldlyness and on the individual dimension of transformation, and the essence of Filipinoness, Suico places everything that is critical of other-worldlyness as drawing on the same epistemological dualism that would also form the foundation for fundamentalist positions, namely the dichotomization of matter and spirit imposed by Western colonizers. Thus, he reverses the charge, indicting Pentecostals' detractors of being a hindrance to true liberation and development, given their non-holistic attitude. In other words, those who betray the nation are not the Pentecostals who are portrayed as inherently empowering, albeit they lack a proper theology that leads to the full realization of such an empowerment for national development. The true betrayers are those who criticize Pentecostals' focus on the other-worldly dimension. Given that according to both Suico and the detractors of Pentecostals, the liberation and development is something that has to be achieved by the Filipinos on their own culture's terms, Suico's interpretation of the deplored other-worldly focus as evidence of a holistic understanding of human being, essential to Filipinoness (as also the detractors would admit), reverses the charge of betraying the Filipinos. Pentecostals' emphasis on individual healing and church growth, according to Suico, proves the Filipino Pentecostals' true holistic outlook and their compatibility with the Filipino culture. Conversely, those who criticize Pentecostals' other-worldly practice criticize Filipino culture as such and become a hindrance to the development of the Philippines on Filipino terms. In this framework, his own Pentecostal theology is staged as an approach that works outside such a dualist framework and thus as an approach that is originally free from the heritage of colonial knowledge production (10–32). He thus portrays Pentecostalism as especially sensitive to Filipino culture, loyal to the national project, and consequently most promising for liberation, empowerment, transformation, and development of the Philippines. This discussion, however, blurs the distinction between an ideal of Pentecostalism, based on his own theological standpoint, and an empirical Pentecostalism as found on the ground.

(Re-)Organizing the history of Philippine Pentecostalism

This indeterminate and inconsistent use of the notion of Pentecostalism is found also in the chapter in which Suico sets out to give an account of the history of Philippine Pentecostalism. Notably, this chapter represents the first contextualization of the actual object of his research. While the outline offered in the introduction announces a chronological account (8), the chapter does not follow a chronological order. He begins by giving a historical account of one particular church that for Suico represents the "independent churches," which according to him are of a more recent date than the "classical Pentecostal" ones founded by US missionaries. Even here, the AG, which in his view the oldest Pentecostal churches belong to and whose missionaries from the United States are the pioneers of Philippine Pentecostalism, is mentioned last (67–78). Thus he first elaborates extensively on Jesus Is Lord (JIL), established in the late 1970s by Eddie Villanueva, then goes on to briefly sketch the Church of the Foursquare Gospel, the Church of God, and finally elaborates expansively on the AG. In this framework the account on the AG functions both as denominational history and as meta-narrative, in which the aforementioned churches are located following a three-wave approach: *first*, the period of establishment and special growth of classical Pentecostal churches, i.e., the 1950s and 1960s; *secondly*, the rise of Charismatic fellowships and independent groups, which, according to Suico, is the reason why the AG growth was periodically hampered, i.e., the 1970s and 1980s; *thirdly*, the present period, i.e., the 1990s onwards, which, according to Suico, sees a new boom of AG churches. Suico concludes this paragraph with the triumphalist note: "Despite the lack of proper record keeping, there is little doubt that the Assemblies of God in the Philippines has experienced remarkable growth through the years" (74). He then proceeds to discuss the two case-study churches, both a product of the 1970s and 1980s. The first is International Charismatic Service (ICS) founded by US missionary Paul Klahr in 1975 out of a worship service conducted in a five-star hotel,[22] which, Suico remarks, "was one of the first in the Pentecostal movement which made a successful attempt to penetrate middle and upper class people in the society" (74).[23] His other case study explores the Christ Is the Answer Assemblies of God founded in 1983 by Jerry Cruz, a medical doctor. The church is located in Manila and caters mostly to low-income families (76).

This partial inversion of chronological order and its teleological integration in the account on the AG represents a (re-)organization of history, which, however, is nowhere explained or even reflected. Thus, it calls on the one hand for a closer look at how independent churches are presented in this account. On the other, it calls for a consideration of how they relate to what Suico claims is their classical counterpart, with which they share features that allow for presuming "independent" and "classical" to be one single entity distinct from others. Thirdly, it calls for a consideration of the function they have in his study.

Co-opting Jesus Is Lord

Suico's description of JIL is the account of a church that is decidedly political and that shows a remarkable social engagement. Along several other activities, Suico mentions extensive social programs, schools, and political rallies (including People Power) organized by Eddie Villanueva, the founder of JIL. This is a strong contradiction to the opening statement in which Pentecostals' sociopolitical involvement was only at the microlevel and which was presented as the rationale for the study as such. Suico takes no efforts to explain how this exception relates to the rule,[24] but implies that the social and political activities of JIL are rooted in the Spirit experience elaborated in the first chapter, thus inferring that all other churches who subscribe to this specific experience share the same social and political attitude, provided that they obtain proper knowledge of their experience and are given a theology to live according to this knowledge. Accordingly he goes on elaborating on the history of the other churches that are all relocated in the history of the AG. Its exceptional character notwithstanding, the JIL's story is presented as an organic part of the AG history, while *mutatis mutandis* JIL's characteristics become the characteristics of AG, or rather the lens in which certain characteristics seen at the microlevel ought to be interpreted.

From Scuio's account of JIL it is evident that the immediate context of the common perception mentioned in the opening sections (that Pentecostals are fundamentalists and indifferent to social change), which is hitherto the only content-filled definition of Pentecostalism available, is not and cannot be JIL. This raises the question of why JIL was chosen as an example for what Suico calls "independent churches." It suggests that rather than JIL (and perhaps the independent churches), from among the churches mentioned in Suico's historical account the AG is the first and foremost addressee of said allegation, which the whole study offers to be apology, correction, and manifesto of. Yet Suico makes remarkable efforts to widen this notion of Pentecostalism. According to Suico's introduction, "Pentecostal" is used by detractors of Pentecostalism with reference to churches like the AG, rather than JIL. Yet in the historical chapter, Suico construes his account in order to make JIL tacitly become bearer of the same name as does the AG, namely "Pentecostal." As a result, JIL becomes also bearer of the connotation attached to said name, and most important, the addressee of the allegation attached to it. Thus, JIL is made equivalent to AG both on an abstract level and with regard to the name "Pentecostal." It is also made equivalent with regard to the definitory outside, namely the concrete detractors who accuse the AG of high treason. AG's antagonist becomes JIL's antagonist, which merges AG and JIL into a single identity against a common enemy.

Albeit Suico emphasizes a few elements of discontinuity and difference between independent and classical, he claims that the similarities and equivalences would outweigh the differences. Yet, what would these similarities be, given the case that the only available definition for Pentecostal endorsed by Suico is the antagonism between AG and its detractors on the issue of sociopolitical indifference? In sum, Suico's equivalence postulated between AG, representing the classical churches, and JIL, representing the independent churches, appears to have no other base than the wish to create a united front. It is a co-option that seeks to construct what it names and claims.

Co-option and hegemony

As shown in the previous section, the rationale for Suico's study is the allegation perpetuated by detractors of AG (and other churches), namely that the AG would be indifferent to what might bring holistic and sustainable social change to the crises-ridden Republic of the Philippines. From this point of view, the whole study could have been written without mentioning JIL, or at least without mentioning it at such a prominent place. Yet the fact that JIL is there and that it is given such significance begs the question, for a yet closer look at what the place of JIL in Suico's narrative and agenda is. What function does JIL have in the narrative with which Suico promotes his project of transformational development for the Philippines?

First and most perspicuously, it serves as an apology. If the case study was insufficient, JIL would certainly prove to potential detractors of the AG that there is no necessary relationship between Pentecostalism and fundamentalism. In other words, it demonstrates that being Pentecostal does not necessarily equal refraining from political engagement as understood by Suico and his dialogue partners.[25] Suico's interest, therefore, is not whether JIL understands itself as Pentecostal or feels the need for a theology of transformation based on an experience claimed to be Pentecostal, but to bail out his own denomination, the AG, whose public image he seems to be trying to change.

Secondly, JIL's superfluous inclusion in the category of Pentecostalism, as far as the explicit argument of the study is concerned, serves to make the problem that actually only concerns Suico and the AG a problem of a larger body of churches and thus serves to unite them under the hegemony of Suico's own theology and sociopolitical agenda. With regard to his theological agenda, Suico does not conceal that he claims to speak for Philippine Pentecostalism in general and that he hopes for as many churches as possible to subscribe to his theological insights. His theology of transformation, which he claims represents a middle position, however, is not only an attempt to reorganize the AG's standing in what in the Philippine context is still strongly dominated by the divide between fundamentalist (read: anti-patriotic, paternalist, conservative) and liberal (read: ecumenical, progressive, etc.) Protestants. It is also a move to reorganize the divide along the notion of "holistic mission" and therefore convince "fundamentalists" within his own camp, who shy away from everything that is labeled liberal and ecumenical, that accepting his theology of transformation is not a contradiction to their Pentecostalness. Less obvious, it is also the subtle attempt to mainstream the experience of the Holy Spirit by naming it and locating it within a wider, although not all too dogmatic, AG doctrinal framework. This is evidenced by the emphasis on Spirit baptism and on Spirit baptism in connection with tongues as initial evidence (19), which is read into the "Declaration of Faith (Jesus Is Lord Church)" attached as an appendix (226–227).

With regard to his sociopolitical agenda, it is not clear what its content is. What is clear, however, is that his sociopolitical agenda needs clout in order to be carried out, which Suico admits himself (208). Thus, the need to name a problem (read: the common detractor and enemy), to stage this problem to be that of many, and proffering oneself as solution, along with one's own history claimed to be the history of many.

This agenda is also present in his (re-)organization of the history of Philippine Pentecostalism. A reorganization that conceals the fact that in 1983 Villanueva founded the Philippines for Jesus Movement (PJM) because of stark disagreements with Pentecostal churches, such as the AG or the Church of the Foursquare Gospel, on several topics both doctrinal and organizational, but also regarding sociopolitical matters. From PJM's perspective, these Pentecostal churches were closer to conservative evangelicals (which Suico would not count as Pentecostal),[26] with whom the Assemblies of God had established the Philippine Council of Fundamental Churches in 1964. Against what according to Villanueva was institutionalized denominationalism and outdated Pentecostalism, with inherently paternalist structures stemming from a failed emancipation from US missionaries, PJM was conceived as a network of independent churches that were doctrinally flexible enough to even include the Oneness United Pentecostal Church, regarded as a sect by the classical Pentecostals. Furthermore, PJM formulated its *reason d'*être explicitly as a mission to raise an awareness about social, economic, and political issues.[27] By choosing JIL as the first example of Philippine Pentecostalism in his historical contextualization, Suico makes this "progressiveness" appear in continuity to the AG.

Thus, the Pentecostalism from which Suico claims to draw his empirical data and which he claims to speak for is no more than a name attached to the AG (and presumably other "classical churches"). He then tries to baptize the "independent churches" into his definition of Pentecostalism, in order to give them a collective self-consciousness and to empower them to become subject to *one*—his own—theological and sociopolitical agenda. Rather than simply being an empirical object of research, as Suico claims, "Pentecostalism" as a category should be considered the result of Suico's specific reading and reorganization of the history of Philippine Pentecostalism. Pentecostalism as Suico uses this name is therefore something his work attempts to create by naming and claiming different churches to be Pentecostal as the AG is Pentecostal.

NAMING THE IMPOSSIBLE OBJECT AND THE MAKING OF A PENTECOSTAL PEOPLE

It is difficult to state whether Suico's endeavor to prove to the presumed detractors of the AG and other churches that Pentecostals should not be regarded as betrayers of the Philippine nation vis-à-vis the crises has been successful or not. The fact that most AG believers up until today reject the name "Pentecostal," hints to the contrary.

As far as his aim to give the various churches that according to him share a common spirituality a name that enables them to become a movement in and for itself, united against allegedly common detractors, empowered by a theological agenda based on his understanding of the Holy Spirit experience, and assembled around a sociopolitical agenda envisioned in his study, is concerned, it was partially successful. Albeit it is difficult to assess how far this project has been promoted outside academia, it is difficult to imagine that Suico, himself active in the teaching ministry and well connected with other church leaders, would not have tried to propagate it further. Field research indicates a wide reception of phrases and buzz-words clustered around the term "transformation," although this does not seem to result in collaborative action. Rather it is used to accuse neighbors of being not transformational (not kingdom-minded, etc.), if for example the proposal for a common evangelistic campaign or social event is not accepted or "transfer members" from another church are welcomed. Still, it may be argued that studies like this may have contributed to reinforcing and popularizing the trend among churches associated with the PCEC, to theologize on society and politics.[28] In any case, the attempt to establish a relation between such an approach to understanding the role of the church vis-à-vis politics and society and the name "Pentecostal," found in the publications of the Asia Pacific Theological Seminary,[29] has failed. Rather than succeeding in redefining the name Pentecostalism, the contrary seems to be the case: Pentecostalism has become a derogatory term, it has morphed into a name hardly anybody wants to be identified with, not even ordinary AG pastors and members themselves.

Suico's study was submitted twelve months before the 2004 Philippine national elections, in which Villanueva ran for president. It is difficult to find out the precise when and how of his decision to run for presidential office. Yet there is strong evidence that in late 2001 there were concrete plans to form a "born-again bloc" in analogy to various already existing Catholic and mainline Protestant blocs in the Philippines, in order to enhance their influence in the coming Philippine government and the public. PCEC leaders as well as bishops of the member denominations (such as the AG, Foursquare, etc.) were divided in the question to what extent it would be appropriate to officially endorse a specific presidential candidate, not to speak of fielding their own candidate. PJM leaders, on the contrary, had created the Task Force for Change Movement (which included some PCEC people as well) and were pushing this topic.

Against this background Suico's work and his attempt to "construc[t] the [PC] 'people,'" or movement,[30] could be read as the theological rationale for the formation of a Pentecostal bloc uniting PJM and other independents and those PCEC members he calls classical and independent Pentecostals while recommending himself as the theologian of choice for such a movement.[31] The name Pentecostal, and *mutatis mutandis* his decided drawing on spirituality, experience, and theological literature termed as Pentecostal (as distinct from merely evangelical, albeit not opposed to it), indeed represents a free space, a niche within the Philippine religious landscape, which, contrary to Latin America, his theology could have filled with hardly any competing parties. When the Task Force for Change Movement agreed to field Villanueva as presidential candidate, the PCEC criticized this decision strongly, explaining its opposition with reference to the separation between church and state. Several leaders of classical denominations followed suit (Villanueva, personal interview, March 10, 2013). Others have suggested the PCEC had good relations with then president Gloria Macapagal-Arroyo (who eventually became president albeit being accused of fraud) and did not want to jeopardize this privileged position.[32] Yet, while a number of AG leaders supported Villanueva in 2004, attempts to create a united Pentecostal movement that would include independent churches by giving them a specifically Pentecostal theology were not successful. The differences (and hostilities) among the various churches and leaders were too strong

and the connotation attached to the name Pentecostal too negative in order to be able to unite various leaders. As far as JIL and
PJM were concerned, there was no need for a Pentecostal theology
of transformation, given that among the teaching arm of PJM, the
Intercessors for the Philippines, there had already been a certain
tradition of theologizing on church, society, and politics that was
partially received also by leaders of classical Pentecostals, given the
public influence of JIL, which Suico himself attests in drawing on
JIL as example.[33] To them, identifying with the name Pentecostal
would not have brought any advantages.

In 2001, as Suico correctly states, Villanueva was among those
who publicly called on Joseph Estrada to resign. The rallies, preceded by what the Catholic Church had called "a Jericho march,"
and the rallies known as EDSA II eventually brought Macapagal-
Arroyo to power. After Villanueva had lost against Macapagal-
Arroyo in an election overshadowed by notable election fraud, he
organized a protest rally to expose the corruption involved. Most
AG pastors who had supported him on the base of a holistic theology of transformation regarded this as "a rebellious act," while
differentiating this from a legitimate protest, such as the EDSA I
rallies. The PCEC leaders who were rewarded for their more or less
tacit loyalty to Macapagal-Arroyo raised serious criticism against
Villanueva too. Still others started to prepare the 2010 campaign.
During this campaign Villanueva forged an alliance with several
Muslim groups, among those Nur Misuari, founder of the Moro
National Liberation Front and old-time symbol of the armed
struggle for a Muslim Mindanao.[34] He also invited Eid Kabalu,
then speaker of the Moro Islamic Liberation Front (MILF), to
assist the signing of a covenant, in which he pledged to take the
concern of the Muslims and those of the Bangsamoro Islamic
Armed Forces. Along with other reasons, Kabalu's participation in

said meeting led to the latter's suspension as MILF spokesperson
(Kabalu, personal interview, May 24, 2013).[35] While some regarded
this as a compromise of faith, many others considered it "mere poli-
ticking" and smiled at it. Still others regarded this as a token of a
truly holistic mission and heralded a "moral revolution for peace
and righteousness," a slogan that could also be read on Villanueva's
campaign placards. Both on the national and local levels, transformation was a catchword for trying to mobilize voters throughout
campaigns in both periods, among Christians and Muslims alike,
yet no articulation or leader emerged as to make it a name that
might have been attractive enough so as to allow significant clout
to identify with. In interviews conducted by the researcher after the
election defeat of 2010, both Villanueva himself and Nur Misuari
seemed uneasy to talk about what brought them together in 2010.
According to Misuari, "We needed each other. That's all" (Misuari,
personal interview, May 5, 2013).

Coming back to the question of whether we are witnessing the
demise of Pentecostalism, the answer is: on the ground, Philippine
Pentecostalism as understood, redefined, named, and claimed by
Suico never did exist; it existed only in the minds of some members
of denominational intelligentsia and researchers as an (im-)possible
object.

CONCLUSION: A HISTORY OF THE NAME

As religious studies scholar Michael Bergunder has argued,[36] ever
since Walter Hollenweger's monumental work published in 1969
established Pentecostalism as an object of research, Pentecostal
studies have in large parts also been identity politics.[37] And even
before Hollenweger's publication, anthropological studies on *evan-
gelicós* in Latin America published by Emílio Willems and Christian
Lalive d'Epinay have made claims concerning the Latin American

sociopolitical status quo and the future of the countries in which the studies had been conducted respectively—based on the specter of a coherent movement.[38] The diversity of churches subsumed under the name Pentecostalism and the overdeterminatedness of the name have intimated the specter of a coherent movement and at least implicitly invited prognoses with respect to the "modernization and democratization" of Latin America, positive (Willems) or negative (d'Epinay).

On the ground, ordinary believers and leaders reject the name Pentecostal as well as PC. It has never shed its association with neo-colonial relations with the United States, resulting from the historical proximity of some churches with North American missionaries, nor did it shed the idea that people identified by that name are seductive of the poor and indifferent to social change. Another association the name Pentecostal was not able to shake off is the image of Pentecostals as uneducated lower class people praying "at the top of one's voice and shouting hysterically,"[39] hinted to by Suico in relation to the expansion of the AG among the "middle and upper class people of society" (74). Attempts to renew the face of Philippine Pentecostalism and the attempt to make it attractive for churches rejecting this name and co-opting them and their achievements under this name can so far not be considered successful. As far as Suico's own work is concerned, the redefinition of the name Pentecostal, as well as the attempt to create through such a redefinition a people willing to unify under the name Pentecostal and under the hegemonic theological and political agenda proposed by Suico, did not encounter positive feedback.[40]

What implications can be drawn from this (pseudo-)demise of Pentecostalism in the Philippines for researchers on Pentecostalism? First and foremost, it calls for a higher self-containment among scholars, and a more disciplined reflection on how PC is researched and defined. It calls for a critical assessment about which context it is supposed to speak about and what agendas are connected to it. (One might wish this to be taken as a suggestion to leaders of churches and to their intelligentsia, especially when it comes to statistics.) It challenges the researchers to consider the limits of the concept of a PC movement in the Philippines, especially when it comes to selecting empirical data and case studies. This is especially crucial, if the discussion aims at discussing sociopolitical themes and drawing conclusions for the Philippine society at large, given the alleged numerical strength and growth rate of the specter. Furthermore, it calls for an approach that conceptualizes PC in a way that is able to measure up to the instability and fluidity of the (group-)identities in question, which are most often those who do not fit into other classifications, good or bad as they were. While the fact that certain believers and groups do not fit into other classifications may give reason to consider them under one single name (e.g., Pentecostal), it would be a disservice to both, to the academy and to the participants of said groups, to treat them in a way that elides their heterogeneity, even more so if social and political claims are implied.

Bergunder has therefore proposed an approach that conceptualizes its research object along formal criteria. According to this approach, Pentecostal/Pentecostalism should be regarded as a mere name, whose history has to be reconstructed from within the context that is to be studied. In a nutshell, such a "history of the name"[41] would begin with asking when, where, how, and by whom the name Pentecostal (or PC) has been used and discussed as a phenomenon, empirical entity, research object, or even specter.[42] Such an approach would then continue to reflect on what data is used to discuss whatever the name PC is said to mean in a given context. From this point of view Pentecostal studies are critical investigations that deconstruct connections made by scholars, media, and participants, between people, events, articulations and actions, on the one hand, and evaluations and conclusions regarding the people, events, articulations, and actions in question, on the other. Therefore, along with discussing the agendas implied, such an approach brings to the fore alternative narratives and positions and opens a space for further discussion.

The present chapter has been a contribution to such a study of the history of the name "Pentecostal" in the specific context of the Philippines through a critique of Suico's work. As such, this chapter too is not free from the zeal to convert differences into equivalences at the cost of excluding subjects and co-opting them for the authors' own narrative. Therefore, it should be understood as an invitation to *relecture,* to critically assess what has been written here and to bring to the fore yet other alternative voices.[43]

Part IV: Oceania

Chapter 15

Joined Hands: Asian Influence on Australian Pentecostal Identity

Denise A. Austin

T HERE HAS BEEN much discussion recently in university and government circles about "Australia in the Asian Century."[1] Although the concept of "Asian" was originally an imagined product of imperialism, contemporary trends have allowed for a more "transnational consciousness."[2] Paralleling these debates has been academic scholarship describing Asian Pentecostalism as the new "first force"[3] and "southward face"[4] of global Christianity. Hence, Amos Yong distinguishes between classical "Pentecostal" and wider contemporary "Pentecostal" expression.[5] Yet the obvious link between "Australia in Asia" and Asian Pentecostalism has not yet been examined. I find this curious considering my own research, as well as my personal spiritual journey, which has included: being mentored by an elderly overseas Chinese intercessor, short- and long-term missions involvement in Asia, attending large multicultural churches, encouraging my children in cross-cultural school programs, working in a college with intentional Asian engagement, and finding inspiration from Charismatic, Asian-born preachers. So, using primary and secondary data gathered from a wide range of sources and reflecting on it in the light of my own spiritual journey, this essay argues that Asian influences have been vital in shaping the identity of Pentecostalism in Australia through raising cultural awareness, encouraging social engagement, nurturing academic appreciation, and inspiring an expansive global vision.

CULTURAL AWARENESS

Firstly, Australian Pentecostal identity has developed a sharpened cultural awareness through the medium of overseas missionaries to Asia. Pentecostalism appeared in Australia from as early as 1907[6]— just six years after the introduction of the Immigration Restriction Act (or "White Australia" policy).[7] Despite deep racial tensions, Pentecostal emphasis on racial unity,[8] mutual ritual performance,[9] and experiential spirituality[10] allowed for unprecedented missions opportunities. Mary Kum Sou (Wong Yen) Yeung (1888–1971) defied her triple marginalization as a female Chinese Pentecostal to become an outstanding missionary and preacher.[11] Although widowed three times and challenged with caring for her eight children, Mary spent more than forty years pioneering successful churches, schools, refugee shelters, kindergartens, and aged care homes in China and Hong Kong.[12] During her sporadic intervals living in Australia, she preached in urban and rural centers across Australia and New Zealand in various denominations, including Assemblies of God in Australia (AGA), Foursquare Full Gospel Church, Apostolic Church, and Churches of Christ Chinese Mission.[13] In 1973, two years after Mary's death, the "White Australia" policy was officially abolished.[14] Although Mary was likely the first Australian of Asian heritage to "go out in the power of the Spirit," there have been many others who have brought mutual benefit and increased cultural awareness between Asian and Australian Pentecostalism.

Post-World War II racism was entrenched in Australia, but overseas missionary reports continued to bring greater cultural sensitivity to Pentecostal congregations. Much of the media representation equated "Asia" with non-Christian, as seen in a 1950 *The Bulletin* article that insisted: "[w]e are a European people....Our religious faith and our national philosophy, and our whole way of life are alien to Asia."[15] Similarly, B. A. Santamaria, leader of the National Civic Council, warned: "...too many people confuse our duty to behave as Christians towards Asians with a belief that all civilizations are in reality equal."[16] In 1960, amid this volatile context, Marie Smith (1915–1971) chose to return to her childhood home of Japan to continue the missionary work of her parents.[17] Japanese Pentecostal groups were flourishing,[18] and Marie became a prominent preacher throughout the nation.[19] She was also a frequent contributor to the AGA magazine, *Australian Evangel*, describing at one point: "There was a real Pentecostal fervor throughout the meetings. One thrilled at the sight of 800 Christians gathered on Sunday morning."[20] Again she wrote: "...the rice is in its early ripening stage—ready to harvest. Japan, too, is ripe for the sickle. Whose shall it be—that of the Gospel or Communism?"[21] Such reports kept the hearts of her readers attuned to the needs of their fallen foe. Interestingly, attitudes in the broader Australian community also began to change, with migration policies easing in 1966.[22] When Smith died unexpectedly in Japan, in 1971, over two hundred people attended her funeral, including leading representatives of the Assemblies of God in the United States and the Assemblies of God in Japan.[23] As the first AGA missionary to Japan, Smith's devotion to its people and her inspiring example of cultural empathy to the congregations at home contributed toward the cultural awareness of Australian Pentecostal identity. Since then, many other missionary reports have similarly enlightened Australian congregations.

SOCIAL ENGAGEMENT

Asian migrant communities have also increased a passion for social engagement in Australian Pentecostal congregations. The number of Asian-born residents in Australia has doubled in the past decade to over two million (or 6 percent of the population),[24] with well over 300,000 Australian-born youth with Asian migrant parents.[25] The volatile political environment during that time, such as the "Hansonism" phenomenon, has urged greater civic participation by Asian migrants.[26] Kwai Hang Ng suggests recent immigrants use Christianity as a social mechanism to imbibe their new ethnic identification.[27] Churches often function as "second families" helping migrants to cope with the new environment.[28] A leading example of the impact of Pentecostal migrant work is International City Church (ICC) in Fortitude Valley, Brisbane. In 1983 it was pioneered by Malaysian-born restaurant owners David and Jeannie Mok.[29] ICC eventually grew to around eight hundred people, encompassing over sixty nationalities. The church operates a Multicultural Community Centre to assist new migrants and refugees, as well as Asian Pacific Institute, which comprises the International Christian College and a Cross-Cultural Training Centre.[30] Services include language, cooking and craft classes, assistance with accommodation and employment, private counseling, and advocacy in cases of discrimination or legal issues. In June 2013 Jeannie Mok was awarded the Order of Australia Medal by the Governor General of Australia as part of the Queen's Birthday list of honors in recognition of her work among multicultural communities in Queensland and beyond.[31] Clearly the social engagement aspect of Pentecostal identity in Australia has been shaped by such prominent Asian migrant congregations and is modeled in many other multicultural and ethnic churches around the nation.

The missional social engagement ethos of Australian

Pentecostal identity has also been nurtured through the example of Asian Pentecostal business people.[32] Peter L. Berger argues that Pentecostalism "as a vehicle of cultural globalization" actually facilitates economic participation.[33] The growing phenomenon of Pentecostal/Charismatic teaching on the relationship between Christianity and business are empowering Asian business people to have a significant impact in Australia.[34] Just a few examples provide a snapshot of a phenomenon that has been multiplied many times over around Australia. In 1984 a Hong Kong couple established First Fruits Company in Brisbane "as a reminder to put God first in everything."[35] They later expanded work into a large property development company, commenting: "...the Lord does not just bless us so we can live a better life but to give to build His kingdom. So that's why I am always reminded of that. Look, the Lord has blessed us, we have to bless the others. That's the way we should live."[36] Another couple originally from Hong Kong have run restaurants, photography shops, property development companies, and teacher training colleges in Australia.[37] They state: "...We never say we are too busy in business to do church work. And we never say we are too busy in church work to do business."[38] Following this model, they pioneered the Pentecostal Brisbane Christian Cantonese Church at Kedron, as well as Gospel Advancement Centre, which is an outreach to Chinese non-Christians. Similarly, one Guangzhou-born Pentecostal woman views her family business as an opportunity to "glorify God," printing "Jesus is Lord" on their business letterheads and business cards.[39] She employs non-Christians as a form of outreach, and many employees, as well as customers, have become involved in church life. Through these examples it can be seen that Chinese business people are shaping Australian Pentecostal identity by actively engaging in their local communities through their business ventures.

ACADEMIC APPRECIATION

Another fascinating by-product of Asian Pentecostal influence has been a growing appreciation for a broader academic education. Historically, anti-intellectualism dominated Pentecostal teaching, warning parishioners that education would cause them to "lose the fire" or "dry up."[40] Originally Pentecostal education focused on ministerial training but later expanded to include schools and universities.[41] Still, Pentecostal pedagogy was focused on experiential practice.[42] In Australia, Pentecostal/Charismatic schools initially sought to isolate their students from the "worldly" effects of state school education and "shelter" Christian children from society.[43] However, a more expanded worldview can be seen in Ron Woolley, principal of Citipointe Christian College (formerly Christian Outreach College Brisbane—COCB), established in 1977.[44] That same year Woolley received a life-defining prophetic prayer from Yonggi Cho's mother-in-law, Choi Ja-Shil, during her tour of regional New South Wales. So Woolley later decided to visit their Yoido Full Gospel Church in Seoul, South Korea.[45] Interestingly, 1977 was also the year that Yonggi Cho was guest speaker at the AGA national conference where a shock leadership swing saw the movement fully embrace the interdenominational Charismatic renewal.[46] In 1983 Woolley became principal of COCB, and after a deep spiritual experience in Korea, he determined to impart to his students an international perspective. His thinking was similar to John Ingelson's findings that if Australia wanted to participate in and benefit from the emerging Asia region, deeper cultural understanding was needed.[47] Woolley embraced this mandate through various means: becoming a founding member of Asia Pacific Federation of Christian Schools (APFCS); forming sister-school relationships with Christian schools in South Korea, Japan, and Indonesia; establishing Christian Outreach International College

(COIC) for international students; and developing the International Student Outreach Program for COCB students to experience a cultural exchange.[48] This enlarged worldview saw remarkable results. By 1996 COCB had grown to be one of the largest schools in Queensland and the largest single campus Christian school in Australia.[49] In the *1999 College Annual* Woolley wrote: "We must encourage our students to think in global terms. It is likely that in the future, working overseas will become as common as working interstate is today."[50] He maintains: "It is important that our students be exposed to other cultures and to overseas students....Without such exposure, our students will not realize the global nature of the 21st century world."[51] Now, just as in many other Christian schools around the country, rather than isolating students from the world, the goal is to provide a holistic academic education—including an embrace of Asia.

There is also clear evidence that Asian Pentecostalism has penetrated into higher education in Australia. Anthony Milner, dean of Asian Studies at the Australian National University, argues that the long-standing relationships between Australian and Asian scholars offer them "the opportunity to become intellectual brokers."[52] Similarly, Melbourne University's Asia Institute reports: "We have become so integrated with the Asia region...in economics; in education links, we are very much tied to the region in our strategic interests."[53] Once again this is evidenced by strategic Korean influences. In 1996 the AGA national training center, Southern Cross College (SCC—later renamed Alphacrucis College), established a Korean campus.[54] It was led by former businessman and pastor David Kwon, who had a burden to train Pentecostal workers to reach the fifty thousand Koreans in Sydney. No doubt he also saw the market advantage of Australia as a center for education, with Asian students numbering nearly one hundred thousand or almost two-thirds of all overseas students.[55] So, Kwon contacted his friend and SCC president David Cartledge, who had served on the international reference board for Yonggi Cho's Church Growth Institute since 1978.[56] Within two years Kwon had established a quarterly four-day Korean pastors training seminar, attracting up to five hundred pastors from across Australia.[57] Eventually the SCC Korean campus became the first in Australia to offer fully accredited certificate IV, diploma, and advanced diploma in ministry delivered totally in the Korean language.[58] This ultimately developed into accredited bachelor's and master's degrees. Indeed, the development of a bachelor of applied theology (Korean) by Alphacrucis College saw the first fully integrated, extensively argued theology "mirror" program anywhere in the sector.[59] Comparing it to many other similar institutes, Korean program director Yang Yong Sun noted: "The difference is Alphacrucis has a very strong Pentecostal life and spirit."[60] Through the influence of such leading Korean Australian academics, Australian Pentecostalism had developed a broader identity base that allowed for excellence in Languages Other Than English (LOTE) higher education.

GLOBAL VISION

Australian Pentecostal identity has also been fashioned through the expansive vision of Charismatic Asian leaders. Wolfgang Vondey believes Pentecostalism is in a "process" of going beyond its cultural heritage and morphing into a new global culture.[61] Brian Howell adds that both the "global" and "local" interconnectivity of Pentecostal communities creates links that define identity.[62] This is evidenced through American-based Asian preachers, such as Sue and Ché Ahn, founders of Harvest International Ministry—a network of over twenty thousand churches, ministries, and organizations in around fifty nations.[63] Similarly, Sam Chand's mission "to help pastors succeed" was outworked at the Australian Christian Churches national conference in May 2013.[64] However, Barbara Watson Andaya goes further by revealing that Pentecostalism is actually proving to strengthen wider connections and break down nationalistic divisiveness.[65] She writes:

> The similarity of these church environments and the affluent hubs of Seoul and Singapore have enabled new circuits of charismatic preaching that both affirm the regionality of Asian Christianity while simultaneously locating Pentecostalism firmly within the worldwide movement.[66]

The dominance of Singaporean Pentecostalism[67] and its influence in Australia can be seen in the example of Joseph Prince, pastor of the thirty-thousand-member New Creation Church.[68] At the 2012 Hillsong Conference in Sydney, Prince told the twenty-one-thousand-strong audience: "It is one thing for us to assemble. It is another thing for us to be gathered....I have a strong sense that this Hillsong conference is a prophet conference....Only eternity will tell how many lives are impacted because of this conference."[69] Clearly, his message resonated with those gathered, as he was invited back for the 2015 Hillsong Conference. Advertising for merchandise from Adelaide's prominent Influencers Conference promised:

> Want to grow in your personal revelation of God's grace and undeserved favor? Be an effective influencer for Christ? Then let Joseph Prince establish you on the rock-solid foundation of Christ on which to build your life and ministry...you will be empowered to profoundly impact your family, your ministry and your nation for His glory![70]

Prince is also host of *Destined to Reign* television program, which airs on the Australian Christian Channel twice a day Mondays

to Fridays, as well prime time on Sundays.[71] This supports the
argument of Pradip N. Thomas and Philip Lee that televangelism provides a global platform for religious identity formation.[72]
Charismatic Asian preachers such as Joseph Prince are infusing
Australian Pentecostal identity with an international perspective.

Finally, Asian leaders are showing Australian Pentecostals that
persecution can foster global unity. As Wonsuk Ma and Julia
C. Ma reveal, Asian Pentecostalism brings a vital contribution
because it has flourished in many places that are openly hostile to
Christianity.[73] In 2011, noted "Brother Yun" of the underground
house church movement in China conducted a tour of Australia.[74] In
a fascinating show of multicultural unity, his preaching in Bethany
Sydney Church (Geregja Bethany Indonesia) at the Powerhouse
Museum was translated from Chinese, into English, and then into
Indonesian. He stated:

> God has sent us as messengers for this morning—let's
> join hands for this catch of fishes which are coming to the
> kingdom of God.... There is no need to fight in the boat any-
> more about who is right and who is wrong. Let's join hands
> for the greatest harvest of the history of the church![75]

The importance of "joining hands" was also highlighted by two
converted Indonesian imams, who held strategic Pentecostal meetings throughout Australia encouraging interreligious sensitivity
when ministering to Islamic people.[76] Another preacher who has
endured opposition, including the bombing of his church in Kuala
Lumpur, is Ong Sek Leang.[77] As chairman of the 23rd Pentecostal
World Conference held in Kuala Lumpur in August 2013, he wrote:
"I believe the theme for this conference, 'In One Accord...rallying,
reaching, and releasing the next generation' is a prophetic call of
our Lord Jesus Christ to inspire, equip, and connect everyone, of
every age group for a strategic thrust to build His church."[78] With

scores of Australian delegates attending this conference, such connections were certainly strengthened. Key Asian leaders who have experienced oppression because of their faith provide another vital element in shaping global Pentecostal perspectives in Australia.

CONCLUSION

This chapter has explored a range of ways in which Asian Pentecostalism has been instrumental in the formation of Australian Pentecostal identity. From as early as the 1920s outstanding missionaries, such as Mary Yeung, were promulgating culturally sensitive compassion for the peoples of China. Experienced AGA missionary Marie Smith also challenged Australian assemblies to put aside the hurts of war and pray for revival in Japan. With the abolition of the White Australia policy, Asian immigrant churches, such as International City Church, became hotbeds for social engagement and care for the disenfranchised. The long-standing Korean influence in Australia has also been evident in increasing cross-cultural academic appreciation in both youth and adult education. With global communications expanding exponentially in the twenty-first-century jet age, Charismatic Asian preachers are also bringing an expanded global vision through multimedia megachurch conferences and stories from the persecuted church. These varied forms of interaction open up not only fresh research directions regarding "Australia in the Asian Church Century" but also a greater hunger to be empowered in the Holy Spirit as the church of the global century.

Chapter 16

Australian Pentecostalism: Origins, Developments, and Trends

Shane Clifton

T HE STORY OF Australian Pentecostalism is illustrative of the religious transitions and trends that have constituted the movement as a globalized spirituality. Australia is not merely a recipient of North American religion but, rather, uniquely indigenizes global trends and contributes to their development and propagation. This chapter describes the emergence of the Pentecostal movement in Australia, paying particular attention to the ways in which it has changed over time. Since the story is really too big to tell (and I apologize upfront for the myriad of important things I have ignored), it can only provide a series of vignettes that represent key moments and transitions. It also highlights points of ambiguity, intending to stimulate dialogue about the opportunities and the challenges facing the movement as it makes its way into its second century of ministry.

EARLY REVIVALS

The first Australian Pentecostal (that we know of) was Sarah Jane Lancaster. Born in 1858, Lancaster was a Methodist lay preacher who developed an interest in "divine healing" that she learned from a Seventh-day Adventist pastor. In 1906 she received a pamphlet from England entitled "Back to Pentecost," which encouraged her to seek after the baptism in the Spirit. In 1908 she was baptized in the Spirit with the evidence of tongues, and on New Year's Eve 1909 she led a prayer meeting at Good News Hall in Richmond, Melbourne, that went on into the New Year and beyond. According to her published testimony, "for six weeks such a glorious revival continued night and day, that we never entered our home again."[1] In fact, the upstairs section of the hall was converted into a home that the Lancasters would live in for the remainder of their lives. From that base she established a local church (later named Apostolic Faith Mission [AFM]) and promoted Pentecostal spirituality throughout the nation. Her founding impact on Australian Pentecostalism is lovingly summed up by Barry Chant:

> Wherever we look in the first twenty years of Australian Pentecostal history, the imprint of Sarah Jane (Jeannie) Lancaster (1858–1934) can be found.... From Perth to Cairns, she was involved in evangelism, church planting, preaching and prayer. She proclaimed the Word on street corners. She handed out tracts. She talked with strangers. She conducted meetings in halls and houses. She communicated with people of all ages. She edited a magazine. She published thousands of tracts. She engaged in welfare work with the poor. She prayed for the sick. She encouraged people to be filled with the Spirit. She eschewed the things of the world for the things of God. Perhaps most significant of all, she was a woman of integrity, prizing love, sacrifice, unity and honesty above all else. Australian Pentecostalism is her enduring legacy.[2]

Lancaster grounded her preaching on the fourfold gospel (Jesus saves, heals, baptizes in Spirit, and is coming again), with a particular emphasis on healing (and the typical suspicion of medicine).[3] Like Pentecostalism globally, she had a restorationist outlook that prioritized the Scriptures and rejected tradition and creed. Importantly, her role as the spiritual mother[4] of Australian Pentecostalism informed the underlying values of the movement, and continues to act as a prophetic symbol, a reminder of the radical and transforming power of the Spirit. It is not without significance that Australian Pentecostalism was founded by a woman, a mother of seven and a grandmother. While she was the (informal) leader of the loose-knit movement, "over half the Pentecostal congregations functioning by 1930 were established and led by women."[5] This was testimony to the radical impact of Pentecostal revival and the challenge it posed to traditional attitudes, values, and hierarchies. During the 1920s her role as leader of the church came under fire from those who advocated male leadership. Lancaster's reply, published in her *Good News* magazine, is evidence of the potency of her first-wave feminism:

> For the Holy Spirit makes the bodies of women His temple, as well as those of men; He speaks and acts through either sex at His own sweet will, declaring that "As many as have been baptized into Christ...have put on Christ...there is, therefore, neither male or female, for ye are all ONE in Christ Jesus (Gal. 3:26, 27)." The capitals are ours, to emphasise a truth which man, proud man, will rarely entertain, for just as Jewish Christians in the days of Paul found it hard to believe the glorious Fact that the Christ of God had torn down the middle wall of partition between the Gentiles and themselves...so to-day the pride of man forbids his acceptance of the grace of God toward those women upon whom He has poured His Spirit, thus making men and women one in Christ.[6]

Lancaster's challenge to gender hierarchies was accompanied by a similar desire to overcome divisions in the church. Indeed, she understood baptism in the Spirit as tearing down the boundary markers of denomination and creed, and she advocated a unity of love in the Spirit that was able to accommodate doctrinal differences. As she observed, "unity can only be achieved by meeting together and enjoying liberty in the Spirit."[7] This ecumenical impulse was to be sorely tested, particularly since Lancaster rejected the doctrine of the Trinity. In fact, she held a (unique) twofold distinction in God; conflating the Father and the Spirit, and distinguishing the person of the Son. She also held an annihilationalist eschatology that was learned from Seventh-Day Adventist friends. For Lancaster, the difference between her theology and that of her Pentecostal sisters and brothers—most of whom accepted orthodox doctrine—was incidental, subsumed by the love of Jesus and unity in the Spirit.[8]

DENOMINATIONAL FORMATION

The ideal of spiritual unity led Lancaster to declare that "the APOSTOLIC FAITH MISSION is NOT another CHURCH [sic],"[9] sensing that the label "church" was divisive. Preferring to speak of "the body as an organism, not an organization,"[10] for most of its life the AFM assembly had little in the way of formal structures. There was no written constitution, no ordination, and no one given the label pastor; Lancaster was "Mother," and everyone else "Brother" and "Sister." As the number of Pentecostal assemblies in the country grew, however, it became apparent that some level of organization was needed to provide leadership and to facilitate and organize shared missionary work. In 1927 fifteen churches and about eighty delegates met together in Melbourne and formed the Apostolic Faith Mission of Australia. As a concession to conservatives, the first president was New Zealander John Adams, with Lancaster appointed vice president (all the other members of the council were men).

The AFM fellowship did not last long. There were various issues, not least concerns about Lancaster's doctrinal position, which had been brewing since an earlier visit by Aimee Semple McPherson, who had been invited to Australia by Lancaster but then refused to share the stage with a "heretic."[11] By 1929 a large number of assemblies had withdrawn, including all the churches from Queensland, who reformed under the banner the Assemblies of God Queensland (AGQ). The newly appointed president, George Burns, gave the opening address, ironically entitled "The Need for Unity and Love." He went on to observe:

> That unity amongst God's saints is desirable and right goes without saying, but let it always be remembered that the "unity" the Lord Jesus prayed for was a "unity in truth." Unity may be obtained at too high a cost.[12]

Unity was to continue to prove a challenge. In 1930 the guest speaker at the AGQ conference was the evangelist William Booth-Clibborn (grandson of the founders of The Salvation Army). Following the conference and with the support of the local churches, Booth-Clibborn conducted an evangelistic campaign in Brisbane that soon gathered large crowds. His ministry was advertised as involving "master music, modern methods, and matchless methods"[13] (a description that might just as easily be given to Hillsong almost a century later). Soon after, Booth-Clibborn purchased a building and established a church, Glad Tidings Tabernacle (today pastored by Wayne Alcorn, the national president of the AOG/ACC), and did so independently of the AGQ—although reunification occurred a decade later.

Meanwhile, in Melbourne American evangelist A. C. Valdez had come to hold revival meetings with Lancaster, but, like Semple McPherson, heard about her "heresy" and so moved to a hall in the neighboring suburb of Sunshine. The ensuing "Sunshine Revival" led to the founding of The Pentecostal Church in Australia (PCA), organized according to what Valdez declared was "the truth of church government"—essentially the typical free-church democracy of the Assemblies of God (AOG) and Foursquare Pentecostal movements in America (itself borrowed from Methodism).[14] The PCA preached the fourfold gospel, with an emphasis on the experience of the Spirit. So noisy were its "tarrying" prayer meetings that the church built a brick soundproof room to minimize the complaints of neighbors.[15] The PCA went on to plant churches throughout Victoria and in Sydney and published the *Australian Evangel*, a monthly magazine that carried transcripts of sermons, reports from missionaries and churches, and testimonies.

In 1930 the Apostolic Church (originally founded in Great Britain and tracing its origins to the Welsh revival) established a congregation in Perth, and in the years that followed planted churches in most Australian capital cities and various country towns.[16] In 1934 an Apostolic Assembly opened in the neighborhood of the PCA, and many of its key members left to join the new church.[17] From the outside it would have been hard to distinguish the ministry of the two churches, with their common doctrine and emphasis on the power of Jesus to heal and baptize in the Spirit. The distinction, however, was to be found in its conception of leadership and authority, with the apostolic emphasis on the fivefold office of the apostle, prophet, evangelist, pastor, and teacher. The PCA was particular concerned about the governmental authority of the church apostle, as well as the authority granted the spiritual guidance given by recognized prophets, and in the years that followed the antagonism between these churches mediated against any attempted reconciliation. Whether the issue was really governance and spiritual practices (in fact, the churches had much more in common than in distinction) or the more practical problem of competition—the two brands of Pentecostalism competing in the same marketplace—is moot.

This is not to suggest that the ecumenical and unifying impulse of early Pentecostalism was entirely undone. In 1937 the AGQ and the PCA in Sydney and Melbourne came together to form the Assemblies of God in Australia (AGA), "a fellowship of Pentecostal Assemblies in voluntary co-operation, on terms of equality, as self-contained and self-governed Christian Assemblies, uniting for aggressive evangelism, unity, fellowship, order, discipline, and other purposes."[18] It was a grassroots fellowship organized from the bottom up; Spirit-filled congregations were responsible for selecting pastors and elders at the local level, and local churches retained their autonomy and elected the leadership of the fellowship. Of particular importance for the fellowship as a whole were two related endeavors; ministry training and missions, at home and abroad. The former saw the establishment of Commonwealth Bible College (later to become Southern Cross College and then Alphacrucis College), which had the responsibility of training pastors and missionaries. The story of the college is outside the scope of this essay (see Denise Austin *Our College*[19]), as is the fellowship's missionary activity. By way of example, the AGA focused much of its missionary work on Papua New Guinea, founding a fellowship of churches that, by the turn of the twentieth century, had planted over nine hundred assemblies reaching hundreds of indigenous tribal groups.[20]

I have described the formation and establishment of the AGA in *Pentecostal Churches in Transition*.[21] In the four decades that followed, the fellowship grew from a national constituency of 1,482 people in 38 churches (1937) to 9,446 people in 152 churches (1977). The AGA was not the only Pentecostal denomination in the nation. The Apostolic Church (mentioned above) had about 35 assemblies by 1983.[22] The International Church of the Foursquare Gospel, founded in 1931 as a church split from Lancaster's AFM, had about 40 assemblies by 1984.[23] In 1945 debates within the AGA about British Israel teaching saw the establishment of the breakaway Christian Revival Crusade,[24] a movement that was to experience some revival in the '60s and '70s (having dispensed with British Israelism), so that by 1984 it could boast a constituency of approximately 19,000 people.[25] (Author's note: Obtaining comparative data for Pentecostal denominations prior to the Charismatic renewal has proven difficult, hence the statistics above are not directly correlated by date but provide indicative information.) It is not possible to tell the story of all of these fellowships in this essay, and for that purpose I would highly recommend Barry Chant's *Heart of Fire*.

CHURCH GROWTH

Notwithstanding the many advancements of Australian Pentecostalism in the early and middle decades of the twentieth century, by the 1970s Pentecostal churches constituted a tiny proportion of the Australian Christian landscape. This was to change dramatically in the late 1970s, with the Charismatic renewal providing the impetus for change.

In the AGA there was initial resistance to the movement. The tension between the elder and more conservative office bearers (including the general superintendent Ralph Reed) and the younger pastors that had embraced Charismatic ministry (such as David Cartledge and Andrew Evans) resulted in the convening of a special conference of the general presbytery in 1972, called to address the issues of "dancing, deliverance, and prostration" and ban Charismatic ministers from speaking in AGA churches. Reed and the executives had theological concerns about the Charismatic focus on the demonic, as well as the consequent deliverance ministry, arguing that Christians could not be demon possessed. In retrospect, a debate about the terms "possession" and "influence" seems finicky, but the issue was really about matters of worship practice and concerns about the supposed excesses of Charismatic prophecy and Charismatic spirituality. Dancing, for example, was seen as indecorous, although such a conclusion had perhaps forgotten that the prayer meetings of first-generation Pentecostals had disturbed neighbors and required the construction of soundproof rooms. Be that as it may, the issue was not resolved at the 1972 presbytery, with a split vote indicative of the prevailing tension.[26]

In the years that followed, those churches that embraced the Charismatic movement experienced substantial growth. Cartledge, for example, pastored a congregation in the country town of Townsville that grew to more than a thousand members, while in Adelaide, Andrew Evans experienced similar "revival."[27] Reg Klimionok grew Garden City Church in Brisbane to a congregation also heading toward one-thousand-strong membership. By the time of the 1977 national conference the fruits of the Charismatic renewal—especially in terms of church growth—were obvious, and there was impetus for change. Yonggi Cho was invited to be guest speaker, and his modeling of Charismatic-style prophecy and obvious embrace of the ministry of the Charismatic pastors became a further endorsement.[28] When the movement voted for its leadership, Ralph Reed was replaced by Andrew Evans as the general superintendent, and David Cartledge and Reg Klimionok were elected to the executive council. This leadership change marked a point of transition in the AGA approach to leadership and church ministry, which was to facilitate rapid growth and dramatic ecclesiological change. The extent of this transition is mapped out in the charts and graphs that follow:

FIGURE 1: AGA/ACC GROWTH[29]

	Constituents	Churches	Average Size	Annual Growth
1977	9,446	152	62	0 percent
1979	10,854	171	63	7 percent
1981	23,857	235	102	60 percent
1983	37,500	325	115	29 percent
1985	51,655	392	132	19 percent
1987	71,335	517	138	19 percent
1989	81,440	549	148	7 percent
1991	88,560	621	143	4 percent
1993	97,654	676	144	5 percent
1995	108,247	762	142	5 percent
1997	115,912	826	140	4 percent
1999	131,426	822	160	7 percent
2001	155,247	859	181	9 percent
2003	160,399	1,000	160	2 percent
2005	186,488	1,062	176	8 percent
2007	214,195	1,118	192	7 percent
2009	225,403	1,092	206	3 percent
2011	236,610	1,066	222	2 percent
2012	255,547	1,061	241	8 percent

FIGURE 2: AGA/ACC ATTENDANCE CHART

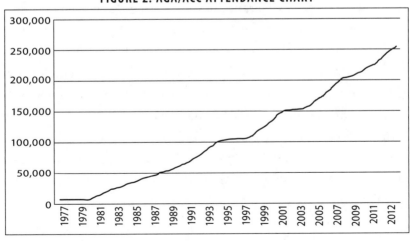

The growth of the AGA is made even more remarkable when considered in the light of the decline of religious attendance in Australia during the same period: in 1977, 29 percent of Australians attended church at least once a month, a figure that had declined to 15 percent by 2011.[30] This growth has multifaceted explanation. It goes without saying that Pentecostal churches were to be the beneficiaries of the Charismatic renewal, as many mainline churches resisted the spirituality engendered by the Charismatic movement, and Charismatically renewed people switched their attendance to Pentecostal assemblies. This is not, however, the whole story, as is apparent by the continued growth of the movement long after Charismatic renewal ebbed.

I shall consider other explanations for growth presently, but before doing so it is also worth noting that the Charismatic renewal birthed new Charismatic/Pentecostal movements. The Christian Outreach Centre (COC) began in Brisbane in 1974 through the Charismatic ministry of Charles Taylor, who soon gathered together a congregation numbering in the hundreds, most drawn from mainline churches, especially from Methodism, as well as a large number of Catholics and people switching from the more conservative AGA assemblies.[31] The COC, whose doctrine and theology mirrored traditional Pentecostalism, with its spiritual practice molded by the exuberance of the Charismatic movement, went on to plant churches throughout Brisbane and then in other States. By 2010 it had 138 churches and 23,000 attenders.[32] Christian City Church (now C3) was founded in 1980 by New Zealanders Phil and Chris Pringle. Once again, it is a Charismatic church with relatively traditional Pentecostal theology, characterized by its contemporary style of worship. It now has 96 churches in Australia with a membership of around 15,000. It has also planted churches in more than thirty-five nations and has more than 300 churches worldwide.[33]

Taken altogether, Pentecostalism in Australia has grown from a relatively marginal denomination to now having the largest number of people attending church on a weekly basis, excepting the Catholic Church.[34] While on the one hand it is virtually impossible to do justice to the description or analysis of the diverse spirituality of Pentecostal assemblies, on the other hand there are shared ecclesiological and theological trends that provide some of the explanation for the movement's growth. These trends set out both the opportunities and challenges facing Pentecostalism as it moves forward.

TREND 1: FROM CONGREGATIONALISM TO THE RISE OF THE MULTI-CENTERED MEGACHURCH

Prior to the 1970s almost every Pentecostal congregation was organized according to standard congregational forms of governance (except the Apostolic Church). By the turn of the twentieth century almost all AGA and C3 churches had ecclesial authority vested in the visionary leadership of the senior pastor and an expert board of management, without any formal congregational membership or voting rights.[35] The biggest single cause of this transition was the arrival of Frank Houston in Sydney, along with the subsequent influence of his son Brian.

In 1976 Frank Houston was the general superintendent of the Assemblies of God in New Zealand and pastor of a congregation of more than one thousand people, when he felt called to move to Sydney, planting the Christian Life Centre (CLC) in July 1977. Within the year the church had gathered a congregation of thousands. In terms of church organization, in New Zealand, Houston had grown tired managing a large church under the constraints of congregationalism, so when he planted in Sydney, he established the church with a form of governance more typical of a Presbyterian church: managed by way of a board of elders under the leadership of the senior pastor. Houston had intended to plant independently but was convinced by Evans and Cartledge to join with the Assemblies of God. When he later joined the AGA National Executive and was appointed to lead the movement in New South Wales, the CLC Constitution became the standard form adopted by new church plants. And since most of the movement's growth occurred after that time, it wasn't long before most churches had either been planted using, or adopting, the new structure.[36]

In ecumenical terms it is noteworthy that this change in AGA polity was a movement toward the structures of the Apostolic Church. Indeed, the change wasn't merely a matter of formality but, rather, facilitated a fundamental transition of the way in which church structure and culture was envisaged. David Cartledge has described this as the "Apostolic Revolution," which he says handed ecclesial power from "deacon-possessed" congregations to apostolic leaders, and so freed the church to modernize and respond quickly to the rapidly changing religious and secular climate of contemporary Australia.[37] Cartledge's book title and analysis borrows from the church growth theories of Peter Wagner (e.g., *The New Apostolic Churches*[38]), which have rightly been repudiated as hermeneutically naive and sociologically inept. But if Wagner's apostolic nonsense is set aside, Cartledge's point is that emphasizing leadership facilitated changes in the organizational structures of Pentecostal churches that enabled it to capitalize on the influx of people from the Charismatic renewal and, when that renewal faded, to continue to mold the vision, shape, and culture of churches to facilitate further growth.

The most recent expression of that changing shape is the multi-campus megachurch. Once again Hillsong has led the way. In 1999 Frank Houston resigned his ministry and, rather than appoint a replacement pastor, the church was handed over to the leadership of Brian, with Hillsong becoming one church in two locations.

Over time it established extension services throughout the city of Sydney; in 2007 it took over MacArthur Christian Life Centre, then describing itself as having three campuses and a series of extension services (the distinction seems to be one of relative priority). In 2009 Garden City Church in Brisbane had a congregation numbering more than two thousand when it was merged with Hillsong. In 2012 Hillsong planted a church in Melbourne, managing to gather more than one thousand people at the first service. All of these churches are led by Houston as senior pastor and are governed by a single eldership/board and a common financial administration. The connection between the churches is made practical by rotating the preaching roster and frequent live video-casting of sermons to all campuses, which rotate musicians and share a roster of songs, and an annual cycle of events (revision weekends, Hillsong conference, Colour Conference, etc.).[39]

It is also the case that Hillsong has gone international, with campuses in London, Kiev, Cape Town, New York City, Moscow, Stockholm, Paris, Konstanz, Amsterdam, and Copenhagen (a list that is likely to be out of date when this article is read), with multi-campuses and extensions in each of those cities. Brian (and Bobby) Houston are the senior pastors of the entire conglomerate, and the church operates with a global board. There is perhaps some irony in the long-standing theme of Hillsong conference, "championing the cause of the local church."[40] Indeed, it could be argued that the emerging structure of Hillsong church represents a move away from the grassroots (bottom-up) ecclesiology that has normally framed Pentecostal churches toward a hierarchical (top-down) quasi-episcopalianism.

Hillsong is self-evidently a unique global phenomena, but its influence on other Australian Pentecostal churches should not be underestimated. The Appendix provides a summary of twelve other multicampus megachurches led by pastors who currently serve on the AGA national and state executives—and this list does not cover all such churches. This development goes some way toward explaining the increase in the average size of AGA congregations from 62 in 1977 to 241 in 2012. (See Figure 1.)

There might be various ways to judge these developments, and while such analysis will need to be left to another time (see also *Pentecostal Churches in Transition*), it is at least important to recognize the practical nature of these changes. That is to say, these developments can't simply be decried as a move away from the ideals of the priesthood of all believers (even if such criticism is warranted) without recognizing that these new leadership models have worked, at least insofar as church growth is concerned. I suspect it would also be possible to find an economic explanation for some of the changes; the increase in the average size of congregations reflects the costs of "doing church" and the benefits to be found in achieving economies of scale. Further, the comprehensive studies of congregational spirituality conducted by the National Church Life Survey continue to show that Australian Pentecostal churches do comparatively well when it comes to the qualities that typically indicate church health (see Figure 3), a fact that suggests that most people attending these churches don't *feel* disempowered by their exclusion from the structures of church power. (Of course, those who feel differently have most likely moved on.)

FIGURE 3: MARKERS OF THE QUALITIES OF CHURCH LIFE[41]

	AGA	All Pentecostal	Other Churches
Growth in faith	69%	67%	49%
Devotions a few times per week	84%	83%	74%
God the most important reality in life	78%	78%	61%
Strong sense of belonging	73%	71%	56%
Strong commitment to vision	60%	59%	39%
Gifts and skills encouraged	73%	71%	60%

TREND 2: BECOMING THE "CONTEMPORARY" CHURCH

In focusing on ecclesial authority in the hand of visionary leaders, Pentecostal churches have also deliberately modernized. While early Pentecostalism lived on the margins of culture (often as complete outsiders), Australian Pentecostals have embraced the surrounding culture, seeking to make the church "contemporary," "relevant," and "attractive"—terms that are ubiquitous on church websites:

- In our [ACC] churches you'll find vibrant, contemporary Christians who love the Lord Jesus Christ and express our love in lively praise and worship. (http://www.acc.org.au/)

- Hillsong Church is an exciting, contemporary ministry. Sunday morning services incorporate a casual atmosphere, a blended style of praise and worship music, and relevant teaching. (http://hillsong.org/about-hillsong/what-to-expect)

- C3 Church Cairns is part of a contemporary church movement where faith is expressed in a bright, relevant and enthusiastic way. (http://c3churchcairns.org/)

This pursuit of relevance is also evident in the names given to churches, such as Edge, Influencers, Inspire, iSee, Planetshakers. (See Appendix.) In 2007—the final year of Brian Houston's ten-year tenure as president—the Assemblies of God in Australia changed its name to the Australian Christian Churches, expressly for the purpose of establishing a brand that would be easier to sell than the former name.

The significance of branding is obvious when it comes to

Hillsong.[42] When founded in 1985, it took its name from its location in Castle Hill—Hills Christian Life Centre. As its music-based conference Hillsong gained traction in the global Christian market, the church appropriated the emerging brand as representative for the whole. Its music, message, services, and events are all intentionally shaped to communicate the style and values of the brand. Across all the Australian campuses, Hillsong mirrors its stage decorations, with services held in darkened auditoriums, equipped with concert lighting and smoke machines, surrounded by giant screens that magnify the event, bringing the (mostly young and trendy) singers and musicians close to the audience. The music is constantly being updated and draws its inspiration from a blending of gospel with contemporary rock and dance. Presiding over the event are superstar preachers—if not Brian and Bobby Houston, then Joel A'Bell, Robert Ferguson, or an internationally famous guest.

The obvious question is whether this contemporary branding (be it that of Hillsong or any other ACC or C3 church) is anything more than collusion with commercial culture. In *Pentecostal Churches in Transition* I drew on the work of Ben Myers to distinguish between weak and strong syncretism; the former is vital to a missionary church, since it contextualizes the gospel, whereas the latter embodies the culture so completely that it empties the gospel of its meaning and prophetic voice.[43] Obviously brand-conscious Australian Pentecostalism is syncretistic—deliberately so. The issue is whether it does more than simply reiterate commercial culture, but, instead, draws on that culture and thereafter disrupts and transforms it according to the values of the kingdom of God.

Trend 3: From Other-Worldly to This-Worldly Redemption— and a Feminine Case Study

The charge of syncretism is most often heard in reference to the movement's attitude to money and, in particular, its so-called prosperity gospel. This is well-worn ground, and there is no need to repeat it here. Recently Marion Maddox extended the criticism, arguing that "Hillsong makes a religious duty of conspicuous consumption—one's body, image and lifestyle are a walking evangelistic billboard."[44] Her particular target was the women's ministry, especially the Colour Conference (that doubles as the women's conference for Hillsong and the ACC fellowship), which she believes promotes a version of feminine beauty that is tied to the commercialism of the contemporary fashion industry: "Hillsong women are literally born to shop—because not to shop is to thwart one's God-given destiny."[45] She goes on to argue that this brand of "princess" femininity is deeply ambiguous: on the one hand seeking to value and empower women, on the other hand promoting a version femininity that capitulates to the shallow objectifications of our sexualized culture, caters to male desires, and presumes male leadership.

In response, Matthew Del Nevo argues persuasively that in focusing on Hillsong's overlap with culture, Maddox has failed to see the extent to which Hillsong provides an alternate space:

> We live in a consumerist culture which seems totalizing (or wanting to be if it is not total yet) and Hillsong are within this culture.…This is where Hillsong starts, and its speakers demonstrate thorough literacy in the consumerist idiom, but the ministry is not about that. On the contrary, it pulls them inwardly free of the projections on them. Hillsong women's ministry does great things for women, and ultimately represents

an alternative spiritual space. It isn't really about hair and make-up at all, that is just a hook in to something much deeper.[46]

What Maddox (along with many an outside observer) has failed to credit is that Hillsong women are prominent and influential (which is not the case in many churches). The stated purpose of the Colour Conference is "placing value upon womanhood so that women can place value upon fellow humanity," and this goal has seen a local focus on projects to promote the self-esteem of girls in schools and counter bullying, and internationally, on supporting the ministry of Compassion Australia, establishing projects to build homes for orphans and widows in Africa, and so on.[47]

CONCLUSION

The point here is not to focus on Hillsong women per se, but to consider their ministry as representative of the Australian Pentecostalism more broadly. If taken in the light of our starting point, there remains a priority given to the empowerment and place of women in Pentecostal ministry. What is new is the nature of that ministry, from the narrower constraints of the fourfold gospel to an understanding of soteriology that transcends the soul and embraces the world, of healing that utilizes science/medicine and is framed socially, of baptism in the Spirit concerned less with tongues and holiness and more with personal flourishing, of an optimistic rather than pessimistic eschatology, looking to transform this world rather than see it end. Exactly how these developments are to be judged, and what they mean for the future, is open for discussion and debate.

MULTICAMPUS MEGACHURCHES

The following is a selection of multicampus megachurches, identifying their senior partner and locations, drawn from the national and state executive leadership of the Australian Christian churches.

- Hillsong (http://hillsong.com/): Brian Houston, located in Sydney (three campuses and twelve extension services meeting around the city), Brisbane, and Melbourne in Australia. It also has campuses in London, Kiev, Cape Town, New York City, Moscow, Stockholm, Paris, Konstanz, Amsterdam, Melbourne, and Copenhagen—with multicampuses and extensions in each of those cities.

Adelaide:

- Influencers Church (www.influencers.church): Ashley Evans, three campuses in Adelaide, one campus in Perth, plus international campus in Atlanta
- Edge Church: Danny Guglielmucci, two campuses in Adelaide, and one in Melbourne, plus campus in Bristol UK

New South Wales:

- Inspire (http://www.inspirechurch.org/): John McMartin, three campuses in Liverpool, Macarthur, Ingleburn
- Shirelive (http://www.shirelive.com/): Mike Murphy, three campuses in Sutherland, Brighton le Sands, Newtown
- Lighthouse Church (http://lighthousechurch.com.au/): Paul Bartlett, two campuses Wollongong, Shellharbour

Queensland:

- Hope Centre (http://www.hopecentre.com/): Wayne Alcorn, one church with many locations; Brisbane, Jindalee, Brisbane North, Sunnybank, Logan, Moreton
- iSee Church (https://www.iseechurch.com/), Paul & Jo Geerling, four Brisbane campuses, Eight Mile Plains, Taigum, Seventeen Mile Rocks, South Brisbane
- Calvary Christian church (http://calvarycc.org.au/sc/): James MacPherson, Townsville, Ipswich, Sunshine Coast.

Victoria:

- Enjoy Church (http://www.enjoychurch.com.au/): Shane Baxter, two campuses in Melbourne plus Gippsland, Bendigo and Ballarat.
- Planet Shakers (http://www.planetshakers.com/index.html): Russell Evans, two campuses in Melbourne, one in Geelong, and one international campus in Cape Town

Western Australia

- Centrepoint Church (http://www.centrepointchurch.com.au) Joel Chelliah, two campuses in Perth—Cockburn and in Gosnells
- Globalheart Church (http://globalheartchurch.com/): Gerard Keehan, two campuses in Perth—Joondalup and Bentley

Chapter 17

From Corner Shop to Boutique Franchise: The Dilemmas of Australian Pentecostalism

Mark Hutchinson

T HERE IS A growing literature on the inadequacy of the Azusa Street revival as a template for global Pentecostalism. The claim for Los Angeles as the beginning point of Pentecostalism is essentially based on four things: primacy (as the earliest such outbreak), centrality (as the center either from which other movements spread out or from which, through literature etc., they are influenced), continuity (with the major Pentecostal traditions of today), and singularity (it is uniquely an example of a globally engaged, socially transformative, internationally important Pentecostalism). Most of this literature (such as Joe Creech's very good work)[1] undermines the ambit claim by pointing out that there were many other instances of Pentecostal outbreak before Azusa Street. Even more recent work is demonstrating that the very idea of continuity is undermined, first by the continuity of *other* movements with contemporary Pentecostalism (the nineteenth century healing movement, for example), and secondly by the growing literature demonstrating that Azusa Street was itself in a line of continuity that flowed back through Dowie and others to a Irvingite/Celtic revivalist tradition, which is proving to be more directly connected to modern Pentecostalism than some have thought.[2]

Centrality is undermined as an idea, because it is demonstrable that in many national movements (such as Australia) Azusa Street was of minimal influence until much later in their development, when Americanization connected indigenous movements to its mythos.

It is my intention herein to deal with the issue of *singularity* or, as it appears in the Australian context, the *dilemmas* of Australian Pentecostalism.[3] Those dilemmas start, in an intellectual sense, with the observation—discovered and rediscovered by a disbelieving Australian public sector to their own surprise from time to time—that Australian Pentecostalism is not American. It is not American either in origins or (largely) in development. Most importantly, however, like many religious bodies in colonized and later globalized settings, it exists in part through its negotiation of the larger conversation between Australian and American cultures, now counter-posing, now absorbing, the influences of globalized cultures. In other words, in the global reflexive space that we share with Canadians in particular, "not being American" is part of what being an Australian Pentecostal is about.

The role of Azusa Street as a symbol, as opposed to Azusa Street as an event and/or historical process, is illustrative of this dilemma. In our inevitable mutual regard we try, of course, not to offend. Azusa Street in much literature has moved from being "*the* Pentecostal outbreak" to being "symbolic" of something larger.[4] It is often we colonials (either of the British Empire or the American) who are at fault for this—undermining the canonicity of Azusa Street often seems like the logical place to begin in reconstructing other national stories. For others, the symbolic nature of Azusa Street provides a convenient source of shorthand statements that conflate the huge mass of historical data into readily usable theological maxims. (At worst, they are an excuse not to read the historical literature in any depth.) "At Azusa Street, the race line was washed away," I read on a recent Canadian Pentecostal website. Well, yes, but what does that mean? For Canadian Pentecostals, race was not a *formative* Pentecostal issue until the rise of postwar multiculturalism and First Nations rights campaigns—in other words, the appropriation of Azusa Street in this context is strictly anachronistic and has more to do with the subsequent dominance of American publishing houses than with historical applicability. Race was a formative issue in the United States,[5] Brazil,[6] South Africa,[7] and to some degree in New Zealand,[8] but it was not such an issue in the urban Pentecostalism that emerged in Australia. Indeed, one would have to say that nationalism/culturalism was more the issue in the Korean setting. This raises the question—does this new historiography merely represent a repackaging of the American metanarrative into more nuanced regional and national accounts, or do we have a larger job to do in considering the methodological basis of Pentecostal historiography? There is probably a role for both, with the former eventually demonstrating the necessity of the latter. As a whole, Pentecostals are progressing from retrieving their own histories to developing tertiary accounts, such as theologies. Short of the reconsideration currently in process in mainstream sociology (largely the result of reconsidering the nature of secularization theory), there is as yet no broadscale attempt to engage, for instance, with the epistemological issues raised by considering socially evident movements of the Spirit outside modernist categories (such as the nation-state, denomination-sect typologies, and even fundamentalism and liberalism). That modern equivalent of the medieval realism/nominalism debate, the difference/différènce debate that has dominated French thought[9] for instance, has left no marks on the informing categories in Australian Pentecostal self-reflection.[10]

THE CONTEXTUAL DIFFÉRÈNCE OF
AUSTRALIAN PENTECOSTALISM

In Australia, like most of the rest of the world outside of America, the historiography of Pentecostalism is poorly developed. Apart from the seminal work of Barry Chant and my own attempts to expand this through biography and focused histories, most of the current running is with the theologians. This is probably unfortunate, given the fact that the sort of grounded theology that needs to be done in Australia needs a concurrent development of historical sources and secondary literature on which to build. Nevertheless, the Australian experience demonstrates how national expressions of Pentecostalism are fundamentally different to the Azusa Street model. Even when they use the same words and express the same behaviors, the underlying assumptions diverge. This is certainly the case in Australia between 1870 and 1970, though it becomes moderated after the impact of the global Charismatic movement in the 1970s. First, as Chant has shown, Australian Pentecostalism starts much earlier than Azusa Street and is certainly present as practice and theology among Methodists and The Salvation Army revivalists in the 1870s and 1880s. This is not the same as the argument made by Dayton that preceding movements (such as Keswick, the healing movements, etc.) form a sort of "*pre*-Pentecostal tinderbox." Rather, it is to say that the idea of Pentecostalism somehow "starting" in 1906 is a misconception. The emergence of Good News Hall in Melbourne from 1909 is essentially not a shift in behaviors at all from that which had been experienced in Methodist prayer meetings and Salvationist rallies. While they were outside the mainstream denominations, the same might be said of The Salvation Army in Australia during the 1880s, and certainly Good News Hall contemporaries did not respond to Sarah Jane Lancaster's activities any differently from when she was a Methodist visitor.

Further, the society in which Lancaster and her contemporaries were working was quite different from that of Los Angeles in 1906. While Americans talk about the deism of Thomas Jefferson and the *possible* effect of the Enlightenment upon the American Revolution, there is no doubt about the neoclassical foundations of Australia. Australia was founded later, as (in the words of Patrick O'Farrell) "the first post-Christian country of modern times." Early Australian Pentecostals were in no doubt about this—they were outposts in a foreign country, snatching individuals from the jaws of hell just prior to the return of Jesus, rather than remnants of a former Christian country striving to bring about a restoration of some lost Christian hegemony. One finds very little evidence of what we might call "civic" Christendom ideas amongst Australian Pentecostals until the Charismatic movement of the 1960s, when the Logos Foundation imports them from New Zealand, and begins to fill them with imported (and often contradictory) American content (particularly that of Rushdoony, who visited Australia several times in the 1980s). Instead, Australian Pentecostal churches have been typified by corporate/gathered church models, negotiating between the central figure of the Charismatic pastor and the "prophethood of all believers."[11] It is the emergence from this ecclesial form that, as I will discuss below, creates some of the contemporary dilemmas for Australian Pentecostals.

The contextual factors for the growth of Australian Pentecostalism are familiar to every Australian school child—distance and the size of the population.[12] These factors have dominated Australian thought, but also politics and culture, since the nineteenth century. Distance impacted upon Australian Pentecostalism because of the filters that it imposed upon migration and the circulation of ideas. For Pentecostal pastors, distance was not mediated as it was for other denominations through the circulation of scientific and other literature—by definition, the movement was lower-middle-class, pragmatist, and largely unaffected by literature outside that by Herbert Booth, J. Hudson Taylor, or their circles. There were also many European religious traditions that did not make it to Australia, because their carriers chose the closer, less expensive option of going to North America. Consequently the holiness tradition in Australia is weaker than it was in the United States, and heavily filtered through English Keswick and by the self-selecting vectors of missionaries who were passing through on their way to China, India, or the Pacific. It is not until the mid-1920s that, through the work of A. C. Valdez and Kelso Glover, Azusa Street had any appreciable impact on Australia, and then it was by two people who were on the edge of mainstream Pentecostalism in the United States and closer to the Foursquare tradition. Both of these individuals would go on to have significant impacts upon the rise of the global Charismatic movement and the consequent influence of the Latter Rain movement. Again, distance was important—both of them came from their native California because of the interaction between an Australian (Mary Ayers) and American missions promoters such as Carrie Judd Montgomery. Even this Azusa Street influence was attenuated by distance, one of its contributing strands thereby becoming more dominant over the others. This was a continuing factor throughout Australian Pentecostal history. Australia tended to get an idiosyncratic slice of the itinerant ministries that left America and a much more representative one of those that left Britain—Lester Sumrall, for example, became a major flashpoint for conflict in the early history of the Australian Assemblies of God when he was discovered to be circulating amongst Queensland churches without the newly formed national body's permission. The contribution of British teachers (Donald Gee, Howard Carter, Aeron Morgan, etc.) would remain strong up until the 1960s and become a bone of contention thereafter precisely because of the Americanization of Australian culture *during* the 1960s.

It was not only distance to Australia, however, that imposed a filter on the influences that came to bear, but also the sheer distance between locations. The marked difference in social and ecclesiological attitudes found between Queensland and Victoria, for example, through at least until the death of C. L. Greenwood (1969), were a constant source of tension within the Assemblies of God. More regional movements—such as the Christian Revival Crusade, strong in South Australia and Victoria, or later the Christian Outreach Centres, strong in Queensland—were regional precisely because of the distances. Again, there was a filtering effect. When Oral Roberts came to Australia in the 1950s, he visited Sydney and Melbourne, and so left a comparatively small mark upon Australian Pentecostalism until the mainstreaming effects of the Charismatic movement in the 1970s.[13] When Billy Graham came three years later, he had the organizational muscle and strategic insight to overcome distances by procuring dedicated landlines that could project his preaching into the many rural and even urban centers where he could not otherwise afford to go.[14]

The size of the population is also related to the factor of distance. Australia is the size of the continental United States, with only 10 percent of its population. Pentecostalism in its early phase was strong in the rural centers (due to the impact of local revivals, such as the Macnade revival of 1924, and the establishment of a key center in Parkes, NSW, in 1917). While the urban churches were relatively larger, there tended to be only one or two major churches in each city, none of them any larger than three hundred congregants up until the 1970s. This provided significant impetus to the rise of the pastor evangelist as a key figure in Australian Pentecostalism, a forerunner to the Charismatic leader figure in the megachurches

that began to develop in Australia from the late 1970s. Early pastors
in the Assemblies of God, for instance, could not afford to stay in
one place—regional evangelism was rarely primarily about church
planting and largely about earning enough to stay in full-time ministry. Australian towns were dominated by the "big four" denominations that (for Anglicans, Presbyterians, and Methodists) had
achieved some form of social legitimacy either through de facto
establishment under the Bourke government in the 1830s, or (for
Catholics) through the institutionalized presence of Catholicism
in unions, schools, and societies. Government preference—which
was to deal with the smallest range of religious options possible—
was reinforced by initial and chain migration (which reinforced the
dominance of British traditions up until the 1940s). Pentecostalism
was a new corner shop with a home delivery service in a town that
already featured four large, though increasingly indistinguishable,
supermarkets. This meant that Australian pastors needed to be
mobile, adaptable, and Charismatically inclined, ready to leave an
impact before they moved on. Early ecclesiology suited this interaction between the voluntary society and the peregrinating pastors:
few churches up until the 1940s appointed their pastors for more
than a year, and many of them for less. Doing Pentecostal church
in Australia was one continuing revival crusade, with teaching content largely imported from Britain (with Gee, Wiggins, Wallace,
and others) and, only in the post-World War II period, from the
United States (Frank and Inez Sturgeon, for example, who were
tasked with establishing the national AOG's Bible college in 1948).
The same trends have been noted, for the same reasons, among
other Protestant traditions in Australia, which until at least the
1980s demonstrated weaknesses in the teaching of Christian disci-
plines other than Bible or missions.[15]

THE PROBLEMATIC DIFFÉRÈNCE OF
AUSTRALIAN PENTECOSTALISM

Such contextual understandings point to the core of the matter. While race or gender may have been among, or even *the*, significant issues in North America, by the time that Pentecostalism emerged in Australia, race had been relativized by the marginalization of a relatively much smaller aboriginal population in the southeast corner and by the expulsion of South Sea islander workers from the cane industry in Queensland's north.[16] It was not that, intellectually speaking, it should not have been an issue, and indeed Reconciliation is in contemporary Australia a definitional issue for the nation: until the 1960s, however, it was not a matter of present concern for most Australian Pentecostals (Queensland and northern NSW excepted). Gender was an emerging societal issue, but first-wave feminism was still largely incorporated within the evangelical churches and had been temporarily defused by the near dominance of Methodist social reformism in New South Wales and the linked and early institution in Australia of the franchise for women. In this British progressivist, and increasingly secularist, culture women still felt that they could vote themselves into equality.[17] Instead, the defining crises in Australian Pentecostalism were the delay of the *parousia* through the 1940s and the fading of the Charismatic movement at the end of the 1970s.

While common to all institutionalising movements, Pentecostal or not, the delay of the *parousia* in Australian Pentecostalism raised the same issues that it did in the early church. On the one hand it forced institutionalization of the movements, while on the other hand it lingered on as a challenge to a movement that did not have the intellectual resources to come up with alternatives. Under James Wallace, a Scottish Bible teacher, the development of the national Bible college as a "soul winning" and church-planting institution acted as an anodyne to the emerging problem of the "tarrying of the Lord,"[18] but was not ultimately a solution. It is for this reason that tensions continue to emerge between the Charismatic individuals at the heart of local churches and the attempt by the gray-beards of the movement to maintain a Methodist connexional form through the 1950s and 1960s. If Jesus was not coming back immediately, what was the purpose of the movement? Eventually this broke out in the 1977 AOG National Conference, where victory essentially went to the Charismatic leaders.

The growth of Pentecostal churches after that period was remarkable: from a total of around seven thousand members in the mid-1970s, from 1979 (when the formal transdenominational Charismatic movement begins to collapse in Australia) the Assemblies of God in Australia grew by in excess of thirteen thousand members every reporting period (reflecting the two years between national conferences), and would continue to do so until the mid-2000s. Around the more significant Charismatic leaders there emerged the megachurches, patterns among which have been widely read as confirming the change in direction in the 1970s.[19] The AOG now forms fully two-thirds of all denominationally affiliated Australian Pentecostals; approximately 15 percent of Australian AOG members attend megachurches, and almost all the significant continuing growth is to be found in churches of a thousand or more members. While there are significant urbanization and globalization issues at play, the direct *entente* that was formed in the 1970s rotated around a displacement of the *parousia* as a core theological concern, for what former movement General Superintendent Andrew Evans called "the gift man."[20] The interesting thing about this *entente* was that it was built upon the transparent evidence of growth amongst churches run by Charismatic individuals (Evans, Klimionok, Cartledge among the leaders), a legitimacy that lasted through the change of leadership toward other megachurch pastors in the early 1990s. In Weberian terms, the change when Brian Houston became president in 1997 was from Evans' "gift man" to Houston's "flourishing man," from individual to institutional charisma.[21] By the mid-2000s, however, it was clear that the fruit of the 1970s Charismatic movement was no longer bleeding out of the mainstream denominations, which had (as in the Catholic Church) either come to a successful *modus vivendi* or (as with Sydney Anglicans) had suppressed Charismatics in their main centers.[22] The megachurches continue to have significant forward thrust, but, with large "back doors" are increasingly reliant upon attracting members from amongst fellow denominational churches, or extending their networked solutions into globalized settings that will permit them to continue to grow elsewhere.

The problem remains, however, that neither the theological challenge of the movement's sense of self (linked to its eschatological heritage) nor the organizational challenge of finding a sustainable solution for increasingly institutionalized churches (or at least one that does also not rely upon the assumption of the universal availability of Charismatic leaders) have been adequately met. The rise of the pastor evangelist and his or her successor, the Charismatic leader, was a response to the pragmatic contextual issues facing Australian Pentecostalism. They were not fundamentally the result of changes of theology. Moreover, the majority approach to dealing with the *parousia* is simply not to mention it. The Assemblies of God statement of faith was progressively broadened to where it is largely now expressed in such terms as "We believe that the Lord Jesus Christ is coming back again as He promised." Full stop.[23] Likewise, core beliefs and practices such as speaking in tongues and Charismatic gifts are increasingly the property of leadership, rather than the common property of ecclesial communities, or squeezed out of the public expression of churches altogether in order to support the shift from a congregational form to a developing civic religiousness. While these were shifts in practice developed to deal with the alternative ecclesial settings of megachurches, the theological consequences have not really been dealt with, nor are there many channels for discussion or theological influence should in fact appropriate solutions arise.

Such developments leave the movement adrift from its early twentieth-century assumptions and hanging on to its experientialism while waiting for new theological syntheses to come along. Intellectually this was probably not a bad place to start; indeed, in the history of spiritualities, it is an essential place to start. It has also proven to be an effective mechanism in global settings— Australian denominations such as the Assemblies of God and Christian City Church have extension churches all over the world, most notably through the Hillsong network (with churches in London, Kiev, Cape Town, New York, Moscow, Stockholm, Paris, Konstanz, Amsterdam, and Copenhagen) and the C3 network (with over three hundred churches worldwide), but also extensive COC works in the Pacific (some three hundred fifty at last count). Each of these claims in excess of thirty thousand converts apiece in their global networks per year. It is probably not sufficient as a *place* to *end*, however, if Pentecostalism is to remain a living tradition in Australia. It would be possible for Australian Pentecostalism to be wildly successful overseas or even in the globally engaged sectors of Australian society, and have almost no impact on its context. There is some recognition of this in the largest of the Pentecostal movements, the Assemblies of God. Over the past few years there has been a change in leadership, which has seen the rigorist insistence on the regionalization of denominational functions come into crisis, and the leadership shift back toward those who have a more movement orientation. The core functions of the *national* movement—missions and education—are still somewhat adrift and sidelined by local and regional church control. After the appointment of Wayne Alcorn as leader, there has been some drift back toward the center—for reasons of effectiveness and financial stability for the national administration, if for no other reason. The intellectual challenges, however, remain, as do the generational challenges. Almost all the major movements in Australia (saving only the CRC) experienced their first significant growth in the 1970s. There is now a notable generational bubble in leadership that is demanding succession planning. Inevitably, the shift from churches run by Charismatic founders to a younger but more legal-rational generation without the necessary legitimization of the Charismatic halo, however, is causing some disruption. Again, the delay in the *parousia* and the question of the nature and function of Charismatic gifts are at the center of the issue.

In 2009 a megachurch-associated social welfare agency based on an American model collapsed in a welter of accusations of "widespread abuse" and financial irregularity. As the *Sydney Morning Herald* reported:

> Allegations of widespread abuse at Mercy Ministries group homes appear finally to have caught up with the fundamentalist Christian group, which has announced it will close its Sydney home on October 31, citing "extreme financial challenges and a steady drop in our support base."[24]

Of course, it was the *Herald* itself that had taken up the allegations, printed them as fact, and undermined the financial support for the ministry, so if the newspaper believed in prophecy, here was a self-fulfilling one of classic proportions. The case, however, demonstrates the issues facing Australian Pentecostalism more generally. To extend the metaphor, in a sense, the movement started as a corner shop in a town with four well-established supermarkets. Since then, both the town has become gentrified, with Australia moving from being a commodities exporter to a dual economy where commodities export is balanced by Australia's emergence as a center for Asian service industries. Not surprisingly, therefore, a whole group of other boutique shops have sprung up in the meantime—everything from Buddhist coffee shops to Muslim evening wear boutiques—even as Pentecostal corner shops have spread all over the town. Some are now so big so as to themselves become small supermarket chains or franchises. Others continue to differentiate themselves according to product: some are filling stations, others comfortable little local bars, yet others offering complete makeovers or primary health services. The decline of the traditional religious supermarkets, however, has left Australian Pentecostal churches in the position of not only defending their own practices but also of seeking for something to say in the public square.

With the rapid shift toward civic forms of Pentecostalism in Australia—as can be seen in widespread competition for government social welfare funds and the increasingly central position taken by social welfare activities (Hope Rwanda, support for Compassion International, increasing engagement with World Vision, etc.)— the issue of public intellectual engagement will come to the fore. The collapse of Mercy Ministries demonstrated the exposure that churches can experience when they lack intellectually engaged professional traditions going in, and effective forms of public apologetics coming out. The case was a classic example of a Pentecostal megachurch caught in the transition between corporate and civic forms of action, without the intellectual resources to manage the shift. The lack of intellectual resources, related specifically to the drift at the center of the movement from its theological moorings— no longer narrowly separationist, but also not committed to a fully orbed approach to intellectual engagement—leaves the movement largely to absorb ideas on a pragmatic basis rather than to think them through. The movement's incipient dilemmas (what to do with the *parousia* and gifts, and what to do with ecclesial authority and the organizing principles that follow from it) are now, therefore, the cause of a larger dilemma—what do Australian Pentecostals, now a significant element in Christian self-identification as a whole in the country, have to "say" to the larger society?

Chapter 18

Transforming Pentecostalism: Some Reflections on the Changing Shape of Pentecostalism in Aotearoa-New Zealand

Brett Knowles

IN 2000 THE author was visited in his office at the University of Otago by a former Assemblies of God pastor who had founded a number of assemblies during his ministry in New Zealand and Australia. During our conversation this pastor stated that, despite his twenty-seven years in the movement, he had not been in a Pentecostal church since 1986. Naturally the author asked him why he had left. "Oh," he replied, "I didn't leave the Pentecostal movement—it left me!" This comment provided a catalyst for more than ten years of research, leading ultimately to the recent publication of *Transforming Pentecostalism: The Changing Shape of New Zealand Pentecostalism.*[1] This article summarizes that research.

Church historian Martin Marty has offered an illuminating analogy—using the environmental metaphors of hurricanes and glaciers—to categorize the change in American religion in the fifty years from 1935 to 1985.[2] He observes that "both hurricane and glacial forces leave altered [religious] landscapes."[3] The "hurricane," he argues, represents sudden, drastic change, the product of clearly identifiable catalytic events such as, for example, the Second Vatican Council from 1962 to 1965. By contrast, the "glacier" represents a process of gradual, subtle change—a slow, cumulative progression of attitudes and orientations that may not be attributable to any specific causative event or series of events. These "glacial" forces are much more difficult to identify than those of the "hurricane," but are also more important and powerful in influencing and shaping the course of history.

The transformation of New Zealand Pentecostalism owes much to these "glacial" processes. After nearly two decades of obscurity, the early movement emerged as a small sectarian cluster of churches following English Pentecostal evangelist Smith Wigglesworth's campaigns here in the 1920s. These were generally characterized by their divisiveness and small size, their suspicion of the outside world, and by their lack of influence on the wider society. Assemblies of God historian Ian Clark describes New Zealand Pentecostals up to the end of the 1950s as "at best a marginal grouping within society,"[4] vividly portraying them as:

> ...a very small and a very ingrown movement. They were making all sorts of efforts to break out of a very constricted kind of a mode, but I think in modern terms, they were *totally irrelevant*. That would be a good way of describing it. Nice people, who met in little upstairs halls above a butcher shop (things like that).... [They] met at Oddfellows' Halls and that sort of thing, and it really was pretty grotty....[5]

However, this "constricted...mode" was not entirely due to Pentecostal sectarianism. Laurie Murray, an Assemblies of God worker in Timaru in 1959–1960, described his Pentecostal congregation in quite unflattering terms. They were "about half-a-dozen old-timers who had either just managed to hold on in the face of general despising and rejection; or maybe their forthright and ever-exuberant witness had frightened people for miles around."[6] While there is an element of self-mockery in Murray's account, it

makes the point that there was a general public antipathy toward
Pentecostalism. This aversion was especially acute with evangelicals[7] and led to a policy of exclusion, in part due to a deep misunderstanding of Pentecostal practices.[8] Nevertheless, a change
of attitude was beginning to emerge. In this respect, the landmark illustrated article on the "Third Force in Christendom" in
Life magazine in 1958 contributed to the beginnings of a clearer
public perception of Pentecostals.[9] Another significant factor was
their increased public visibility, brought about by a new wave of
Pentecostal evangelism.

PENTECOSTAL METAMORPHOSIS

It seems ironic that the foundations for Pentecostal expansion in the
1960s were laid by a sectarian schism from the Pentecostal Church
of New Zealand in 1946. This led to the eventual creation of a minis-
cule network of radically independent "Latter Rain" churches. This
group was significant in that its lack of organizational impediments
gave it freedom to respond to new opportunities more rapidly than
other, more denominational Pentecostal churches were able to do.
American evangelist Tommy Hicks' visit to New Zealand in late
1957 sparked a wave of "tent evangelism," the most prominent examples of this being Latter Rain–oriented Rob Wheeler and his colleagues.[10] The real evangelistic breakthrough, however, came with
a spectacularly successful healing campaign conducted by independent American evangelist A. S. Worley in Timaru in June and
July 1960. More than six hundred people were converted during the
five-week campaign in this religiously conservative town. This success created a "launching pad" for further independent Pentecostal
evangelism in the South Island (which complemented the campaigns of Wheeler and his colleagues in the North Island). By
1965 this network of independent Latter Rain–oriented Pentecostal

churches had grown from six to more than sixty in just five years and was beginning to coalesce into a movement of "Indigenous Churches."[11] Wheeler commented that, at the height of this expansion, "at one stage, between Ron Coady [in the South Island] and myself [in the North Island], we were opening a new church every two weeks."[12] The spectacular growth of these churches in the 1960s would be matched by that of other Pentecostal churches (particularly the Assemblies of God) in the next two decades.

This expansion in the 1960s and 1970s created one of the strongest Pentecostal movements in the English-speaking world,[13] the impact of which was extended by the effects of the Charismatic movement. This had a wide influence in the mainstream churches and did much to diminish Pentecostal sectarianism, accelerate Pentecostal rapprochement, and foster Pentecostal "respectability." These changes of attitude led eventually to a landmark conference at Snell's Beach in Auckland in 1975 that finally brought about reconciliation between the main Pentecostal groups, ending decades of antagonism. A significant organizational change resulting from this rapprochement was the formation of an umbrella group, the Associated Pentecostal Churches of New Zealand, to represent all Pentecostal churches in New Zealand. This was established to foster Pentecostal unity and to enable united delegations to government on the declining moral state of society.

As the 1970s progressed, Pentecostal moralist activism became more pronounced; this reflected a largely unconscious shift of attitude. Most conservative evangelicals held premillennial views, believing that the world was doomed to become progressively more degenerate, with the climax of evil coming just before the Second Coming of Christ. In the light of this pessimistic worldview, there was little point in attempting to change the world, since it was, by its very nature, irredeemable. The rise of the new moralist movements implied a move away from this worldview, although most evangelicals (including Pentecostals) seemed unaware that their activism was in fact at variance with their eschatology.[14] In New Zealand this new activism culminated in the landmark 1985 petition against the Homosexual Law Reform Bill. This petition was, by far, the largest ever in New Zealand history, receiving 815,000 signatures,[15] but was summarily rejected by the Labour Government, which was determined to implement its program of social and economic change. Since the Pentecostal movement was in the vanguard of this opposition, the rejection of the petition represented a defeat of almost apocalyptic proportions, a moralist Armageddon in which the forces of righteousness lost. Consequently there was strong Pentecostal support of, and in some cases, candidacy for, the two Christian political parties that emerged in the late 1980s and 1990s.[16] Nevertheless, such activism was rather more muted than was the case in the 1980s.

The sense of confidence and Pentecostal dynamism manifest in the campaign against the Homosexual Law Reform Bill was reflected in some of the music produced in the movement in the mid-1980s.[17] This perception of numbers and power culminated in the nationwide "Rise Up" campaign of 1990, which attempted to make an evangelistic impact on the consciousness of the average New Zealander. However, little resulted from the campaign, and, apart from pockets of vigorous growth in Auckland and several other centers,[18] Pentecostal growth and enthusiasm began to plateau in the 1990s. This leveling off had already begun in the previous decade, with the beginnings of references in Pentecostal archival material to "burnout," "disillusionment," and "discouragement."[19] There were several reasons for this. Firstly, the mantle of leadership by now was passing from the pioneer generation (who had been involved in the revivalism of the 1960s) to second-generation leadership (some of whom had transferred into the movement from Charismatic churches). This new leadership generally did not have the spiritual stature of the movement's pioneers. Secondly, Pentecostal churches became more managerial and entrepreneurial,[20] in contrast to the Spirit-led ethos that had characterized their earlier days. Leadership patterns became predicated on techniques such as "church growth,"[21] rather than on a dependence on the Holy Spirit. This transition was paralleled, in the eyes of many of the movement's earlier participants, by superficiality and a loss of spiritual power,[22] and by a decline of spontaneity and freedom (which was paralleled by increasing inflexibility on the part of its leadership).[23]

A final element of change in New Zealand Pentecostalism was the numbers of people exiting the movement. This exodus went largely unnoticed, but when it *was* remarked, it was attributed to "backsliding" and to younger people losing their faith and departing the church. However, sociologist Alan Jamieson has shown (in a highly significant study, based on interviews with more a hundred adult leavers from evangelical, Pentecostal, and Charismatic churches), that this was not the case. The average period of time spent in these churches by Jamieson's respondents was 15.8 years; 94 percent had been involved in some form of church leadership, and 36 percent had undertaken part-time or full-time theological study.[24] He interprets this exodus as a quest for individual spiritual growth: many such leavers looked back at the Pentecostal church with affection, while recognizing that its conformist nature meant that it has taken them as far as it could in their spiritual journey. Jamieson also found that few people had left the church because of what he calls "meta-grumbles";[25] most maintained—at least in part—elements of Pentecostal faith that their erstwhile fellow believers considered that they had left behind.

PENTECOSTALISM IN THE PRESENT DAY

Given these trends, what is the present situation of Pentecostalism in Aotearoa-New Zealand? Here the data is ambiguous. The latest census figures—from the 2013 Census—identifies the movement as the fifth largest denominational grouping in New Zealand. It is also highly visible, with at least four large New Zealand Pentecostal churches broadcasting on national television. There are a number of Pentecostal megachurches[26] (particularly in Auckland) and many smaller churches in regional and provincial centers. Nevertheless, it is noteworthy that the number of Pentecostal respondents dropped by 6.51 percent (from 79,635 to 74,439 adherents) between the 2006 and 2013 Censuses. Although the combined returns for the "Pentecostal: not further defined" and "Pentecostal: not elsewhere classified" categories increased by 14.21 percent from 42,066 to 48,042 adherents, those for the specified Pentecostal denominations decreased over the seven-year period. In total, this figure fell from 37,569 to 26,397 (a decline of 29.74 percent). This might indicate that institutional forms of Pentecostalism are weakening.

Pentecostal churches in New Zealand have also suffered division and disintegration over the last fifteen years. The Associated Pentecostal Churches of New Zealand, after dwindling for years, was eventually disbanded in 2003. Several large "flagship" Pentecostal churches left their denominations in the 1990s and 2000s.[27] There were also wider defections, with about thirty Samoan Assemblies of God seceding from their parent body in 2005, leading to ongoing legal and constitutional conflict. The Apostolic Church lost nine of its churches to the Destiny Church in 2003. This loss was partly explained by the fact that Bishop Brian Tamaki, Destiny's leader, had formerly been an apostle in the Apostolic Church before leaving that movement in 1994. In addition, the trend noted by Jamieson in the 1990s (i.e., of evangelicals, Pentecostals, and Charismatics leaving their churches) continued with many of these ending up in a network of small informal house-fellowship groups. Professor Peter Lineham estimates that there are up to six hundred of these groups in Auckland alone and that their rise constitutes a major change in the shape of New Zealand church life.[28]

A comparison of denominational listings from the last Associated Pentecostal Churches of New Zealand Pastors Directory (2001–2002)[29] and current websites for the various New Zealand Pentecostal churches[30] yields quantitative evidence of this decline. This is summarized in Table 1.

On analysis of this data, several trends immediately become apparent. The number of churches had declined in the majority of Pentecostal denominations between 2002 and 2012, in some cases precipitously. Overall, the decline was just over 8.5 percent (from 701 to 641 churches) over the ten years. In general, the larger denominations were hardest hit: the four largest Pentecostal groups (which comprised 75 percent of the total number of congregations) declined 19.89 percent from 528 to 423 churches. Two denominations declined more than 40 percent, while there were three others with decreases of between 30 percent and 40 percent. In the case of those Pentecostal groups that do appear to have increased during the decade, this data was not as positive as it looked. The Samoan Assemblies of God were locked in a vigorous legal battle for control of church assets with their former parent body, the Assemblies of God.[31] The Destiny Church grew from 5 to 10 churches, but this included a secession of 9 churches from the Apostolic Church in 2003; evidently not all of these churches had survived the transfer to Destiny.

TABLE 1: COMPARISON OF PENTECOSTAL CHURCHES
2002–2012
(categorized into growing and declining churches and sorted in order of size at 2002)

Pentecostal Body	Number of Churches				Comment
	2002	2012	Change	%	
Assemblies of God	261	233	-28	-10.73%	Schism of about 30 Samoan Assemblies of God churches in 2005
New Life Churches of New Zealand	108	93	-15	-13.89%	
Apostolic Churches (renamed ACTs Churches)	99	56	-43	-43.43%	Schism of 9 churches to Destiny in 2003
Elim Churches	60	41	-19	-31.67%	
Other churches (not specified)	33	30	-3	-9.09%	
Vineyard Churches	26	16	-10	-38.46%	
International Convention of Faith Ministries	19	18	-1	-5.26%	
Christian Revival Crusade Churches	12	8	-4	-33.33%	
Christian Outreach Centres	11	6	-5	-45.45%	
Millennium Ministries	7		-7	-100.00%	No data available for 2012
Christian Covenant Churches	5	0	-5	-100.00%	Closed; churches transferred to other groups
Associated Fellowships	3		-3	-100.00%	No data available for 2012

Pentecostal Body	Number of Churches				Comment
	2002	2012	Change	%	
Rhema Churches	0	0	0		Perhaps previously closed (awaiting further research)
Network of Christian Ministries	25	29	4	16.00%	
LinkNZ	15	19	4	26.67%	
Christian City Churches	9	16	7	77.78%	
Destiny Churches	5	10	5	100.00%	
Celebration Centres	2	7	5	250.00%	
Christian Life Churches	1	6	5	500.00%	
Samoan Assemblies of God in New Zealand	0	45[32]	45		About 30 of these churches had split from the Assemblies of God in 2005.
City Impact Churches	0	5	5		New group (split off from New Life Churches)
New Frontiers Churches	0	3	3		New group
Total	701	641	-60	-8.56%	

The Christian Life Centres increased from 1 to 6 churches by 2012, but this merely reflected the suburbanization of a large central city church. Furthermore, some of the new groups that emerged appear to have done so as secessions from other Pentecostal bodies. These changes appear to indicate that New Zealand Pentecostal growth was more a product of the "circulation of the saints" (to use the classic term of sociologists Bibby and Brinkerhof[33]) than of evangelism. This characteristic, together with the exodus of long-term participants from Pentecostal churches, represent worrying "straws in the wind" for New Zealand Pentecostalism.

So (to paraphrase a folk song from the 1960s), where have all the "Penties" gone? Firstly, the growth of urban Pentecostal mega-churches might indicate that smaller churches have been absorbed into larger bodies.[34] However, an analysis of Pentecostals belonging in each location reveals that the number of Pentecostal churches in the Auckland supercity (the location of many of these large mega-churches) had declined by 6.44 percent between 2002 and 2012. In other urban centers of more than 100,000 people (Hamilton, Tauranga, Napier/Hastings, Wellington, Christchurch, and Dunedin) the decline was 8.94 percent. In the provincial towns of less than 100,000 people (which were less likely to have mega-churches), this was greater still: 23.75 percent overall.[35] Six of the sixteen provincial areas (Northland, Waikato, Bay of Plenty, Gisborne, Tasman, and the Chatham Islands) had drops of more than 30 percent in the number of Pentecostal churches. The fall-offs in these more sparsely populated locations (where few mega-churches were located) were therefore unlikely to be due to a gravitational accretion to larger Pentecostal churches. A second factor (which has already been noted) is the trend toward informal house-fellowship groups. In part, this appears to reflect a rejection of Pentecostal institutionalism and an attempt to return to the less structured models of the 1960s and 1970s. This is indicative of a wider trend in New Zealand society, particularly with regards to institutional belonging. A third trend is the Pentecostal "leavening" of mainstream churches. This appears to reverse that of the 1960s and 1970s, when people left mainstream churches for Pentecostal groups.

A survey of four mainstream churches in Dunedin in 2013[36] produced the following results:

TABLE 2: PREVIOUS PENTECOSTAL INVOLVEMENT OF
CURRENT MAINSTREAM CHURCH MEMBERS

Church	Number of previous Pentecostal members	% of previous Pentecostal members in respondents	Weighted average length of participation in Pentecostal movement (in years)
Presbyterian (n = 82)	42	51.22%	6.92
Baptist (n = 163)	81	49.69%	7.15
Anglican (n = 27)	5	18.52%	12.70
Methodist (n = 14)	2	14.29%	1.75
Average (n = 71.5)	32.5	45.45%	7.21

This data shows that, on the average, more than 45 percent of
these churches' present congregations had previously been members of, or participants in, Pentecostal churches. This proportion was higher in the larger churches in the survey. The average
length of participation in Pentecostal churches was 7.21 years; a
number of respondents had been in the movement for more than
20 years. Several of these had held pastoral offices (and in one case,
the responsibility for national ministry training in a Pentecostal
denomination). It is therefore clear that there has been a noticeable exodus from Pentecostal to mainstream churches over the last
two decades and that these ex-Pentecostals have enriched the life
of the receiving churches. The effect of this has been to reinforce
the impact of the Charismatic movement and to "Pentecostalize"

aspects of mainstream church life, particularly in the areas of music and worship styles.

THE WIDER CONTEXT

Church attendance in the Western world has declined steadily since the 1960s, leading British historian of religion Hugh McLeod to refer to "the Religious Crisis of the 1960s."[37] Various reasons have been offered to explain this phenomenon, the two most prominent being the shift from modernity to postmodernity and the advance of secularization. French philosopher Jean-François Lyotard defines postmodernism as an "incredulity towards metanarratives,"[38] that is, a denial of overarching interpretative frameworks (such as "progress") or teleological goals.[39] This "incredulity" rejects the notion that the human race is following any particular course of development.[40] All such explanations become the results of an imposed subjectivism. History therefore becomes atomized and relativized, with the emphasis shifting from macrohistory to microhistory.[41] This, of course, undercuts all claims to institutional authority (which, in the case of the Christian church, are built upon the macrohistorical foundations of Scripture and tradition). However, this philosophy is not universally accepted as an explanation of the changes taking place in today's world, nor, I argue, is it logically consistent. Indeed, one could ask the question: Might not the movement from modernity to postmodernity *itself* be construed as having elements of a metanarrative? If this is the case, then Lyotard's "incredulity towards metanarratives" becomes self-contradictory. And while there is no doubt that institutional authority has been challenged since the 1960s, this did not necessarily lead to a general anarchy. As I will shortly argue, authority has been *deinstitutionalized* and *relocated*, rather than rejected outright.

A second, widely held explanation for the decline of religious authority in the Western world is secularization. Sociologist Bryan Wilson has defined this as "the process whereby religious thinking, practice and institutions lose social significance."[42] There is now a large body of literature by historians and sociologists that attempts to explain the religious crisis of the 1960s in terms of the secularization process.[43] In New Zealand this theory is widely accepted, largely due to the dominant influence of religious scholars Lloyd Geering and Jim Veitch, who are usually the scholars quoted by the media on religious subjects. But as sociologist David Martin has perceptively pointed out, proponents of this thesis tend to present it in *prescriptive*, rather than *descriptive* terms—i.e., secularization is what *should* be happening, rather than what *is* happening.[44]

The inconvenient truth is, as theologian Harvey Cox has noted, that "today it is secularity, not spirituality, that may be headed for extinction."[45] Other scholars also refer to the resacralizing of the world and to the "Spirituality Revolution" that is now emerging.[46] And, even among those scholars who continue to accept that the secularization process is to some extent valid, there is a circumscription of its influence and effect. Thus:

> ...instead of secularisation as an event "after Christendom," ...we have secularisation as a set of dynamics "within Christendom."...Where religion has flourished in the west...it has done so by breaking out of the didactic mode of territorial Christendom....Decline does not mean death—the difference is important.[47]

The tide of secularization now appears to be turning, both within New Zealand and overseas, and the ultimate secularity of society is much less assured.[48] It is increasingly being recognized that religion has not died out as the secularists had predicted and, indeed, that religious beliefs continue to be strongly held and spirituality to be strongly pursued. In New Zealand the practice of Māori *karakia* ("prayers," "incantations") and ceremonies such as the lifting of *tapu* ("spiritual restrictions") at public functions is an example of religiosity "coming through the backdoor," to the secularists' dismay.[49] Furthermore, as Bruce Knox (former executive director of the Bible College of New Zealand) has shown, interest in theological education has grown in New Zealand. The number of students taking theological subjects at tertiary institutions in this country increased by 98 percent between 1988 and 1999—this at a time when church rolls were continuing to fall.[50] Knox concludes that this points to the continuing existence of active inquiry into Christian things and thus challenges the popular view that Christianity is in decline in New Zealand.[51]

Secularization appears to reflect a *reorientation*, rather than a *relinquishing*, of religious belief. As will be seen, this is manifest not in the falling-off of spirituality and the death of Christianity, but in *the decline of the institutions that have characterized it*. One factor that frequently is overlooked by proponents of the secularization theory is that the process of institutional decline is not limited to religious bodies. Suspicion toward institutions is manifest both in a dwindling core of committed "membership" and in a reluctance to accept institutional claims of authority. While this is most marked in the decline of church membership, this phobia of commitment is reflected elsewhere also. Sociologist Kevin Ward has drawn an illuminating analogy from rugby football (which has the status of a "national religion" in New Zealand). He observes that although membership of rugby clubs in this country declined from 400,000 in 1970 to 120,000 by 2000, enthusiasm for the game remains widespread.[52] Ward finds the same phenomenon—i.e., of participation, but not membership—replicated in running clubs.[53] In other words, the decline in membership does not reflect a lack of interest, but *rather a reluctance to commit to the institutions that service this interest.*

The suspicion of institutions and the reluctance to commit to membership in them therefore extends much further than religious groups and is paralleled by a rejection of bureaucratic modes of authority. This diminution of authority is mirrored in altered modes of behavior. This is particularly the case with those based upon traditional forms of religious or church authority (for example, "no sex before marriage"). The churches are therefore fighting a losing battle to maintain traditional social mores, since their institutional authority is no longer universally accepted in the public arena.[54] It should be noted carefully, however, that this declining authority is not due to the process of secularization *per se*, but rather to the wider process of declining institutional—i.e., bureaucratic— authority. Furthermore, it is not a process peculiar to the churches, but is more pervasive, affecting all organizations and institutions of authority.

Nevertheless, this rejection of authority was neither total nor universal. The point at issue was the institution. As I have argued elsewhere,[55] the suspicion of institutional forms of authority during the 1960s represents a *relocation* rather than a *rejection* of authority. In the later 1960s particularly the youth culture was marked by a resistance to collectively imposed forms of authority. This involved the repudiation of traditional "institutional" standards of conduct, with the location of authority being both *personalized* and *internalized*: "Do your own thing!" and "If it feels good, do it!" This dependence on internal forms of authority was based on personal awareness and experience, either as an individual or as part of a group. However, this shift should not be overemphasized, since elements of conventionality and continuity also continued in the 1960s. The "Youth Counterculture" of the later 1960s was not as pronounced, militant, or oppositional in New Zealand as was the case overseas. Nevertheless, it did mark the beginnings of a relocation of authority away from traditional, external, institutions toward an internalized, autonomous authority. Or, to put it another way, it represented a rejection of bureaucratic modes of power and a move toward personalized and individualized—i.e., Charismatic—sources of authority. This contributed to the expansion of the Pentecostal and Charismatic movements. Less institutional forms of Christianity thus both reflected and benefited from these attitudinal shifts, and the rise of the Pentecostal and Charismatic movements has paralleled the decline of mainstream, institutional Christianity worldwide. These changes indicate, not a decay of Christian spirituality, but rather a deinstitutionalization and relocation of Christian participation. Profound changes *are* taking place in the institutional character of Christianity, but—as church historian Dominic Erdozain emphasizes—this does necessarily not mean its demise.[56] As with American author Mark Twain, reports of its death have been greatly exaggerated.

PENTECOSTAL PROSPECTS

A number of "glacial" shifts have taken place in the religiosity of the Western world. I have commented on the suspicion of institutions that has been evident in the increasing institutional decline since the late 1960s. I have also noted that spirituality is continuing outside the institutions that have traditionally serviced it and that these changes represent the *relocation*—rather than the *rejection*—of authority. This internalization of religious authority has obvious affinities with Charismatic forms of Christianity, although it carries its own dangers in hyperindividualism and in cults of personality. In New Zealand these changes have resulted in the realignment of longstanding Pentecostal networks, the rise of megachurches in the larger urban centers, and the emergence of a growing network of house churches. There has also been a significant leavening of mainstream churches as Pentecostals transfer their membership to them, possibly because of increased opportunities for ongoing individual spiritual development.

What is the significance of these changes for the future of Pentecostalism in Aotearoa-New Zealand? The rise of urban mega-churches might indicate a possible trajectory for the movement, although there are considerable risks associated with this. These churches depend to a great extent on the person of the Charismatic leader and therefore face routinization of their charisma on the transmission of that leadership to the next generation. It seems to the author that these churches are in fact falling into the trap of institutionalization—and this at a time when institutions are under suspicion. Conversely, the decline of Pentecostal denominations and churches in the first decade of the twenty-first century is a trend in the opposite direction. Together with the waning intensity of spiritual experience, this indicates a certain degree of Pentecostal malaise.

Nevertheless, there are some positive indications for the future. In the wider community there is some recovery of the youth idealism that had characterized the 1960s and that contributed to Pentecostal expansion in that decade. A Dunedin high school principal recently commented to the author that many pupils at her school are heavily involved in voluntary community and service projects. She observed that this is a schoolwide phenomenon and is not limited to Pentecostal or Christian young people.[57] Elsewhere, there are specific Christian manifestations of this reemerging commitment, with young people becoming involved in service agencies such as Servants and living and working in Asian urban slums.[58] Others are participating in new communal lifestyles such as Urban

Monasticism and in social assistance projects in their local communities. One group of Dunedin Christians has recently purchased a discontinued primary school campus and plan to build a community of low-cost family "cohouses,"[59] using the main school buildings as a community center.[60] These local examples reflect a wider trend of engagement in community-based social ministries and a holistic understanding of the Christian gospel.[61] Although these developments are not confined to Pentecostalism, they do reflect changing perceptions of the Holy Spirit's work in the world. These idealistic young people are often highly educated—in some cases, holding doctoral degrees—and are fully committed to following the Holy Spirit both within and beyond their churches. The strengths of the Pentecostal movement lie in its adaptability and in its democratization of spiritual power. These characteristics, together with the continued public interest in spirituality (although not in the institutions which service it), indicate opportunities for it at a grassroots level. After all, the power of Pentecostalism lies, as its adherents believe, not in an institutional channel but in the Holy Spirit as the wind that blows where it will, both inside and outside organizational boundaries. The key for the movement's survival and ongoing effectiveness is therefore to maintain a dependence on, and sensitivity to, the divine Spirit. Church history is replete with examples of the "hurricane" force of God's Spirit coming suddenly and unexpectedly upon individual (and collective) acts of faith and obedience to God's leading. The future of the Pentecostal movement will depend on its participants' willingness to take small steps such as these.

Part V: Roman Catholicism and Other Theological Themes

Chapter 19

Roman Catholic Charismatic Renewal in Asia: Implications and Opportunities

Jonathan Y. Tan

THE BIRTH OF renewal Christianity is the most momentous development of Christianity in the twentieth century. Beginning with the incipient Pentecostal revival in 1901 at Charles F. Parham's Bethel Bible School in Topeka, Kansas, that was marked by ecstatic outbursts of *glossolalia* or speaking in tongues, leading to the famed Azusa Street Revival that began on April 9, 1906, under the dynamic leadership of the African American preacher William J. Seymour, the Pentecostal movement has grown beyond its initial roots into a truly global movement that has penetrated into the established or mainline churches as the Charismatic movement from the 1960s onward. Without a doubt, the Charismatic movement has swept through much of Asia, transforming Asian Christianity in the wider Catholic Church. Asia joins Africa and Latin America in having a sizeable number of Pentecostal and Charismatic Christians, with a significant number of Charismatic Christians in the Philippines, India, China, Korea, and Southeast Asia. While Charismatic Christians retain their various denominational affiliations, they nevertheless share the same emphasis on the gifts of the Spirit, including a deep and fervent religious experience, baptism in the Spirit, speaking in tongues or *glossolalia*, healings and miracles, prophecy, signs and wonders, as well as a renewed life in the Holy Spirit, which acts as a signpost and guide in their daily lives.

The Roman Catholic Charismatic renewal movement took root in Asia in the late 1960s, in the aftermath of the Second Vatican Council (1962–1965) that transformed the Roman Catholic Church in Asia and elsewhere. Like their Pentecostal and Charismatic counterparts, Charismatic Catholics emphasize a new faith life through baptism in the Spirit and receiving and sharing the gifts of the Spirit, including *glossolalia*, prophecy, healing, and miracles. Since the nascent Charismatic movement caught fire among Asian Catholics in the 1970s, it has experienced tremendous growth throughout the region. According to the latest statistics compiled by the Vatican-backed International Catholic Charismatic Renewal Services (ICCRS), there are nearly fourteen thousand Charismatic prayer groups in the Asian Church, with an estimated 15 percent of Asian Catholics involved in the Catholic Charismatic Renewal Movement (CCRM). Asia comes second after Latin America, which has an estimated 16 percent of Catholics involved in the CCRM.[1]

The CCRM in Asia received a big boost in 1994 with the formation of the Catholic Charismatic Council for Asia-Pacific under the aegis of the ICCRS. As a result of the efforts of various local leaders in building and promoting the CCRM within various regions of Asia, the tremendous growth of the CCRM throughout Asia caught the attention of the ICCRS, which established the ICCRS Sub-Committee for Asia-Oceania (ISAO) in December 2006 at a meeting in Singapore that drew participants from fourteen countries in the Asia-Oceania region. The ISAO organized the First Asia-Oceania Catholic Charismatic Renewal Leaders' Conference in Jakarta, Indonesia, from September 14–18, 2008, which drew 525 CCRM leaders from twenty-one countries in the Asia-Oceania region and marked an important milestone in the awakening of the Spirit in the revival of the Asian Catholic Church. This was followed by the establishment of the Gulf Catholic Charismatic Renewal Services (GCCRS) and an inaugural conference from December 7–9, 2008, that drew 1,800 leaders from Bahrain, Kuwait, Oman, Qatar, Saudi Arabia, and the United Arab Emirates under the banner "Let the Fire Fall Again." In turn, this paved the way for Asia to have the honor of hosting in South Korea from June 2–9, 2009, the International Catholic Charismatic Leaders' Conference. This was the first time that this global conference was held outside of Italy in Asia. Drawing participants from forty-three countries around the world, this conference culminated in a Charismatic prayer rally that drew around fifty thousand participants. This was an important milestone and coming of age for the CCRM in Asia, enabling Asia to take its place alongside Latin America and Africa as regions where the CCRM is growing and thriving.[2]

As space does not permit an extended discussion of the growth and significance of the CCRM in various regions throughout Asia, this essay focuses on two case studies of the CCRM in Asia, namely the El Shaddai movement in the Philippines and the *Khristbhakta* movement in Northern India. It will highlight the principal elements of these two movements, explore their significance, and consider their theological implications and challenges for the Catholic Church on new ways of creating and constituting ecclesial communities that are inspired by the Holy Spirit working among the subaltern masses of Asia.

PHILIPPINES

As a country with the highest concentration of Catholics in Asia, Philippines has witnessed the tremendous growth of the CCRM since the 1970s. Stanley Burgess observes that the Catholic

Charismatic movement has grown tremendously in the Philippines, drawing more than 11.5 million participants since taking root in the Philippines in 1969 when Brother Aquinas and Mother Marie Angela started Charismatic prayer groups.[3] He notes that the success of these Charismatic fellowships among Filipino Catholics prompted the Filipino bishops to co-opt these independent groups within the broader framework of the Catholic Church. This paved the way for the formation of vibrant groups such as El Shaddai, Couples for Christ, the Community of God's Little Children, and *Bukas Loob Sa Diyos* (Open to the Spirit of God).

Among the various CCRM groups in the Philippines, the most prominent among them is the El Shaddai movement.[4] Established in 1981 by Brother Mike Velarde, El Shaddai swept like wildfire among Filipino Catholics, garnering a following of about eleven million within fifteen years, with chapters in nearly every province in the Philippines and more than thirty-five countries around the world.[5] Filipino Catholics, with their flair for baroque exuberance,[6] find the personal and emotive intensity of El Shaddai's *gawain* or weekly lay-led Charismatic prayer meetings with laying on of hands, miracles and faith healings, and exorcisms highly attractive, in contrast to the impersonal and dry "soberness and sense"[7] of the official liturgies of the Roman Rite.

Wiegele describes El Shaddai's *gawain* or weekly Charismatic prayer meetings as highly emotional and cathartic events involving a lot of singing that is led by a choir and praise band, "sharing" or testifying by El Shaddai members, dramatic sermonizing by a visiting preacher, praying in tongues, and the preacher laying hands on members for healing, casting out evil spirits, or slaying participants in the Holy Spirit.[8] She suggests that in these weekly *gawain*, El Shaddai's Charismatic lay healers exercise traditional shaman-like functions.[9] It appears that as far as the ordinary Filipinos who attend these *gawain* perceive El Shaddai's layer healers as replacing local folk healers or *yakal* in exorcizing spirits and healing ailments.[10]

More interestingly, Wiegele observes that the *gawain* incorporates ritual elements of the Mass as a form of *mimicry* of the official liturgy, thereby maintaining orthodoxy while pursuing innovation, especially with the lay prayer leader-healer imitating the ritual actions of the priest in an official liturgical ritual. Her detailed observation of a *gawain* in a neighborhood in the heart of Metro Manila that she calls "Sinag" highlights the lay leader's *mimicry* of his ordained counterpart's ritual actions:

> There are, however, certain ceremonial elements of the *gawain* in Sinag that mimic the Catholic mass. During one Sinag *gawain*, there was a sort of table that resembled an altar in a Catholic Church. Consisting of a table covered with white cloth, it was placed at the front of the meeting place (in this case the paved, enclosed schoolyard) in what would be the "stage" area. The preacher placed a glass of water (presumably to moisten his throat) on the table and laid a folded white handkerchief neatly across the top of the glass, mimicking the holy chalice of wine and water, with the cloth, on a priest's altar. On this table were two candles as well as a crucifix on a stand with a rosary draped over it—again references to the Catholic altar. Holding the Bible over his head with both hands, as a priest often does, the preacher entered. He then kissed the Bible ceremoniously (again mimicking a priest) before turning around to address the group. Before preaching, the man turned his back to the crowd, faced the bare cement wall of the schoolyard, and bowed his head in a short prayer. To my research assistant, this was amusing. When the priest does this he is facing both the holy tabernacle and the crucifix in a symbolic gesture; the El Shaddai preacher was facing a cement wall. It was done in such a way, however, that any practicing Catholic would have recognized

the liturgical parallels. The borrowed ritual elements seemed to give the novice preacher, an unschooled man in his early twenties, an aura of legitimacy.[11]

One important difference separates the *gawain* from the official liturgical rites; that is, the *gawain* provide space for and empower laity from the subaltern Filipino classes as prophets, exorcists, and healers. More importantly, this empowerment of the laity has kindled the fire that led to the explosive growth of the El Shaddai movement across the globe. Where Filipino migrant workers go, they inevitably bring El Shaddai with them. In the Middle East, where there are severe restrictions on the establishment of parishes and missions, the lay leaders of the El Shaddai movement have been able to circumvent official restrictions on clerical presence to keep the Christian faith alive and strong among the Filipino migrant workers who labor under significant hardship and miserable working conditions across the Middle East.

INDIA

In his seminal essay surveying the emergence and growth of Pentecostalism in India,[12] Stanley Burgess notes that that the Catholic Charismatic renewal began in India in 1972 when Minoo Engineer, a young Parsi student at Fordham University, participated in the Catholic Charismatic fellowship and was converted to the Catholic faith. When he returned to India, he planted the seeds of the Charismatic renewal among Indian Catholics. His efforts were complemented by two Indian Jesuit priests, Fuster and Bertie Philips, who became Charismatic during their studies in the United States and, upon returning to India, established Catholic Charismatic prayer fellowships, beginning with Mumbai before spreading throughout India. Burgess also highlights the outreach of the popular Indian Catholic Charismatic healer and preacher from

Kerala, Mathew Naickomparambil, who has established the Divine Retreat Centre in Potta to facilitate his ministry to the growing community of Indian Charismatic Catholics.[13]

Amidst the various Catholic Charismatic groups in India, the one group that stands out because of its profound ecclesiological implications for the Asian Catholic Church is the *Khristbhakta* Movement.[14] *Khristbhaktas* are Indian devotees of *Yesubhagavan* (Christ Jesus) as their *Satguru*, that is, the true Lord and teacher who shall lead them along the path of new life and spiritual growth. They draw spiritual nourishment from Christian ashrams, maintaining a dual belonging or hybridized identity as followers of Christ and His gospel while not formally seeking baptism and church membership, in order to retain their Hindu identities.[15] Although the *Khristbhaktas* are not, strictly speaking, Catholics as they have neither sought baptism nor participate in the traditional Catholic sacramental life, nonetheless they demonstrate the future direction of hybridized or dual/multiple-belonging Indian Catholic Charismatic faith and practice that confounds the institutional structures and boundaries of classical forms of Christian identity and church membership that first emerged in Late Antique Europe.

The *Khristbhakta* movement is the vision and brainchild of Fr. Anil Dev, an Indian Catholic priest and missioner of the Indian Missionary Society (IMS), who started the movement in 1993 at Matridham Ashram. Founded and operated by the IMS in the midst of the Hindu heartland of Varanasi, Matridham Ashram represents a unique Indian Catholic experiment at providing a liminal space for hybridized Hindu *bhakti* (devotional) and Indian Catholic Charismatic expressions of spiritual formation and faith development. Since then, the *Khristbhakta* movement has spread among the subaltern Dalits and Tribals in the northern region of India. According to the IMS missioner Jerome Sylvester, who undertook an ethnographical study of the *Khristbhakta* movement, a survey conducted between 2003 and 2007 reveals that the Scheduled Castes comprise about 37.3 percent of the *Khristbhaktas*. Sylvester further notes that the majority of *Khristbhaktas* are from the subaltern communities of Dalits and Tribals in India.[16] While Matridham Ashram remains the spiritual heartland of the *Khristbhakta* movement, newer communities have emerged across northern India, including Jeevan Dham (Faridabad, near New Delhi), Yesu Darbar (Allahabad), Jabalpur (Madhya Pradesh), Uttar Pradesh, Ranchi (Jharkhand), Patna (Bihar), and Haryana.[17]

Eschewing the path of baptism for membership in the Indian Catholic Church, most *Khristbhaktas* opt to maintain a hybridized identity, remaining in the *liminal* space of the interstices between Hinduism and Charismatic Christianity, participating in weekly Charismatic prayer meetings with laying of hands and healings called *satsangs* that combine aspects of rituals of liturgical tradition with devotionals (*bhakti*), feasting (*melâ*), healing, and exorcisms that are led by lay leaders called *aguwas*.[18] The *satsangs* are well attended and numbers grow as a result of testimonies of miracles and healings by participants. From his fieldwork among the *Khristbhaktas*, the IMS missioner Jerome Sylvester notes that the *Khristbhaktas* seek to combine traditional Indian devotional practices with devotional and ritual elements from the Charismatic movement.[19] Sylvester unpacks the implications of the *Khristbhakta* Movement as follows:

> The Khristbhaktas are trying to create a social space for themselves in different ways by affirming their experience in Christ. They have found the Khristbhakta Movement as one of the channels. Emancipation and empowerment become the driving force that draws them to the Movement. They find support and shelter in features of free association in the

Satsang. The movement is free in every sense of the word, no membership and no limiting structures.[20]

Concluding Theological Reflections

One unifying thread that binds the Filipino El Shaddai Charismatics and the Indian *Khristbhaktas* is that many of them hail primarily from the subaltern classes[21] of their communities that are confronting the challenges of postcolonialism, postmodernism, and globalization that are rapidly transforming the world around them. Moreover, both examples as discussed above also reveal the complexities of multiple belongings and hybridized identities[22] that challenge the homogeneity of the ecclesiological vision of the Catholic Church. By putting at the center of their faith life their hybridized devotional and popular ritual practices rather than the church's official liturgy, these subaltern Asians are challenging the hegemony of a Eurocentric and Roman-centric vision of church. This has profound implications, especially as the center of Christianity has shifted away from Rome and Europe to the Two-Thirds World.[23]

Moreover, if ecclesial identity and communion with Rome is the center of a fully lived Catholic experience, one has to ask how the official church could incorporate the Christ-followers from the subaltern masses across Asia who have accepted Jesus but choose to live out their faith in an alternate *hybridized* ecclesial world that synthesizes folk and popular identity markers with the gospel message within the Charismatic praxis of renewal Christianity. Although Jerome Sylvester made these remarks in the context of *Khristbhaktas*, they are pertinent to the marginal status of other subaltern groups, who reject official ecclesial identities for hybridized identities:

The subaltern struggle against caste and class can be well
understood against the background of heterodox and antisys-
temic movements. Those who are at the margins negotiate the
porous borders in their search of a new identity and empowerment. Khristbhaktas negotiate the borders of faith and culture
for empowerment against social exclusion and marginalization from the liminal position of Hinduism and Christianity.[24]

In response, one could discount two extreme solutions, i.e.,
monolithic uniformity and chaotic heterogeneity. Monolithic uniformity insists on homogeneity at the expense of healthy diversity
and differences, while chaotic heterogeneity accentuates differences
without seeking a middle ground that is *sine qua non* for community building. This essay proposes that the middle way between
monolithic uniformity and chaotic heterogeneity would be a *catholicity* that eschews uniformity, maintaining a connection with the
universal church while also affirming the real particularities of the
local concerns. Indeed, Asian Catholics are faced with the tension
of balancing the *catholicity* of the church on the one hand and the
particularities of their own lives together with their complexities,
nuances, and hybridities on the other hand. By *catholicity*, I refer to
the US ecclesiologist Joseph Komonchak's definition of catholicity
as "a fullness or wholeness which reflects and embodies the fullness
of the gifts of God's salvation in Christ and embraces the totality of
human life and culture."[25] As Komonchak explains:

> Theological reflection on the catholicity attributed to the
> Church in the Creed has varied over the ages. Reviews of this
> tradition present it as varying between emphasis on "quali-
> tative wholeness" and stress on "extensive universality," the
> former dominant in patristic and medieval thought, the latter
> in post-Reformation apologetical argument. The last two cen-
> turies have seen a recovery of the earlier, patristic qualitative

notion of catholicity which has now supplemented or even supplanted the apologetical argument from geography.[26]

Moreover, Komonchak insists that "catholicity is not simply variety, but a *variety integrated,* made a whole, a recapitulation of all things, persons, and cultures *under the headship of Christ and in the unity of the Spirit*" (emphasis added).[27] Here, Komonchak gives the Holy Spirit an important role in uniting and integrating diversity and pluralism within the catholicity of Christ's church on earth. In doing so, he builds upon the understanding of catholicity as "a common effort to attain fullness in unity" that was outlined by the Second Vatican Council in its Dogmatic Constitution on the Church, *Lumen Gentium* (LG):

> This character of universality which adorns the People of God is a gift from the Lord himself. By reason of it, the Catholic Church strives energetically and constantly to bring all humanity with all its riches back to Christ its Head in the unity of his Spirit. In virtue of this catholicity each individual part of the Church contributes through its special gifts to the good of the other parts and of the whole Church. Thus through the common sharing of gifts and through the *common effort to attain fullness in unity,* the whole and each of the parts receive increase.[28]

Reading LG 13 and Komonchak together would suggest that Asian Catholics should consider privileging a *catholicity* that balances the extremes of monolithic uniformity with Rome on the one hand and chaotic heterogeneity on the other hand. Moreover, the paradigm of catholicity expresses beautifully the unitive in-gathering of believers that took place at Pentecost under the inspiration of the Holy Spirit, where everyone present heard the good news of Jesus Christ being proclaimed to them *in their own languages.* As the Acts of the Apostles describes it:

And how is it that we hear, each of us, in our own native
language? Parthians, Medes, Elamites, and residents of
Mesopotamia, Judea and Cappadocia, Pontus and Asia,
Phrygia and Pamphylia, Egypt and the parts of Libya
belonging to Cyrene, and visitors from Rome, both Jews and
proselytes, Cretans and Arabs—in our own languages we hear
them speaking about God's deeds of power.

—ACTS 2:9–11, NRSV

Clearly, social, cultural, and other particularities need not be
suppressed in order to receive the gospel and follow Christ. The
bystanders were not asked to give up their languages, ethnicities,
cultures, and traditions to hear the gospel in Hebrew or Aramaic,
the earliest languages of the Christian church. Indeed, it appeared
to have been divinely willed that under the inspiration of the Holy
Spirit, catholicity amidst diversity and plurality, rather than homogeneous uniformity, was to be the hallmark of the fledging church
from the moment of its birth at Pentecost. In other words, without
the diversity and plurality of Asian communities, including subaltern communities in the fullness of their marginal status, multiple belongings, and hybridized identities, there can be no true
catholicity.

To conclude, a renewed Asian Catholic Church would also be
nourished by the rich diversity and plurality of popular devotions,
of which the diverse variety of Charismatic prayer meetings and
their rituals of *glossolalia*, healing, miracles, and prophecies are
examples *par excellence* of popular devotions that are inspired by
the Holy Spirit to draw the Asian peoples closer to Jesus Christ
and His good news of salvation. The importance of popular devotions in general and Charismatic devotional practices in particular
should not be underrated. Popular devotions are able to provide
a multifaceted window that would enable one to glimpse into the
mind of the *sensus fidelium* and the ethos of a community that

is outside the grasp of formal and normative ecclesial structures. Popular devotions also empower the subaltern Asians to express their faith, piety, and spirituality in a manner that is often beyond the case of official ecclesial control, as is the case with Charismatic prayer meetings in its various local forms and practices. Be it the El Shaddai's *gawain* or the Khristbaktas' *satsangs*, it is the same Spirit that unites the variety of gifts, services, and activities for the greater glory of God and the common good of all (1 Cor. 12:1–11), thereby transcending past precedents to uncover new ways of constituting ecclesial communities in the name of Christ Jesus.

Chapter 20

Unleashing the Dragon: Exploration of the Possible Impact of Chinese Confucian Culture on Pentecostal Hermeneutics

Jacqueline Grey

THE PROPHETIC WRITINGS of the Old Testament provide a record of the messages of Yahweh communicated through the mediator of the prophet to a particular person or people group within the history of ancient Israel.[1] Generally these messages were directed to the community contemporary with the prophet to provide guidance or warning of possible future events. This chapter will explore prophetic writings and the role of the prophetic in two ways. First, it will attempt to emulate the role of the Old Testament prophet to speak to the contemporary community in discerning possible future trends and trajectories of Pentecostalism. The possible trend explored in this essay is the emergence of Chinese Confucian culture as an influencing factor within Pentecostalism. Second, it will explore the potential impact of Confucian-influenced readings of Scripture for Pentecostals through a reading of the prophetic text of Joel 2:28–32.[2] A fundamental though controversial tenet within the discussion of Pentecostal hermeneutics is the role of experience. While this discussion emphasises the importance of experience as the lens through which Pentecostals read

Scripture, it will reflect on the role of culture[3] in forming experience and, by implication, its influence in the reading process.

While Chinese culture and language is generally observed to have had an influential impact on the history and development of its surrounding cultures within Asia, in more recent decades China has grown in its international influence, particularly in the economic and political spheres. For the majority of countries in the Asia-Pacific region, including Australia, China is a major (if not *the* major) trading partner.[4] What is still to be seen is the emerging influence of China's "soft power,"[5] that is, the subtle export of its culture and values. This is primarily exported through entertainment, technology, and literature. While Western influence (particularly the United States) dominates these fields through the "soft culture" of entertainment and literature, its influence may begin to decline as Asian nations, such as China and India, develop and increase export of their own local industries. In particular, China has become a primary producer of manufactured goods within the global context, so the next step is for China to become a primary producer of cultural and intellectual goods. A unique element that Chinese culture offers in its production of cultural and intellectual goods stems from its tradition of Confucianism. Although this tradition, in terms of ritual application, has been in recent generations disrupted by Communist influences in mainland China, Confucianism is still an important underpinning of Chinese cultural values.[6] This tradition remains a major factor in the defining of contemporary Chinese culture.

It must be noted from the outset that there are enormous challenges in exploring this topic of the emergence of Chinese Confucian culture as an influencing factor within Asia and, by implication, Asian Pentecostalism. For example, is Chinese Confucian culture to be defined geographically and politically, that is, confined to mainland China rather than the significant Chinese communities located elsewhere? Or is Chinese Confucian culture to be understood as the cultural values implicit in the cultural values of a community, including cultures such as Korean? My response is that all of the above can actually be included in a definition of Chinese Confucian culture. However, to simplify the discussion, I will focus primarily on Chinese Confucian culture as a set of ideals and values exported from mainland China. My own location in the discussion is that of an Australian female Pentecostal observing the growing influence of China within the broader global economy and political spheres. The engagement of countries such as Australia with Chinese language and culture is not new. The anticipated growth of China's tiger economy can be seen in the introduction over the last two decades of Mandarin and Cantonese taught as a second language to many Australian students, including myself. This exposure to Chinese language and literature and its underpinning Confucian tradition is likely to increase. While there is no doubt that the increasing interaction between China and Western countries will result in the exporting of Western values to China, there has generally tended to be little expectation among Western nations for the reverse: that Chinese language and ideas will influence beyond its borders and impact the West. The potential is for the transformation of dominant Western cultures through the influence of Chinese values. As Baogang He writes, "In terms of a cultural encounter, the interaction of culture A with culture B reduces the uniqueness of each culture."[7] Western ideas and values may begin to be altered through exposure to and interaction with Chinese Confucian culture.

This essay suggests that the increasing interaction with mainland China through globalization and the growth of the Chinese economy will result in an increasing number of people or countries being exposed to and sharing common values with those developed in China. As mainland China increases the exporting of its culture and literature through "soft culture," Chinese Confucian culture will begin to influence cultures outside its borders. Baogang He calls this the "universalization" or "globalization" of Chinese values and characteristics.[8] As prophets of the future of Pentecostalism, this calls us to question: What if Chinese characteristics became more integrated into a broader global culture? How might Western values, such as democracy, be transformed through the interaction with Chinese Confucian culture? What implications does this have for how Christians and, especially Pentecostals, read Scripture and do theology?

GLOBALIZATION AND CHINESE CONFUCIAN CULTURE

The globalization of Chinese Confucian culture would offer a coming together of Western and Chinese values. It is anticipated that the fusion of Chinese culture with Western culture would form a third unique alternative, or hybrid. What are some of the specific values that would be fused in this enterprise? How would they be evaluated? A fusion of cultures would involve combining seemingly disparate values, such as Confucian filial piety and its tendency toward authoritarianism with Western democracy. It would blend the virtue of benevolence with individualism. While Western culture measures motives and intent, Confucianism measures the outcome. Relationships are emphasised over personal (that is, individual) ambition. Prestige and status, which tend to be allocated to men, are honored in the Confucian tradition over the Western ideal of the equality of the genders. The question at large is not can these two traditions mix, but *how* will they mix? What will become common values and what will be abandoned in the fusion of these two cultures to form a unique alternative? This also raises the issue

of how this fusion could and should be evaluated. As Ormerod and
Clifton note, "It is not good enough to simply observe the phenomenon of an emerging global culture, to trace its movements, to mark
out its boundaries. Should it be encouraged and what form should
it take? Or should it be rejected, and if so why?"[9] How does one
evaluate an emerging global culture? This is no simple task; culture is a multilayered reality.[10] For some Pentecostal scholars, the
approach is to compare the current or developing culture with its
original expression. This restorationist approach, in which the origins of Pentecostalism[11] are idealized, is popular in contemporary
Pentecostal studies, particularly the study of Pentecostal hermeneutics. Scholars such as McQueen and Archer[12] have retrieved
early Pentecostal readings of Scripture in the attempt to eluci-
date the core of Pentecostalism. While they do not assume that a
simple retrieving of early Pentecostal readings of Scripture will provide a Weberian pure vision of the religion, they do suggest that a
second *naiveté*—based on the retrieval of a selected reading of early
Pentecostalism—can provide a re-vision that embraces the initial
vision yet expands it for the contemporary context. This assumes
a normative understanding of early Pentecostalism; that is, that
the original community of the Azusa Street Revival[13] provides the
permanent ideal to be achieved, albeit with improvements. This
restorationist approach fails to identify the role of culture, particularly North American culture in the early twentieth century,
upon this idealized expression of Pentecostalism. It assumes that,
to some extent, the original Pentecostal community embodied the
pure expression of the religion. However, as Ormerod and Clifton
note, there has never been a "pure" form of Christianity that was
unrelated to some preexisting cultural matrix. In the same way,
neither has there ever been a "pure" form of Pentecostalism; if anything, Pentecostalism has been incubated in the culture of North

America. Now, with its center shifting to the global south, it can be expected that Pentecostalism will be changed by or adapt to exposure to other cultures.

What kind of impact might an emerging hybrid culture have upon Pentecostalism? This chapter will evaluate the possible emerging fusion of Chinese culture with Western culture in the light of the ideals of the vision of Pentecostalism expressed in its origins and transformed through the globalized culture. The ideals of the vision of Pentecostalism are emphasised as the democratization of the Spirit and emphasis on immediate encounter with God. To envision what this new enculturation might look like—the fusing of these two disparate cultural systems in the globalization of Chinese culture and its implications for Pentecostalism—it will be imagined through the reading of a prophetic text: Joel 2:28–32.

Joel in Pentecostal Interpretation

The prophet Joel envisions a worshipping community, located during the post-exilic period and centered on the routine operation of the temple in Jerusalem. Elizabeth Achtemeier notes the twin themes of God's judgment of human sin and grace that dominate the book. The experience of judgment and grace overflow from humanity into the broader creation. Destruction is not the destiny of God's covenant people, but grace.[14] Judgment is envisioned in cosmic imagery as Joel describes the coming judgment of the day of the Lord. This terminology of the "Day of the Lord" draws on the apocalyptic tradition of Amos, Isaiah, and Ezekiel. Yet this is not just an update of the earlier tradition; Joel offers not only a rescue from this terrible devastation but also a reversal. In response to the repentance and lamentation of the people (Joel 2:18),[15] the land will be restored. As judgment was envisioned through the cosmic and natural realms, so will God's benevolent salvation be known. Joel

2:28–32 then describes the signs that will accompany the apocalyptic in-breaking of God's rule. By these signs the people will
know the day of the Lord. The day of the Lord will be preceded
by supernatural signs in both the cosmic and natural spheres. The
motifs of fire, darkness, the veiling of the sun and moon are cosmic
signs of God's supremacy and rule. Not the least of the signs is the
outpouring of God's Spirit. The goal of this restoration is relational;
God will be known in experiential encounter. Joel invites hope for
a future community of prophets.[16] Pentecostal scholar McQueen
emphasises the role of the direct speech of Yahweh in the Book of
Joel, and the exchange with the people of Judah.[17] This emphasis
has enormous implications for the Pentecostal community that
seeks to hear and know God (like the Judean community) through
direct encounter.

A key message of Joel 2:28–32 to the community is: just as
God has spoken directly to the prophet, so will the Spirit of God
be given to the covenant community. The outpouring of Spirit
is promised in response to the lamentation and repentance of
the people.[18] This promise of the Spirit in Joel fulfils the Mosaic
longing for all people to hear God's voice (Num. 11:29). As the Spirit
of prophecy was given to Moses's elders to authenticate their leadership and authority, so the Spirit will be given to Joel's community. Similarly, the goal of the giving of the promises of salvation
(including the promise of the Spirit) for Joel is that the people may
know Yahweh. Knowing Yahweh and hearing Yahweh are inex-
tricably linked.[19] As McQueen writes, "the enablement of all the
people of Judah to prophesy means that all will have immediate
knowledge of Yahweh."[20] This has tremendous implications for the
Pentecostal community that reads this promise through the lens of
Luke-Acts and the democratization of the Spirit. Achtemeier notes
that while Acts emphasises that this promise of the Spirit is given

to those of all the nations, Joel does not offer this outpouring of the Spirit as a universal gift but limits its offer specifically to the covenant people.[21] However, within the boundary of the community of covenant people, there are no limits.

Joel describes the outpouring of the Spirit on "all flesh." As McQueen points out, defining "all flesh" as the people of Judah emphasizes the "flesh" aspect of the recipients, that is, those who are weak and marginalized.[22] He writes:

> The contrast is thus between the privileged status of selected individuals who received the spirit of Yahweh in the past and the "democratization" of the spirit upon all persons in the community of Judah in the future. Privileges based upon gender or age or social standing will end when the spirit poured out.[23]

This group of Spirit-gifted people in Joel are not just elders, nor men, but includes young people, women, and slaves—those normally outside the power structures of the community. In this new exodus, the inclusive prophetic vocation will be gifted to daughters and sons, old and young, to allow each member of the community to hear directly from God rather than be confined to the exclusive prophet. The Spirit will enable Joel's community the full range of prophetical experience: to have dreams, to have visions, and to prophesy. This signifies an intimacy with God, known previously exclusively to the prophets, now available for the whole community.[24] No longer will a prophet be required to mediate God's message and guidance to the people; they will relate to God directly. The Spirit will no longer be given to a select minority but will be available for the whole community. This activity and democratization of the Spirit is a sign that the day of the Lord is near. According to Acts 2, this was fulfilled on the Day of Pentecost. This is a gracious, benevolent gift; even the ability to call on the name of the Lord is enabled by the Spirit. In God's grace, those to whom God has given the Spirit are able to call upon the name of the Lord.[25] To call on the name of the Lord means to live by God's will and guidance, rather than our own. Each member of the community is to call on God constantly for guidance and empowering, not just in times of trouble, but continually as part of their relational obedience.[26]

CHINESE CONFUCIAN CONTRIBUTIONS TO JOEL INTERPRETATION

In the light of this, what might a global Chinese Confucian reading of Joel 2:28–32 offer, and how might it challenge some of the presuppositions of either Western or Pentecostal cultures? A prominent feature of Western cultures is the emphasis on democracy. Foundational to democracy is belief in the common equality and inherent value of each recognized person within the community. It may be understood as the diffusion of power from one ruler to the majority. The Western democratic system emphasizes rights as inherent to the person; it means that the person is entitled to his or her right, including the right to do wrong, or even evil. For traditional Confucianism, rights originate with the state and are not inherent to the person. Rights for the individual do exist, particularly the right to be heard, but it is not an individualistic theory of rights. Instead, Confucianism emphasises the existence and development of community as the priority over the individual right to do wrong. As Baogang He asserts, "According to Confucianism, individuals are social beings and have duties to their communities and societies."[27] He notes that, in comparison, an individualistic starting point for rights has great difficulty in balancing rights and duties as rights are considered intrinsic to the person regardless of their willingness or unwillingness to accept their responsibilities. In this sense, Confucianism emphasises the priority of compassion over individual rights. This, according to He, can promote the enterprise of human rights. To fuse these seemingly incongruent values of filial piety and the Confucian respect for authority with democracy may lead to a new and transformed understanding of democracy, a democracy in which individual rights coexist with responsibility for the other. Rather than democracy being the servant of factionalism, its fusion with Confucianism can introduce a concern for the interests and welfare of the whole community, and not merely an individual's own narrow interests. In this sense, morally autonomous individuals are responsible for the fate of the nation and community.[28]

According to McQueen, there is a need for a re-visioning or renewal of Pentecostalism to its initial vision, that is, an eschatological orientation and apocalyptic spirituality. He writes, "Most critiques of contemporary Pentecostalism from both inside and outside the movement point to an accommodation of the middle-class American values of individualism and consumerism as the reason for the waning of such a radical vision."[29] Instead, for Pentecostals, there is a responsibility for each believer to be a witness of truth. According to McQueen, the foundation of this responsibility is located in the belief in the priesthood and prophethood of all believers. The giving of the Spirit at Pentecost to all people regardless of gender, class, or age (in fulfilment of the prophet Joel) is foundational to this understanding of the prophethood of all believers. As McQueen notes, "According to the book of Joel and the New Testament vision, the Spirit-filled community is characterised by equality and justice. Equality of race, class, and gender is deeply rooted in the biblical and historical heritage of Pentecostalism."[30] In this sense Pentecostalism has a natural ally with Western democracy. The cross-section of society anticipated in Joel represents not just diversity but unity. Westerners see the

outpouring of the Spirit as a democratic right as all within the
community can now hear God's voice and not just the exclusive
prophet. Of course, McQueen goes on to note that for this to be a
reality, it requires each member of the Pentecostal community to
be an active participant in the prophetic experiment of hearing and
mediating God's voice.[31] It is possible to be given the Spirit and do
nothing with it.[32] Therefore it is not just a right for each member
of the community to hear the Spirit, but also a responsibility. What
was previously a privilege of a few in the Old Testament has been
made the privilege of many. Therefore, the democratization of the
prophetic experience is a right, responsibility, and a privilege. This
is where Pentecostalism can also find an ally with a global Chinese
Confucian culture. A reading of Joel 2:28–32 through the lens of
a global Chinese Confucian culture would emphasize both the
right and responsibility of each member of the community that has
received the Spirit.

A corollary of this reading is the possible impact on the role
and function of the leader within the Pentecostal community. This
seems to go against the grain of Chinese Confucianism with its
emphasis on authoritarian leadership and filial piety. Yet perhaps a
fusion with Western democracy will result in a third reading: If all
people are hearing God's voice, what is the role of the leader? Like
Confucian culture, ancient Israel was a patriarchal society. At the
top of the social structure of ancient Israel (like the Confucian tradition) stood the free, older male. As Dillard highlights, most of the
prophets of the Old Testament actually fit this category.[33] Within
this stratified and authoritarian community Moses expressed the
desire that all people would be prophets. For Moses, the sharing
of the prophetic role did not undermine or threaten his leadership.
Instead, the desire for the whole community to hear God's voice
would transform the role of the leader. Shared prophetic authority

for Moses had a judicial function.[34] His deputies were to be judges in discerning God's guidance and will in disputes within the community.[35]

Yet while all people are prophets, not all are leaders. Pentecostalism has had a tendency to emphasize one over the other; democratization of the Spirit has been seen as mutually exclusive to leadership. You can either have shared prophetic authority or centralized leadership. What a global Chinese Confucian reading of Joel 2:28–32 might offer is the balancing of these two approaches. With its notion of filial piety—respect for elders—this third alternative might offer a new perspective of the role of the leader within Pentecostalism. If, in this prophethood of believers,[36] the people are empowered to hear God's voice (that is, discern God's will), they do not need a judge over legal ordinances but a judge or facilitator of relationship and communication. Community is important for Pentecostals; it is not enough for an individual to seek a message from God in a vacuum. If they are to be a community of prophets, it then requires that each recipient of a prophetic message is able to communicate it with another, and by implication, requires them to be in some kind of relationship whereby the message can be heard, weighed, and possibly received. This requires engagement in and with the community. As McQueen notes, "One interpreter never speaks the final word. Privatised reason can take the interpreter only so far. Communal wisdom takes us further."[37] Leadership then would be focused on the facilitation of the complexity of community relationships. It is possible to hold in tension a respect for both leadership authority and the democratization of prophetic authority.

A final way that a global Chinese Confucian reading of Joel 2:28–32 might contribute to our understanding of the passage is to consider the description of the Spirit. The Spirit of God is described as being "poured out" like water. As Dillard notes, "the Spirit of God is commonly associated with water in the Bible, and the means of investiture is often associated with pouring."[38] According to many social linguists, such as Lakoff and Johnson, metaphors have both a conceptual and experiential basis.[39] Conceptually it is a comparison for the purposes of explanation between a known idea and an unknown idea. Experientially metaphors are not innocent but often reflect the actual experience of the speakers. Lakoff and Johnson provide the example of argument as war not because it is convenient for explaining the unknown of argument by the known of war, but because an argument is experienced like a war in which the speaker defends themselves whilst attacking another.

Within Joel 2:28–32 the Spirit is poured out like water. Within Chinese popular religion, water is the source of life.[40] There are five basic elements (metal, wood, water, fire, and earth) considered foundational for life. Water, within this system of thinking, is essential for life, but is also a symbol of change.[41] The movement of water can be smooth, forceful, unstoppable, and not only powerful but also a generator of power. A Chinese saying, speaking of the political power of masses, says: "Water can keep a boat afloat; it can also overturn it."[42] However, as water is also transparent and colorless, it is also seen in Chinese language and the Confucian tradition as a picture of purity. As a word symbolizes the idea or process, the pouring out of the Spirit in a global Chinese Confucian reading suggests a forceful movement in the same way as the democratic power of the community to either uphold or revolutionize a government. This linking of democracy with the forceful nature of water reminds contemporary Pentecostals that the development of the prophethood of believers in Joel and later Acts, with its rights and responsibilities of the community in hearing God's voice, is the powerful work of the Spirit swelling to destabilize the assumed social structures.

What this metaphor of the pouring out of the Spirit emphasizes is the role of experience. Interestingly, for the Confucian tradition, experience is important. This has immediate connection with Pentecostal hermeneutics in which the experience and encounter of God is not just valued but the goal of the reading event. For many Pentecostals, hearing God's voice and guidance is the goal of reading Scripture. Reading is not just for conceptual purposes (that is, to better understand an unknown idea); it is also to understand the experience of the writers and to somehow mirror or live out a comparable experience. A global Chinese Confucian reading of Joel 2:28–32 can reinforce this value of experience and seek to reflect the vision of the prophet in seeking the forceful pouring out of God's Spirit on all the community.

The importance of experience can be seen throughout this chapter. As noted above, while the discussions of Pentecostal hermeneutics have emphasised the importance of experience as the lens through which Scripture is read, there has been little consideration of how culture influences experience and, by implication, influences the reading process. What this essay attempts to demonstrate through its discussion is that culture and language not only provide the conceptual framework (that is, to structure and communicate ideas) but also frame experience. The exposure of different cultures to one another results in a fusion of ideas, experiences, and expectations. This, in turn, impacts the reading process as the experience through which Scripture is read has been transformed. Therefore the impact of an emerging global Chinese Confucian culture has considerable implications for the future of Pentecostalism. As this reading of Joel 2:28–32 suggests, a global Chinese Confucian reading—seen through the experience of Western democracy and Confucian tradition—has the potential to reinforce the right of all believers to hear directly from the Spirit whilst congruently maintaining the priority of community, which similarly requires the responsibility of all believers to hear directly from the Spirit. Through its fusion of experience it invites respect for both leadership authority and the democratization of prophetic authority. It also anticipates the outpouring of the Spirit as a powerful force to destabilize assumed social structures. In this sense, it connects with the earlier experience of Pentecostalism as a revisionist social movement in which young women from Kansas see visions and older, blind African American men see dreams. Perhaps a global Chinese Confucian reading can help renew Pentecostalism and realign it with its values of the prophethood of all believers.

Chapter 21

Pentecostalism at the Crossroads

Simon Chan

IN A FALLEN world every religious movement has its bright and shadow sides in varying degrees of combination. But the ambiguity is particularly acute when extraordinary phenomena are involved. The problem is not new. Already in the early history of Israel we encounter the ambiguity of Charismatic prophecy in Saul, the first king of Israel. Prophecy occurred at the beginning of Saul's kingship as a vindication of his calling (1 Sam. 10:9–11), but also near the end of his reign when he was in a backslidden state (1 Sam. 19:23–24). This is why claims to extraordinary phenomena have been subject to more rigorous discernment in the Christian tradition.[1] Both the New Testament (1 Cor. 14; 1 Thess. 5) and the early Christian tradition underscore the necessity of discernment of prophets and prophecy. In the *Didache*, a late first- or early second-century church document, we read that although prophets were accorded special recognition by being given the liberty to pray without following the prescribed text at the Eucharist, yet when they took liberties with the church by asking for money, they were regarded as false prophets.[2] With a long history of discerning extraordinary phenomena, one would expect some consensus when it comes to evaluating the modern Pentecostal/Charismatic phenomenon, yet surprisingly we seem to encounter sharply differing views. Historical and sociological studies have tended to be generous, whereas theological studies have been somewhat cautious, if not critical. This ambivalence is symptomatic of a movement that has reached a critical crossroads.

PENTECOSTALISM'S SELECTIVE ADAPTATION TO CULTURE

On the positive side, Pentecostalism has shown a remarkable ability to adapt selectively to different cultures. According to historian Grant Wacker, it does this by holding together in creative tension the "pragmatic" and "primitivist" impulses. This dialectic is aptly summed up in the title of his book: *Heaven Below*.[3] Putting it more prosaically, Pentecostalism has made use of and adapted itself to certain aspects of culture while rejecting other aspects in such a manner as not to lose its focus on the Transcendent. This selective adaptation to culture is not unique to Pentecostalism. Evangelicals in previous centuries faced a similar challenge and adopted a similar approach.[4]

Pentecostal historian William Kay has noted how Pentecostals in Britain have selectively adapted to modernity.[5] Kay redefines modernity to include a more fluid "psychological modernity" in addition to the "classical modernity" represented by men like Descartes and Newton. Wesley was in many ways shaped by this fluid modernity: for instance, his emphasis on experience owes much to Romanticism. Pentecostalism also draws from this experiential tradition in addition to many other features of modernity, such as its qualified egalitarianism (female leadership, racial integration) and activism (evangelism, mission).

The study of Bernice Martin brings out this selective adaptation in the Latin American context.[6] Martin notes that unlike the Pentecostal movement in the West, in Latin America it moves from pre- to postmodern culture without going through the modern or Enlightenment phase. But it still retains some elements of the pre-modern that makes it highly adaptable in the postmodern climate.[7] In the squalid conditions created by a postmodern and postindustrial economy, Pentecostalism gives to individuals the means to make choices to break out of those oppressive conditions, not by such grand schemes as dismantling structural evils (à la liberation theology) but through *personal* empowerment to change their immediate surroundings.[8]

The advantage of Martin's analysis is that it takes into consideration what actually goes on at the grassroots, thus giving her work a more nuanced picture often missed in elitist accounts; e.g., Pentecostalism in the latter is often understood as a form of totalitarianism (authoritarian leadership, mind control, etc.), but what is often ignored is the experience of freedom and social mobility that comes from participation in the movement.[9] Martin highlights a number of paradoxes to explain the Pentecostals' success. One, they stress individual initiative as well as voluntary association. Leaders are authoritarian, but within the community there is freedom, including the freedom to form a new church.[10] The freedom and spontaneity Martin notes belies the common perception that Pentecostals are like other fundamentalists who fear to exercise freedom in a postmodern culture and find security in legalistic conformity to rules (such as the doctrine of inerrancy, strict personal holiness codes, etc.). Martin argues that for Pentecostals the holiness codes are freely embraced because it is a sign of freedom from fatalism.[11] Another paradox is the Pentecostals' use of modern media technology while resisting its hedonism and other excesses.[12] Along similar lines, Donald Miller and Tetsunao Yamamori have noted the positive social impact that global Pentecostalism has had, including prosperity gospel preachers even though their *modus operandi* may be questionable.[13]

The adoption of certain aspects of modernity also accounts for the phenomenal growth of churches in Asia. According to Hong Yong-gi, the megachurch is essentially the creative application of "McDonalization," the spiritual counterpart of a successful modern business enterprise. They have been able to make the best use of modernity by infusing it with the experience of transcendence through their Charismatic leaders and programs such as mass early morning prayer meetings. Hong believes that theological integrity is preserved as long as the megachurches maintain a healthy tension between "McDonaldization" and "charismatization."

Andrew Walker's analysis, however, reveals the ambivalent relation of the Charismatic movement to modernity.[14] With Martin, Walker sees Pentecostals as playing a positive role in Latin America as modernizing agents. They not only use modern media to good effect, but also help the poor and disinherited in their social mobility and integrate them into the mainstream of social life.[15] In Walker's view, the modern Charismatic movement is not so much a reversion to "pre-modern" worldview, nor is it a reaction against modernity à la Niebuhr (Christ against culture); rather, it is either "reluctantly modern" or enthusiastically modern.[16] Pentecostals in the initial revival were indeed anti-modern and world-denying, as reflected in their premillennial eschatology, but over time they have become "an unwilling symbolic carrier of modernity as well as falling prey to the secularizing tendencies of the modern world."[17]

Pentecostalism, despite its overt rejection of modernity, is shaped by modernity. Even though its early alignment with fundamentalism was only a form of legitimation, it does not quite escape the grip of modernity, since fundamentalism too is based on a rationalistic epistemology.[18] Perhaps it may be truer to say that

Pentecostalism is shaped by modernity in some respects (such as its *modus operandi*, its use of mass media, etc.) but not in others, such as its supernaturalistic worldview, as noted by Martin.

The neo-Pentecostals or Charismatics, on the other hand, are much more thoroughly plugged into late modernity as seen in their "preoccupation with therapy and self-fulfilment," while their "hedonistic individualism replaced ascetic individualism" of the earlier Pentecostals.[19] Walker also notes the quick mutation of the newer Pentecostal/Charismatic movements and the tendency of some classical Pentecostal churches to become more and more like the Charismatics, such as Kensington Temple, a classical Elim Pentecostal Church in London.[20] The Toronto Blessing represents the end of the Charismatic phenomenon that "has drunk deeply at the well of modern cultural forms," resulting in "a disintegration of liturgical and Biblical norms."[21] Theologically, this phenomenon dovetails with Schleiermacher's liberal theology with its primary concern for self and personal experience.[22] Walker's account is particularly helpful in alerting us to the rapid mutation of Pentecostalism from a movement that adapted (reluctantly) to modernity while retaining its spiritual robustness to a series of rapidly changing phenomena reflecting the values of late modernity and postmodernity. Although Walker considers his work a "sociological reflection," it offers trenchant critiques based on theological considerations.[23] And when theological criteria are applied, the picture that emerges is somewhat mixed.

THEOLOGICAL CRITIQUES OF PENTECOSTALISM

Tom Smail locates the basic problem of much of the newer Charismatics in the two-stage Pentecostal model of the Christian life.[24] The first stage is the work of Christ to bring salvation; the second stage is the work of the Spirit to empower the believer for service. By separating the work of Christ and the work of the Spirit and treating the latter as, practically, a higher form of spiritual life, the resulting tendency is to exult in the *theologia gloriae* without the *theologia crucis*. In short, early Pentecostals lacked a robust Trinitarian theology to hold together the work of Christ and the work of the Spirit. This is not a new critique, but was made earlier by Peter Hocken.[25] The separate works of grace produce a number of problematic bifurcations. First, the person of the Spirit is separated from the person of Christ, with some focusing on the person of the Spirit (e.g., Yonggi Cho) and others on Christ (Oneness Pentecostals).[26] Second, the gifts of the Spirit (1 Cor. 12–14) are separated from the gifts of Christ (Eph. 4), with some gravitating toward the former, resulting in chaotic freedom of the Spirit, and others, in reaction, focusing on the authority of Christ exercised through the five "ministry gifts," especially apostles and prophets. The latter has a long history in the Pentecostal movement, but quickly mutated into various forms of authoritarianism: the Latter Rain in the 1940s, the Shepherding movement in the 1970s, and lately the "apostles" of Peter Wagner.[27]

The consequence of a *theologia gloriae* is an over-realized eschatology that finds its most current expression in the "Third Wave." Early Pentecostals, by aligning with dispensational premillennialism, retained a strong eschatological reserve. But with the "charismatized" evangelicals of the Third Wave the shaky balance between the "already" and the "not yet" is decisively tilted in favor of the "already." The results are all too familiar; i.e. the gospels of "signs and wonders," prosperity, positive confession, and the fixation on extraordinary phenomena (gold dust, visions of angels, etc.). One could argue that the prosperity gospel in the affluent West is quite different when transplanted in the poverty-stricken Majority World. In the former, it panders to human greed; in the latter, it is the inspiration for upward social mobility.[28] One could further argue that some forms of the prosperity gospel are better nuanced by incorporating a concept of delayed blessing: God's blessing may come "slowly"; thus one has to work hard and leave the blessing to God's timing.[29] The truth of the matter, however, is that in whatever context the health-and-wealth gospel is preached, it will fail sooner—or later, if one believes in delayed fulfillment. In a world still tainted by the effects of sin, a theology of glory will *inevitably* fail because it raises the expectation of *ultimate* fulfillment in this age. Whatever work the Spirit does in this present age, it must be grounded in the crucified Christ. Only a "Pascal model" can sufficiently address the complexity of the Christian life in a fallen world.[30]

Another ramification of an over-realized eschatology is its implicit dualism.[31] If God has *already* accomplished salvation and healing, then the only reason for sickness is doubt or the devil. Healing and sickness are understood in terms of the stark dualism of either faith or doubt, God or Satan. If God did not do it, then it must be the devil. Thus when David Watson, a prominent Anglican Charismatic with a successful healing ministry, died of cancer, one Charismatic declared that the devil murdered him.[32] In the dualist's scheme of things, there is an "integral unity" of sickness, doubt and the devil.[33]

It is in light of these overarching theological presuppositions found in some forms of the Charismatic movement today that we must further nuance our theological assessment. Space permits us to highlight only a few issues. Take the issue of authority. Bernice Martin shows the creative side of Pentecostalism's treatment of authority. While the Pentecostal church maintains the Pauline male leadership in the church, it frees women to exercise the prophetic gifts of the Spirit, thus maintaining "two modes of spiritual

authority held in creative tension."[34] This way of understanding
spiritual authority may be closer to the biblical conception (contra
Western egalitarianism). But there is a problematic aspect seen in
the Third Wavers. To them authority is no longer about whether
the pastor should be male or female, but a kind of overriding spiritual authority of "apostles" created by a special council of apostles
based on new "revelations." Epistemologically, Wagner is no different from the prosperity teachers who rely on a special *"rhema*
word" conveyed directly to the believer apart from Scripture. Such
"revelations" could only be described as gnostic.[35]

Another issue is worship. From a sociological perspective, contemporary worship has a lot to be said for it. It provides a bridge for
young people who otherwise would not step into the church. But
more importantly, there is a deep spirituality involved in Charismatic
worship, at least in the initial phase of the renewal movement in the
1960s.[36] Many who had experienced renewal at that time could testify to the deep impact of singing that "engages the deep primal
emotions at the hidden centre of our being in our self-offering to
the living God."[37] But in this area too the Charismatic movement
has mutated rapidly. Theologically the problems are serious and
many. The wide range of components that make up worship found
in most Christian traditions including earlier Pentecostals', such as
confession of sin, intercession, and testimonies, are all but gone.
Worship is reduced to "praise."[38] The theology of glory without the
theology of the cross is now extended to worship.[39] Lester Ruth,
in an analysis of some of the most popular contemporary songs
that make up a significant part of Charismatic worship, notes that
they are generally weak in Trinitarian reference and soteriologically
thin. Their songs almost invariably express one's own private experience of God, with little awareness of ecclesial or corporate life.[40]

So, despite the attractiveness of "contemporary worship," there are serious defects that could only lead to serious malformation of Christians in the long term. The church historian Daniel H. Williams recounts a visit to such a church and observes, among other things, that it "caters to short attention spans and relies heavily on stimulating emotional highs during the service"; the elements of the Lord's Supper were "hurriedly handed around" without so much as reading the words of institution; their worship songs contained an "extremely limited" vocabulary; etc.[41] If "the rule of praying is the rule of faith," such worship reveals serious theological impoverishment and a woefully defective ecclesiology. Perhaps what is most alarming is that Williams's observation of a contemporary worship service in North America can be seen in "charismatized" churches of all sizes around in the world. It is not peculiar to any one culture, much as K-pop and Hillsongs have become globalized.

Yet another issue that urgently needs addressing is prophecy. Increasingly we are seeing self-styled prophets who have a "prophetic word" for anyone and any occasion. What is alarming is the unquestioning way in which it is received. The explanation underlying such naivety is both cultural and theological. There is already a predisposition in some cultures to seek out "supernatural" sources of information. In many parts of Asia, Buddhists and Taoists consult fortune-tellers; Christians seek out prophets. But the problem is also theological. William Kay has noted the intimate connection between the dispensational eschatology of John Nelson Darby and the Pentecostal movement.[42] But the connection is more than historical. They share a spiritual affinity with respect to prophecy. The former's literalistic interpretation is a specific application of Scottish commonsense philosophy: what appears in the text is what *is*. This has tended to foster an uncritical attitude toward prophecy. If the true interpretation is always the literal one (unless absurd), there can be no possibility of an alternative view. But where the dispensationalists are content to apply the literal interpretation to prophecies in the Bible, the Pentecostal/Charismatics have extended this dispensational hermeneutic to contemporary prophecy. The response to a "prophetic word" especially coming from an authoritative figure is unqualified acceptance. But when prophecy fails, the result is devastating. This was the case with the LoveSingapore movement, which at its height attracted thousands of Christians including not a few prominent church leaders. But it quickly dissipated when a prophecy by a renowned Latin American evangelist that Singapore would see a mass conversion of two million souls by December 2001 failed to materialize.[43]

Many scholars have noted the deep spiritual affinities between Pentecostalism and primal religions, and here again we see both positive and negative ramifications. In Southeast Asia, Singaporean sociologist Daniel Goh has shown how Charismatic worship involves, among other things, the transfiguration of Chinese religious rites to distinguish them from Christian worship forms.[44] In Japan Mark Mullins has shown how certain Japanese indigenous Christian movements of Pentecostal origins have adapted Shinto and Confucian ancestral rituals for specifically Christian ends, and in so doing have expanded our understanding of the doctrine of the communion of saints.[45] These are creative and positive developments. In contrast, followers of Third Wavers in Asia seem to have eschewed any form of contextualization by demonizing many traditional beliefs, practices, and even artifacts associated with non-Christian religions, such as the Chinese dragon and acupuncture. They seem to be promoting a "pure" gospel free of cultural accretions. Yet their anti-cultural stance is based on an uncritical acceptance of a non-Christian worldview regarding the existence and organization of spiritual hierarchies and territorial spirits. Thus what seems like a rejection of culture turns out to be based on the unquestioning acceptance of some other aspects of a religious worldview quite foreign to Christianity.[46]

LOOKING AT THE FUTURE

It is clear that different approaches to the Pentecostal/Charismatic movement have generated different results. This is because each asks a different set of questions. A movement that attracts masses of people and creates upward social mobility would be considered a social good. But if upward social mobility includes an understanding that it is the Christian's birthright to be rich and healthy, and therefore poverty and sickness reveal a lack of faith in God, then the question we must raise is whether good, practical outcomes have been achieved at the expense of sound biblical norms. And what are the long-term consequences when biblical norms are violated?

If the Pentecostal/Charismatic movement is more than a sociological movement, we need theological criteria to assess it adequately. How, for example, do we assess the practice of marketing the gospel? There are obvious social benefits deriving from mass conversion as a result of effective marketing. But theologically, how has marketing the gospel affected the gospel itself? The question is entirely appropriate if, as Marshal McLuhan reminded us, the medium *is* the message. But the case is still far from settled. For some, marketing suggests the creative adaptation of a modern mode of operation that could genuinely advance God's kingdom as long as it is balanced by openness to transcendence (as argued by Hong Yong-gi). For others, marketing the gospel reflects the efficiency and control that modernity enables, giving to people a sense of godlike sovereignty that belongs only to God.[47]

We need, therefore, more than just the ability to maintain a sense of mystery and transcendence while using the tools of modernity as

Hong recommends. Openness to the supernatural alone is not sufficient; we need to discern between true and false spiritual manifestations. In short, "charismatization" itself has become a problem. In some Charismatic circles it has become a tool for pragmatic ends, a kind of "spiritual technology" that could be replicated at will.[48] The late Tan-Chow May Ling's study of the LoveSingapore movement in the 1990s has shown quite clearly its tendency to trivialize the gospel by turning central gospel practices into "strategic practices" for instrumental ends.[49] This is no longer a case of creative adaptation to culture but accommodation to the postmodern *Zeitgeist*. Underlying their bold programs and grand strategies is a *theologia gloriae* without a *theologia crucis*.

If theology is a map, we need a good and reliable one.[50] But where do we get such a map? The theological map that we can rely on is the product of generations of Christians who had gone ahead of us. They had charted the territory, posted road signs, marked danger spots, etc. In short, good theology is the result of the cumulative wisdom of the faithful in the church—what the Catholic Church calls the *sensus fidei* (the sense of the faith),[51] and what the Orthodox call the living tradition.[52] The problem of Pentecostal/ Charismatics today is that they have an extremely short memory shaped by the Internet culture and a neurotic concern for cultural relevance. As a result, they have become the victims of passing theological fads. With no long-term memory, there is no enduring Christian and ecclesial identity either. This is the primary reason for its rapid mutation.

What the future holds for Pentecostal/Charismatic Christianity in the twenty-first century will depend on which direction it chooses to go. Its future will depend largely on how it reckons with two central foci of biblical pneumatology. First, the Spirit is the firstfruits of the new creation; Pentecostal/Charismatics are quite right, therefore, to believe in an open and expanding future. Yet paradoxically, in anticipating the coming age, we groan with the rest of the fallen creation (Rom. 8:22-23). The Spirit who is the power of the future also moves us to act in solidarity with the sufferings and pain of this world. The failure of modern Charismatics is keeping this paradox in focus. Second, the Spirit is the Spirit of the Father and the Son. If the Spirit is leading the church into new experiences, these new experiences are developments from what the Spirit has already revealed to us in the past. This does not mean that the future is merely a repeat of the past, but that if it is the genuine work of the Spirit, it has a Trinitarian shape and trajectory.[53]

Two processes must be present if the church is to negotiate successfully in a rapidly changing world: retrieval of resources from the past that shape her basic identity (*ressourcement*) and regular updating in light of new contextual situations (*aggiornamento*). The two must always go together and follow in that order. Without the prerequisite of *ressourcement, aggiornamento* could easily end up with the church capitulating to the spirit of the age.[54]

Notes

THE MANY TONGUES OF ASIAN AND OCEANIAN PENTECOSTALISMS:
AN INTRODUCTION AND SOME THEOLOGICAL PROGNOSTICATIONS

1. Perhaps beginning with Walter J. Hollenweger, "An Introduction to Pentecostalisms," *Journal of Beliefs and Values* 25, no 2 (2004): 125–137; cf.
   Daniel Chiquete, "Latin American Pentecostalisms and Western Postmodernism," *International Review of Mission* 92, no. 364 (January 2003):
   29–39.

2. See, e.g., Peter C. Phan, *Christianities in Asia* (Malden, MA, and Oxford:
   Wiley-Blackwell, 2011).

3. John C. England, et al., eds., *Asian Christian Theologies: A Research
   Guide to Authors, Movements, Sources*, 3 vols. (Maryknoll: Orbis Books,
   2005).

4. Much of the material in this paragraph is common knowledge, easily
   verifiable in multiple sources; that nation-states come and go and that
   many of these ethnic groups inhabit spaces more technically considered
   as "territories" which categorizations are dynamically shifting depending
   on a variety of factors makes any accurate consideration of these matters
   subject to continual review.

5. Acts 2:9–11 specifies groups hailing from these locations or areas: Par-
   thia, Mede, Elam, Mesopotamia, Judea, Cappadocia, Pontus, Asia,
   Phrygia, Pamphylia, Egypt, Libya, Cyrene, Rome, Israel (reference here is
   to Jews in general), the wider Mediterranean world (reference is to proselytes, who are Greek-speaking converts to Judaism), Crete, and Arabia.

6. For further discussion of this matter in Acts 2, see my *The Spirit Poured
   Out on All Flesh: Pentecostalism and the Possibility of Global Theology*
   (Grand Rapids: Baker Academic, 2005), 198–199.

7. We have no chapter on Pentecostalisms in Western Asia in this book;
   however, a chapter on Pentecostalism in Israel is planned for the volume
   on Europe and North America.

8. Statistics from Todd M. Johnson and Kenneth R. Ross, eds., *Atlas of
   Global Christianity 1910–2010* (Edinburgh: Edinburgh University Press,
   2009), 136 and 103, although it should be noted that these figures include
   "renewalists" among and with Pentecostals, the former being a much
   more elastic category that includes Charismatic Christians of many sorts;

such inclusiveness is consistent with the overarching parameters for this book, however. (See the discussion further below.)

9. For the Pentecostal concern with syncretism, see Julie C. Ma and Wonsuk Ma, *Mission in the Spirit: Towards a Pentecostal/Charismatic Missiology* (Oxford: Regnum, and Eugene, OR: Wipf & Stock, 2010), ch. 14.

10. Any kind of empirically based comparison would be difficult to come by. A sampling of the scholarly literature, however—e.g., Philip Jenkins, *The Next Christendom: The Coming Global Christianity* (Oxford: Oxford University Press, 2002)—suggests that the expansive diversification of world Christianity is intertwined with marked Pentecostalization and charismatization, and this phenomenon fuels any argument forthcoming about overall trends in these directions vis-à-vis either Pentecostal or evangelical movements.

11. Aloysius Pieris, for example, thus talks about Buddhism as a *metacosmic* religion, but of its diversified *cosmic* manifestations on the ground when melded with local or indigenous traditions; see Pieris, *An Asian Theology of Liberation* (Maryknoll: Orbis Books, 1988), esp. 71–74.

12. As persuasively argued by Harvey G. Cox, *Fire From Heaven: The Rise of Pentecostal Spirituality and the Reshaping of Religion in the 21st Century* (Reading, MA: Addison Wesley, 1995).

13. Walter J. Hollenweger, *Pentecostalism: Origins and Developments Worldwide* (Peabody, MA: Hendrickson Publishers, 1997), 132–141.

14. For an instance of the former, see my book, *Pneumatology and the Christian-Buddhist Dialogue: Does the Spirit Blow Through the Middle Way?* Studies in Systematic Theology 11 (Leiden and Boston: Brill, 2012), esp. part III; regarding the latter, see, Paul L. Swanson, ed., *Pentecostalism and Shamanism in Asia*, Nanzan Institute for Religion & Culture Symposium 16 (Nagoya, Japan: Nanzan Institute for Religion & Culture Symposium, 2013).

15. E.g., Geomon K. George, *Religious Pluralism: Challenges for Pentecostalism in India* (Bangalore: Centre for Contemporary Christianity, 2006), and Ivan Satyavrata, *God Has Not Left Himself Without Witness* (Oxford: Regnum, and Eugene, OR: Wipf & Stock, 2011); it is for this same reason that much of my theological work has been devoted to thinking about the questions of cultural and religious pluralism, such as Yong, *Hospitality and the Other: Pentecost, Christian Practices, and the Neighbor*, Faith Meets Faith series (Maryknoll, NY: Orbis Books, 2008).

16. E.g., Tan-Chow May Ling, *Pentecostal Theology in the Twenty-First Century: Engaging with Multifaith Singapore* (Burlington, VT, and Aldershot, UK: Ashgate, 2007).

17. Compare, therefore, *Readings in Malaysian Church and Mission* (Malaysia: Pustaka SUPES, 1992), and Mark Andrew Robinson, "Pentecostalism in Urban Java: A Study of Religious Change, 1980–2006" (PhD thesis, University of Queensland, 2008).

18. See Christl Kessler, and Jürgen Rüland, *Give Jesus a Hand! Charismatic Christians: Populist Religion and Politics in the Philippines* (Manila: Ateneo de Manila University Press, 2008).

19. I begin to gesture toward such a pluralistic political theology in dialogue with global Pentecostal movements in my book *In the Days of Caesar: Pentecostalism and Political Theology* (Grand Rapids, MI, and Cambridge, UK: William B. Eerdmans Publishing Company, 2010).

20. E.g., V. V. Thomas, *Dalit Pentecostalism: Spirituality of the Empowered Poor* (Bangalore: Asian Trading Corporation, 2008).

21. See Nanlai Cao, "Urban Property as Spiritual Resource: The Prosperity Gospel in Coastal China," in Katherine Attanasi and Amos Yong, eds., *Pentecostalism and Prosperity: The Socioeconomics of the Global Charismatic Movement*, Christianities of the World 1 (New York: Palgrave Macmillan, 2012), 151–170; cf. Cao, *Constructing China's Jerusalem: Christians, Power, and Place in Contemporary Wenzhou* (Stanford: Stanford University Press, 2010).

22. Michael Wilkinson, ed., *Global Pentecostal Movements: Migration, Mission, and Public Religion*, International Studies in Religion and Society 14 (Leiden and Boston: Brill, 2014).

23. See my *In the Days of Caesar*, §§1.2 and 7.1. The literature on Pentecostal globalization is growing: Murray W. Dempster, Byron D. Klaus, and Douglas Petersen, eds., *The Globalization of Pentecostalism: A Religion Made to Travel* (Oxford and Irvine, CA: Regnum, 1999); Sturla J. Stålsett, ed., *Spirits of Globalization: The Growth of Pentecostalism and Experiential Spiritualities in a Global Age* (London: SCM Press, 2006); and Steven M. Studebaker, ed., *Pentecostalism and Globalization: The Impact of Globalization on Pentecostal Theology and Ministry* (Eugene, OR: Wipf & Stock, 2010), among other inquiries.

24. See Pradip Ninan Thomas, *Strong Religion, Zealous Media: Christian Fundamentalism and Communication in India* (Los Angeles: SAGE, 2008), and Jonathan D. James, *McDonalisation, Masala McGospel and*

Om Economics: Televangelism in Contemporary India (New Delhi: SAGE Publications, 2010)—the former exploring more South Asian and North American connections while the latter focuses more on Indian-Australasian interfaces.

25. See Monique Ingalls and Amos Yong, eds., *The Spirit of Praise: Music and Worship in Global Pentecostal/Charismatic Christianity* (University Park, PA: Penn State University Press, 2015), including the chapter 10 by Mark Evans, "Hillsong Abroad: Tracing the Songlines of Contemporary Pentecostal Music."

26. Leading the way here is Australian Pentecostal theologian Shane Clifton; see his coauthored book, Neil J. Ormerod and Shane Clifton, *Globalization and the Mission of the Church*, Ecclesiological Investigations 6 (Leiden and Boston: Brill, 2011).

27. The leading voice at this point is Nigerian Pentecostal social ethicist, Nimi Wariboko; see his books *The Charismatic City and the Public Resurgence of Religion: A Pentecostal Social Ethics of Cosmopolitan Urban Life*, CHARIS: Christianity and Renewal—Interdisciplinary Studies 2 (New York: Palgrave Macmillan, 2014), and *Economics in Spirit and in Truth: A Moral Philosophy of Finance* (New York: Palgrave Macmillan, 2014).

28. This can be discerned across many of the chapters in Allan Anderson and Edmond Tang, eds., *Asian and Pentecostal: The Charismatic Face of Christianity in Asia* (London: Regnum International, and Baguio City, Philippines: Asia Pacific Theological Seminary Press, 2005).

29. Katharine L. Wiegele, *Investing in Miracles: El Shaddai and the Transformation of Popular Catholicism in the Philippines* (Honolulu: University of Hawaii Press, 2004).

30. See Jakob Egeris Thorsen, *Charismatic Practice and Catholic Parish Life: The Incipient Pentecostalization of the Church in Guatemala and Latin America*, Global Pentecostal and Charismatic Studies 17 (Leiden and Boston: Brill, 2015), which describes what is happening in these terms as applied to Latin American Catholicism, although the trends are unmistakable also in especially the Asian context. In Oceania, one might speak more accurately about the Pentecostalization or charismatization of Oceanian Evangelicalism instead.

31. E.g., as discussed by Lutheran Charismatic theologian Wilfred J. Samuel, *Charismatic Folk Christianity: 'A Storm in the Flower'— Reflections on*

Post-Charismatic Trends (Kota Kinabalu, Malaysia: Sabah Theological Seminary, 2003).

32. The Chinese case is related to the isolation of the church during the communist period, but see Luke Wesley, *The Church in China: Persecuted, Pentecostal, and Powerful* (Baguio City, Philippines: AJPS Press, 2004); for the Indian scene, see P. Solomon Raj, *A Christian Folk-Religion in India: A Study of the Small Church Movement in Andhra Pradesh, with a Special Reference to the Bible Mission of Devadas* (Frankfurt and New York: Peter Lang, 1986), and Michael Bergunder, *The South Indian Pentecostal Movement in the Twentieth Century* (Grand Rapids, MI: William B. Eerdmans Publishing Company, 2008).

33. There is precious little available research on Pentecostalism in these parts of the world. We might hope, for instance, that Marcin Rzepka, "Facing History: Iranian Pentecostals on the Move" (unpublished paper presented to the Annual Meeting of the Society for Pentecostal Studies, Southeastern University, Lakeland, Florida, 12–14 March 2015), will find the light of publication sometime soon. A few other studies are also available on countries that are not discussed in this volume. On Charismatic renewal in Pakistan, we can consult Oddbjørn Leirvik, "Charismatic Mission, Miracles and Faith-Based Diplomacy: The Case of Aril Edvardsen," in Sturla J. Stålsett, ed., *Spirits of Globalization: The Growth of Pentecostalism and Experiential Spiritualities in a Global Age* (London: SCM Press, 2006), 131–144. Myanmar is covered by Khua Khai Chin, "Pentecostalism in Myanmar: An Overview," *Asian Journal of Pentecostal Studies* 5, no. 1 (2002): 51–71, and Saw Tint Sann Oo, "The History of the Assemblies of God Theological Education in Myanmar: Development of the Assemblies of God Bible Schools," *Asian Journal of Pentecostal Studies* 17, no. 2 (2014): 187–206. See also Bal Krishna Sharma, "A History of the Pentecostal Movement in Nepal," *Asian Journal of Pentecostal Studies* 4, no. 2 (2001): 295–306. Last but not least for our purposes, Melanesian Pentecostalism has been studied by anthropologists—e.g., Joel Robbins, *Becoming Sinners: Christianity and Moral Torment in a Papua New Guinea Society* (Berkeley: University of California Press, 2004), and Richard Eves, "Pentecostal Dreaming and Technologies of Governmentality in a Melanesian Society," *American Ethnologist* 3, no. 4 (2011): 758–773; cf. also the missiological study of Theodor Ahrens, "'The Flower Fair Has Thorns as Well': Nativistic Millennialism in Melanesia as a Pastoral and Missiological Issue," *Missiology* 13, no. 1 (1985): 61–80.

34. Readers can profit further from these chapters by consulting the authors' other works, including but not limited to Giovanni Maltese, *Geisterfahrer zwischen Transzendenz und Immanenz: Die Erfahrungsbegriffe in den pfingstlich-charismatischen Theologien von Terry L. Cross und Amos Yong im Vergleich* [Experiences of the Spirit between Transcendence and Immanence: A Comparison of the Concept of Experience in the Pentecostal/Charismatic Theologies of Terry L. Cross and Amos Yong], Kirche—Konfession—Religion 61 (Göttingen: V&R Unipress, 2013); Jörg Haustein and Giovanni Maltese, hg., *Handbuch pfingstliche und charismatische Theologie* [Handbook of Pentecostal and Charismatic Theology] (Göttingen, Germany: Vandenhoeck & Ruprecht, 2014); Simon Chan, *Pentecostal Theology and the Christian Spiritual Tradition* (Sheffield: Sheffield Academic Press, 2000); and Simon Chan, *Pentecostal Ecclesiology: An Essay on the Development of Doctrine* (Blandford Forum, UK: Deo Publishing, 2011).

35. There is not only an Acts 29 network of churches (see www.Acts29network.org), but this notion has also been adapted by Pentecostal theologians—e.g., Pamela M. S. Holmes, "Acts 29 and Authority: Towards a Pentecostal Feminist Hermeneutic of Liberation," in Michael Wilkinson and Steven M. Studebaker, eds., *A Liberating Spirit: Pentecostals and Social Action in North America* (Eugene, OR: Pickwick Publications, 2010), 185–209.

36. Those interested can also consult my own extensive efforts to bring Pentecostal theology into its second generation—e.g., Yong, *Spirit-Word-Community: Theological Hermeneutics in Trinitarian Perspective*, New Critical Thinking in Religion, Theology and Biblical Studies Series (Burlington, VT, and Aldershot, UK: Ashgate Publishing Ltd.; reprint: Eugene, OR: Wipf & Stock Publishers, 2002); *The Spirit of Creation: Modern Science and Divine Action in the Pentecostal/Charismatic Imagination*, Pentecostal Manifestos 4 (Grand Rapids, MI, and Cambridge, UK: William B. Eerdmans Publishing Company, 2011); *Spirit of Love: A Trinitarian Theology of Grace* (Waco, TX: Baylor University Press, 2012); *The Missiological Spirit: Christian Mission Theology for the Third Millennium Global Context* (Eugene, OR: Cascade Books, 2014); *The Dialogical Spirit: Christian Reason and Theological Method for the Third Millennium* (Eugene, OR: Cascade Books, 2014); and *Renewing Christian Theology: Systematics for a Global Christianity*, images and commentary by Jonathan A. Anderson (Waco, TX: Baylor University Press, 2014), besides the aforementioned *The Spirit Poured Out on All Flesh* and *In the Days of*

Caesar: Pentecostalism and Political Theology, among other monographs and edited volumes.

CHAPTER 1
CHRISTOLOGICAL NUANCES IN BHIL PENTECOSTAL THEOLOGY

1. David Barrett, George T. Kurien, and Todd M. Johnson, eds., *World Christian Encyclopedia: A Comparative Study of Churches and Religion in the Modern World*, 2nd ed. (Delhi: Oxford University Press, 2005), I.360.

2. Roger E. Hedland, "Editorial—Pentecostalism," *Dharma Deepika* 6, no. 2 (July–December 2002): 2.

3. Bhils are primarily an *Adivasi* (the first inhabitants) people of Central India. They speak the Bhil languages, a subgroup of the Western Zone of the Indo-Aryan languages. It is estimated that there are 6.7 million Bhil people of India. Geographically they are scattered all over the states of Gujarat, Madhya Pradesh, Chhattisgarh, Maharashtra, and Rajasthan. The Bhil are mainly a community of settled farmers, with a significant minority who are landless agricultural labourers. A significant subsidiary occupation remains hunting and gathering. The Bhil are now largely Hindu. They worship tribal deities such as *Mogra Deo* and *Sitla Matta*. However, since 1960s the Pentecostal revival has made inroads into the Bhil community. It is now estimated that there are over 300,000 Bhil tribal believers. See A. T. Cherian, "Pentecostal Revival, the Key to Church Growth," *Filadelfia Jyoti*, Souvenir (Udaipur, India: FBC, 2006), and Alexander T. Daniel, *The Impact of Christian Mission on the Socio-Cultural Life of the Bhil Tribe in Rajasthan* (New Delhi: ISPCK/SALTDC, 2012), for detailed discusion.

4. G. H. Lang, *The Histories and Diaries of an Indian Christian: J. C. Aroolapen* (London: M. F. Robinson & Co. 1939), 173ff.

5. For example, Alfred Garr and Lillian Garr (Calcutta, December 1906); T. B. Barratt of Norway (Coonoor, 1908), Mary Weems Chapman (Madras, 1908); George E. Berg (South India, 1908); R. F. Cook (1913), and others represented the denominational Pentecostalism.

6. K. E. Abraham, *IPC Praaramba Varshangal* [The Early Years of IPC], 2nd ed. (Kumbanad, India: K. E. Abraham Foundation, 1986); *Yesukristhuvinte Eliya Dassan* [The Humble servant of Jesus Christ—Autobiography of Pastor K. E. Abraham], 3rd ed. (Kumbanad, India: K. E. Abraham Foundation, 2001).

7. Allan H. Anderson, "Revising Pentecostal History in Global Perspective," in Allan H. Anderson and Edmond Tang, eds., *Asian and Pentecostal: The Charismatic Face of Christianity in Asia* (Carlisle: Regnum Books International, 2005), 153.

8. A. C. George, *Trailblazers for God: A History of the Assemblies of God in India* (Bangalore: SABC, 2004), 34; Robin Boyd, *Church History of Gujarat* (Madras: The Christian Literature Society, 1981), 110.

9. See McGee, "'Latter Rain' Falling in the East: Early Twentieth-Century Pentecostalism in India and the Debate over Speaking in Tongues," *Church History* 68, no. 3 (1999): 649; cf. Helen S. Dyer, ed., *Revival in India 1905-1906* (Akola, Maharashtra: Alliance Publications, 1987), 37-49. Also Allan Anderson, *Spreading Fires: The Missionary Nature of Early Pentecostalism* (London: SCM, 2007), 83; Michael Bergunder, *The South Indian Pentecostal Movement in the Twentieth Century*, Studies in the History of Christian Missions (Grand Rapids, MI: Eerdmans, 2008), 24; and R. V. Burgess, "Pandita Ramabai: A Woman for All Season," *Asia Journal of Pentecostal Studies* 9, no. 2 (2006): 183-198.

10. The revival in the Presbyterian Church had several elements of Pentecostal expressions, such as praying aloud, singing, dancing, trembling, and being slain in the Spirit. Believers began to confess their sins and participate in passionate worship and even, probably, spoke in tongues. See O. L. Snaitang, "The Indigenous Pentecostal Movement in Northeast India," *Dharma Deepika* 6, no. 2 (2002): 5-11; cf. McGee, "'Latter Rain' Falling in the East," 649; T. Nongsiej, "Revival Movement in Khasi-Jaintia Hills," in O. L. Snaitang, ed., *Churches of Indigenous Origin in Northeast India* (Delhi: ISPCK, 2000), 32-34.

11. The revival spread to places like Dehra Dun, Almora, Moradabad, and Allahabad. See J. Edwin Orr, *Evangelical Awakening in South Asia* (Minneapolis: Bethany Fellowship, 1975), 144-154; Basil Miller, *Praying Hyde: A Man of Prayer* (Grand Rapids, MI: Zondervan Publishing House, 1943); and John C. B. Webster, *The Christian Community and Change in Nineteenth Century North India* (Delhi: Macmillian, 1976), 231.

12. Gary B. McGee, "The Calcutta Revival of 1907 and the Reformulation of Charles Parham's Bible Evidence Doctrine," *Asia Journal of Pentecostal Studies* 6, no. 1 (2003): 123.

13. Allan H. Anderson, *An Introduction to Pentecostalism: Global Charismatic Christianity* (Cambridge: Cambridge University Press, 2004), 124; also Anderson, *Spreading Fires*, 88; Bergunder, *The South Indian*

Pentecostal Movement in the Twentieth Century, 24; and Stanley M. Burgess, "Pentecostalism in India: An Overview," *Asia Journal of Pentecostal Studies* 4, no. 1 (2001): 91–92.

14. See M. T. Cherian, *Hindutva Agenda and Minority Rights: A Christian Response* (Bangalore: Centre for Contemporary Christianity, 2007), 155–205. See also C. V. Mathew, *Saffron Mission: A Historical Analysis of Modern Hindu Missionary Ideologies and Practices* (New Delhi: ISPCK, 1999); Anderson, *Spreading Fires*, 90; Paulson Pulikottil, "Emergence of Indian Pentecostalism," *Dharma Deepika* 6, no. 2 (2002): 52; Gary B. McGee, "Missions, Overseas (North American Pentecostal)," in Stanley M. Burgess and Eduard van der Maas, eds., *New International Dictionary of Pentecostal and Charismatic Movements* (Grand Rapids, MI: Zondervan, 2002), 896; and Wessly Lukose, *A Contextual Missiology of the Spirit: Pentecostalism in Rajasthan, India* (Oxford: Regnum Books, 2013), 113.

15. See Shaibu Abraham, "Ordinary Pentecostal Theology" (PhD thesis, University of Birmingham, United Kingdom, 2011), 148–157; also Lukose, *Contextual Missiology*, 60.

16. M. K. Chacko was the first pioneer Pentecostal missionary who went from Kerala to North India in 1937, followed by Kurien Thomas in 1943, who established Pentecostal churches. Similarly, another Pentecostal pioneer, P. S. Samuel, began mission work in Raipur, Chhattisgarh, in 1949, among the local tribal people. See *M. K. Chacko, An Autobiography* (Delhi: Pastor M. K. Chacko, 1976), 9–10; Kurien Thomas, *God's Trailblazer in India and around the World* (Itarsi: India, 1986), 22; Mathew, *Kerala Penthecosthu Charithram*, 273; and H. Wilfred, "In Fond Memory of P. S. Samuel," *Hallelujah* 11, no. 12 (15 June 2006): 6–7. Several missionaries from Kerala came to various parts of the north and established Pentecostal churches in North India and among the tribals. George Thomas Paradeshi from Kerala, who had a special gift as regards healing and exorcism, came to Nadiad in Gujarat in the 1970s. Paradeshi and his first convert, Dr. Raj, who used to visit eastern Surat, Dang, and Navapur in Maharashtra frequently for missionary work in the seventies and eighties, had made great impact among the Gamaitti, Mauchi, and Vasave. However, the spiritual revival kindled in the ministry of Paradeshi faded in the long run because it did not establish churches and had traces of syncreticism. See Finny Philip, "The Thomas Mathews

Revolution," *Cross and Crown* 36, no. 1 (Nov 2005–March 2006): 20, and Mathew, *Kerala Penthecosthu Charithram*, 191.

17. Lukose, *Contextual Missiology*, 60.

18. Ibid., 60–61.

19. Thomas Thonnakkal, *Marubhoomiyile Appostalan* [The Apostle of the Desert: A Biography of Thomas Mathews] (Udaipur, India: Cross and Crown, 2004), 46; Thomson Thomas Kaithamangalam, *Marubhoomiyil Thalarathu* [Not Tired in the Desert: A Biography of Thomas Mathew] (Udaipur, India: Cross and Crown Publications, 1996), 17; and Roger Simmons, *Vision Mission and a Movement: The Story of Dr. Thomas Mathews and the Native Missionary Movement* (Richardson, TX: Native Missionary Movement, 2008), 26.

20. Here its focus is not on the functions and roles of Christ generally, as is seen in the traditional offices of prophet, priest, and king, but with specific reference to the experience of believers of the ministry of Christ in salvation, sanctification, healing, and so forth.

21. Abraham, "Ordinary Pentecostal Theology," 35–40.

22. Building on the recent research done by the faculty of Filadelfia Bible College, this essay is an attempt to look at the Christological formulation of Bhil Pentecostals in the north of India. See Abraham T. Cherian, "A Study of the Religion of the Bhils of Jhadol Taluk in Udaipur, Rajasthan and Their Response to Christian Faith in the Post-Independent Period" (MTh Thesis, Asian Institute of Theology, Bangalore, India, 2001), and "Contribution of Churches and Missions to the Bhils of Rajasthan" (PhD Thesis, Asian Institute of Theology, Bangalore, India, 2005); Lukose, *Contextual Missiology*; and Abraham, "Ordinary Pentecostal Theology."

23. For detailed discussion see Ram Ahuja, "Religion of the Bhils, a Sociological Analysis," in P. M. Chacko, ed., *Tribal Communities and Social Change* (New Delhi: Sage, 2005), 148–157.

24. See Paul G. Hiebert, "The Flaw of the Excluded Middle," *Missiology* 10, no. 1 (1982): 35–47. Many traditional cultures have worldviews with three zones. The upper zone has to do with heaven or God. The lower represents the material world we live in. The middle zone is the world of spirits, which is believed to closely interact with the material world.

25. Ahuja, "Religion of the Bhils"; Sathianathan Clarke, *Dalits and Christianity: Subaltern Religion and Liberation Theology in India* (New Delhi: Oxford University Press, 1999), 71; Abraham T. Cherian, "Contribution of Churches and Missions," 42.

26. For a comprehensive understanding of the names of spirits worshipped by various tribal groups in different states of India, see H. H. Risley and E. A. Gait, *Census of India* 1921, Religion (Calcutta: Superintendent Government Printing, India, 1923). See also Abraham T. Cherian, "A Study of the Religion of the Bhils of Jhadol Taluk in Udaipur."

27. Various categories of spirits such as village spirits, clan spirits, and spirits of the ancestors are identified; Shah Ghanshyam, "Conversion, Reconversion and the State: Recent Events in the Dangs," *Economic and Political Weekly* (6 February 1999): 315.

28. Daniel Katapali, "Indigenous Missions and the Savara Tribal Church of Srikakulam," in Roger E. Hedlund, ed., *Christianity Is Indian: The Emergence of an Indigenous Community* (Delhi: ISPCK, 2004), 270; Abraham M. Ayrookhuziel, "Distinctive Characteristics of Folk Traditions," in Gnana Robinson, ed., *Religions of the Marginalised: Towards a Phenomenology and Methodology of Study* (Delhi: ISPCK, 1998), 2–3.

29. See Shah, "Conversion, Reconversion and the State," 312–318, and Sathianathan Clarke, "Reviewing the Religion of the Paraiyar: Ellaiyamman as an Iconic Symbol of Collective Resistance and Emancipatory Mythology," in Robinson, ed., *Religions of the Marginalised: Towards a Phenomenology and Methodology of Study*, 35–53.

30. Prabhakar Joshi, *Ethnography of the Primitive Tribes in Rajasthan* (Jaipur, India: Printwell, 1995), 196.

31. Abraham Cherian, "Contribution of Churches," 42.

32. Hiebert, "Flaw of the Excluded Middle."

33. Clarke, *Dalits and Christianity*, 71.

34. Cherian, "Contribution of Churches," 28.

35. M. C. Raj, *Dalitology* (Tumkur, India: Ambedkar Resource Centre, 2001), 245–246.

36. Cherian, "Contribution of Churches," 41; J. Samuel, "A Study on the Influence of Rajasthan Pentecostal Church in the Socio-Economic Upliftment of the Bhil Tribes in Udaipur District" (MTh thesis, Asian Institute of Theology, Bangalore, India, 2006), 29.

37. Philip Jenkins, *The Next Christendom: The Coming of Global Christianity* (Oxford: Oxford University Press, 2002), 183–184. In the case of Pentecostalism in North India, more than 90 percent of the Pentecostals are from tribal and Dalit backdrop.

38. J. Massey, *Down Trodden: The Struggle of India's Dalits for Identity, Solidarity and Liberation* (Geneva: WCC Publications, 1997), 41–61.

39. See Birgit Meyer, "'Make a Complete Break with the Past': Memory and Post-Colonial Modernity in Ghanaian Pentecostalist Discourse," *Journal of Religion in Africa* 28, no. 3 (1998): 316–349, for further discussion.

40. See Lukose, *Contextual Missiology*, 77; the Bhil believers often confess in their gathering *Athmane mujhe Chudaya* (the Spirit has delivered me) and *Athmane mujhe changa kiya* (the Spirit healed me).

41. See Cherian, "Contribution of Churches."

42. Abraham, "Ordinary Pentecostal Theology," 236–237.

43. Ibid., 195–205.

44. See David Hardiman and Gauri Raje, "Practices of Healing in Tribal Gujarat," *Economic and Political Weekly* (1 March 2008): 49; also see David Hardiman, "Healing, Medical Power and the Poor: Contests in Tribal India," *Economic and Political Weekly* (21 April 2007): 1405-06, and P. G. Abraham, *Caste and Christianity: A Pentecostal Perspective* (Kumbhaza, Kerala: Crown Books, 2003), 116-18.

45. See Rudolf C. Heredia, "No Entry, No Exit: Savarna Aversion towards Dalit Conversion," *Economic and Political Weekly* (9 October 2004): 4546; also see Heredia's *Changing Gods: Rethinking Conversion in India* (New Delhi: Penguin Books, 2007).

46. Abraham, "Ordinary Pentecostal Theology," 206–214.

47. This has resulted in a rapid growth of Pentecostalism among the poor villagers; see Biswamoy Pati, "Identity, Hegemony, Resistance: Conversions in Orissa, 1800–2000," *Economic and Political Weekly* (3 November 2001): 4204.

48. Chad M. Bauman, *Christian Identity and Dalit Religion in Hindu India, 1868-1947* (Grand Rapids, MI: William B. Eerdmans Publishing Company, 2008), 40.

49. Hardiman and Raje, "Practices of Healing in Tribal Gujarat," 49.

50. Abraham, "Ordinary Pentecostal Theology," 215–226.

51. Hardiman and Raje, "Practices of Healing in Tribal Gujarat," 49.

52. Abraham, "Ordinary Pentecostal Theology," 227–235.

53. Ibid., 236–243.

54. Ibid., 243.

55. Ibid., 244–249.

56. See ibid., 250–257, for an elaboration of what is discussed in the remainder of this subsection.

57. Amos Yong, "Going Where the Spirit Goes: Engaging the Spirit(s) in J. C. Ma's Pneumatological Missiology," *Journal of Pentecostal Theology* 10, no. 2 (April 2002): 119.
58. See R. T. France, "The Uniqueness of Christ," *Evangelical Review of Theology* 17, no. 1 (1993): 24, for further discussion.

CHAPTER 2
PENTECOSTALISM IN SRI LANKA

1. Paul G. Hiebert, "The Flaw of the Excluded Middle," *Missiology* 10 (1982): 35–47.
2. A. S. Beaty and W. J. T. Small, *Survey of Missionary Work in Ceylon: Chiefly Relating to Societies* (Colombo: Christian Literature Society for India and Africa, Ceylon Branch, 1926), 6.
3. Tissa Jayatilake, *Sirimavo* (Colombo: Bandaranaike Museum Committee, 2010), 48.
4. Christopher John Fuller, *The Camphor Flame: Popular Hinduism and Society in India* (Princeton: Princeton University Press, 2004), 29
5. K. M. de Silva, *University of Ceylon: History of Ceylon*, vol. 2 (Colombo: University of Ceylon Press, 1973), 230.
6. A. J. Appasamy, *Sundar Singh: A Biography* (London: Lutterworth Press, 1976), 92–99.
7. A. Fay Farley, "A Spiritual Healing Mission Remembered: James Moore Hickson's Christian Healing Mission at Palmerston North, New Zealand, 1923," *Journal of Religious History* 34, no. 1 (2010): 1–19.
8. H. W. Frodsham, *Smith Wigglesworth: Apostle of Faith* (Springfield, MO: Gospel Publishing House, 1972), 79.
9. E. Leembruggen-Kallberg, "Sri Lanka," in Stanley M. Burgess and Eduardo van der Maas, eds., *The New International Dictionary of Pentecostal and Charismatic Movements* (Grand Rapids, MI: Zondervan, 2002), 248–253.
10. Colton Wickramaratne and Hal Donaldson, *My Adventure in Faith* (Colombo: HigherLife Development Services 2007), 27.
11. Allan Anderson, *An Introduction to Pentecostalism: Global Charismatic Christianity* (Cambridge: Cambridge University Press, 2004), 142.
12. It was registered as a Christian Mission in 1924. A. C. Thomas, *The Biography of Pastor Paul* (Chennai: Pentecost Press Trust, 1998), 37.
13. Alwin Alwis was a Sinhalese from Galle. He was an English school master at the time of conversion. He came from a traditional Methodist

family in Galle. Ramankutty Paul was a Malayali who served as a house-hold servant in an Anglican medical doctor's house. Regarding Paul's family background, Paulson Pulikottil states plainly, "Pastor Paul was a Dalit convert of the Ezhava caste from central Kerala"; see Pulikottil, "Ramankutty Paul: A Dalit Contribution to Pentecostalism," in Allan Anderson and Edmond Tang, eds., *Asian and Pentecostal: The Charismatic Face of Christianity in Asia* (Oxford: Regnum Books, 2005), 245.

14. See Walter H. Clifford, "Latter Rain in Ceylon," *Pentecostal Evangel* (May 4, 1940).

15. The structure of these so-called faith homes was different from the American ones in this period. In fact, the faith home of the Ceylon Pentecostal Mission was the collective residence of the full-time pastors and workers of a particular area of ministry. See R. M. Riss, "Faith Homes," in Burgess and van der Maas, eds., *The New International Dictionary of Pentecostal and Charismatic Movements*, 630–632.

16. Howard Wriggins, *Ceylon: Dilemmas of a New Nation* (Princeton: Princeton University Press, 1960), 331–333.

17. Anderson, *An Introduction to Pentecostalism*, 12.

18. Barbro Andreasson, *Svensk Pingstmission i Sri Lanka* [The Swiss Pentecostal Mission to Sri Lanka] (Huddinge, Sweden: MissionsInstitutet, 2003), 52.

19. I. Hexham and K. Poewe-Hexham, "South Africa's Black African Charismatics," in Burgess and van der Maas, eds., *The New International Dictionary of Pentecostal and Charismatic Movements*, 230–231.

20. Michael Dissanayake, *Assemblies of God Bible College, Forty Years After Reawakening, 1971-2011* (Colombo: Evangel Press, 2011).

21. Carrie Pemberton, Kevin Ward, Andrew Wingate and Wilson Sitshebo, *Anglicanism: A Global Communion* (London: Church Publishing Inc., 2000), Foreword.

22. For a scholarly Buddhist perspective, see Sasanka Perera, *New Evangelical Movements and Conflict in South Asia: Sri Lanka and Nepal in Perspective* (Colombo: Regional Centre for Strategic Studies, 1998).

23. Alexandra Owen, "Using Legislation to Protect against Unethical Conversions in Sri Lanka," *J. L. & Religion* 22 (2006-2007): 323–351.

24. Frederica Jansz, "Conversion Confusion," *Sunday Leader* (September 7, 2003).

25. "The Violent Side of Sri Lankan Buddhism (Video)," *Colombo Gazette* (March 11, 2014), http://colombogazette.com/2014/03/11/the-violent -side-of-sri-lankan-buddhism (accessed April 3, 2015).

26. Shanika Sriyananda, "New Laws to Stop Unethical Religious Conversions," *Sunday Observer* (December 21, 2003).

27. G. C. Jackson refers such a class difference in the Protestant church in the 1960s; Graeme C. Jackson, *Basil: Portrait of Missionary* (Colombo: The Ecumenical Institute for Study and Dialogue, 2003).

Chapter 3
Indian Pentecostalism in Kerala and the Disapora: Living Locally Defined Holiness in a Globalized World

1. Stanley M. Burgess, "Development and Growth of Pentecostalism in India (1910–60)," in Stanley M. Burgess and Eduard van der Maas, eds., *The New International Dictionary of Pentecostal and Charismatic Movements* (Grand Rapids, MI: Zondervan, 2002), 122; Saju Mathew, *Kerala Penthecosthu Charithram* [The History of Pentecostalism in Kerala], 2nd ed. (Kottayam, Kerala: Good News Publications, 2007), 36.

2. Mathew, *Kerala Penthecosthu Charithram*, 36, 49; K. E. Abraham, *Yesukristhuvinte Eliya Dassan K. E. Abraham* [Autobiography of Pastor K. E. Abraham], 2nd ed. (Kumbanad, Kerala: K. E. Abraham Foundation, 1983), 180.

3. Abraham, *Yesukristhuvinte Eliya Dassan*, 81.

4. *Sworgeeya Dwoni Bi-Weekly* [Heavenly Echo] 11, no. 18 (September 2013): 1.

5. Mathew, *Kerala Penthecosthu Charithram*, 421.

6. *Moved by the Spirit,* Center for Religion and Civil Culture (Los Angeles: University of California, 2013).

7. Kerala Catholic Charismatic Renewal Services, Emmaus, http://www .emmauskst.org/ (accessed March 13, 2014).

8. Mathew, *Kerala Penthecosthu Charithram*, 425.

9. Anil Kodithottam, "Madhyama Vicharam" [Thoughts on Media], *Believers Journal* 7, no. 1 (January 13, 2014): 12.

10. Mathew, *Kerala Penthecosthu Charithram*, 260–285.

11. Mathews Paul, *Jwalichu Prakashicha Villakku—Pastor K. J. Samuel* [A Light that Shined Brightly—Pastor K. J. Samuel] (Mumbai, India: Suvartha Publications, 1997), 19–23.

12. Samuel Alexander, "India Pentecostal Church: Church Planting Activities in New York," in *India Pentecostal Church New York 1990 Souvenir* (Queens Village, NY: Pentecostal Young People's Association, 1990), 29–31.

13. Thomaskutty, "From Kuwait," in *India Pentecostal Church New York 1990 Souvenir*, 60–61.

14. Abraham, *Yesukristhuvinte Eliya Dassan*, 44

15. Ibid., 88.

16. Ibid., 121.

17. Samkutty Chacko, *Hallelujah* 18, no. 19 (November 1, 2013): 3.

18. P. S. Philip, "Kudiyetta Charithram" [The History of Immigration], in Oommen Ebenezer, ed., *Pentecostal Conference of North American Keralites (PCNAK) Silver Jubilee Souvenir* (Orlando, FL: PCNAK, 2007), 36.

19. Omana Russel, "Empowerment of Malayali Nurses in the United States of America," *Christhava Chintha* [Christian Thought] (June 3, 2013): 6-11.

20. Mathew, *Kerala Penthecosthu Charithram*, 416.

21. Philip, "Kudiyetta Charithram," 36.

22. Mathew, *Kerala Penthecosthu Charithram*, 417.

23. Shaji Karackal, "Malayali Penthecosthu Sabhakalude Charithram" [The History of the Malayali Pentecostal Churches], in Ebenezer, ed., *Pentecostal Conference of North American Keralites (PCNAK) Silver Jubilee Souvenir*, 54–55.

24. Thomas Varghese and Shirley Chacko, "Light of the North West: 25 Years and Moving Ahead," in Sam Podimannil, ed., *The Memoirs: Western Pentecostal Jubilee Conference* (Edmonton, Alberta: Western Pentecostal Jubilee Conference, 2013), 27–30.

25. Karackal, "Malayali Penthecosthu Sabhakalude Charithram," 50–63.

26. Thomson Mathew, "Pentecostal Conference of North American Keralites," in Burgess and van der Maas, eds., *The New International Dictionary of Pentecostal and Charismatic Movements*, 967–968.

27. Varghese and Chacko, "Light of the North West," 27–30.

28. Thomas, "Pinnitta 15 Varshangal Ente Ormayil" [The Last 15 Years in My Memory], in Johnson Zachariah, ed., *North American Church of God (India) Fellowship (NACOG) Crystal Jubilee Souvenir* (Dallas, TX: NACOG, 2010), 30–31.

29. T. C. Mathew, ed., "Editorial," *Pentecostal Youth Fellowship of New Jersey and New York Souvenir, 1995* (Edison, NJ: PYFNJ&NY, 1995).

30. Joy Joseph, "Sunday School Ministry in North America," in Ebenezer, ed., *Pentecostal Conference of North American Keralites (PCNAK) Silver Jubilee Souvenir*, 81–82.

31. S. P. James, "Writers' Forum: A Review," in P. S. Philip, ed., *Kerala Pentecostal Writers' Forum—10th Anniversary Souvenir 1993–2003* (New York: KPWF, 2003), 17.

32. Samkutty Chacko, *Hallelujah* 17, no. 13 (July 1, 2013); Samkutty Chacko, *Hallelujah* 18, no. 20 (November 15, 2013).

33. Samkutty Chacko, *Hallelujah* 18, no. 19 (November 1, 2013): 3.

34. Gary McIntosh, *Taking Your Church to the Next Level: What Got You Here Won't Get You There* (Grand Rapids, MI: Baker Books, 2009).

35. George Stephenson, pastor, International Christian Assembly in Chicago, IL, telephone interview by author, Tulsa, OK, February 14, 2014.

36. Thomson K. Mathew, "American Keralite Churches Must Hire Theology Graduates of US Schools," Agape Partners International, http://agape partners.org/articles/51/1/American-Keralite-Churches-Must-Hire -Theology-Graduates-of-US-Schools/Page1.html (accessed April 3, 2015).

37. "Unnatha Vidyabhyasam Adambaramalla" [Higher Education Is Not a Luxury], *Good News Weekly* 36, no. 31 (August 5, 2013): 2.

38. John Varghese, President, Multi-Media Ministries in Oklahoma City, OK, interview by author, Tulsa, OK, March 2, 2014.

39. Rev. Mathukutty A. Samuel, a pastor in Oklahoma City, OK, and Rev. Joseph Thomaskutty, a minister in Houston, TX, attempted to do this study at Oral Roberts University, Tulsa, OK. Both were unable to complete the research due to personal and congregational reasons.

40. Sam George, "The Silent Exodus of Syrian Churches and the Next Generation from the Indian Immigrant Churches in North America," *Coconut Generation* (blog), February 9, 2013, http://cocogen.wordpress.com /2013/02/09/the-silent-exodus-of-syrian-christians-and-the-next -generation-from-immigrant-churches/ (accessed April 3, 2015); Arun Lakshman, "New Generation Churches 'Poach Devotees' in Kerala," *Rediff News* (November 23, 2010), http://www.rediff.com/news/report /new-generation-churches-poach-devotees-kerala/20101123.htm (accessed April 3, 2015).

41. Ministers who attended a pastors' seminar conducted by the author at the India Pentecostal Church Family Conference held in Rochester, New York, on June 26, 2010, expressed great concern about these issues.

Chapter 4
Pentecostals in China

1. My translation of song 747, "The Wind of the Holy Spirit Will Blow Everywhere," found in Lu Xiaomin, *Xin Ling Zhi Sheng* [Sounds of the Heart] (underground house church publication, 2003), 806.

2. Tony Lambert, *China's Christian Millions* (London: OMF/Monarch Books, 1999), 179.

3. Due to the limitations of space, we are not able to include Chinese Roman Catholics in this study.

4. On the evangelical character of the Chinese church, see Alan Hunter and Kim-Kwong Chan, *Protestantism in Contemporary China* (Cambridge: Cambridge University Press, 1993), 82; Ryan Dunch, "Protestant Christianity in China Today: Fragile, Fragmented, Flourishing," in Stephen Uhalley Jr. and Xiaoxin Wu, eds., *China and Christianity: Burdened Past, Hopeful Future* (London: East Gate/M.E. Sharpe, 2001), 195–216.

5. The emphasis on healing and the miraculous in the Chinese church is noted in Hunter and Chan, *Protestantism*, 85, 145–46; Lambert, *China's Christian Millions*, 112; and Dunch, "Protestant Christianity in China Today: Fragile, Fragmented, Flourishing," 203, 215–16.

6. David Aikman, *Jesus in Beijing: How Christianity Is Transforming China and Changing the Global Balance of Power* (Washington, DC: Regnery Publishing, 2003); Gotthard Oblau, "Pentecostals by Default? Contemporary Christianity in China," in Allan Anderson and Edmond Tang, eds., *Asian and Pentecostal: The Charismatic Face of Christianity in Asia* (Costa Mesa, CA: Regnum, 2005), 411–436; Edmond Tang, "'Yellers' and Healers: Pentecostalism and the Study of Grassroots Christianity in China," in Anderson and Tang, eds., *Asian and Pentecostal: The Charismatic Face of Christianity in Asia*, 467–486; Chen-yang Kao, "The Cultural Revolution and the Post-Missionary Transformation of Protestantism in China" (PhD thesis, University of Lancaster, 2009).

7. We concur with Simon Chan: "an adequate definition of Pentecostalism cannot be restricted to phenomenological description"; see Chan, "Wither Pentecostalism," in Anderson and Tang, eds., *Asian and Pentecostal: The Charismatic Face of Christianity in Asia*, 578.

8. Kao, "Cultural Revolution," 99.

9. I define Pentecostals, then, as those who believe that: the Book of Acts serves as a model for contemporary Christian life and ministry; the baptism in the Holy Spirit (Acts 2:4) is a post-conversion enabling for ministry; and speaking in tongues marks this experience. Neo-Pentecostals affirm all of the above except they reject the notion that tongues serve as a normative sign of baptism in the Spirit. For more on Pentecostal identity and related definitions, see Robert Menzies, *Pentecost: This Story Is Our Story* (Springfield, MO: Gospel Publishing House, 2013), 11–20.

10. Daniel H. Bays, "The Growth of Independent Christianity in China, 1900–1937," in Daniel Bays, ed., *Christianity in China: From the Eighteenth Century to the Present* (Stanford: Stanford University Press, 1996), 309.

11. Ibid., 310; for similar estimates see Hunter and Chan, *Protestantism*, 134n60.

12. Bays, "The Growth of Independent Christianity in China, 1900–1937," 310.

13. Daniel Bays, "Indigenous Protestant Churches in China, 1900–1937: A Pentecostal Case Study," in Steven Kaplan, ed., *Indigenous Responses to Western Christianity* (New York: New York University Press, 1995), 129.

14. Ibid., 130.

15. For further details, see Iap Sian Chin's chapter, "Bernt Berntsen: A Prominent Oneness Pentecostal Pioneer to North China," in this volume.

16. Hunter and Chan, *Protestantism*, 121.

17. Bob Whyte, *Unfinished Encounter: Christianity and China* (London: Fount, 1988), 177; Timothy T. Y. Yeung, "Pentecostalism in China: Past and Present" (paper presented at a conference in Australia on "Asian Pentecostalism," July 8–10, 2013), 11–12.

18. Hunter and Chan, *Protestantism*, 121; on the Jesus Family see also Bays, "The Growth of Independent Christianity in China, 1900–1937," 312.

19. Ibid.

20. Daniel Bays, "Christian Revival in China, 900–1937," in Edith Blumhofer and Randall Balmer, eds., *Modern Christian Revivals* (Urbana: University of Illinois Press, 1993), 171.

21. Paul Lewis, "China," in Stanley M. Burgess, ed., *Encyclopedia of Pentecostal and Charismatic Christianity* (New York: Routledge, 2006), 95.

22. Letter from Mattie Ledbetter to Sadie, dated November 30, 1920, courtesy of the Assemblies of God Archives, Springfield, Missouri.

23. See the brief note on her death entitled, "A Good Fight Finished," in *The Pentecostal Evangel* (March 26, 1938): 7. For more on Mattie Ledbetter's ministry, see Wai Man Leung, "The Impact of Pentecostalism on the Chinese Churches in Hong Kong" (DMin Thesis, Asia Pacific Theological Seminary, Baguio City, Philippines, 2005), 61–64.

24. Tony Lambert, *The Resurrection of the Chinese Church* (Wheaton, IL: OMF/Harold Shaw Publishers, 1994), 154.

25. See also Hunter and Chan, *Protestantism*, 140.

26. Chen-Yang Kao, "The Cultural Revolution and the Emergence of Pentecostal-Style Protestantism in China," *Journal of Contemporary Religion* 24, no. 2 (2009): 174.

27. On the basis of Paul Hattaway's analysis in his *Henan: The Galilee of China*, The First & Blood Series 2 (Carlisle, U.K.: Piquant, 2009), 323–334, I believe a realistic number for Chinese Protestants today is 80 million. According to my definitions offered above, at least half of this number might be accurately described as Pentecostal and two-thirds Pentecostal or neo-Pentecostal.

28. Hunter and Chan, *Protestantism*, 141–163.

29. Fenggang Yang, "Lost in the Market, Saved at MacDonald's: Conversion to Christianity in Urban China," *Journal for the Scientific Study of Religion* 44 (2005): 432.

30. Kao, "Cultural Revolution," 102.

31. Written statement from a questionnaire completed by Chen Bao Chi, a pastor and church leader from Wenzhou, dated March 18, 2014.

32. Although several CGF leaders affirmed the Pentecostal distinctives noted above, a survey of twenty students at their Beijing seminary revealed that only seven viewed tongues as a sign of Spirit baptism, and only nine said that tongues occurred in their churches often or occasionally.

33. These conclusions are supported by: the results of a questionnaire completed by house church leaders from the Fang Cheng Church, Miao's Wenzhou Church, and the China Gospel Fellowship (for a copy of this questionnaire, contact rmenzies@mail2go.net); an interview with the leaders of the Li Xin Church, including the founder, Uncle Zheng; an interview with Dennis Balcombe on October 14, 2014; and my personal observations and conversations in China over the past twenty years.

34. The government-recognized (TSPM) churches tend to be less open to Pentecostal values, although there are notable exceptions. For an analysis of TSPM attitudes, see the book I wrote under a pen name, Luke Wesley,

The Church in China: Persecuted, Pentecostal, and Powerful (Baguio City,
Philippines: Asia Journal of Pentecostal Studies Books, 2004).

35. Hattaway, *Henan*, 282.

36. Ibid., 288.

37. Dennis Balcombe, *China's Opening Door* (Lake Mary, FL: Charisma
House, 2014), 110.

38. A Chinese translation of William W. Menzies and Stanley M. Horton,
Bible Doctrines: A Pentecostal Perspective (Springfield, MO: Logion Press,
1993).

39. Connie Au, "Pentecostalism as Suffering: House Churches in China
(1949–2012)," in Harold D. Hunter and Neil Ormerod, eds., *The Many
Faces of Global Pentecostalism* (Cleveland, TN: CPT Press, 2013), 73–99.

40. The impact of Jackie Pullinger's ministry among drug addicts in Hong
Kong should also be noted. See R. T. Kendall's description of her ministry in chapter 11 of his *Holy Fire* (Lake Mary, FL: Charisma House,
2014).

41. See Tony Lambert, *China's Christian Millions*, 62, for this English translation. I have included the sentence, "In Christ God grants a diversity
of gifts of the Holy Spirit to the church so as to manifest the glory of
Christ," which is found in the Chinese original, but which is omitted in
Lambert's version. This appears to be an editorial oversight.

42. The Chinese characters translated "outpouring" (*jiao guan*) and "filling"
(*chong man*) of the Spirit in this statement are also found in Acts 2:17
("pour out") and Acts 2:4 ("filled") of the *Chinese Union Version* translation, the most widely used Chinese translation of the Bible.

43. The Chinese characters translated by the phrase "do not impose upon"
(*mian qiang*) certainly convey the notion of "force."

44. This may be an attempt to distance themselves from non-trinitarian
Oneness groups, like The True Jesus Christ, who present speaking in
tongues as a necessary sign of salvation.

45. Dunch, "Protestant Christianity in China Today: Fragile, Fragmented,
Flourishing," 215.

46. See also Balcombe, *China's Opening Door*, 188–191.

47. Wesley, *The Church in China*, 91–103.

48. I would like to thank Timothy Yeung, Yee Thamwan, and Don Parrett
for their contributions to this essay, especially for their help in collecting
data from questionnaires and interviews.

CHAPTER 5
BERNT BERNTSEN: A PROMINENT ONENESS
PENTECOSTAL PIONEER TO NORTH CHINA

1. The elder child is a boy, whose name is Henry Bernhand Berntsen. His name can be seen many times in *Popular Gospel Truth*, and many articles in this periodical were written by him. His name has also appeared in Paul Wei's (the major pioneer of TJC's publication) *The True Witness Book of the Holy Spirit*, vols. 1, 3, which says Henry practiced exorcism for Wei's daughter with him. In *Word and Witness* 9, no. 9 (1913): 4, his name is also mentioned as: "Our own son, Henry, a mere boy, is having his call renewed to preach." Those documents show that Henry became an important assistant to Berntsen; however, he later worked for an American-Asiatic underwriter in Hankou. The other child is a daughter named Ruth, who married a missionary named Matron Redmon and sustained Berntsen's mission work in China after Bernsten's death. She was obviously affiliated with the Oneness camp.

2. R. G. Tiedemann, ed., *Handbook of Christianity in China*, vol. 2: *1800–Present* (Leiden and Boston: Brill, 2010), 550.

3. Cecil M. Robeck Jr., *The Azusa Street Mission and Revival* (Nashville: Nelson Electronic, 2006), 260–261.

4. *Apostolic Faith* 1, no. 10 (September 1907): 1.

5. *Apostolic Faith* 1, no. 12 (1908): 3.

6. Robeck, *Azusa Street Mission and Revival*, 261; Tiedemann, *Handbook of Christianity in China*, 550.

7. Robeck, *The Azusa Street Mission and Revival*, 261.

8. See *Popular Gospel Truth* 15 (1917): 1. The preface mentioned that the base of this periodical will move to No.1, Xinglong Street, Qianmengwai, Beijing.

9. Allan Anderson, *Spreading the Fires: The Missionary Nature of Early Pentecostalism* (New York: Orbis Books, 2007), 133. Furthermore, *Popular Gospel Truth* 3 (1914): 5, mentioned this trip to North Europe; in the previous issue his son, Henry, also talked about this trip. His passport shows that he went to Norway, Sweden, and Denmark during the span from April to November 1910. See also *Department Passport Application*.

10. *Pentecostal Testimony* 1, no. 8 (1911): 13.

11. *Pentecostal Testimony* 1, no. 5 (1910): 10–11.

12. Daniel Bays, "Indigenous Protestant Churches in China, 1900–1937: A Pentecostal Case Study," in Steven Kaplan, ed., *Indigenous Responses to*

Western Christianity (New York: New York University Press, 1995), 124–143.

13. R. G. Tiedemann, *Reference Guide to Christian Missionary Societies in China: From the Sixteenth to the Twentieth Century* (New York: M. E. Sharpe, 2009), 121–122. Chinese Christian leader Wang Mingdao witnessed that "Pentecostal churches in China had been Pentecostal Church, Apostolic Faith Mission, Church of God (神的教會 and 上帝教會), now most of them are called Assemblies of God (神召會)." See Wang, *The Fifty Years* (Taipei: Olive Christian Foundation, 1996), 80.

14. *Combined Minutes of the General Council of the Assemblies of God in the United States of America, Canada and Foreign Lands Held at Hot Springs, Ark. April 2-12, and at the Stone Church, Chicago, Ill. November 12-29, 1914*, 13.

15. Gary Tiedemann, "The Origins and Organizational Developments of the Pentecostal Missionary Enterprise in China," *Asia Journal of Pentecostal Studies* 14, no. 1 (2011): 138.

16. Tiedemann, *Handbook of Christianity in China*, 550.

17. Tiedemann, "The Origins and Organizational Developments of the Pentecostal Missionary Enterprise in China," 138–139. I also later received a copy of this passport application; indeed, I found that he was both a PAW and a GOC (Adventist) minister.

18. Tiedemann, *Reference Guide to Christian Mission Societies in China*, 199.

19. *Pentecostal Herald* 21, no. 1 (1946): 8.

20. Wei Yisa, ed., *Commemorating the 30th Anniversary of the True Jesus Church—Special Issue* [English title] (Nanjing: The True Jesus Church General Assembly, 1947), J4.

21. We have no further information about the identity of this elder "Qui" and are unable to be sure if he is a Chinese or a Westerner, but his name appeared in *Popular Gospel Truth* and seems to be one of Berntsen's main assistants.

22. Deng Zhaoming, "Indigenous Chinese Pentecostal Denominations," in Allan Anderson and Edmond Tang, eds., *Asian and Pentecostal: The Charismatic Face of Christianity in Asia* (Oxford: Regnum Books International, 2005), 442; David A. Reed, "Missionary Resources for an Independent Church—Case Study of the True Jesus Church" (presented at the 40th Annual Meeting of the Society for Pentecostal Studies, 2011), 13.

23. Deng, "Indigenous Chinese Pentecostal Denominations," 442: "Shortly thereafter Zhang had a vision that the Sabbath was to be observed and

convinced elder Peterson to change the day of worship to Saturday in July, 1916."

24. *Popular Gospel Truth* 4 (1912): 2.

25. Barnabas Zhang, *Travel Notes of Preaching* [English title] (Nanjing: The True Jesus Church, 1929), 9.

26. Xin is a Chinese, baptized in the Spirit in Shijiazhuang, who came to Beijing from Zhengdingfu, and became an elder of AFM. See *Popular Gospel Truth* 14 (1916): 8.

27. Paul Wei, *True Testimonies of the Holy Spirit* [English title], unpublished, 2. Wei recalled that, "I went to Dong Chen Faith Union next day; upon encountering the pastor in this church, he looked very poor. While he looked poor, morally he seemed to be better than other church's Christians...from that day on, they became close friends, he helped Paul Wei understand a great deal of Bible truth." Also see *Popular Gospel Truth* 13 (1916): 1–2.

28. Wei, *True Testimonies of the Holy Spirit*, 17. In Chinese, pastor is written as 牧師 (*mushi*), and the word "*shi*" means teacher; that is the reason why some Chinese indigenous churches, such as TJC and Little Flock, avoid using this term.

29. Zhang, *Travel Notes of Preaching*, 27.

30. Wei, *Commemorating the 30th Anniversary of the True Jesus Church*, M9–M10.

31. Wang, *The Fifty Years*, 79

32. Ibid., 79–82, 98.

33. Ibid., 93–94.

34. *Popular Gospel Truth* 22 (1920): 3.

35. Walter Hollenweger, *The Pentecostals* (Minneapolis: Augsburg, 1977), 332.

36. Kenneth J. Archer, "Early Pentecostal Biblical Interpretation," *Journal of Pentecostal Theology* 9, no. 18 (2001): 64, 62.

37. Frank D. Macchia, "Baptized in the Spirit: Toward a Global Theology of Spirit Baptism," in Veli-Matti Kärkkäinen, ed., *The Spirit in the World: Emerging Pentecostal Theologies in Global Context* (Grand Rapids, MI: William B. Eerdmans, 2009), 6–7.

38. *Popular Gospel Truth* 13 (1916): 1. Other articles have been written, such as the following: Holy Communion should be routinely held after sunset on Saturday. Keep the Sabbath. Foot washing. Believe in Jesus's healing for every sort of sickness. Seek the Holy Spirit and be proofed by

speaking in tongues. Preaching must be in accordance with the New Testament and the Old Testament.

39. *Popular Gospel Truth* 8 (1915): 1–3.

40. Xie Shundao, *The Doctrine of the Holy Spirit* [English title] (Taichung: Palm Publisher, 1995), 180.

41. *Popular Gospel Truth* 3 (1911): 7; *Popular Gospel Truth* 10 (1916): 3.

42. *Popular Gospel Truth* 12 (1916): 6.

43. *Minutes of the General Council of the Assemblies of God in the United States of America, Canada, and Foreign Lands held at Turner Hall, St. Louis, MO, October 1–10, 1915*, 9–16.

44. Ibid., 5.

45. Ibid., 8.

46. *Minutes of the General Council of the Assemblies of God in the United States of America, Canada, and Foreign Lands held at Bethel Chapel, St. Louis, MO, October 1–7, 1916*, 11–13.

47. William Menzies, *Anointed to Serve: The Story of the Assemblies of God* (Springfield, MO: Gospel Publishing House, 1971), 118.

48. Hollenweger, *Pentecostals*, 32.

49. *Popular Gospel Truth* 13 (1916): 1.

50. *Popular Gospel Truth* 14 (1916): 8.

51. *Popular Gospel Truth* 18 (1918): 7.

52. Tiedemann, *Handbook of Christianity in China*, 550.

53. Xie, *The Doctrine of the Holy Spirit*, 175.

54. Zhang, *Travel Notes of Preaching*, 25.

55. Ibid., 4.

56. Xie, *The Doctrine of the Holy Spirit*, 179, 181.

57. As we see the statement of faith of the official website of this denomination, we find that this Church of God believes in the Trinity of the Godhead and has no Pentecostal background. See General Conference Church of God (Seventh Day), "About Us: Introducing the Church of God (Seventh Day)," http://cog7.org/about/ (accessed April 4, 2015).

58. This article has been partly modified and translated (from the original Chinese) by the author from "Bernt Berntsen: A Study of His Life and Thought with Reference of Oneness Pentecostalism," *Jian Dao* 38 (2012): 33–58. I dedicate it to the memory of my brother in Christ, Dennis Kam (1964–2015), pastor of Full Gospel Assembly, USJ (Subang Jaya), Malaysia.

CHAPTER 6
CONTEMPORARY EXPRESSIONS OF A SPIRIT-LED
CHRISTIAN MOVEMENT: A CHINESE CASE STUDY

1. This chapter engages the study of the Word of Life movement (WOL) in China that was regarded as one of largest house church networks in China with approximately 23 million affiliated believers (according to statistics in *Operation World*, 2001 edition).

2. The model used herein an adapted version of Howard Snyder's paper presented, as the keynote speaker, at the Global Consultation on Pentecost and New Humanity, sponsored by the Center for the Study of World Christian Revitalization Movements at Asbury Theological Seminary in Wilmore, Kentucky, in October 2009. It was later published as "The Pentecostal Renewal of the Church," in Howard Snyder, *Yes in Christ: Wesleyan Reflections on Gospel, Mission and Culture* (Toronto: Clements Academic, 2011), 259–294.

3. See Luke Wesley, "Is Chinese Church Predominantly Pentecostal?" *Asia Journal of Pentecostal Studies* 7, no. 2 (2004): 238.

4. Paul Hattaway and Joy Hattaway, "From the Front Lines with Paul & Joy Hattaway," *Asia Harvest* 2 (March 2002): 2.

5. Snyder, *Yes in Christ*, 285.

6. Some of the data used in this essay, especially the historical data, were also available in some of my earlier publications on the house church movement, i.e. "Inner Dynamics of the Chinese House Church Movement," *Mission Studies* 25, no.2 (2008): 157–184, and *Inside China's House Church Network: The Word of Life Movement and Its Renewing Dynamic* (Lexington: Emeth Press, 2009).

7. Xin, *Inside China's House Church Network*, 159. The *Seven Principles* are the essential biblical themes identified by the community of believers in the WOL church in their spiritual and ministerial practice. These are compiled and edited into the *Truth Practice Curriculum* that is used in different levels of theological education. They are sometimes referred to as "theology of the cross."

8. Patrick Johnstone, *The Future of the Global Church* (Colorado Springs: Biblica, 2011), 225. According to Johnstone, the Jesus/early church model consists of the three basic functions of "local congregations," "Apostolic teams" (or mission agencies), and "leader coaching" (or, theological training). Over time the balance of the three shifted. Johnstone calls for a "restoration of the original balance for the church globally and

locally," and "the three functions working harmoniously and prayerfully together."

9. See Jonathan Chao, *A History of Christianity in Socialist China, 1949-1997* (Taipei: CMI Publishing Co. Ltd, 1997), 522–523.

10. Messengers of the Gospel is a name that has been commonly used among the house church networks that emerged in Central China. It refers to the full-time evangelists, typically sent out by the Gospel Band for frontier evangelism. They were sometimes referred to as itinerant evangelists.

11. Cf. Patrick Jonestone, Robyn Johnstone, and Jason Mandryk, *Operation World* (Cumbria, UK: Paternoster Lifestyle, 2001), 160.

12. Snyder, *Yes in Christ*, 261.

13. Ibid., 262.

14. Ibid., 264.

15. Ibid., 275.

16. WOL Manual I, "Zhen li shi jian ke cheng" [Truth Practice Curriculum, Book 1], (unpublished manuscript, WOL editorial office, 2003).

17. Newman Sze, *Meng xun jiao shi zhuan* [The Biography of Marie Monson] (Culver City, CA: Witness Publishing, 1998), 11–12.

18. Snyder, *Yes in Christ*, 265.

19. Howard A. Snyder, *Models of the Kingdom: Gospel, Culture and Mission in Biblical and Historical Perspective* (Eugene, OR: Wipf and Stock Publishers, 1991), 16.

20. Snyder, *Yes in Christ*, 267.

21. Ibid., 277.

22. Peter Xu, interview by author, 2004, Los Angeles, California.

23. Furnaces of revival refer to house churches in rural areas in central China area that were experiencing small-scale revivals initially that gradually spread out geographically. This was also where one of the seven principles of the WOL theology, Interlink and Fellowship, came to formation. Snyder, *Yes in Christ*, 269.

24. Ibid., 279.

25. Xin, *Inside China's House Church Network*, 169.

26. Snyder, *Yes in Christ*, 281.

27. Peter Xu, interview, 2004.

28. Snyder, *Yes in Christ*, 282.

29. Ibid., 283.

30. "The Confession of Faith" was the first official document created by representatives from four of the largest house church networks in China, which served two purposes primarily: (1) as a practical step in the house church unity movement, and (2) as clarification over controversies, primarily fabricated accusation from the authorities against these large house church groups.

31. Jonathan Chao, trans., "Chinese House Church Confession of Faith," *China Prayer Letter and Ministry Report* 149 (November 1998–February 1999): 2–4.

32. Peter Xu, "The Renewal of the Church and its Dynamic" (transcribed presentation at the annual consultation addressing worldwide revitalization by the Center for the Study of World Christian Revitalization Movements, Wilmore, Kentucky, October 15–18, 2009).

33. Marie Monson, *The Awakening: Revival in China* (London: China Inland Mission, 1961), 54.

34. Snyder, *Yes in Christ*, 270.

35. Ibid.

36. Ibid., 271, italics in original.

37. Ibid., 284.

38. Paul Hattaway, *Back to Jerusalem* (Carlisle: Piquant, 2003), 66.

39. "The Way of the Cross" is the second principle of the WOL theology. It deals with the necessity of suffering of the cross for believers as exemplified by Jesus, the external and internal suffering of walking the way of the cross, so that the salvation of the Lord will be preached to the world.

40. WOL Manual I, "Zhen li shi jian ke cheng," 91.

41. Ibid.

42. Snyder, *Yes in Christ*, 270.

43. Peter Xu, interview, 2004.

44. Snyder, *Yes in Christ*, 290.

CHAPTER 7
PENTECOSTAL AND CHARISMATIC CHRISTIANITY
IN PROTESTANT TAIWAN

1. Murray A. Rubinstein, "Taiwan," in Stanley M. Burgess and Eduard van der Maas, eds., *The New International Dictionary of Pentecostal Charismatic Movement* (Grand Rapids, MI: Zondervan, 2002), 263.

2. R. G. Tiedemann, *Reference Guide to Christian Missionary Societies in China: From the Sixteenth to the Twentieth Century* (New York & London: M. E. Sharpe, 2009), 173.

3. Murray A. Rubinstein failed to show that there are other AG groups besides those related to the United States and wrongly referred to the China Assemblies of God as the Taiwan Assemblies of God, a group that was formed by Finnish missionaries. See Murray A. Rubinstein, "Holy Spirit Taiwan; Pentecostal and Charismatic Christianity in the Republic of China," in Daniel H. Bays, ed., *Christianity in China: From the Eighteenth Century to the Present* (Stanford: Stanford University Press, 1996), 355.

4. Rubinstein, "Holy Spirit Taiwan," 356.

5. The authors use the Pinyin phonetic system for transliterating Chinese characters, except when the individual concerned, or credible publications, have popularized alternative spellings. Such is the case with 顏金龍, who is known both by the aboriginal name Hetai Machi and, in international Assembly of God publications, as Yen Chin Long. See The World Assemblies of God Fellowship Office, *WAGF Connection* (September 2012), http://ag.org/newsletters/wagf/downloads/WAGF -Connection-Sept-2012.pdf (accessed April 4, 2015).

6. Hetai Machi is known for his night-club ministry. See Connie Au, "Justice and Peace for Global Commercial Sex Workers: The Plight of Aboriginal Migrant Women in Taiwan," *The Ecumenical Review* 64, no. 3 (2012): 274.

7. This is common in Finland where Pentecostals, commonly called "Helluntaiherätys," do not register as a denomination. The FFFM is now called Fida International, a name taken in 2001 after integrating with another organization. It is a member of the AG world fellowship. See L. Ahonen, "Finland," in Burgess and van der Maas., eds., *The New International Dictionary of Pentecostal and Charismatic Movements,* 103–104; Tiedemann, *Reference Guide to Christian Missionary Societies in China,* 207.

8. *Pentecostal Evangel,* no. 2753 (1967): 6–7.

9. Zhuang Fei, "History of China Assemblies of God," unpublished manuscript (Taiwan: n.d.), 27.

10. Jieren Li, "A History of the Finnish Free Foreign Mission in Taiwan (1949-1998)" (MA Thesis, ICI University), 75–76, 140. See also Bill and Diana Kelly, interviewed by Connie Au, Toronto, February 28, 2010.

11. Joy Cheng, ed., *Commemorative Volume on the Fiftieth Anniversary of the Mission to Taiwan of China Assemblies of God Taiwan District Council* (Taipei: China Assemblies of God Taiwan District Council, 1999), 50–51.

12. Edith L. Blumhofer, *Restoring the Faith: The Assemblies of God, Pentecostalism, and American Culture* (Champaign: University of Illinois Press, 1993), 72–73.

13. Edith Blumhofer, personal e-mail to Iap Sian-Chin, June 19, 2012.

14. Rodney Stark and Roger Finke, *Act of Faith: Explaining the Human Side of Religion* (Berkeley and Los Angeles: University of California Press, 2000), 36, 193.

15. Allan Anderson, "Varieties, Taxonomies, and Definitions," in Allan Anderson, Michael Bergunder, Andre Droogers, and Cornelis van der Laan, eds., *Studying Global Pentecostalism: Theories and Methods* (Berkeley and Los Angeles: University of California Press, 2010), 18; Anderson added "Older Independent and Spirit Church" to the popular threefold category.

16. Barnabas Zhang has been thought to be one of the earliest pioneers of the TJC. TJC leaders later expelled him for causing splits in the church.

17. *Commemorative Volume on the Thirtieth Anniversary of Mission to Taiwan* (Taichung: The True Jesus Church, 1956), 6, 8.

18. John S. T. Chu, *Taiwan Church Report 2011* (Taichung: Christian Resources Center, 2012), 8.

19. Murray A. Rubinstein, "The New Testament Church and the Taiwanese Protestant Community," in Murray A. Rubinstein, ed., *The Other Taiwan: 1945 to the Present* (New York: M. E. Sharpe, 1994), 445–452.

20. During the 1940s, in Canada, the movement was known as, "new order"; Blumhofer, *Restoring the Faith*, 203–211; Menzies, *Anointed to Serve*, 321–325, 330.

21. Leo Ling-nam Ip (葉嶺楠), Spokesman, Public Relations Office; Director, Missions and Church Planting; Secretary-General, I-Link Association, Bread of Life Christian Church in Taipei (台北靈糧堂), interview by Maurie Sween, tape recording, Taipei, Taiwan, May 5, 2014; "Taipei Ling Liang Church Vision and Core Values" (台北靈糧堂異象及核心價‧簡體版), PowerPoint (Taipei, Taiwan: Bread of Life Church in Taipei Media Center, 2014); "A Brief History of the Church" (教會簡史), video, (Taipei, Taiwan: Bread of Life Church in Taipei Media Center [台北靈糧堂媒體中心], 2013); Taiwan Ministry of

Culture (台灣文化部), "Taipei Bread of Life Christian Church," *Encyclopedia of Taiwan* (台灣大百科全書), 2011, http://taiwanpedia.culture.tw /en/content?ID=4255 (accessed May 27, 2014); see also Maurice Alwyn Sween III, "Chinese Protestant Theologies of Social Ministry in Nationalist Taiwan" (PhD Thesis: University of Edinburgh, 2006), 65.

22. Ernest Chan, interview by Maurie Sween, tape recording, Kaohsiung, Taiwan, May 3, 2014; Agape International Leadership Institute (愛修園國際領袖學院), http://www.agapecenter.net (accessed May 8, 2014); Agape Kaohsiung Leadership Institute (高雄愛修園), http:// kaohsiung.agapecenter.net (accessed May 8, 2014); Zhang Meiyan (張美燕), personal e-mail, December 10, 2014.

23. Sween, "Chinese Protestant Theologies of Social Ministry in Nationalist Taiwan," 56–57, 61.

24. Felix Liu, "The Relationship between Forgiveness and Christian Wholistic Healing in Biblical Study and Pastoral Ministry" (PhD diss., Fuller Theological Seminary School of Intercultural Studies, 1999).

25. Felix Liu, interview by Maurie Sween, telephone, November 14, 2014.

26. Sween, "Chinese Protestant Theologies of Social Ministry in Nationalist Taiwan," 25, 35–36, 48, 50; cf. C. M. Robeck Jr., "Charismatic Movements," in William A. Dyrness and Veli-Matti Kärkkäinen, eds., *Global Dictionary of Theology* (Nottingham: InterVarsity Press, 2008), 150.

27. See Richard Madsen, *Democracy's Dharma: Religious Renaissance and Political Development in Taiwan* (Berkeley: University of California Press, 2007), 12–13, 139; Chi-Ming Lee, "Changes and Challenges for Moral Education in Taiwan," *Journal of Moral Education* 33, no. 4 (2004): 576, 578; Yen-zen Tsai, "Confucian Culture in Contemporary Taiwan and Religious Experiences," in Yen-zen Tsai, ed., *Religious Experiences in Contemporary Taiwan and China* (Taipei: Chengchi University Press, 2013), 143, 146; Sween, "Chinese Protestant Theologies of Social Ministry in Nationalist Taiwan," 32–33, 41–42; and Fong-mao Lee, "The Daoist Priesthood and Secular Society: Two Aspects of Postwar Taiwanese Daoism" (trans. Philip Clart), in Philip Clart and Charles B. Jones, eds., *Religion in Modern Taiwan: Tradition and Innovation in a Changing Society* (Honolulu: University of Hawaii Press, 2003), 126, 133–134, 153–154.

28. Information in this paragraph derives from various chapters in Yen-zen Tsai, ed., *Religious Experiences in Contemporary Taiwan and China* (Taipei: Chengchi University Press, 2013): Ping-yin Kuan, "A Profile of

Religion in Contemporary Taiwan," 18, 32, 39; Hsing-kuang Chao, "Tai-wanese Christianity and Religious Experiences," 118; Chen-yang Kao, "The Religious Experiences of the Non-Religious in Taiwan," 129–130; Ming-hua Yu, "Folk Religion and Religious Experiences in Taiwan," 42–44; Yi-jia Tsai, "Taiwanese Buddhism and Religious Experiences," 60; Cheng-tian Kuo, "Taiwanese Daoism and Religious Experiences," 78, 81, 84. See also Sween, "Chinese Protestant Theologies of Social Ministry in Nationalist Taiwan," 50.

29. Murray A. Rubinstein, "Medium/Message in Taiwan's Mazu-cult Cen-ters: Using 'Time, Space and Word' to Foster Island Wide Spiritual Con-sciousness and Local, Regional, and National Forms of Institutional Identity," in Paul Katz and Murray A. Rubinstein, eds., *Religion and the Formation of Taiwanese Identities* (New York: Palgrave MacMillan, 2003), 213; Avron A. Boretz, "Righteous Brothers and Demon Slayers: Subjectives and Collective Identities in Taiwanese Temple Processions," in Katz and Rubinstein, eds., *Religion and the Formation of Taiwanese Identities*, 220; Fong-mao Lee, "The Daoist Priesthood and Secular Society," 126, 133, 153–154; Madsen, *Democracy's Dharma*, 1, 3–6, 12–15, 136, 153; Christian Jochim, "Carrying Confucianism into the Modern World: The Taiwan Case," in Clart and Jones, eds., *Religion in Modern Taiwan: Tradition and Innovation in a Changing Society*, 72; and Julian Pas, "Stability and Change in Taiwan's Religious Culture," in Clart and Jones, eds., *Religion in Modern Taiwan: Tradition and Innovation in a Changing Society*, 36–39, 42.

30. André Laliberté, "Religious Change and Democratization in Postwar Taiwan: Mainstream Buddhist Organizations and the Kuomingtang, 1947–1996," in Clart and Jones, eds., *Religion in Modern Taiwan: Tra-dition and Innovation in a Changing Society*, 172, 178–179; Madsen, *Democracy's Dharma*, 4, 155–156; Boretz, "Righteous Brothers and Demon Slayers," 232, 240; and Rubinstein, "Medium/Message," 213–214.

31. Masden, *Democracy's Dharma*, 2, 142, 155–156; Chao, "Taiwanese Chris-tianity and Religious Experiences," 109.

32. Madsen, *Democracy's Dharma*, 5–6; Fong-mao Lee, "The Daoist Priest-hood and Secular Society," 132, 136, 138, 141; Noah Buchan, "Taiwan's Folk Temple's Branch Out with a Bang," *Taipei Times* (August 9, 2014), http://www.taipeitimes.com/News/feat/archives/2014/08/09 /2003596986/1 (accessed August 21, 2014); Barbara E. Reed, "Guanyin Narratives—Wartime and Postwar," in Clart and Jones, eds., *Religion in*

Modern Taiwan: Tradition and Innovation in a Changing Society, 187–188, 200–202; and Yi-jia Tsai, "Embodied Modes of Religious Experience in Taiwan," 163–165.

33. Shoki Coe, "Contextualization as the Way Toward Reform," in Boris Anderson, ed., *Recollections and Reflections* (Taiwan: The Rev. Dr. Shoki Coe's Memorial Fund, 1993), 268.

34. Miroslav Volf, *Exclusion and Embrace: A Theological Exploration of Identity, Otherness and Reconciliation* (Nashville: Abingdon Press, 1996), 226–227.

35. Rubinstein, "Taiwan," 262–263.

36. The authors would like to thank Judith Lin (Fuller Theological Seminary) for her editorial assistance.

CHAPTER 8
THE KINGDOM OF GOD IN KOREAN PENTECOSTAL PERSPECTIVE

1. Chai Choon Kim, "The Present Situation and Future Prospects of the Korean Church," in Harold S. Hong, Won Yong Ji, and Chung Choon Kim, eds., *Korea Struggles for Christ: Memorial Symposium for the Eightieth Anniversary of Protestantism in Korea* (Seoul: Christian Literature Society of Korea, 1966), 15.

2. Walter J. Hollenweger, *Pentecostalism: Origins and Developments Worldwide* (Peabody: Hendrickson Publishers Inc., 2005), 105; Harvey Cox, *Fire from Heaven: The Rise of Pentecostal Spirituality and the Reshaping of Religion in the Twenty-First Century* (Reading: Addison-Wesley Publishing Company, 1995), 220–222; Boo-Woong Yoo, *Korean Pentecostalism: Its History and Theology* (Frankfurt am Main: Verlag Peter Lang, 1988), 223; Byoung-Suh Kim, "The Explosive Growth of the Korean Church Today: A Sociological Analysis," *International Review of Mission* 74 (1985): 61–74.

3. Pan Ho Kim, "Paul Tillich and Dr. Yonggi Cho: A Dialogue between Their Respective Theologies of Healing," Young San Theological Institute, ed., *Dr. Yonggi Cho's Ministry & Theology* I (Gunpo: Hansei University Logos, 2008), 362.

4. David Kwan Sun Suh, "A Biographical Sketch of an Asian Theological Consultation," in Yong Bock Kim, ed., *Minjung Theology: People as the Subjects of History* (Singapore: The Commission on Theological Concerns of the Christian Conference of Asia, 1981), 17.

5. Ibid.

6. Byung Mu Ahn, "Jesus and the Minjung in the Gospel of Mark," in Yong Bock Kim, ed., *Minjung Theology*, 148.

7. Compared with the other synoptic Gospels, *ochlos* is used fifty-one times and *laos* thirteen times in the Book of Matthew; in Luke's Gospel, *ochlos* is used forty times and *laos* thirty-five times. Ahn insists that both Matthew and Luke were influenced by Mark. See Byung Mu Ahn, *Galilea ui Yesoo* [Jesus of Galilee] (Seoul: Hankook Sinhak Yeongooso, 2008), 137.

8. Ahn, *Galilea ui Yesoo*, 136–143.

9. Byeong Mu Ahn, "Minjock, Minjung, Gyohoi [Nation, People, and Church]," in Hankook Gidockgyo Gyohoihyubuihoi [The National Council of Churches in Korea], *Hankook Yoeksa Sokui Gidokgyo* [Christianity in Korean History] (Seoul: Giminsa, 1985), 215.

10. David Kwang-sun Suh, *The Korean Minjung in Christ* (Hong Kong: The Christian Confession of Asia, 1991), 78–79.

11. Seon Kwang Seo, *Hankook Gydokgyo Jeongchishinhak ui Jeon Gae* [The Development of Korean Christian Political Theology] (Seoul: Yewha Yeoja Dae Hak Chulpanboo, 1996), 81.

12. Ahn, "Jesus and the Minjung in the Gospel of Mark," 150.

13. Se Yoon Kim, "Is *Minjung* Theology a Christian Theology?" *Calvin Theological Journal* 22, no. 2 (1987): 251–274.

14. Hwa Yung, *Mangoes or Bananas? The Quest for an Authentic Asian Christian Theology* (Oxford: Regnum, 1997), 180-81.

15. "Interview with Yonggi Cho," in *Mokhoi wha Sinhak* [Ministry and Theology] (October 2009): 28–35.

16. Young Hoon Lee, *The Holy Spirit Movement in Korea* (Oxford: Regnum Books International, 2008), 83–85.

17. Joon Gon Kim, "Korea's Total Evangelization Movement," in Ro Bong Rin and Marlin L. Nelson, eds., *Korean Church Growth Explosion: Centennial of the Protestant Church (1884–1984)* (Seoul: Word of Life Press & Asia Theological Association, 1983), 26–28.

18. Lee, *The Holy Spirit Movement in Korea*, 84.

19. Gook Jae Shin Hak Yeon Goo Won [International Theological Institute], *Hananim euy Sunghoi GyoHoiSa* [Church History of Assemblies of God] (Seoul: Seoul Mal Sseum Sa, 1998), 214.

20. Allan Anderson, *An Introduction to Pentecostalism: Global Charismatic Christianity* (Cambridge: Cambridge University Press, 2008), 137–138.

21. Steven J. Land, *Pentecostal Spirituality: A Passion for the Kingdom* (Sheffield: Sheffield Academic Press, 1993), 65.

22. Miroslav Volf, "On Loving with Hope: Eschatology and Social Responsibility," *Transformation* 7, no. 3 (1990): 28.

23. Land, *Pentecostal Spirituality*, 65.

24. Peter Althouse, *Spirit of the Last Days: Pentecostal Eschatology in Conversation with Jürgen Moltmann* (London: T&T Clark International, 2003), 195.

25. Ibid., 4.

26. Jürgen Moltmann, *The Coming of God: Christian Eschatology* (Minneapolis: Fortress Press, 1996), 330.

27. Yonggi Cho, *More Than Numbers: Principles of Church Growth* (Collins, Glasgow: Valley Books Trust, 1983), 78.

28. Kim, "Paul Tillich and Dr. Yonggi Cho," 362.

29. Althouse, *Spirit of the Last Days*, 176.

30. Yonggi Cho, *The Story of Fivefold Gospel for Modern People* (Seoul: Seoul Logos Inc., 1997), 18.

31. Moon Ok Park, "An Eschatological Understanding of Dr. Yonggi Cho's Idea of Divine Healing," in Young San Theological Institute, ed., *Dr. Yonggi Cho's Ministry & Theology I* (Gunpo: Hansei University Logos, 2008), 332.

32. Yonggi Cho, *Praying With Jesus* (Lake Mary, FL: Charisma House, 1988), 50.

33. Anderson, *An Introduction to Pentecostalism*, 228.

34. Ibid.

35. Richard Bauckham, *The Theology of Jürgen Moltmann* (Edinburgh: T&T Clark International, 1995), 106–107.

36. See Jürgen Moltmann, *The Theology of Hope* (Minneapolis: Fortress Press, 1993), 34.

37. Yoo, *Korean Pentecostalism*, 113.

38. Cox, *Fire from Heaven*, 201.

39. Gook Jae Shin Hak Yeon Goo Won [International Theological Institute], *Yoido SoonBokEum Gyo Hoi Ui Shin Ang Gwah Shin Hak* II [The Theology and Faith of Yoido Full Gospel Church] (Seoul: Seoul Seo Jeok, 1993), 98–99.

40. Ig Jin Kim, *History and Theology of Korean Pentecostalism* (Zoetermeer: Boekencentrum Publishing House, 2003), 204–209.

41. Yonggi Cho, *Salvation, Health and Prosperity* (Altamonte Springs, FL: Creation House, 1987), 11.

42. Yonggi Cho, *Oh Jung Bok Eum Kwa Sam Jung Chuk Bok* [Fivefold Gospel and Threefold Blessing] (Seoul: Seoul Mal Sseum Sa, 2002), 145.

43. Yonggi Cho, *Soon Bok Eum Ui Jin Ri* [The Truth of Full Gospel] *I* (Seoul: Young San Chul Pan Sa, 1979), 166–174; and Yonggi Cho, *Oh Jung Bok Eum Kwa Sam Jung Chuk Bok*, 173–192.

44. Hyeon Sung Bae, "Understanding Youngsan's Theological Horizon and Hope," in Hansei University Press, ed., *2004 Young San International Theological Symposium* (Gunpo: Hansei University Press, 2002), 211–214.

45. Rodrigo D. Tano, "Dr. Yonggi Cho's Theology of a Good God," in Young San Theological Institute, ed., *Dr. Yonggi Cho's Ministry & Theology I* (Gunpo: Hansei University Logos, 2008), 24.

46. Cho, *Soon Bok Eum Ui Jin Ri* I, 72–73.

Chapter 9
Toward a History and Theology of Japanese Pentecostalism

1. John W. Juergensen, "Brother John Juergensen at the General Council," *Pentecostal Evangel* (November 11, 1927): 4.

2. Paul Tsuchido Shew, "A Forgotten History: Correcting the Historical Record of the Roots of Pentecostalism in Japan," *Asian Journal of Pentecostal Studies* 5, no. 1 (2002): 23–49; Paul Tsuchido Shew, "History of the Early Pentecostal Movement in Japan: The Roots and Development of the Pre-War Pentecostal Movement in Japan (1907–1945)" (PhD diss., Fuller Theological Seminary, 2003); Paul Tsuchido Shew, "Pentecostals in Japan," in Allan Anderson and Edmon Tang, eds., *Asian and Pentecostal: The Charismatic Face of Christianity in Asia* (Oxford; Baguio City: APTS Press, 2005), 487–508.

3. Masakazu Suzuki, "The Life and Ministry of Kiyoma Yumiyama and the Foundation of Japan Assemblies of God," *Asian Journal of Pentecostal Studies* 9, no. 2 (2006): 220–243; Masakazu Suzuki, "A New Look at the Pre-War History of the Japan Assemblies of God," *Asian Journal of Pentecostal Studies* 4, no. 2 (2001): 239–267; Masakazu Suzuki, "The Origins and the Development of the Japan Assemblies of God: The Foreign and Japanese Workers and Their Ministry (1907 to 1975)" (PhD diss., Bangor University, 2011).

4. David Hymes, "Japan," in Stanley M. Burgess and Eduard van der Mass, eds., *The New International Dictionary of Pentecostal and Charismatic Movements*, (Grand Rapids, MI: Zondervan, 2002), 147–150; Kimio Takaguchi, ed., *Standing on the Word, Led by the Spirit: The First 50 Years*

of the Japan Assemblies of God, trans. Tomoyuki Kisaki (Tokyo: Nihon Assemburiizu obu Goddo Kyodan, 1999).

5. Mark R. Mullins, "Japan," in Peter C. Phan, ed., *Christianities in Asia* (West Sussex: Wiley-Blackwell, 2011), 198.

6. Mark R. Mullins, "Christianity in Contemporary Japanese Society," in Inken Prohl and John K. Nelson, eds., *Handbook of Contemporary Japanese Religions* (Leiden and New York: Brill, 2012), 138.

7. See Noriyuki Miyake, *Belong, Experience, Believe: Pentecostal Mission Strategies for Japan* (Gloucester: Wide Margin, 2011).

8. Mullins, "Christianity in Contemporary Japanese Society," 138.

9. Kikuo Matsunaga "Theological Education in Japan," in Jean S. Stoner, ed., *Preparing for Witness in Context: 1998 Cook Theological Seminar* (Louisville: Presbyterian Publishing House, 1999), 299.

10. John W. Juergensen, "Courageous Missionary Activity," *Pentecostal Evangel* (January 5, 1924): 11.

11. Juergensen, "Brother John Juergensen at the General Council," 4.

12. Suzuki, "The Origins and the Development of the Japan Assemblies of God," 1.

13. Mullins, "Japan," 198.

14. Mark R. Mullins, "Indigenous Christian Movements," in Mark R. Mullins, ed., *Handbook of Christianity in Japan* (Leiden: Brill, 2003), 143.

15. Shew, "History of the Early Pentecostal Movement in Japan," 50.

16. Ibid., 52–53.

17. Suzuki, "The Origins and the Development of the Japan Assemblies of God," 49; Suzuki, "A New Look at the Pre-War History of the Japan Assemblies of God," 246.

18. Suzuki, "The Origins and the Development of the Japan Assemblies of God," 155.

19. Ibid., 342.

20. Shew, "History of the Early Pentecostal Movement in Japan," 289.

21. Ibid., 298.

22. Mikito Nagasawa, "Makuya Pentecostalism: A Survey," *Asian Journal of Pentecostal Studies* 3, no. 2 (2000): 205.

23. Carlo Caldarola, *Christianity: The Japanese Way* (Leiden: Brill, 1979), 3.

24. Mullins, "Christianity in Contemporary Japanese Society," 150.

25. Ibid., 151.

26. Takaguchi, *Standing on the Word, Led by the Spirit*, 185–186.

27. H. Yoshiyama, "21-seiki ni kitaisure nihon no seirei undo [The Holy Spirit Movement in the 21st Century]," *Signs* (2001): 97.

28. J. Nelson Jennings, "Theology in Japan," in Mark R. Mullins, ed., *Handbook of Christianity in Japan* (Leiden: Brill, 2003), 181.

29. Akie Ito, *The Statement of Fundamental Truths: An Exposition* (Tokyo: Japan Assemblies of God, 2000).

30. Shew, *Early History of Pentecostal Movement in Japan*, 154–164.

31. Ibid., 164.

32. Yasunori Aoki, "Coote Family: The History of Oneness Pentecostalism 'United Pentecostal Church in Japan' and Pentecostal Mission Board 'Next Towns Crusade,'" Presented at the 2011 Annual Meeting of the Society for Pentecostal Studies, Memphis, Tennessee, March 10–12, 2011.

33. Miyake, *Belong, Experience, Believe*, 10.

34. Mark R. Mullins, "Japanese Pentecostalism and the World of the Dead: A Study of Cultural Adaptation in Iesu no Mitama Kyodai," *Japanese Journal of Religious Studies* 17, no. 4 (1990): 360.

35. Jun Murai, "Shimei ni Tachite [Standing on the Call]," *Seirei* (April 1, 1940): 2, as quoted by Suzuki, "The Origins and the Development of the Japan Assemblies of God," 363.

36. Suzuki, "The Origins and the Development of the Japan Assemblies of God," 424.

37. Kojika Kawasaki, "Ko Iwasaki Sojiro Kei [Late Brother Sojiro Iwasaki]," *Seirei* (September 1, 1939): 4, as quoted by Suzuki, "The Origins and the Development of the Japan Assemblies of God," 424.

38. Jun Murai, "Nento no Ji [Word for the Beginning of the Year]," *Seirei* (January 1, 1940): 1 as quoted by Suzuki, "The Origins and the Development of the Japan Assemblies of God," 425.

39. Toshio Sato, "The Second Generation," in Yasuo Furuya, ed., *A History of Japanese Theology* (Grand Rapids, MI: Cambridge: William B. Eerdmans Publishing Company, 1997), 58.

40. Mark R. Mullins, *Christianity Made in Japan: A Study of Indigenous Movement* (Honolulu: University of Hawaii Press, 1998), 99.

41. Jun Murai, "Hi izuru katayori Noborumono [One who rises from the east]," *Seirei* (September 1, 1941): 3, as quoted in Suzuki, "The Origins and the Development of the Japan Assemblies of God," 411.

42. Mullins, "Japanese Pentecostalism and the World of the Dead," 362–363.

43. Nagasawa, "Makuya Pentecostalism," 207. See also Mullins, *Christianity Made in Japan*, 37.

44. Mullins, *Christianity Made in Japan*, 127.

45. Ibid., 125.

46. Mullins, "Japan," 210.

47. Suzuki, "The Origins and the Development of the Japan Assemblies of God," 522.

48. Erica Baffelli and Ian Reader, "Impact and Ramifications: The Aftermath of the Aum Affair in the Japanese Religious Context," *Japanese Journal of Religious Studies* 39, no. 1 (2012): 8. See also Mark R. Mullins, "The Legal and Political Fallout of the 'Aum Affair,'" in Robert J. Kisala and Mark R. Mullins, eds., *Religion and Social Crisis in Japan: Understanding Japanese Society through the Aum Affair* (New York: Palgrave, 2001), 71–86.

49. Baffelli and Reader, "Impact and Ramifications," 7–8.

50. Mullins, *Christianity Made in Japan*, 153.

51. Mullins, "Japan," 203.

52. Sato, "The Second Generation," 80. Also Seiichi Yagi, "The Third Generation," in Yasuo Furuya, ed., *A History of Japanese Theology* (Grand Rapids, MI; Cambridge: William B. Eerdmans Publishing Company, 1997), 88.

53. Mullins, *Christianity Made in Japan*, 48.

54. Noriyuki Miyake, "A Challenge to Pentecostal Mission in Japan," *Asian Journal of Pentecostal Studies* 9, no. 1 (2006): 89.

55. Makito Nagasawa, "Religious Truth: From a Cultural Perspective in the Japanese Context," *Journal of Asian Mission* 4, no. 1 (2002): 55.

56. Rick Richardson, *Evangelism Outside the Box: New Ways to Help People Experience in the Good News* (Downers Grove, IL: InterVarsity, 2000), 51, as quoted in Nagasawa, "Religious Truth," 56.

57. Mullins, "Japan," 204.

58. Ibid.

59. Juergensen, "Brother John Juergensen at the General Council," 4.

CHAPTER 10
THE PENTECOSTAL MOVEMENT IN VIETNAM

1. The other four largest religions are Buddhism, Cao Đài, Hoà Hảo, and Islam. Sources used in this paragraph and the next paragraph include: General Statistic Office of Vietnam, *2009 Vietnam Population*

and *Housing Census* (Hà Nội: Tổng Cục Thống Kê, 2009); Thái Phước
Trường, *Hội Thánh Tin Lành Việt Nam: 100 Năm Hình Thành và Phát
Triển* [The Evangelical Church of Vietnam: 100 Years of Forming and
Development] (Hồ Chí Minh City: Hội Thánh Tin Lành Việt Nam Miền
Nam, 2011), 202; Nguyễn Cao Thanh, "Đạo Tin Lành ở Việt Nam từ
1975 đến nay, tư liệu và một số đánh giá ban đầu" [Evangelicalism in
Vietnam From 1975 to the Present: Sources and Initial Comments], The
Government Committee for Religious Affairs, http://btgcp.gov.vn
/Plus.aspx/vi/News/38/0/240/0/2737/ (accessed November 5, 2014).

2. Nguyễn Cao Thanh, "Evangelicalism in Vietnam from 1975 to the
Present."

3. While Vietnamese evangelicals may agree with David Bebbington that
evangelicalism emphasizes the death of Jesus on the cross, the authority
of the Bible, the necessary of conversion, and the importance of evangelism, they add equal emphasis on apocalyptic teaching and holiness
because these teachings inform their view of the society and how they
should live in that society. On Bebbington's definition of evangelicalism,
see his *Evangelicalism in Modern Britain: A History from the 1730s to the
1980s* (London: Unwin Hyman, 1989), 2–17.

4. Vietnamese: *Hội Thánh Tin Lành Việt Nam và Cơ Đốc Truyền Giáo
Hội*. At the present time the ECVN has two denominational bodies, the
ECVN (South) and ECVN (North). Both churches are historically con-
nected to the missionary efforts of the Christian and Missionary Alliance
(C&MA), which came to Vietnam in 1911. For more information, see
Lê Hoàng Phu, "A Short History of the Evangelical Church of Viet Nam
(1911–1965)" (PhD Dissertation, New York University, 1972).

5. A former C&MA missionary and researcher on Vietnamese evangelicalism, Reg Reimer, documented that the Mennonite Central Committee
for medical and social work came to Vietnam in 1954, the Southern Baptists arrived in 1959, and the AG in 1972. See Reimer, *Vietnam's Christians: A Century of Growth in Adversity* (Pasadena, CA: William Carey
Library, 2011), 41.

6. For a categorization of the Vietnamese evangelical groups from a social
research approach, see Nguyễn Cao Thanh, "Evangelicalism in Vietnam
from 1975 to the Present."

7. Pastor Đinh Thiên Tứ of the local evangelical church of Tuy Lý Vương in
Hồ Chí Minh City was credited with developing this cell group system.
Tongues-speaking evangelical pastors who led the early Pentecostal

movement picked up the understanding of the cell group system as one among several valid church models during their pre-1975 seminary training at the ECVN's Nha Trang Bible Institute, with faculty members Reg Reimer and Trương Văn Tốt as key teaching resources. Reimer and Trương Văn Tốt had studied church growth under Donald McGavran at Fuller Theological Seminary in 1970–1971.

8. Lê Thị Hồng Ân, e-mail message to author, November 24, 2014. This may be accurate because the Vietnamese evangelicals had limited overseas contacts in the early 1980s. Also, a group of Vietnamese evangelicals who experienced tongues did visit a Charismatic Catholic priest, Father Đinh Khắc Tiệu, in Hồ Chí Minh City to learn more about the nature of the experience. Given the limited Vietnamese evangelical-Catholic contact in the past, the evangelicals must have exhausted their own sources before they decided to consult a Catholic priest. Additionally, the French Assembly of God missionary, Roland Cosnard, who worked in South Vietnam before 1975, only revisited Vietnam as early as 1986 (or 1988, according to two different sources). Although Cosnard, in his collaboration with a Mrs. Hồng Phước, had significant influence on postwar Vietnamese Pentecostal leaders during his time in Vietnam, his post-1975 first visit appeared to be later than the earliest outbreaks of tongues.

9. The ECVN (South), Church Memo 21/TLH/VP, dated June 24, 1989, quoted in Trần Thái Sơn, "Sau Hai Mươi Năm" [After Twenty Years] (unpublished manuscript, 1995).

10. On the 1971 revival, see Orrel Steinkamp, *The Holy Spirit in Vietnam* (Carol Stream, IL: Creation House, 1973). On the 1938 revival, see Phan Đình Liệu, "Lịch Sử Hội Thánh Tin Lành Việt Nam" [History of the Evangelical Church of Vietnam] (unpublished manuscript, 1966).

11. R. A. Jaffray, "'Speaking in Tongues'—Some Words of Kindly Counsel," *Alliance Magazine* (March 13, 1909). On the C&MA and Pentecostalism, see Charles Nienkirchen, *A. B. Simpson and the Pentecostal Movement* (Peabody, MA: Hendrickson Publishers, 1992); and Paul King, *Genuine Gold: The Cautiously Charismatic Story of the Early Christian and Missionary Alliance* (Tulsa, OK: Word & Spirit Press, 2006).

12. R. A. Jaffray, "South China," *Alliance Review* (1907–1908): 7, 142–143. See also, Nienkirchen, *A. B. Simpson and the Pentecostal Movement*, 88, 125–128, and King, *Genuine Gold*, 102–104.

13. Which led to a generous estimate of postwar AG leader Trần Đình Ái that "there were 10,000 to 15,000 adherents in the AG [in Vietnam] in

1975"; see Trần Đình Ái, "The History of Pentecostalism in Vietnam," paper presented at the 10th anniversary of the Pentecostal movement, Vũng Tàu, August 1998, quoted in Joshua (pseudonym), "Pentecostalism in Vietnam: A History of the AG," *Asian Journal of Pentecostal Studies* 4, no. 2 (2001): 307–326. Note the Vietnamese AG dated the beginning of the Pentecostal movement as late as 1988, bringing it closer to the time its leaders were excommunicated from the ECVN in 1989.

14. On the C&MA's fourfold gospel, see Bernie Van de Walle, *The Heart of the Gospel: A. B. Simpson, the Fourfold Gospel, and Late Nineteenth-Century Evangelical Theology* (Eugene, OR: Pickwick Publications, 2009).

15. The influence of the ECVN on the Pentecostal movement of Vietnam cannot be overemphasized. It was the evangelical pastors and believers who left the ECVN that made up a majority of the early Pentecostals in the 1980s. This historical connection with the ECVN explains why the constitution and structure of many Pentecostal groups are similar to those of the ECVN.

16. For example, E. F. Irwin, *With Christ in Indo-China* (Harrisburg, PA: Christian Publications, Inc., 1937); I. R. Stebbins, *41 Năm Hầu Việc Chúa Với Hội Thánh Tin Lành Việt Nam* [41 Years Serving God with the Evangelical Church of Vietnam] *(1920-1961)* (Hồ Chí Minh City, Vietnam: private publication, 2009).

17. See, for example, Peter Wagner, *Dominion! How Kingdom Action Can Change the World* (Grand Rapids, MI: Chosen Books, 2008).

18. I would like to thank Lê Thị Hồng Ân, Rebecca Mihm, and Reg Reimer for their comments on the early drafts of this essay. I remain fully responsible for any errors.

CHAPTER 11
PENTECOSTALISM IN THAILAND

1. Marten Visser, *Conversion Growth of Protestant Churches in Thailand,* Mission 47 (Zoetermeer, The Netherlands: Uitgeverij Boekencentrum, 2008), 101.

2. Alex Smith, *Siamese Gold: The Church in Thailand* (Bangkok: Kanok Bannasan/OMF Publishers, 1981), 93.

3. Prasit Pongudom, *Prawatsaasat Saphakrischak nai Prathet Thai* [The History of the Church of Christ in Thailand] (Bangkok: The Church of Christ in Thailand, 1984), 83–88.

4. Sook Pongsnoi, "New Life in the Church in Siam," *Missionary Review of the World* 62 (1939): 341–342.

5. Alex Smith (*Sikamises Gold*, 204, 212–213) writes that at the start of World War II Thailand's Christian population was approximately 10,700 consisting of: 9,399 CCT church members, 450 British Churches of Christ members, 100 Brethren Church members, 75 Christian and Missionary Alliance members, 500 Karen Church members, and 50 Anglican Church members. By the end of the war CCT membership had fallen to between 6,000–7,000 members.

6. Dr. Nithi Eowsriwongs, "Yonroi adeet: 175 pee mitchannari Protestant nai Prathet Thai" [Tracing the Past: 175 Years of Protestant Missionaries in Thailand], in Nantachai Mejudhon, ed., *175 pee: Phanthakit Kristasatsana Protestant nai Prathet Thai (K.S. 1828-2003* [175 Years: Protestant Missions Endeavor in Thailand, 1828–2003] (Bangkok: The Fellowship Church in Thailand, 2004), 47.

7. Robert Nishimoto, *Prawat Pentecost lae Kharismatic nai Prathet Thai 1946–1996* [History of Pentecostals and Charismatics in Thailand] (Bangkok: Rock Ltd., 1996), 43–46.

8. Hannu Kettunen, *Thung Ruang Thong* [Golden Fields] (Bangkok: Finnish Free Foreign Mission and Full Gospel Churches in Thailand, 1996), 21–22.

9. Ervin E. Shaffer, *Missions—Thailand: Under the Shade of the Coconut Palms* (Bangkok: Thai Gospel Press, n.d.), 12.

10. Ibid., 18–20; Herbert R. Swanson, "HeRD #364—Thailand's First Pentecostal Church" (April 3, 1997), http://www.herbswanson.com/_get .php?postid=35#364 (accessed February 26, 2015).

11. Jaakko Mäkelä and Khrischak Issara, *The Independent Churches in Thailand: Their Historical Background, Contextual Setting, and Theological Thinking* (Pargas, Finland: Åbo: Åbo Akademi University Press, 2000), 58.

12. Nishimoto, *Prawat Pentecost lae Kharismatic nai Prathet Thai*, 149–150; Mäkelä and Issara, *The Independent Churches in Thailand*, 70, 152.

13. Nishimoto, *Prawat Pentecost lae Kharismatic nai Prathet Thai*, 174–175; Kettunen, *Thung Ruang Thong*, 52–53.

14. Kettunen, *Thung Ruang Thong*, 65–66.

15. Ibid., 88; and Robert Nishimoto, "Pentecost Nai Prethet Thai [Pentecost in Thailand]," in *Krob Roop 10 Pi Phantakit Romyen* [10th Anniversary

of Rom Yen Missions], a ten-year anniversary souvenir brochure (Bangkok: Rom Yen Missions, 1993), 15.

16. Robert Nishimoto, "Survey of Pentecostal Missions in Thailand," spiral-bound manuscript (1993), 7, estimates about six hundred believers.

17. Eowsriwongs, "Yonroiadeet," 64.

18. Unless otherwise noted, here and elsewhere in this chapter, we derive the number of churches in our study from the following website: https://thaichurches.org/directory/denomination/ (accessed May 6, 2015).

19. Full Gospel Assemblies of Thailand "FGAT," http://fgat.christian.in.th /home/index.php (accessed July 27, 2014).

20. Nishimoto, "Survey of Pentecostal Missions in Thailand," 10.

21. Based on an interview with Wirachai Kowae, January 6, 2015.

22. Nishimoto, "Survey of Pentecostal Missions in Thailand," 10.

23. Thailand National Institute for Christ, http://www.angelfire.com/mo3 /tnic/history.html (accessed June 26, 2014).

24. Nishimoto, "Survey of Pentecostal Missions in Thailand," 11.

25. New Covenant Church of Hampton, Virginia, www.ncchampton.org /missions/primary.html (accessed December 6, 2009). New Covenant is the home church that sent the Crooke family to Thailand.

26. Mäkelä and Issara, *The Independent Churches in Thailand*, 88.

27. Again, unless otherwise indicated, the information regarding church numbers identified in this column derives from https://thaichurches .org/directory/denomination/.

28. Using only an Internet search on February 3, 2015, only five UPC churches were mentioned in articles related to their work in Thailand.

29. COC Thailand, "Affiliated Member Churches," http://www.cocthailand .com/ministries/coc-network-member-churches/ (accessed February 12, 2015).

30. ChristianityMalaysia.com, "Touching Hearts and Changing Lives—Vineyard Outreach Dinner," April 21, 2014, http://christianitymalaysia.com /wp/touching-hearts-changing-lives-vineyard-outreach-dinner/ (accessed February 12, 2015).

31. Visser, *Conversion Growth of Protestant Churches in Thailand*, 104.

CHAPTER 12
PENTECOSTALISM IN SINGAPORE AND MALAYSIA:
PAST, PRESENT, AND FUTURE

1. Some helpful resources: Tan-Chow May Ling, *Pentecostal Theology for the Twenty-First Century* (Burlington, VT: Ashgate, 2007); Roger E. Hedlund, "Understanding Southeast Asian Christianity," in Michael Nai-Chiu Poon, ed., *Christian Movements in Southeast Asia* (Singapore: Trinity Theological College and Genesis Books, 2010), 59–100, esp. 73–80 and 89–96; Jin Huat Tan, "Pentecostals and Charismatics in Malaysia and Singapore," in Allan H. Anderson and Edmond Tang, eds., *Asian and Pentecostal*, rev. ed., (Oxford: Regnum, 2011), 227–247; Lana Yiu Lan Khong, *A Study of a Thaumaturgical Charismatic Movement in Singapore*, ed. Michael Nai-Chiu Poon (Singapore: Trinity Theological College, 2012); and Allan Heaton Anderson, "Pentecostalism and Charismatic Movements in Asia," in Felix Wilfred, ed., *The Oxford Handbook of Christianity in Asia* (Oxford: Oxford University Press, 2014), 158–70.

2. Cecil M. Robeck Jr., *Azusa Street Revival* (Nashville: Thomas Nelson, 2006).

3. A. H. Anderson, "Pentecostalism in East Asia: Indigenous Oriental Christianity?," *Pneuma* 22, no. 1 (2000): 115–132; Young-Hoon Lee, "Korean Pentecost: The Great Revival of 1907," *Asian Journal of Pentecostal Studies* 4, no. 1 (2001): 73–83; Hwa Yung, "Endued with Power: The Pentecostal/Charismatic Renewal and the Asian Church in the Twenty-First Century," *Asian Journal of Pentecostal Studies* 6, no. 1 (2003): 63–82, esp. 68–69; and Sung Won Yang, "The Influence of the Revival Movement of 1901–1910 on the Development of Korean Christianity" (PhD diss., Southern Baptist Theological Seminary, 2002).

4. Allan Heaton Anderson, *To the Ends of the Earth: Pentecostalism and the Transformation of World Christianity* (Oxford: Oxford University Press, 2013); idem, "To All Points of the Compass: The Azusa Street Revival and Global Pentecostalism," *Enrichment Journal* (2006), available online at http://www.enrichmentjournal.ag.org/200602/200602_164_AllPoints .cfm (accessed May 6, 2015); and Donald E. Miller, Kimon H. Sargeant, and Richard Flory, eds., *Spirit and Power: The Growth and Global Impact of Pentecostalism* (Oxford: Oxford University Press, 2013).

5. Edmund Kee-Fook Chia, "Malaysia and Singapore," in Peter C. Phan, ed., *Christianities in Asia* (Malden, MA: Blackwell-Wiley, 2011), 77–94; Robbie B. H. Goh, *Christianity in Southeast Asia* (Singapore: ISEAS,

2005), 47–56; John Roxborough, *A History of Christianity in Malaysia* (Singapore: Seminari Theoloji Malaysia and Genesis, 2014).

6. Tan, "Pentecostals and Charismatics in Malaysia and Singapore," 227.

7. Although not cited unless quoted from directly, the rest of this section draws extensively from Tan's comprehensive, "Pentecostals and Charismatics in Malaysia and Singapore"; I will provide supplements where necessary.

8. See "The Origin of the CPM Work in Malaysia and Singapore," *Pentecostal Messenger* (April 2001): 8, 20–21; Chris Thomas, *Diaspora Indians* (Penang: MIEC, 1978).

9. Georg Evers, "'On the Trail of Spices': Christianity in Southeast Asia: Common Traits of the Encounters of Christianity with Societies, Cultures, and Religions in Southeast Asia," in Felix Wilfred, ed., *The Oxford Handbook of Christianity in Asia* (Oxford: Oxford University Press, 2014), 73.

10. Tan-Chow, *Pentecostal Theology*, 18–19.

11. Although there are some indications the seminar took place in 1977, Tan-Chow (*Pentecostal Theology*, 15n4) cites sources saying that the event occurred in 1982.

12. See also Tan Jin-Huat and Ooi Chin Aik, eds., *Pursuit of God's Cause* (Petaling Jaya: National Evangelical Christian Fellowship, 1998), 24.

13. Peter Tan: http://johannministries.com/site/ and autobiography, *The Road to Glory* (Canberra, Australia: Johann Ministries, 2014), available at http://spiritword.net/ebooks/The%20Road%20to%20Glory.pdf (accessed May 6, 2015); Paul Ang Global Vision: http://pagv.org.my/ (accessed May 6, 2015); and David Wong's World Harvest Church, Kuala Lumpur, and GloryWord Seminar (registered in 1988 to operate Ministry Training Institute and Apostolic Program; the school, now known as World Harvest Institute, received its twelfth intake on March 7, 2010): http://www.worldharvest.org.my/ and http://psdavidwong.blogspot.com/ (accessed January 6, 2015).

14. JoyChan.Weebly.com, "I Almost Casted the Stone…Actually I Did!," September 28, 2009, http://joychan.weebly.com/1/post/2009/09/i-almost-casted-the-1st-stoneactually-i-did.html, and his critics, Victory Ministries, "Pastor Peter Tan—Coming Wars and Worldwide Castrophes," http://walthope.wordpress.com/tag/peter-tan/ (accessed January 6, 2015).

15. Unlike Tan, Barbara Watson Andaya, "Christianity in Southeast Asia: Similarity and Differences in a Culturally Diverse Region," in Charles E. Farhadian, ed., *Introducing World Christianity* (Malden, MA: Wiley-Blackwell, 2012), 121, claims that Sidang Injil Borneo's prayer movement at Mount Murud in Sarawak is the mountain spirit continuing the veneration of the dead tradition.

16. Jin Huat Tan, *Planting an Indigenous Church: The Case of the Borneo Evangelical Mission* (Oxford: Regnum Books, 2011).

17. Chinese and Hokkien gospel singer cum pastor Lim Gee Tiong, http://gtlim.com/#about (accessed January 7, 2015).

18. Judy Berinai, "Liturgical Inculturation in Anglican Worship in Light of the Spirituality of the Indigenous People of Sabah, Malaysia" (PhD diss., Oxford Centre for Mission Studies, 2013), 263.

19. National Evangelical Christian Fellowship Malaysia, "Membership," http://www.necf.org.my/index.cfm?&menuid=7 (accessed January 6, 2015).

20. ChristianityMalaysia.com "Celebrating God's Goodness!—Malaysian CARE 35th Anniversary and Thanksgiving," September 17, 2014, http://christianitymalaysia.com/wp/celebrating-gods-goodness-malaysian-care-35th-anniversary-thanksgiving/ (accessed April 4, 2015).

21. E.g., Kar Yong, NT lecturer in Seminari Theologji Malaysia: "Response to Rev Won Kim Kong's Statement," http://myhomilia.blogspot.com/2008/09/response-to-rev-wong-kim-kongs.html (accessed April 4, 2015).

22. Leadership Transformation Academy, http://www.wongkimkong.com/index.cfm?&menuid=21 (accessed January 6, 2015).

23. Ong Sek Leang, "Response from Rev. Ong Sek Leang, Senior Pastor of Metro Tabernacle Church," July, 1, 2013, http://www.youtube.com/watch?v=yNUnjPG-6c8 (accessed May 6, 2015); idem, "Welcome Message from PWC Host Chairman, 23rd Pentecostal World Conference," June 26, 2013, http://www.pwc2013.org/welcome-pwc.html.

24. "Christians Persecuted in Malaysia," January 4, 2014, https://www.youtube.com/watch?v=UkjGkeO1OOE; Krisis and Praxis, "The Beginning of Persecution of Christian Minorities in Malaysia?," January 3, 2014, http://www.krisispraxis.com/archives/2014/01/the-beginning-of-persecution-of-christian-minorities-in-malaysia/ (accessed April 4, 2015).

25. Goh, *Christianity in Southeast Asia*, 35–46; Bobby E. K. Sng, *In His Good Times* (Singapore: Bible Society of Singapore, 2003), esp. 37–38,

133–137. In Singapore, Anglicans are regarded as Protestants although English Reformation differs from the European Protestant Reformation and the Radical Reformers' development.

26. Daniel P. S. Goh, "State and Social Christianity in Post-Colonial Singapore," *Sojourn: Journal of Social Issues in Southeast Asia* 25, no. 1 (2010): 54.

27. I draw variously in the next two paragraphs on Tan-Chow, *Pentecostal Theology*, 18–19.

28. Singapore Pentecostal churches abbreviated as AG instead of Malaysian Pentecostal use, AOG.

29. Tan, "Pentecostals and Charismatics in Malaysia and Singapore," 233.

30. Tung Ling Bible School Board of Directors, http://www.tungling.org.sg /our-people/ (accessed January 8, 2015).

31. Khong, *Study of a Thaumaturgical Charismatic Movement*, 28–31, traced the Charismatic renewal to American attorney-turned-evangelist Herbert Mjorud to the Lutheran missionaries, the Anglican Church, and the Roman Catholics; see also Michael Poon and Malcom Tan, eds., *The Clock Tower Story* (Singapore: Trinity Theological College, 2011).

32. James Wong, "A Pioneer's Reflection," November 1, 2008, http://www .tungling.org.sg/a-pioneers-reflection-canon-james-wong/ (accessed January 8, 2015).

33. Tan-Chow, *Pentecostal Theology*, 20n16, citing from T. R. Doraisamy, ed., *Forever Beginning* (Singapore: The Methodist Church in Singapore, 1985), 135.

34. "What Is Pentecostalism?," http://www.methodist.org.sg/~methodis /index.php/home/public-square/1179-what-is-Pentecostalism (accessed January 8, 2015).

35. Tan, "Pentecostals and Charismatics in Malaysia and Singapore," 241; Jeffrey Tsang and Susan Tsang, *Acts of the Holy Spirit at Church of Our Saviour* (Singapore: Armour Publishing, 2012), 15–16. Professor Khoo Oon Teik, founder of the National Kidney Foundation, Singapore, and who established nephrology in Singapore General Hospital, also experienced the Charismatic touch while attending The Methodist Church in Singapore. See Alvin Chua, "Khoo Oon Teik," *SingaporeInfopedia*, http:// eresources.nlb.gov.sg/infopedia/articles/SIP_1558_2009-08-29 .html (accessed January 8, 2015).

36. Tan-Chow, *Pentecostal Theology*, 19; Tsang and Tsang, *Acts of the Holy Spirit*, 15–16, 23–26; Daniel P. S. Goh, "Pluralist Secularism and the

Displacements of Christian Proselytizing in Singapore," in Juliana Finucane and R. Michael Feener, eds., *Proselytizing and the Limits of Religious Pluralism in Contemporary Asia* (Singapore: Springer Science+Business Media Singapore, 2014), 125–146, at 137; Michael J. McClymond, "Charismatic Renewal and Neo-Pentecostalism: From North American Origins to Global Permutations," in Cecil M. Robeck Jr. and Amos Yong, eds., *The Cambridge Companion to Pentecostalism* (Cambridge: Cambridge University Press, 2014), 39.

37. Tsang and Tsang, *Acts of the Holy Spirit*, 15–16, 26–29, 33.

38. "Festival of Praise," http://www.guidinglight.com/encyclopedia/F /Festival_of_Praise/ (accessed January 8, 2015).

39. This is notwithstanding Bishop Chew's claim that Anglicanism has more in common with Pentecostals than with the progressive ethos of the Church of England. See Laurie Thompson, "A Model of Reciprocity in Anglicanism: The Consecration and Enthronement of the Revd. Dr. John Chew Hiang Chea, April 25, 2000 at St. Andrews' Cathedral, Singapore," *Anglican and Episcopal History* 70, no. 4 (2001): 527–532.

40. LSBC, http://www.lsbc.org.sg/about-us/; BBTC: http://bbtc.com.sg /history/ (accessed January 9, 2015). I have excluded Bethesda Cathedral since its Charismatic ethos is not normally perceived as aligned with member churches of the Brethren Network Fellowship, Singapore. Also, one has to wonder, would it be possible for the Church of Singapore (formerly Brethren in its roots) to rekindle fellowship with the Brethren, some of whom have become more welcoming of moderate Charismatic renewal?

41. Church of the Nativity of the Blessed Virgin Mary, "Charismatic Renewal Movement," http://nativitychurchsingapore.org/?page_id=745 (accessed January 8, 2015). Khong, *Study of a Thaumaturgical Charismatic Movement*, 29–30, claims Anglican influence on Catholic Charismatic renewal.

42. Church of the Nativity of the Blessed Virgin Mary, "Charismatic Renewal Movement"; The Burning Bush, "About the Burning Bush Charismatic Prayer Group," http://www.burningbush.sg/about/index .htm (accessed January 8, 2015).

43. Roman Catholic Archdiocese of Singapore, "Archdiocesan Catholic Council for Ecumenical Dialogue (ACCED), http://www.veritas.org.sg /catholic_directory_group_detail.php?GroupID=327&TypeDesc= Commissions&pageTitle=Archdiocesan%20Catholic%20Council%20

for%20Ecumenical%20Dialogue%20 (accessed January 8, 2015). Methodist André de Winne's "An Underlying Intolerance," observed this bigotry from his encounter with Singapore Protestants: "An Underlying Intolerance," July 3, 2013, http://methodist.org.sg/index.php/home/public -square/1338-an-underlying-intolerance (accessed January 9, 2015).

44. CBCP News, "Singapore Catholics, Protestants Jointly Hold Healing Service," October 25, 2014, http://www.cbcpnews.com/cbcpnews/?p=43986 (accessed January 8, 2015).

45. Goh, "Pluralist Secularism and Displacements," 133.

46. New Creation Church, "Factsheet on New Creation Church's Business Entities," August 26, 2014, http://r.newcreation.org.sg/storage/factsheet .pdf (accessed January 9, 2015).

47. Goh, "Pluralist Secularism and Displacements," 130–132; Khong, *Study of a Thaumaturgical Charismatic Movement*, 44–45.

48. Terence Chong, "Christian, Evangelicals and Public Morality in Singapore," *ISEAS Perspective* 17 (March 17, 2014): 1–11; Khong was responding to the progressive proposals like Kenneth Paul Tan and Gary Jack Jin Lee, "Imagining the Gay Community in Singapore," *Critical Asian Studies* 39, no. 2 (2007): 179–204.

49. Goh, "Pluralist Secularism and Displacements," 131.

50. Jean DeBernardi, "Asia's Antioch: Prayer and Proselytism in Singapore," in Rosalind I. J. Hackett, ed., *Proselytization Revisited* (London: Equinox, 2008), 279.

51. Goh, "Pluralist Secularism and Displacements," 134–136; *The Straits Times*, "Trial of City Harvest Church Leaders Resumes," http://www .straitstimes.com/chc_funds_case (accessed January 9, 2015). See also CHC Special Notices, http://www.chc.org.sg/#!special-notices/ and http:// www.chc.org.sg/#!chc-dna/ (accessed 9 January 2015).

52. Rivers of Life Ministry, Ltd., College of Prophets, http://gallery .mailchimp.com/9ca6d4dbf5b7fda1d2742cced/files/Prospectus.3.pdf (accessed January 6, 2015). These former Malaysian pastors include Rev. Dr. Steven Francis, Rev. Dr. Roy Muttiah (Cornerstone Glory Church), and Rev. Dr. Collin Gordon (Trinity Community Centre, Petaling Jaya).

53. GoForth brings together largely evangelical mission bodies such as Crus (formerly Campus Crusade for Christ), HealthServe, Lausanne Committee for World Evangelization, Interserve, Operations Mobilization (OM), ORTV, Overseas Missionary Fellowship (OMF), Southeast Asia Unreached People Groups Network (SEALINK), SEANET, SIM,

TWR-Asia, Wycliffe Bible Translators, and many other organizations as part of the 'National Missions Movement in Singapore," http://www .goforth.org.sg/index.php/en/about-goforth1 (accessed January 9, 2015).

54. Statue in the Singapore Government, Attorney General's Chambers, July 31, 2011, http://statutes.agc.gov.sg/aol/search/display/view.w3p;page =0;query=DocId%3A77026343-e30d-40e2-a32e-b1f5d46c5bd7%20%20 Status%3Ainforce%20Depth%3A0;rec=0;whole=yes (accessed January 9, 2015).

55. "International Religious Freedom Report for 2011" and "2012," US Department of State, Bureau of Democracy, Human Rights and Labor, http://www.state.gov/documents/organization/192873.pdf and http:// www.state.gov/documents/organization/208476.pdf (accessed January 9, 2015).

56. Still awaiting the Asia and Europe in a Global Context forum B21 report on "Transcultural Dynamics of Pentecostalism: Pentecostal Christianity between Globalization and Localized Spheres in Singapore and the Straits," led by Katja Rakow, and supported by Esther Naemi Rebekka Berg and Matthias Deininger; see Cluster of Excellence: Asia and Europe in a Global Context, "B21 Transcultural Dynamics of Pentecostalism," http:// Seoul: Seoul Mal Sseum Sa, www.asia-europe.uni-heidelberg .de/en/research/b-public-spheres/b21-transcultural-dynamics-of -Pentecostalism.html (accessed January 8, 2015).

57. Richard Magnus, "The Christian Role in a Pluralistic Society, with Specific Reference to Singapore," in Michael Nai-Chiu Poon, ed., *Pilgrims and Citizens* (Adelaide: ATF Press, 2006), 169–178; Roland Chia, "Christian Witness in the Public Square: Retrospection and Prospection," in Michael Nai-Chiu Poon, ed., *Engaging Society* (Singapore: Trinity Theological College, 2013), 133–150.

58. Terence Chong, "Filling the Moral Void: The Christian Right and the State in Singapore," *Journal of Contemporary Asia* 41, no. 4 (2011): 566–583; Terence Chong and Yew-Foong Hui, *Different Under God* (Singapore: Institute of Southeast Asian Studies, 2013).

59. Goh, "Pluralist Secularism and Displacements," 138.

60. Gerard Jacobs, *The Pursuit and Acquisition of Health and Wealth* (Christchurch: Wisebuys NZ Books, 2006); Johnson T. K. Lim, *Health and Wealth Gospel* (Singapore: FaithNWorks, 2009).

61. This matter is the subject of Goh, "Pluralist Secularism and Displacements."

62. Sng, *In His Good Times*, 202–204; Anonymous, "Fundamentalism in Singapore," unpublished paper, 4, 6–9, http://www.calvarypandan.sg/images /CBS/History%20of%20Fundamentalism%20in%20Singapore.pdf (accessed January 9, 2015). Other related literature can be found at http:// www.calvarypandan.sg/other-seminarstalks.

63. Simon Chan, "LoveSingapore—Stone Soup? Review of May Ling Tan-Chow, *Pentecostal Theology for the Twenty-First Century*," *H-Pentecostalism* (December 2007), http://www.h-net.org/reviews /showrev.php?id=13966 (accessed January 9, 2015).

64. "Amazing Holy Spirit in Singapore!!," February 2, 2012, https://www .youtube.com/watch?v=iH_d_ktnKW4; "Pentecostalism in Singapore— Megachurches and Contemporary Christianity," September 19, 2013, https://www.youtube.com/watch?v=fx2qlG8UBhM (accessed February 1, 2015).

65. Johnson T. K. Lim, ed., *Holy Spirit* (Singapore: Word N Works, 2015).

66. Terence Chong and Daniel P. S. Goh, "Asian Pentecostalism," in Bryan S. Turner and Oscar Salemink, eds., *Routledge Handbook of Religions in Asia* (New York: Routledge, 2015), 412–415.

67. Yung, *Mangoes or Bananas? The Quest for an Authentic Asian Christian Theology* (Oxford: Regnum International, 1997).

68. Barbara Watson Andaya, "Contexualizing the Global: Exploring the Roots of Pentecostalism in Malaysia and Indonesia," paper presented at the Management and Marketing of Global Religions symposium at the National Museum of Ethnology, August 11–14, 2009, available online at http://www.360doc.com/content/14/0715/17/11096586_394607353.shtml (accessed February 1, 2014).

69. S. E. Ackerman, "The Language of Religious Innovation: Spirit Possession and Exorcism in a Malaysian Catholic Pentecostal Movement," *Journal of Anthropological Research* 37, no. 1 (1981): 90–100; idem, "Experimentation and Renewal among Malaysian Christians: Charismatic Movement in Kuala Lumpur and Petaling Jaya," *Asian Journal of Social Science* 12 no. 12 (1984): 35–48; Chia, "Malaysia and Singapore," 84–87; Ida Lim, "Three Things We Learned From Malaysia's 'Allah' Case," *MalaymailOnline*, January 25, 2015, http://www.themalaymail online.com/malaysia/article/three-things-we-learned-from-malaysias -allah-case (accessed February 3, 2015).

70. Trinity Theological College, "Centre for the Study of Christianity in Asia," http://www.ttc.edu.sg/academics/centres/csca/ (accessed February 1, 2015).

71. However, Tan Kong Beng, "Leadership Formation and Training in Malaysia," in Michael Nai-Chiu Poon, ed., *Church Partnerships in Asia* (Singapore: Trinity Theological College, 2011), 169–177, sees the many seminaries in Malaysia as an unproductive over-stretching of the churches' resources.

72. *Herald Malaysia Online*, "Looking Towards the Future With Hope," August 14, 2014, http://www.heraldmalaysia.com/newscategory/news/Looking-towards-the-future-with-hope/20486/5/ (accessed February 1, 2015).

73. There are contesting reports: "Church Growth in Singapore," November 2, 2013, http://singaporereligion.com/; or eleven-part article on mega-church growth in Singapore, July 17, 2010, http://junmingumich.blogspot.com/2010/07/many-recent-articles-on-churches-in.html (accessed February 1, 2015).

74. Luis Bush, "The Unfinished Task: It Can Be Done," AD2000.org, http://www.ad2000.org/tut0701.htm (accessed February 1, 2015).

75. Chia, "Malaysia and Singapore," 82–83. I am not negating that some forms of localized worship are observable in Singapore and Malaysia megachurches.

76. Some of Islam-Christian dialogue in Malaysia amid the nation's sensitive interreligious and governmental approaches have been analyzed by a rising Presbyterian observer in Singapore: Sze Zeng, "About," http://szezeng.blogspot.com/p/about-me.html (accessed February 2, 2015).

77. For instance, see Roland Chia, "Preserving Religious Peace in Multi-religious Singapore," paper presented at the Ethos Institute for Public Christianity of the National Council of Churches Singapore, Trinity Theological College Singapore and The Bible Society of Singapore, December 16, 2014, available at http://ethosinstitute.sg/preserving-religious-peace-in-multi-religious-singapore/ (accessed February 2, 2015).

78. Chia, "Malaysia and Singapore," 85–87.

79. Goh, "Pluralist Secularism and the Displacements," 126.

80. Open Doors, "2015 World Watch List," https://www.opendoorsusa.org/christian-persecution/world-watch-list/ (accessed February 2, 2015).

81. Li Ann Thio, "Religion in the Public Sphere of Singapore: Wall of Division or Public Square," in Wade Roof Clark, ed., *Religious Pluralism and Civil Society* (Oxford: Bardwell Press, 2008), 73–104.

82. Mark Chan, "Narcissistic Spirituality and Its Impact on Christian Public Engagement," in Michael Nai-Chiu Poon, ed., *Engaging Society* (Singapore: Trinity Theological College, 2013), 83–97.

83. Michael Nai-Chiu Poon, *Religion and Governance for Social Harmony in Singapore* (Singapore: Trinity Theological College, 2012); Leong Weng Kam, "PM Lee Lauds Methodist Church's Contributions to Singapore," October 31, 2014, http://www.methodist.org.sg/index.php/home/special -feature/1191-pm-lee-lauds-methodist-churchs-contributions-to -singapore (accessed February 2, 2015).

84. Poon, ed., *Engaging Society*, especially essays by Daniel Koh, "Middle Axioms and Social Engagement in a Plural Society," and Roland Chia, "Christian Witness in the Public Square: Retrospection and Prospection," chapters 6 and 7 respectively; cf. Daniel Kok and Kiem-Kiok Kwa, eds., *Issues of Law and Justice in Singapore* (Singapore: Armour Publishing, 2009).

85. My appreciation to Ms. Esther Ng Ailey for proofreading the original draft, and to Professors Vinson Synan and Amos Yong for this invitation to write about and for churches in my country of origin.

CHAPTER 13
AMERICAN MISSIONARIES AND PENTECOSTAL THEOLOGICAL EDUCATION IN INDONESIA

1. This is taken from the latest census in 2010 by the Indonesian Bureau of Statistics. For a more detailed information, see Biro Pusat Statistik, "Penduduk Menurut Kelompok Umur Dan Agama Yang Dianut," 2010, http:// sp2010.bps.go.id/index.php/site/tabel?tid=320&wid=0.

2. En-Chieh Chao, "Born-Again Cosmopolitan: Pentecostalism and Its Expressive Religiosity Resonates with a New Generation of Christians," *Inside Indonesia* (December 2012), http://www.insideindonesia.org /current-edition/born-again-cosmopolitan.

3. This chapter will focus mainly on the works of Assemblies of God missionaries in Indonesia. There are two reasons for this: (1) I am personally more familiar with Indonesian Assemblies of God than other denominations. I was born in a Pentecostal pastor's family, was raised in this denomination, am a product of an Assemblies of God Bible school, and

have worked as a denominational Bible school professor and pastor. (2) The archive from the Assemblies of God World Missions has been very helpful to uncover the dynamic of missionaries work. I am well aware that Indonesian Assemblies of God is far from being the "representative" of the entire Pentecostal movement in Indonesia. Yet due to space limitation, I focus on the Assemblies of God.

4. Mary Louise Pratt, *Imperial Eyes: Travel Writing and Transculturation* (London and New York: Routledge, 1992), 4.

5. Ibid., 6.

6. The additional insight from an Australian historian, Lynette Russell, is quite helpful as well that "cross-cultural encounters produce boundaries and frontiers. These are spaces both physical and intellectual, which are never neutrally positioned, but are assertive, contested, and dialogic. Boundaries and frontiers are sometimes negotiated, sometimes violent and often are structured by convention and protocol that are not immediately obvious to those standing on either one side or the other." See Lynette Russell, "Introduction," in Lynette Russell, ed., *Colonial Frontiers: Indigenous-European Encounters in Settler Societies* (Manchester: Manchester University Press, 2001), 1.

7. Pratt, *Imperial Eyes*, 6.

8. Ibid.

9. Ibid.

10. The first European colonial empire that came to Indonesia was actually not Dutch, but Portuguese in April 1511. Then the Dutch came to Indonesia in 1595. The coming of Islam was even earlier than the Europeans. For further discussion, see M. C. Ricklefs, *A History of Modern Indonesia Since C. 1200*, 3rd ed. (Stanford, CA: Stanford University Press, 2001), chapter 3.

11. See Cornelius van der Laan, "Johan Thiessen and Margaretha Alt and the Birth of Pentecostalism in Indonesia," *PentecoStudies: An Interdisciplinary Journal for Research on the Pentecostal and Charismatic Movements* 11, no. 2 (2012): 151ff; David A. Reed, "From Bethel Temple, Seattle to Bethel Church of Indonesia: Missionary Legacy of an Independent Church," in Michael Wilkinson, ed., *Global Pentecostal Movements: Migration, Mission, and Public Religion* (Leiden, Netherlands: Brill, 2012) 93–115; Trinidad E. Seleky, "A History of Pentecostal Movement in Indonesia," *Asian Journal of Pentecostal Studies* 4, no. 1 (2001): 135ff.; Mark Robinson, "The Growth of Indonesian Pentecostalism," in Allan

Anderson and Edmond Tang, eds., *Asian and Pentecostal: The Charismatic Face of Christianity in Asia* (Oxford, UK: Regnum International, 2005), 331.

12. See unknown author, "Mission Emphasis Week Observance Is Planned," *The Argus Press* (October 3, 1985): 3.
13. Kenneth McComber, "There's No Place Like Home," *The Missionary Challenge* (June 1954), Assemblies of God World Missions Archive.
14. Ibid., 16.
15. Ibid., 17.
16. Ibid., italics in original.
17. Ibid.
18. Ibid.
19. In the same vein, Robert Miles and Malcolm Brown have pointed out beautifully that when a representation is produced, it does not only define the other but also the self. So, the project of othering affects both directions. Their comment is worth quoting in full:

    > Migration, determined by the interrelation of production, trade and warfare, has been a precondition for the meeting of human individuals and groups over thousands of years. In the course of this interaction, imagery, beliefs and evaluations about the Other have been generated and reproduced in order to explain the appearance and behaviour of those with whom contact has been established, and to formulate a strategy for interaction and reaction. The consequence has been the production of 'representations'...of the Other, images and beliefs which categorise people in terms of real or attributed differences when compared with Self ('Us'). There is, therefore, a dialectic of Self and Other in which the attributed characteristics of Other refract contrasting characteristics of Self, and vice versa. This is frequently a theme of cultural analyses of 'identity' or 'identities', which are not simply 'biographical' or 'reflexive projects'...because our representations of the Other are important ingredients of our own identities.

    For further discussion, see Robert Miles and Malcolm Brown, *Racism*, 2nd ed., Key Ideas (London: Routledge, 2003), 19.
20. Harold Skoog and R. B. Caveness, "In the East Indies," October 1948, 14, Assemblies of God World Missions Archive.
21. Frantz Fanon, *Black Skin, White Masks*, trans. Charles Lam Markmann (London: Pluto Press, 1991), 147.
22. Pratt, *Imperial Eyes*, 7.
23. Skoog and Caveness, "In the East Indies," 14.

24. Paul W. Lewis, "Indonesia," in Stanley M. Burgess and Eduard van der Maas, eds., *The New International Dictionary of Pentecostal and Charismatic Movements* (Grand Rapids, MI: Zondervan, 2002), 129.

25. Ibid.

26. Kenneth Short G., "Report of the Dutch East Indies" (presented at the Missionary Conference, Springfield, MO, March 16, 1943), 9.

27. Ibid., 9–10.

28. Ibid., 11.

29. John C. Tinsman, "Report from the Moluccas," January 15, 1949, Assemblies of God World Missions Archive.

30. R. M. Devin, "Letter to Noel Perkin Concerning Moluccan Bible Institute," August 8, 1947, Assemblies of God World Missions Archive.

31. Leonardo E. Lanphear, "The Outpouring in Minahasa," March 1, 1953, Assemblies of God World Missions Archive.

32. Unknown author, "Sunday School in Djakarta," *The Missionary Challenge* (March 1952): 7, Assemblies of God World Missions Archive.

33. Ibid., 22.

34. Raymond A. Busby and Leonardo E. Lanphear, "Batavia Bible Institute," May 6, 1950, Assemblies of God World Missions Archive.

35. Unknown author, "Indonesian Victories," *The Missionary Challenge* (October 1953), Assemblies of God World Missions Archive.

36. Unknown author, "This Month's Challenge: Revival Center, Djakarta, Indonesia," *World Challenge* (October 1957), Assemblies of God World Missions Archive.

37. Unknown author, "Know Your Mission Fields: Indonesia," *The Missionary Challenge* (June 1954): 25, Assemblies of God World Missions Archive.

38. Harold R. Carlblom, "Report to M. L. Ketcham" (April 28, 1959): 2.

39. Pratt, *Imperial Eyes*, 27.

40. Edna M. Devin, "Indonesian Work Advancing," *The Pentecostal Evangel* (September 2, 1956), Assemblies of God World Missions Archive.

41. Phillip Douglas Chapman, "The Whole Gospel for the Whole World: A History of the Bible School Movement Within American Pentecostalism, 1880–1920" (PhD diss., Michigan State University, 2008), 23–24.

42. "BAN-PT Akreditasi STT Sayabhakti," *Malang Post* (November 17, 2013).

43. Some schools (e.g., *Sekolah Tinggi Teologi Ekklesia* in Jakarta) have abandoned the dormitory system. Students live off campus, and there is no

strict daily regimen except for academic regulations. Other schools are beginning to start satellite programs where classes are offered on offsite campuses.

44. Michel Foucault's concept of the prison system as a means of creating a disciplinary society is apparent in this model of theological education. See Michel Foucault, *Discipline and Punish: The Birth of the Prison*, 2nd ed. (New York: Vintage Books, 1995).

45. See John F. Walvoord, *Penggenapan Nubuatan Masa Kini - Akhir Jaman* (Malang, Indonesia: Gandum Mas, 1996), translation of *Major Bible Prophecies* (New York: HarperCollins, 1994); Charles C. Ryrie, *Dispensationalism: Dari Zaman Ke Zaman* (Malang, Indonesia: Gandum Mas, 2005), translation of *Dispensationalism Today* (Chicago: Moody Press, 1965).

46. Gani Wiyono, "Ratu Adil: A Javanese Face of Jesus?," *Journal of Asian Mission* 1, no. 1 (1999): 65–66.

47. Ibid., 66.

48. Ibid.

49. Ibid., 74–79.

50. Agustinus Dermawan, "The Spirit in Creation and Environmental Stewardship: A Preliminary Pentecostal Response toward Ecological Theology," *Asian Journal of Pentecostal Studies* 6, no. 2 (2003): 199–217.

51. Ibid., 205–206.

52. See "Sejarah Sekolah Tinggi Teologi Satyabhakti," http://www.sttsati.org/index.php/home/tentang-sati-menu/sejarah-menu (accessed December 8, 2013). It is worth noting also that not only the leadership of the schools was held by American missionaries but also the entire organization of Indonesian Assemblies of God. The organizational structure of Indonesian Assemblies of God itself is a duplication of the American model. Kenneth Short, the first Assemblies of God missionary in Indonesia, wrote that "the organization [Indonesian Assemblies of God] should be patterned as nearly as possible after the same general plan as the Assemblies of God in America" (see Short, "Report of the Dutch East Indies," 19). It was only in April 1959 that the general superintendent position was transferred to an Indonesian. Here is the list of leadership of Indonesian Assemblies of God in the first four General Councils:

    1. The first General Council in Jakarta (January 1–5, 1951)

        • General Superintendent: Ralph Mitchell Devin

        • Assistant General Superintendent: Raymond A. B. Busby

- Secretary and Treasurer: Leonardo E. Lanphear

2. The second General Council in Tomohon, North Sulawesi (July 5–9, 1952)

  - General Superintendent: John C. Tinsman
  - Assistant General Superintendent: Harold R. Carlblom
  - Secretary and Treasurer: Leonardo E. Lanphear

3. The third General Council in Malang, East Java (January 16–21, 1956)

  - General Superintendent: Harold R. Carlblom
  - Assistant General Superintendent: Raymond A. B. Busby
  - Secretary and Treasurer: Leonardo E. Lanphear.
  - Assistant to Secretary and Treasurer: Soemardi Stefanus

4. The fourth General Council Convention in Jakarta (April 21–25, 1959)

  - General Superintendent: Soemardi Stefanus
  - Assistant General Superintendent: Paul Tehupuring
  - Secretary and Treasurer: K.L. Tobing
  - Assistant to Secretary and Treasurer: Ie Sing Gwan (Imam Sugriwo)

Right after the transition from American leadership to Indonesians, Harold R. Carlblom, the third general superintendent, wrote this to M. L. Ketcham:

> Well, our conference has come and gone, and it was an historic one, for as I wired you yesterday, ALL INDONESIAN OFFICERS, indeed makes history for the Assemblies of God in Indonesia.... Only one thing that I am sorry for is that you were not here to also witness it all.... Bro. Stefanus clearly stood out as a recognized leader among the brethren and when there was debate he rose to speak, there was unusual silence, feeling that his words would be words of wisdom, which they usually were. We all marveled at him. We feel that he will make a good chairman and he has shown such a humble spirit in it all. He wept when he gave his acceptance speech and revealed clearly that he knew the greatness of the responsibility resting on him and a willingness to be advised and helped. They (rather Stefanus suggested) asked to have it appear in the minutes (not in the constitution-B-ls) that they wanted Ray and myself to be in a position as "advisors" to them. This was all voluntary, with no grading of prompting on our parts for which we were extremely happy. Bro. Stefanus said that he will send copies of all letters of importance and seek our opinions (even when we go home on furlough), which certainly is nice and shows a wonderful attitude.

So it seems clearly that even though the national leadership positions had been in the hand of Indonesians, there was still a certain dependency on the missionaries as the "advisors." The power negotiation is always an ongoing process between Indonesians and foreign missionaries. See "Letter from Harold R. Carlblom to M. L. Ketcham," April 28, 1959; for further discussion see also Gani Wiyono, "A Sketch of the History of the Assemblies of God of Indonesia (Gereja Sidang-Sidang Jemaat Allah)" (ThM thesis, Asia Pacific Theological Seminary, 2004).

53. For further discussion, see Franz Magnis-Suseno, *Javanese Ethics and World-View: The Javanese Idea of the Good Life* (Jakarta: Gramedia Pustaka Utama, 1997).

54. Gani Wiyono, "Pentecostals in Indonesia," in Anderson and Tang, eds., *Asian and Pentecostal: The Charismatic Face of Christianity in Asia*, 319.

55. Jan S. Aritonang, "The Spectacular Growth of the Third Stream: The Evangelicals and Pentecostals," in Jan S. Aritonang and Karel A. Steenbrink, eds., *A History of Christianity in Indonesia*, Studies in Christian Mission 35 (Leiden: Brill, 2008), 878.

56. Margaret M. Poloma, "The Spirit Bade Me Go: Pentecostalism and Global Religion," Hartford Institute for Religious Research, http://hirr.hartsem.edu/research/Pentecostalism_polomaart1.html (accessed December 6, 2013).

CHAPTER 14
THE DEMISE OF PENTECOSTALISM IN THE PHILIPPIANS: NAMING AND CLAIMING THE IMPOSSIBLE OBJECT AND THE POLITICS OF EMPOWERMENT IN PENTECOSTAL STUDIES

1. David B. Barrett, ed., *World Christian Encyclopedia: A Comparative Study of Churches and Religions in the Modern World, AD 1900–2000* (Nairobi: Oxford University Press, 1982), 562–563.

2. See David B. Barrett, George Thomas Kurian, and Todd M. Johnson, eds., *World Christian Encyclopedia: A Comparative Survey of Churches and Religions in the Modern World*, 2nd ed. (Oxford: Oxford University Press, 2001), I.594.

3. Research Center Pew, *Pew Forum: 10 Nation Survey of Renewalists (2006): Pew Forum on Religion & Public Life 10 Nation Survey of Renewalists. Final Topline, 2006, Data Released December 1, 2007* (Washington, DC: Pew Research Group, December 1, 2007), 4, available at http://www.pewforum.org/files/2006/10/Pentecostals-topline-06.pdf (accessed May 6, 2015). According to a survey conducted by German scholars of social and political science Christl Kessler and Jürgen Rüland

published in 2006, 19 percent of the total Philippine population partici-
pates in the PC movement; see Christl Kessler and Jürgen Rüland, *Give
Jesus a Hand! Charismatic Christians: Populist Religion and Politics in
the Philippines* (Quezon City: Ateneo de Manila University Press, 2008),
93; cf. Christl Kessler and Jürgen Rüland, "Responses to Rapid Social
Change: Populist Religion in the Philippines," *Pacific Affairs* 79, no. 1
(2006): 73–96, and Christl Kessler, "Charismatic Christians: Genuinely
Religious, Genuinely Modern," *Philippine Studies: Historical and Ethno-
graphic Viewpoints* 54, no. 4 (2006): 560–584.

4. The research project was sponsored by the German Research Foundation
and conducted by the Department of History of Religion and Intercultural Theology at the University of Heidelberg. For more information on
the project, see: http://rmserv.wt.uni-heidelberg.de/webrm/Forschung
/fs-pfingstbewegung/pfingstbewegung-philippinen (accessed May 6,
2015).

5. During the last years the Philippine General Council of the Assemblies
of God underwent a major crisis resulting in a schism with at least two
big factions claiming to represent the denomination as a whole. And
while the website run by the faction close to the US Assemblies of God
does not seem to shy away from the term "Pentecostal," the other major
faction produces only two hits of the term "Pentecostal" or "Pentecos-
talism" on their homepage (see"Home (PGCAG)," PGCAG | The Offi-
cial Website of the Philippines General Council of the Assemblies of
God, http://pgcag.org/ (accessed March 28, 2014); "Philippines General
Council of the Assemblies of God (PGCAG)," PGCAG | The Official
Website of the Philippines General Council of the Assemblies of God,
https://pgcag.wordpress.com/home/ (accessed January 27, 2015), The
scholar discussed below is affiliated with the faction that is backed by
the US Assemblies of God. At the time of the work analyzed below, this
schism had not yet happened.

6. It seems noteworthy that especially anthropological publications recently
begin to include the term "evangelical" in their titles; see, for example,
Simon Coleman and Rosalind I. J. Hackett, eds., *The Anthropology of
Global Pentecostalism and Evangelicalism* (New York: New York University Press, 2015). On the other hand, the discussion of a "Pentecostalization of Christianity," which is sometimes even extended to
a Pentecostalization of society and politics, seems to indicate "Pentecostal" as a catch-all phrase, making the term analytically weak. See, for

example, Cephas Omenyo, "From the Fringes to the Centre: Pentecostalization of the Mainline Churches in Ghana," *Exchange* 34, no. 1 (2005): 39–60; Henri Gooren, "The Pentecostalization of Religion and Society in Latin America," *Exchange* 39, no. 4 (2010): 355–376; and Timothy J. Steigenga, "Pentecostalization, Politics, and Religious Change in Guatemala: New Approaches to Old Questions," *PentecoStudies: An Interdisciplinary Journal for Research on the Pentecostal and Charismatic Movements* 13, no. 1 (2014): 9–34. Recently, however there seems to be an attempt by some leaders to form a bloc within the Philippine Council of Evangelical Churches (PCEC). The PCEC, however, sees itself as explicit counterpart to the Catholic Bishops Conference in the Philippines (CBCP) under which most groups labeled Charismatic renewal groups are organized, rendering the description of the partners of PCEC as "Charismatic" problematic. The relation between the PCEC and many leaders usually subsumed under PC remains full of tensions, not least due to reasons related to politics, which were most blatant in the 2004 and 2010 elections, when Eddie Villanueva ran as a presidential candidate against the advice of the most PCEC leaders, who in 2004 endorsed Gloria Macapagal-Arroyo. Several personal interviews conducted by Maltese in 2013 with different people directly involved show that attempts of reconciliation, including a foot-washing ceremony organized by Wyden King and the Movement for National Transformation/NFS in the wake of Villanueva's senatorial bid for the 2013 midterm elections, did not resolve the deeper lying disagreements and conflicts.

7. There have been attempts to introduce "renewal movement" as a new term to describe these groups; see, for example, Pew, *Pew Forum: 10 Nation Survey of Renewalists (2006): Pew Forum on Religion & Public Life 10 Nation Survey of Renewalists, Final Topline, 2006; data released December 1, 2007.* However, despite the fact that often these groups do indeed often claim to represent an "original" or most genuine form of Christianity, such attempts have all in all not been successful. In addition, it should be noted that "renewal" itself is a term too common to allow for distinctions within the spectrum of Christian churches, while any attempt to define it more clearly runs the risk of opening another gap between scholarly representation and self-description, as is the case with the term "PC." There simply is no common agenda for the term "renewal." Whereas for one group "renewal" might mean endorsing the practice of speaking in tongues, for other groups it is the very rejection of the practice of speaking in tongues that characterizes "renewal," since

speaking in tongues is associated with "irrational emotionalism of lower class people," as one of the research participants put it. Yet another way to define Pentecostalism on the basis of formal (not substantial) criteria has been proposed by Michael Bergunder, "The Cultural Turn," in Allan Anderson, et al., eds., *Studying Global Pentecostalism: Theories and Methods* (Berkeley: University of California Press, 2010), 51–73.

8. See, for example, Julie C. Ma, *When the Spirit Meets the Spirits: Pente-costal Ministry Among the Kankana-Ey Tribe in the Philippines*, Studien Zur Interkulturellen Geschichte Des Christentums 118 (Frankfurt am Main and New York: P. Lang, 2000); Kessler and Rüland, *Give Jesus a Hand!*; Katharine L. Wiegele, *Investing in Miracles: El Shaddai and the Transformation of Popular Catholicism in the Philippines* (Honolulu: University of Hawai'i Press, 2005); Jae Yong Jeong, "Filipino Indepen-dent Pentecostalism and Empowered Biblical Transformation," in Allan Anderson and Edmond Tang, eds., *Asian and Pentecostal: The Charis-matic Face of Christianity in Asia* (Oxford, UK, and Costa Mesa, CA; Baguio City, Philippines: Regnum Books International and APTS Press, 2005), 385–407; Joseph R. L. Suico, "Pentecostalism in the Philippines," in Anderson and Tang, eds., *Asian and Pentecostal: The Charismatic Face of Christianity in Asia*, 345–362; and Julie C. Ma and Wonsuk Ma, *Mission in the Spirit: Towards a Pentecostal/Charismatic Missiology* (Eugene, OR: Wipf & Stock, 2010). The most study that has been most influential on recent literature has been David Martin, *Tongues of Fire: The Explosion of Protestantism in Latin America* (Oxford: Blackwell, 1990).

9. Cf. political scientist Ruth Marshall, who states "In their accounts of the world and history, Pentecostals challenge the orderings of historians, anthropologists, political scientists [...] and anthropological or social scientific explanations can also be the object of explicit protest by Char-ismatics and evangelicals"; Ruth Marshall, "Christianity, Anthropology, Politics," *Current Anthropology* 55, no. S10 (2014): 346.

10. See, e.g., William M. Esposo, "Does the Catholic Church Recognize Its Greater Crisis?," Philstar.com, June 15, 2008, http://www.philstar.com /opinion/67676/does-catholic-church-recognize-its-greater-crisis (accessed May 6, 2015); Wiegele, *Investing in Miracles*, 81–83.

11. Kessler and Rüland, *Give Jesus a Hand!*, 153.

12. Wonsuk Ma, "Asian (Classical) Pentecostal Theology in Context," in Anderson and Tang, eds., *Asian and Pentecostal: The Charismatic Face of Christianity in Asia*, 59.

13. Kessler and Rüland, *Give Jesus a Hand!*, 189.

14. Ibid., 164.

15. Ibid., 189–207.

16. Donald E. Miller and Tetsunao Yamamori, *Global Pentecostalism: The New Face of Christian Social Engagement* (Berkeley, CA: University of California Press, 2007), 160–161, 168; Joel A. Tejedo, *Sambayanihan: How Filipino Pentecostals Build Communities in the Philippine* (Baguio City: Computerized Clean Print, 2011); Joel A. Tejedo, "The Economic Participation of Filipino Pentecostals: A Case of Selected Assemblies of God Business People in the Philippines," *Asian Journal of Pentecostal Studies* 16, no. 1 (2013): 3–16.

17. See, for example, Jeong, "Filipino Independent Pentecostalism and Empowered Biblical Transformation"; Wiegele, *Investing in Miracles*; Kessler and Rüland, *Give Jesus a Hand!*; David S. Lim, "Consolidating Democracy: Filipino Evangelicals between People Power Events, 1986–2001," in David Halloran Lumsdaine, ed., *Evangelical Christianity and Democracy in Asia* (Oxford: Oxford University Press, 2009), 235–277; Ma and Ma, *Mission in the Spirit*.

18. Martin, *Tongues of Fire*, 234.

19. Joseph R. L. Suico, "Institutional and Individualistic Dimensions of Transformational Development: The Case of Pentecostal Churches in the Philippines" (PhD thesis, University of Wales, Bangor, 2003); all references to this work will be made parenthetically by page or section number. Suico uses the name PC only few times (e.g., 76); he generally speaks of Pentecostal (capitalized). As we will see, however, he oscillates between a definition of Pentecostalism that includes Charismatics and one that does not, while his tendency is on the latter.

20. Joseph R. L. Suico, "Pentecostalism and Social Change," *Asian Journal of Pentecostal Studies* 8, no. 2 (July 2005): 195–213.

21. Averell U. Aragon, "The Philippine Council of Evangelical Churches," in Anne C. Kwantes, ed., *Chapters in Philippine Church History* (Colorado Springs, CO: International Academic Publishers, 2002), 369–389; Floyd T. Cunningham, "Diversities Within Post-War Philippine Protestantism," *The Mediator* 5, no. 1 (2003): 43–145.

22. A friend of Korean megachurch pastor Yonggi Cho, Klahr arranged a meeting between Cho and Ferdinand Marcos. Klahr comments on this meeting as follows: "Dr. Cho being in the Philippines attracted the news media and because of the popularity of Dr. Cho and through the assistance of Bishop George Castro, we had a meeting with the President of the Philippines. President Marcos wanted to meet the famous Preacher from Korea. The meeting with the President was excellent and several of us were asked to have a photograph taken with the President." Paul Klahr, "My Life: 'Do You Know That Jesus Loves You?,'" n.d., http:// klahrskorner.org/chapter7.html (accessed May 6, 2015). The meeting is not dated, but it must have been during martial law in the late 1970s since in the early 1980s Klahr returned to the United States.

23. As Suico notes, the church underwent several schisms. According to Julie and Wonsuk Ma (*Mission in the Spirit*, 135), ICS was started as Asian Christian Charismatic Fellowship in 1981. Both of churches seem to have disaffiliated from the AG. Howevever, none of the several AG leaders who were contacted by the author commented on the disaffiliation, besides conjectures that both churches are no more with the AG.

24. Suico simply refers to a particular theology inherited from America as reason for the church's agenda. He does not, however, elaborate on this theology any further, besides giving a short reference in a footnote concerning a document called "The 13 Declaration of Faith (Jesus Is Lord Church)" (226–227n68). Yet a close look at said declaration shows that, contrary to documents such as the "The 16 Fundamental Truths of the Assemblies of God" (219–220), this "declaration" does not contain any doctrinal statements. It merely consists of Bible verses, to which probably any Christian who acknowledges Scriptures as an important document would be able to subscribe to.

25. Suico does not take into consideration that a retreat or the insistence on a quietist attitude could be read as a political option too; cf. Amos Yong, *In the Days of Caesar: Pentecostalism and Political Theology* (Grand Rapids, MI: Eerdmans, 2010); Andreas Heuser, "Encoding Caesar's Realm: Variants of Spiritual Warfare Politics in Africa," in Martin Lindhardt, ed., *Pentecostalism in Africa Presence and Impact of Pneumatic Christianity in Postcolonial Societies*, Global Pentecostal and Charismatic Studies 15 (Leiden: Brill, 2014), 270–290.

26. Wonsuk Ma, "Philippines for Jesus Movement," in Stanley M. Burgess and Gary B. McGee, eds., *The New International Dictionary of*

Pentecostal and Charismatic Movements, rev. and exp. ed. (Grand Rapids, MI: Zondervan, 2002), 988.

27. Ibid.

28. Groundbreaking in this regard have been the works of the *Institute for Studies in Asian Church and Culture*, for example Melba Padilla Maggay, *The Gospel in Filipino Context* (Mandaluyong, Metro Manila: OMF Literature, 1987); Melba Padilla Maggay, *Pagbalik Loob: Moral Recovery and Cultural Reaffirmation* (Quezon City; Quezon City: Akademya ng Kultura at Sikolohiyang Pilipino and Institute for Studies in Asian Church and Culture, 1993); Melba Padilla Maggay, *Communicating Cross-Culturally: Towards a New Context for Missions in the Philippines* (Quezon City: New Day Publishers, 1989); Melba Padilla Maggay, *Filipino Religious Consciousness: Some Implications to Missions* (Quezon City: Institute for Studies in Asian Church and Culture, 1999). See also Lim, "Consolidating Democracy," 255.

29. See, for example, the AG-dominated *Asian Journal of Pentecostal Studies*; cf. also Anderson and Tang, eds., *Asian and Pentecostal*.

30. Ernesto Laclau, *On Populist Reason* (London: Verso, 2007), 67–128.

31. Albeit Suico's case study is about social engagement; his emphasis on politics proper represents a significant shift compared to his masters thesis, which proposed a Pentecostal "Strategy of Social Action," see Joseph R. L. Suico, "A Strategy of Social Action: A Filipino Pentecostal Perspective" (MA thesis, Asia Pacific Theological Seminary, 1993).

32. Cf. Romel R. Bagares and Averell U. Aragon, "The PCEC and the Fight Against Corruption in the Philippines: A Call for Self-Reflection and Re-Direction" (September 5, 2011), http://de.scribd.com/doc/64361687/The -PCEC-and-Corruption.

33. See for example, Zenaida S. Badua, *Redeeming the Land: The Philippine Experience* (Manila: All-Nations Publishing, 1993).

34. Sonja Grigat, *Umkämpfte Herrschaft Eine figurationssoziologische Untersuchung des Friedensprozesses in Mindanao*, Micropolitics of Violence [Contested Lordship: A Study of the Peace Process in Mindanao from the Perspective of Fugurational Sociology] (Frankfurt: Campus Verlag, 2014), 136–138.

35. Ryan D. Rosauro, "MILF Suspends Top Leader Kabalu for Meeting with Candidates," *Philippine Daily Inquirer* (April 14, 2010), sec. Inquirer Politics.

36. Bergunder, "The Cultural Turn."

37. Walter J. Hollenweger, *Enthusiastisches Christentum: die Pfingstbewegung in Geschichte und Gegenwart* [Charismatic Christianity: The Pentecostal Movement in History and in the Present] (Wuppertal / Zürich: Theologischer Verlag, Brockhaus; Zwingli-Verlag, 1969).

38. Emílio Willems, *Followers of the New Faith: Culture Change and the Rise of Protestantism in Brazil and Chile* (Nashville, TN: Vanderbilt University Press, 1967); Christian Lalive d'Epinay, *Haven of the Masses: A Study of the Pentecostal Movement in Chile* (London: Lutterworth, 1969); another influential work that is to be mentioned in this context is Martin, *Tongues of Fire*.

39. Luther Jeremiah Oconer, "The Culto Pentecostal Story: Holiness Revivalism and the Making of Philippine Methodist Identity, 1899–1965" (PhD thesis, Drew University, 2009), 173.

40. As already mentioned, as far as the name *Charismatic* is concerned (left out by Suico), believers refute it because it seems to be increasingly reserved for Catholics and therefore disliked by most non-Catholic believers, who consider themselves a minority and still nurture reservations toward Catholic practices they perceive as unbiblical, even among the mainline churches. An example of such reservations even among so-called ecumenical Protestants can be found in Lila Ramos Shanani, "The Papal Visit: A Protestant Perspective," *PhilSTAR.com* (January 19, 2015), sec. Opinion, at http://www.philstar.com/opinion /2015/01/19/1414524/papal-visit-protestant-perspective (accessed May 6, 2015).

41. Michael Bergunder, "What Is Religion? The Unexplained Subject Matter of Religious Studies," *Method and Theory in the Study of Religion* 26, no. 3 (2014): 259.

42. For works that have applied this approach, see for example Jörg Haustein, *Writing Religious History: The Historiography of Ethiopian Pentecostalism* (Wiesbaden: Otto Harrasowitz, 2011), and Yan A. Suarsana, "Inventing Pentecostalism: Pandita Ramabai and the Mukti Revival From a Post-Colonial Perspective," *PentecoStudies* 13, no. 2 (2014): 173–196.

43. We are indebted to Esther Berg and Ulrich Göppel for very helpful comments on an earlier draft of this chapter.

CHAPTER 15
JOINED HANDS: ASIAN INFLUENCE ON
AUSTRALIAN PENTECOSTAL IDENTITY

1. David Walker and Agnieszka Sobocinska, "Introduction: Australia's Asia," in David Walker and Agnieszka Sobocinska, eds., *Australia's Asia: From Yellow Peril to Asian Century* (Perth: University of Western Australia Press, 2012), 2; *Australia's Asian Context in the Asian Century: A One-Day Research Workshop*, University of New South Wales (12 July 2013), http://www.arts.unsw.edu.au/news-and-events/australia-s-asian -context-in-the-asian-century-a-one-day-research-workshop-2083.html (accessed June 23, 2013); Robert Ayson, "China Central? Australia's Asia Strategy," *The International Spectator: Italian Journal of International Affairs* 44, no. 2 (2009): 25; David Walker, "National Narratives: Australia in Asia," *Media History* 8, no. 1 (2002): 73.

2. Prasenjit Duara, "Asia Redux: Conceptualizing a Region of Our Times," *The Journal of Asian Studies* 69, no. 4 (November 2010): 977.

3. John Mansford Prior, "The Challenge of the Pentecostals in Asia Part One: Pentecostal Movements in Asia," *Exchange* 36 (2007): 14; Allan Anderson, "Revising Pentecostal History in Global Perspective," in Allan Anderson and Edmond Tang, eds., *Asian and Pentecostal: The Charismatic Face of Christianity in Asia* (Baguio City, Philippines: APTS Press, and Oxford: Regnum Books International, 2005), 147; Andrew F. Walls, "Eusebius Tries Again: Reconceiving the Study of Christian History," *International Bulletin of Missionary Research* 24, no. 3 (July 2000): 105.

4. Julius Bautista, "About Face: Asian Christianity in the Context of Southern Expansion," in Julius Bautista and Francis Khek Gee Lim, eds., *Christianity and the State in Asia: Complicity and Conflict* (Florence, KY: Routledge, 2009), 202–215.

5. Amos Yong, *The Spirit Poured Out on All Flesh: Pentecostalism and the Possibility of Global Theology* (Grand Rapids, MI: Baker Academic, 2005), 18–19.

6. "Pentecost in Australia," *The Apostolic Faith* 2, no. 13 (May 1908): 1.

7. "The History," *Fact Sheet 8—Abolition of the "White Australia" Policy*, http://www.immi.gov.au/media/fact-sheets/08abolition.htm (accessed June 26, 2013).

8. Veli-Matti Kärkkäinen, "Identity and Plurality: A Pentecostal/ Charismatic Perspective," *International Review of Mission* 91, no. 363 (March 2009): 501.

9. Joel Robbins, "The Obvious Aspects of Pentecostalism: Ritual and Pentecostal Globalization," in Martin Lindhardt, ed., *Practicing the Faith: The Ritual Life of Pentecostal/Charismatic Christians* (New York: Berghahn Books, 2011), 56.

10. David Martin, *Pentecostalism: The World Their Parish* (Oxford: Blackwell Publishers, 2002), 157.

11. See Denise A. Austin, "Mary Yeung: The Ordinary Life of an Extraordinary Australian Chinese Pentecostal—Part I and II," *Asian Journal Pentecostal Studies* 16, no. 2 (August 2013): 99-137.

12. "Pentecostal," *The Advertiser* (Adelaide) (Saturday, June 8, 1935): 8, http://trove.nla.gov.au/ndp/del/article/40050578?searchTerm=%22Wong%20Yen%22%20Pentecostal&searchLimits= (accessed February 23, 2012); Mary Yeung, Letter to Oriental Full Gospel Church Melbourne (June 1959); William Wing Young Chen, *The Mission Work of Bro. & Sis. C. N. Yeung;* "Welcome to the Mission Covenant Church of Hong Kong," *The Mission Covenant Church,* http://www.mcc.org.hk/english.htm (accessed April 28, 2012); Mary Yeung, Letter to Oriental Full Gospel Church Melbourne (June 1959).

13. "Revival Tidings: Sr Yeung's Visit Made a Blessing," http://webjournals.alphacrucis.edu.au/journals/AEGTM/1940-april/revival-tidings-sr-yeungs-visit-made-a-blessing/ (accessed April 30, 2012).

14. Alena Lee, personal e-mail correspondence with Denise Austin, June 15, 2012.

15. Cited in Geoffrey Blainey, "Australia and Asia: Expresso Democracy in a Satay Region," *The National Interest* (Winter 1995/1996): 74.

16. B. A. Santamaria, "A Pacific Confederation," *Quadrant* 2, no. 21 (1962): 27.

17. Ichikawa Maki, "Smith, Marie Bertha (1915–1971)," *Australasian Dictionary of Pentecostal and Charismatic Movements,* http://webjournals.ac.edu.au/journals/ADPCM/q-to-z/smith-marie-bertha-1915-1971/ (accessed June 23, 2013).

18. Paul Tsuchido Shew, "Pentecostals in Japan," in Anderson and Tang, eds., *Asian and Pentecostal: The Charismatic Face of Christianity in Asia,* 498.

19. Marie Smith, "Japan," *The Australian Evangel and Glad Tidings Messenger* 21, no. 2 (February 1964): 3–4; Marie Smith, "Japanese Convention," *The Australian Evangel and Glad Tidings Messenger* 18, no. 7 (1961): 11.

20. Smith, "Japanese Convention," 10.

21. Marie Smith, "Facets of Japanese Life," *The Australian Evangel and Glad Tidings Messenger* 19, no. 10 (1962): 23.
22. "The History," *Fact Sheet 8—Abolition of the "White Australia" Policy*.
23. *Minutes of Meeting—Assemblies of God in Australia Eighteenth Biennial Commonwealth Conference* (Ringwood VIC: April 22–28, 1971), 7.
24. Tim Colebatch, "Asian Migration a Tour de Force," *The Age* (June 17, 2011), http://www.theage.com.au/national/asian-migration-a-tour-de-force-20110616-1g62x.html (accessed June 23, 2013).
25. Asian Studies Association of Australia, *Maximizing Australia's Asia Knowledge: Repositioning and Renewal of a National Asset* (Melbourne: Asian Studies Association of Australia, 2002), 9.
26. Perera Suvendrini, "The Level Playing Field: Hansonism, Globalisation and Racism," *Race and Class*, http://static.highbeam.com/r/raceandclass/october011998/thelevelplayingfieldhansonismglobalisationracismpa/ (accessed October 1, 1998); Wang Gungwu, *The Chinese Overseas: From Earthbound China to the Quest for Autonomy* (Cambridge MA: Harvard University Press, 2000), 99.
27. Kwai Hang Ng, "Seeking the Christian Tutelage: Agency and Culture in Chinese Immigrants' Conversion to Christianity," *Sociology of Religion* 63, no. 2 (2002): 195-214.
28. Rogelia Pe-Pua, Mitchell, Iredale, and Castles, *Astronaut Families and Parachute Children: The Cycle of Migration Between Hong Kong and Australia* (Canberra: Australian Government Publishing Service, 1996), 37; W. David Stevens, "Spreading the Word: Religious Beliefs and the Evolution of Immigrant Congregations," *Sociology of Religion* 65, no. 2 (Summer 2004): 121.
29. Janice Boddy, personal interview with Denise Austin, Brisbane, May 18, 2009.
30. "Multicultural Community Centre," International City Church, http://www.iccbrisbane.org/community/multicultural-community-centre/ (accessed December 24, 2010); "History," International City Church, http://www.iccbrisbane.org/about-us/our-history/ (accessed June 26, 2013).
31. Jeannie Mok, e-mail correspondence to Denise Austin, group e-mail, June 25, 2013.
32. For further details see Denise A. Austin, *"Kingdom-Minded" People: Christian Identity and the Contributions of Chinese Business Christians* (Leiden: Brill, 2011).

33. Cited in Peter L. Berger, "Introduction: The Cultural Dynamics of Globalization," in Peter L. Berger and Samuel P. Huntington, eds., *Many Globalizations: Cultural Diversity in the Contemporary World* (Oxford: Oxford University Press, 2002), 8.

34. Crown Financial Ministries, "Teaching People God's Financial Principles," http://www.crown.org (accessed June 7, 2004); Rick Boxx, "Whose Code of Ethics Are You Following?," International CBMC: Monday Manna, www.cbmcint.org (accessed April 26, 2004); Jeff van Duzer and Tim Dearborn, "The Profit of God: Finding the Christian Path in Business," *Christianity Today*, http://www.christianitytoday.com/ct/2003/002/2.42.html (accessed April 7, 2015); Ed Silvoso, *Anointed for Business* (Ventura: Regal Books, 2002), 33; Tony Carnes, "The Silicon Valley Saints: High-tech Christian Executives Are Bringing Biblical Values Into a Mecca of Mammon," *Christianity Today*, http://www.christianitytoday.com/ct/2001/010/1.34.html (accessed April 7, 2015).

35. Ming Hon, personal interview with Denise Austin, Brisbane, June 3, 2003.

36. Ibid.

37. Larry Lee, personal interview with Denise Austin, Brisbane, May 20, 2003.

38. Ibid.

39. Rebecca Liesegang, personal interview with Denise Austin, Brisbane, June 4, 2003.

40. Donald Gee, "I Wish I'd Been to Bible School," *Australian Evangel* 19, no. 7 (1962): 13.

41. William K. Kay, "Pentecostal Education," *Journal of Beliefs and Values* 25, no. 2 (August 2004): 229–239.

42. Denise A. Austin and David Perry, "From Jerusalem to Athens: A Journey of Pentecostal Pedagogy in Australia," *Journal of Adult Theological Education* 12, no. 1 (May 2015): 3.7.

43. Sam Hey, "God in the Suburbs and Beyond: The Emergence of an Australian Megachurch and Denomination" (PhD thesis, Griffith University, 2010).

44. See Denise A. Austin, "Of Which I Was Part: Pastor Ron Woolley, Australia," in Wanda Bigham, Graham Leo, and Won Sul Lee, eds., *Teaching the Truth in Dynamic Times: Australia, Japan, Korea, Pakistan* (Seoul: Asia-Pacific Federation of Christian Schools, 2004), 9–69.

45. John Mansford Prior, "The Challenge of the Pentecostals in Asia, Part One: Pentecostal Movements in Asia," *Exchange* 36 (2007): 20.

46. Philip B. Duncan, *The Charismatic Tide* (Sydney: Glenburn, 1978), available also online at http://webjournals.ac.edu.au/journals/EB/the-charismatic-tide-duncan/the-charismatic-tide-ch-7/ (accessed April 7 2015); Shane Clifton, "Pragmatic Ecclesiology: The Apostolic Revolution and the Ecclesiology of the Assemblies of God in Australia," *Australasian Pentecostal Studies* 9 (2005/6): 23–47, available at http://webjournals.ac.edu.au/journals/aps/issue-9/03-the-apostolic-revolution-and-the-ecclesiology-o/ (accessed August 12, 2011).

47. John Ingelson, "Australia in Asia," *Asian Studies Review* 23, no. 1 (1999): 93.

48. Ron Woolley, personal interview with Denise Austin, Brisbane, May 30, 2003.

49. *Christian Outreach College, Mansfield 1996 Annual*, 4.

50. *Christian Outreach College, Brisbane 1999 Annual*, 4.

51. Woolley, personal interview with Denise Austin.

52. Asian Studies Association of Australia, *Maximizing Australia's Asia Knowledge: Repositioning and Renewal of a National Asset* (Melbourne: Asian Studies Association of Australia, 2002), 5.

53. Jeff Waters, "Academic Howard Nathan Says Australia's Race Relations Changed 'Immeasurably for the Better,'" ABCNews.net, June 20, 2013, http://www.abc.net.au/news/2013-06-20/former-judge-fails-australias-improved-race-relations/4769422 (accessed June 22, 2013).

54. David Kwon, e-mail correspondence with Denise Austin, October 9, 2012.

55. Asian Studies Association of Australia, *Maximizing Australia's Asia Knowledge*, 5.

56. Mark Hutchinson, "Cartledge, David Frederick (1940–2005)," http://webjournals.alphacrucis.edu.au/journals/ADPCM/a-to-d/cartledge-david-frederick-1940-2005/ (accessed December 20, 2011).

57. *Southern Cross College Administration Board Minutes of Meeting* (2000), 8.

58. *Southern Cross College NewsUpdate* 2 (April 1999): 3.

59. Denise A. Austin, *Our College: A History of the National Training College of Australian Christian Churches (Assemblies of God in Australia)* (Sydney: Australian Pentecostal Studies, 2013), 284.

60. Yang Yong Sun, personal interview with Denise Austin, Parramatta NSW, April 19, 2012.

61. Wolfgang Vondey, *Beyond Pentecostalism: The Crisis of Global Christianity and the Renewal of the Theological Agenda* (Grand Rapids, MI: William B. Eerdmans Publishing, 2010), 7.

62. Brian Howell, "Practical Belief and the Localization of Christianity: Pentecostal and denominational Christianity in Global/Local Perspective," *Religion* 33, no. 3 (2003): 239.

63. "Our Mission," Harvest International Ministry, http://www.harvestim .org/index.php?a=about&s=vision&ss=who-we-are (accessed June 28, 2013).

64. "Dr Sam Chand," *Leadership E-Mag* 2 (2013), 4.

65. Barbara Watson Andaya, "Response to Prasenjit Duara, 'Asia Redux'," *Journal of Asian Studies* 69, no. 4 (November 2010): 1019.

66. Ibid., 1020.

67. Daniel P.S. Goh, "State and Social Christianity in Post-Colonial Singapore," *Sojourn: Journal of Social Issues in Southeast Asia* 25, no. 1 (April 2010): 54.

68. "Joseph Prince," Joseph Prince Ministries, http://www.josephprince.org /About_Joseph_And_Wendy.html?active=about (accessed June 28, 2013).

69. "Joseph Prince Speaking at Hillsong Conference 2012," http://www .youtube.com/watch?v=ELd1L0qYeO8 (accessed June 30, 2013).

70. "Influencers Conference-Live@Paradise Community Church, Australia (DVD Album-NTSC)," Joseph Prince Ministries, https://www .josephprince.org/store/influencers-conference-live-paradise-community -church-australia/ (accessed June 30, 2013).

71. "Joseph Prince: Destined to Reign," Australian Christian Channel, http:// www.acctv.com.au/program.php?intid=3123 (accessed June 30, 2013).

72. Pradip N. Thomas and Philip Lee, "Global and Local Televangelism: An Introduction," in Pradip N. Thomas and Philip Lee, eds., *Global and Local Televangelism* (New York: Palgrave Macmillan, 2012), 1.

73. Wonsuk Ma and Julia C. Ma, "Jesus Christ in Asia: Our Journey with Him as Pentecostal Believers," *International Review of Mission* 94, no. 375 (October 2005): 493.

74. "Brother Yun Brisbane Australia November 2011 Part II," http://www .youtube.com/watch?v=57ptqQ997d8 (accessed July 1, 2013).

75. "Brother Yun at Bethany Sydney Church Part IV," http://www.youtube .com/watch?v=8gu1V9ceXPI (accessed July 1, 2013).

76. Observations by Denise Austin, April 2013.

77. Ong Sek Leang, "Response from Rev. Ong Sek Leang, Senior Pastor of Metro Tabernacle Church," http://www.youtube.com/watch ?v=yNUnjPG-6c8 (accessed July 1, 2013).

78. Ong Sek Leang, "Welcome Message from PWC Host Chairman, 23rd Pentecostal World Conference," http://www.pwc2013.org/welcome-pwc .html (accessed June 26, 2013).

CHAPTER 16
AUSTRALIAN PENTECOSTALISM: ORIGINS,
DEVELOPMENTS, AND TRENDS

1. Sarah Jane Lancaster, "The History of Good News Hall," cited in Shane Clifton, *Pentecostal Churches in Transition: Analysing the Developing Ecclesiology of the Assemblies of God in Australia* (Leiden, The Netherlands: Brill, 2009), 54.

2. Barry Chant, "The Spirit of Pentecost: The Origins and Development of the Pentecostal Movement in Australia, 1870-1939" (PhD thesis, Macquarrie University, 1999), 213.

3. Ibid., 114.

4. She was affectionately known as Mother Lancaster (ibid., 60).

5. Ibid., 3.

6. Sarah Jane Lancaster, *Good News* 17, no. 10 (October 1926): 11, cited in Chant, "The Spirit of Pentecost," 265.

7. Lancaster, *Good News* (January 1913): 7, cited in Clifton, *Pentecostal Churches in Transition*, 59.

8. For a fuller discussion of Lancaster and Pentecostal ecumenism, see Shane Clifton, "Ecumenism from the Bottom Up: A Pentecostal Perspective," *Journal of Ecumenical Studies* 47, no. 4 (Fall 2012): 576–592.

9. Lancaster, *Good News* 17, no. 10 (October 1926): 10, cited in Clifton, *Pentecostal Churches in Transition*, 58.

10. Lancaster, "By One Spirit," *Good News* 18 (July 1927): 10, cited in Clifton, *Pentecostal Churches in Transition*, 66.

11. Clifton, *Pentecostal Churches in Transition*, 56.

12. George E. Burns, "Assemblies of God–Queensland," *Australian Evangel* 4, no. 12 (June 1930); 10, cited in Clifton, *Pentecostal Churches in Transition*, 82.

13. Clifton, *Pentecostal Churches in Transition*, 83.

14. Ibid., 88.

15. Ibid., 89.

16. Barry Chant, *Heart of Fire: The Story of Australian Pentecostalism*, 2nd ed. (fully revised) (Adelaide: The House of Tabor, 1984), 165–180.

17. Clifton, *Pentecostal Churches in Transition*, 93.

18. The Assemblies of God in Australia, United Constitution 1943, cited in Clifton, *Pentecostal Churches in Transition*, 101.

19. Denise A. Austin, *Our College: A History of the National College of Australian Christian Churches (Assemblies of God in Australia)* (Sydney: Australasian Pentecostal Studies, 2013).

20. George Forbes, *A Church on Fire: The Story of the Assemblies of God of Papua New Guinea* (Melbourne: Mission Mobiliser International, 2001).

21. See also Chant, *Heart of Fire*. Also Denis Smith and Gwen Smith, *A River Is Flowing* (Adelaide: Assemblies of God in Australia, 1987).

22. Chant, *Heart of Fire*, 178.

23. Ibid., 160.

24. This was a teaching popular among Pentecostals in the years immediately following the war, in which it was believed that the Anglo-Saxon race was descended from the northern tribes of Israel that were disbursed during the destruction of the northern kingdom. See Clifton, *Pentecostal Churches in Transition*, 103.

25. Chant, *Heart of Fire*, 197.

26. Clifton, *Pentecostal Churches in Transition*, 144–146.

27. Ibid., 143.

28. David Cartledge, *The Apostolic Revolution: The Restoration of Apostles and Prophets in the Assemblies of God in Australia* (Sydney: Paraclete Institute, 2000), 93–97.

29. Data constructed from the annual census report of the Australian Christian churches.

30. Ruth Powell, et al., *Enriching Church Life: A Guide to Results from National Church Life Survey Is for Local Churches* (Sydney: Mirrabooka, 2012), 71. Also Philip Hughes, "Are Australians 'Losing Their Religion'?," *Pointers: Bulletin of the Christian Research Association* 20, no. 2 (June 2010), http://search.informit.com.au/documentSummary;dn=16915109469 5960;res=IELHSS (accessed May 6, 2015).

31. Sam Hey, "God in the Suburbs and Beyond: The Emergence of an Australian Megachurch and Denomination" (PhD thesis, Griffith University,

2011), 161–163, http://trove.nla.gov.au/version/184284326 (accessed May 6, 2015).

32. Ibid., 157.

33. These numbers are difficult to pin down and have been taken from a video presentation on http://c3churchglobal.com/about-c3church (accessed May 6, 2015).

34. In 2001 the National Church Life Survey listed Pentecostalism as having the third highest weekly attendance figures (behind the Catholic and Anglican churches)—John Bellamy and Keith Castle, "2001 Church Attendance Estimates," *NCLS Occasional Paper* 3 (2004): www .ncls.org.au/download/doc2270/NCLSOccasionalPaper3.pdf (accessed June 7, 2013). Since that time Pentecostalism has almost doubled its attendance—so it can be presumed to have reached second place. However, the NCLS chart of 2001 has not yet been updated.

35. For the AGA see Clifton, *Pentecostal Churches in Transition*, 156–157. For C3 see http://c3churchglobal.com/about-c3church. COC churches retained congregational structures (Hey, "God in the Suburbs," 287), largely because the movement was established prior to the arrival of Frank Houston and without his direct impact thereafter.

36. Clifton, *Pentecostal Churches in Transition*, 156–157.

37. Cartledge, *The Apostolic Revolution*.

38. C. Peter Wagner, *The New Apostolic Churches* (Glendale: Regal Books, 2000).

39. Some of this information is difficult to source. Details of the corporate governance in Australia is set out an online at http://myhillsong.com /corporate-goverance (accessed May 30, 2013). Other information has been learned by me as an attender of the South West campus and lecturer of the Alphacrucis campus located at Hillsong Baulkham Hills.

40. Stated on Hillsong.com (accessed May 30, 2013).

41. Chart constructed from information in Powell, et al., *Enriching Church Life*.

42. For an exploration of the Hillsong brand, see Robin Hicks, "Hillsong—Australia's Most Powerful Brand," *mUmBRELLA*, July 26, 2012, http:// mumbrella.com.au/hillsong-australias-most-powerful-brand-104506.

43. Clifton, *Pentecostal Churches in Transition*, 194–195. See also Ben F. Meyer, *The Early Christians: Their World Mission and Self-Discovery* (Wilmington: Glazier, 1986).

44. Marion Maddox, "Prosper, Consume and Be Saved," *Critical Research on Religion* 1, no. 1 (April 1, 2013): 110.

45. Ibid., 112.

46. An extended discussion between Marion Maddox and Matthew Del Nevo took place on my blog, http://shaneclifton.com/2013/05/17 /hillsong-church-and-marion-maddox/.

47. "Welcome Home," Hillsong, http://hillsong.com.s3-website-ap -southeast-2.amazonaws.com/ (accessed April 5, 2015).

CHAPTER 17
FROM CORNER SHOP TO BOUTIQUE FRANCHISE: THE
DILEMMAS OF AUSTRALIAN PENTECOSTALISM

1. See Joe Creech, "Visions of Glory: The Place of the Azusa Street Revival in Pentecostal History," *Church History* 65, no. 3 (September 1996): 405–424.

2. See William D. Faupel, "Theological Influences on the Teachings and Practices of John Alexander Dowie," *Pneuma* 29, no. 2, (2007): 226–253; and my own, "Edward Irving's Antipodean Shadow," *Australasian Pentecostal Studies* 10 (2009): http://webjournals.ac.edu.au/journals/aps/issue -10/edward-irvings-antipodean-shadow/ (accessed May 6, 2015).

3. By "dilemmas" is intended the sort of institutional tensions pointed to by Thomas O'Dea, as originally spelled out in his "Five Dilemmas in the Institutionalization of Religion," *Journal for the Scientific Study of Religion* 1, no. 1 (October 1961): 30–41.

4. Adam Stewart, "A Canadian Azusa? The Implications of the Hebden Mission for Pentecostal Historiography," in Michael Wilkinson and Peter Althouse, eds., *Winds From the North: Canadian Contributions to the Pentecostal Movement* (Leiden and Boston: Brill, 2010), 17.

5. William Purinton, "Review of *Afro-Pentecostalism: Black Pentecostal and Charismatic Christianity in History and Culture* and *Black Fire: One Hundred Years of African American Pentecostalism*," *International Bulletin of Missionary Research* 36, no. 2 (April 2012): 104–105.

6. John Burdick, "What is the Color of the Holy Spirit? Pentecostalism and Black Identity in Brazil," *Latin American Research Review* 34, no. 2 (1999): 109–131.

7. Allan Anderson, "'Walking in the Spirit': The Complexity of Belonging in Two Pentecostal Churches in Durban, South Africa," *African Studies Review* 50, no. 3 (December 2007): 207–208; Glen Thompson,

"'Transported Away': The Spirituality and Piety of Charismatic Christianity in South Africa (1976–1994)," *Journal of Theology for Southern Africa* 118 (March 2004): 128–145.

8. Anthony Hubbard, "Destiny Delivers a Wake-Up Call," *Sunday Star-Times* (Wellington), (August 29, 2004): 10.

9. Todd May, *Reconsidering Difference: Nancy, Derrida, Levinas, and Deleuze* (University Park, PA: Pennsylvania State University Press, 1997), 2.

10. Elsewhere, as the Pentecostal Politics of Space and Power project based in Padova, Italy, shows, such categories are beginning to flow out of critical cultures in Europe.

11. This has since been picked up by Roger Stronstad—e.g., his work *The Prophethood of All Believers: A Study in Luke's Charismatic Theology* (Sheffield: Sheffield Academic Press, 1999)—but was a common concept amongst Pentecostal pastors and teachers in the 1970s and 1980s, among whom David Parker at Alphacrucis College is probably the best example.

12. Hence the importance of a book such as Geoffrey Blainey's *Tyranny of Distance* (Melbourne: Sun Books, 1966) in establishing an Australian nationalist school of historiography.

13. David Harrell, *Oral Roberts: An American Life* (Indianapolis: Indiana University Press, 1985), 73–75, places the Melbourne experience of rejection by Australian unionists at the heart of Roberts' understanding of his broadening ministry.

14. Billy Graham, *Just As I Am: The Autobiography of Billy Graham* (San Franisco: HarperSanFrancisco/Zondervan, 1997).

15. See, for instance, Geoffrey R. Treloar, ed., *The Furtherance of Religious Beliefs* (Sydney: Centre for the Study of Australian Christianity, 1997).

16. Viz. Ross Laurie, "Reporting on Race: White Australia, Immigration and the Popular Press in the 1920s," *Journal of the Royal Historical Society of Queensland* 18, no. 10 (April 2004): 420–431.

17. Jessica Paten, "Coppertails and Silvertails: Queensland Women and Their Struggle for the Political Franchise, 1889–1905," *Queensland Review* 12, no. 2 (November 2005): 23–50.

18. See the history of Alphacrucis College by Denise A. Austin, *Our College: A History of the National Training College of Australian Christian Churches (Assemblies of God in Australia)* (Sydney: Australian Pentecostal Studies, 2013).

469

19. See David Cartledge, *The Apostolic Revolution: The Restoration of Apostles and Prophets in the Assemblies of God in Australia* (Sydney: Paraclete Institute, 2000); and more recently, Andrew Evans, in http://www.acc .org.au/NewsMedia/ACCENTMagazine.aspx.

20. See "Cartledge, David Frederick (1940–2005)," http://webjournals.ac.edu .au/journals/ADPCM/a-to-d/cartledge-david-frederick-1940-2005/ (accessed May 6, 2015); and A. Evans, Interview with Mark Hutchinson, October 9, 2009, Pentecostal Heritage Centre, Alphacrucis College, Sydney.

21. Evans is always referred to in AOG circles as "Andrew," rather than as the pastor of Paradise Church, Adelaide. Brian Houston, on the other hand, is seen as the embodiment of Hillsong Church, and his incumbency as part of the influence of Hillsong on the larger movement. For the theory behind routinization, see Robert C. Tucker, "The Theory of Charismatic Leadership," *Daedalus* 97, no. 3 (1968): 731–756, and more recently Reinhard Bendix, *Max Weber: An Intellectual Portrait*, vol. 2 (New York: Routledge), 312–313.

22. The Uniting Church has continued to bleed its Charismatic wing over issues such as the ordination of homosexual clergy. While a significant proportion of the Australian population in the early twentieth century, however, such numbers are not now a significant contribution to the Pentecostal movement.

23. ACC website, http://www.acc.org.au/AboutUs/WhatWeBelieve.aspx.

24. Ruth Pollard, "Mercy Ministries Home to Close," *Sydney Morning Herald* (October 28, 2009), http://www.acc.org.au/about-us/ (accessed April 27, 2015).

CHAPTER 18
TRANSFORMING PENTECOSTALISM: SOME REFLECTIONS ON THE CHANGING SHAPE OF PENTECOSTALISM IN AOTEAROA-NEW ZEALAND

1. Brett Knowles, *Transforming Pentecostalism: The Changing Shape of New Zealand Pentecostalism* (Lexington, KY: Emeth Press, 2014). Missiologists will recognize an allusion to David Bosch's magisterial book, *Transforming Mission: Paradigm Shifts in Theology of Mission* (Maryknoll: Orbis Books, 1991), in which he argues that the missionary movement is not only a movement that transforms; it is also a movement that is itself being transformed. The same, I argue, is true of Pentecostalism.

2. Martin E. Marty, "Introduction: Religion in America 1935–1985," in David W. Lotz, Donald W. Shriver Jr., and John F. Wilson, eds., *Altered Landscapes: Christianity in America 1935–1985* (Grand Rapids, MI: William B. Eerdmans Publishing Company, 1989), 1–16.

3. Ibid., 1.

4. Ian Clark, *Pentecost at the Ends of the Earth: The History of the Assemblies of God in New Zealand (1927–2003)* (Blenheim, NZ: Christian Road Ministries, 2007), 93.

5. Ian Clark, interview, February 28, 1990, cited in Brett Knowles, *The History of a New Zealand Pentecostal Movement: The New Life Churches of New Zealand from 1946 to 1979*, Studies in Religion and Society 45 (Lewiston, NY: Edwin Mellen Press, 2000), 47, emphasis as cited. Clark was specifically referring to the Assemblies of God (of which he was for some years general secretary). His observation is, however, valid for the whole Pentecostal movement.

6. Laurie Murray, *Where to World 1977?* (Palmerston North, NZ: By the author, 1977), 25.

7. Peter J. Lineham, "Tongues Must Cease: The Brethren and the Charismatic Movement in New Zealand," *Christian Brethren Research Journal* 34 (November 1983): 16–17.

8. For other examples of this misunderstanding of, and opposition to, Pentecostalism before the mid-1960s, see W. Luke Worsfold, "Subsequence, Prophecy and Church Order in the Apostolic Church, New Zealand" (DPhil thesis, Victoria University of Wellington, 2004), 44–47.

9. "Photographic Essay, 'The Third Force in Christendom: Gospel-Singing, Doomsday-Preaching Sects Emerge as a Mighty Movement in World Religion,' Photographed for *Life* by Carl Mydans," *Life* 44, no. 23 (June 9, 1958): 113–121; Henry P. Van Dusen, "Force's Lessons for Others," *Life* 44, no. 23 (June 9, 1958): 122–124.

10. Ray Bloomfield and Frank Houston of the Assemblies of God were also enjoying marked success among Māori in the Waiomio Valley in rural Northland in 1958 and 1959.

11. Eventually renamed the "New Life Churches of New Zealand" in 1988.

12. Rob Wheeler, interview, cited in Knowles, *The History of a New Zealand Pentecostal Movement*, 116.

13. Peter Lineham, "When the Roll Is Called Up Yonder, Who'll be There?," in Douglas J. Pratt, ed., *Rescue the Perishing: Comparative Perspectives in*

Evangelicalism and Revivalism, Waikato Studies in Religion 1 (Auckland: College Communications, 1989), 16.

14. See Richard Russell, "The Growing Crisis of the Evangelical World-View and its Resolutions" (MA thesis, Bristol University, 1973), 98–100; also (in the context of the American "New Christian Right"), Robert C. Liebman and Robert Wuthnow, eds., *The New Christian Right: Mobilization and* Legitimation (New York: Aldine Publishing Company, 1983).

15. "Day in the House," *Otago Daily Times* (September 25, 1985): 5. Member of Parliament Graeme Lee called it "the largest petition in the history of this Parliament—on a comparative [per capita] basis, the largest of any Parliament in the world." *New Zealand Parliamentary Debates*, 466, no. 6978 (September 24, 1985). It represented nearly a quarter of the total population of New Zealand at the time.

16. The most high-profile Pentecostal candidacy was that of Rob Wheeler, who stood for the National Party against Helen Clark (later prime minister of New Zealand) in the Mount Albert seat in the 1987 election. Stephen Stratford, "Christians Awake! Join the National Party, Save New Zealand," *Metro* (November 1986): 124–137; Brian Rudman, "For God and National," *New Zealand Listener* (March 28, 1987): 28–29.

17. Brett Knowles, "'From the Ends of the Earth We Hear Songs': Music as an Indicator of New Zealand Pentecostal Theology and Spirituality," *The Spirit and Church* 3, no. 2 (November 2001): 227–249. The article was also (with permission) published online in four parts in *Australian Pentecostal Studies Journal* 5–6 (April 2002), http://aps.webjournals.org /Issues.asp?index=9&id={CE149387-42E6-48C3-801C-7ED675022C60} (accessed May 27, 2005).

18. For examples from the 1980s, see Jack Leigh, "Getting Religion," *New Zealand Women's Weekly* (July 8, 1985): 59–62; Jonathon Harper, "The Church That's Taking Over Auckland," *Metro* (November 1983): 122–135; Tania Evans, "God Almighty," *New Outlook* 14 (January/February 1985): 22–30; Yvonne Dasler, "Then They Came to Elim," *New Zealand Listener* (April 24, 1982): 18–21.

19. Cited in Brett Knowles, "Some Aspects of the History of the New Life Churches of New Zealand 1960–1990" (PhD thesis, University of Otago, 1994), 279n86. For the Charismatic movement, see Donald Battley, "Charismatic Renewal: A View from the Inside," *Ecumenical Review* 38 (1986): 49.

20. Jamieson notes that "the CEO model often espoused by church leaders appears to have more in common with the authoritarian, profit-driven corporate leadership style of the 1980s than that of corporate CEOs I meet with today." Alan Jamieson, *A Churchless Faith: Faith Journeys beyond Evangelical, Pentecostal and Charismatic Churches* (Wellington: Philip Garside Publishing, 2000), 163n1.

21. Ibid., 33–34.

22. Luke Worsfold, "Subsequence, Prophecy and Church Order," 104–105, 119; cited also in Knowles, *Transforming Pentecostalism*, 212–213.

23. David Shearer to All *ICNZ* [Indigenous Churches of New Zealand] Regional Representatives, September 15, 1986, *BKRP* [Brett Knowles Research Papers], cited in Knowles, *Transforming Pentecostalism*, 213.

24. Jamieson, *A Churchless Faith*, 16–18.

25. I.e., questions about the deep-rooted foundations of the faith itself; ibid., 69.

26. For a discussion of megachurches in New Zealand, see Peter Lineham, *Destiny: The Life and Times of a Self-Made Apostle* (Auckland: Penguin, 2013), 60–62, 165–66. See also idem, "Three Types of Church," in Ree Boddé and Hugh Kempster, eds., *Thinking Outside the Square* (Auckland: St. Columba's Press & Journeyings, 2003), especially 204–206, 216–219; and Philip Matthews, "Gimme That Big-Time Religion," *New Zealand Listener* (November 23, 2002): 28–30.

27. For example, the Auckland Victory Christian Centre and the West City Christian Centre from the Assemblies of God (Clark, *Pentecost at the Ends of the Earth*, 235, 252) and Majestic House (the Christchurch New Life Centre) from the New Life Churches of New Zealand.

28. Peter Lineham, cited in Darryl Hutchinson, "Rethinking Religion," TV3 "The Nation," Saturday, April 3, 2010, 11:00 a.m.

29. Associated Pentecostal Churches of New Zealand, "Pastors Directory, 2001/2002" (Christchurch: Associated Pentecostal Churches of New Zealand, 2001).

30. Apostolic/Acts Churches, http://www.apostolic.org.nz/churches/ (accessed March 21, 2012); Assemblies of God Churches, http://www.agnz.org/find-a-church/ (accessed May 6, 2015); Christian City Churches (C3 Churches), http://www.c3churchglobal.com/church/5/25 (accessed May 6, 2015); Celebration Centres, http://www.celebrationcentre.com (accessed May 6, 2015); Christian Life Churches, http://www.lifenz.org/church (accessed May 6, 2015); Christian Outreach Centres Churches

(advised by Bruce Currie, Dunedin, April 25, 2012); Christian Revival Crusade Churches, http://www.crcnz.org/ (accessed May 6, 2015); City Impact Churches, http://www.cityimpactchurch.com/locations (accessed May 6, 2015); Destiny Churches, http://www.destinychurch.org.nz/ (accessed May 6, 2015); Elim Churches, http://www.elim.org.nz/about /church_locator.aspx (accessed May 6, 2015); International Convention of Faith Ministries, http://www.icfm.org/ (accessed May 6, 2015); Network of Christian Ministries Churches, http://www.thenetwork.org.nz/the network/Members.html (accessed May 6, 2015); New Frontiers Churches, http://newfrontierstogether.org/Groups/103229/Newfrontiers/Worldwide /New_Zealand/New_Zealand.apx (accessed May 6, 2015); New Life Churches of New Zealand, http://newlife.org.nz/directory/churches/ (accessed May 6, 2015); Samoan Assemblies of God Churches in New Zealand, http://en.wikipedia.org/wiki/Samoan_Assemblies_of_God_ churches_in_New_Zealand (accessed May 6, 2015); Vineyard Churches, http://www.vineyard.org.nz/churches/ (accessed May 6, 2015).

31. Louisa Cleave, "Churches' Call Divides Flock," *New Zealand Herald* (August 7, 2007), http://www.nzherald.co.nz/nz/news/article.cfm?c_ id=1&objectid=10456213 (accessed February 22, 2013).

32. The Samoan Assemblies of God in New Zealand claimed 135 churches on their Wikipedia website in 2013. However, this figure should be viewed with extreme suspicion, since more than 40 of the churches in this listing are also listed under identical or similar names on the Assemblies of God website; others appear to exist only on paper. There were also legal and constitutional issues over which organizational authority these churches came under. It is unlikely that all the churches claimed by the Samoan Assemblies of God in New Zealand actually existed or were affiliated with it. See Cleave, "Churches' Call Divides Flock." This article refers to 85 Samoan Assemblies of God churches in New Zealand, of which 40 were linked to the parent Assemblies of God; this gives a figure of 45 Samoan churches aligned with the breakaway group as at 2007. This number has been taken as a safer estimate than the 135 claimed in the Wikipedia website.

33. Reginald W. Bibby and Merlin B. Brinkerhof, "The Circulation of the Saints: A Study of People Who Join Conservative Churches," *Journal for the Scientific Study of Religion* 12 (1973): 273–283.

34. An example of this occurred in the early 1990s, when an Elim pastor moved to Christchurch to open a large "city church." The immediate result

was the closure of six suburban Elim churches in Christchurch as their members transferred to the new church.

35. These figures exclude the effect of the Samoan Assemblies of God, since figures for this group were unreliable and the location of its churches could not be verified. See note 31 above.

36. Brett Knowles, Research Project on New Zealand Pentecostalism, March 3, 2013. The survey asked respondents if they had ever been a member of, or participant in, a Pentecostal church, and if so, for how long. Catholic and Brethren churches were also approached, but did not take part in the survey.

37. Hugh McLeod, *The Religious Crisis of the 1960s* (Oxford: Oxford University Press, 1998).

38. Jean-François Lyotard, *The Postmodern Condition: A Report on Knowledge*, trans. Geoff Bennington and Brian Massumi, with foreword by Frederic Jameson (Manchester: Manchester University Press, 2004), xxiv. Original French text from idem, *La Condition Postmoderne*, Collection Critique (Paris: Les Edition de Minuit, 1979), 7.

39. Examples of these include the Christian belief in the eschatological kingdom of God; the Marxist idea of the inexorable dialectical advance of history, leading to the triumph of the revolutionary proletariat and the advent of the classless society; the scientific notions of evolution and scientific progress; and the Hegelian concept of the development and realization of Absolute Spirit, leading to the kingdom of the Spirit.

40. Willie Thompson, *Postmodernism and History* (Houndmills, UK: Palgrave Macmillan, 2004), 18.

41. Ibid., 25.

42. Bryan Wilson, *Religion in Secular Society: A Sociological Comment* (London: C. A. Watts, 1966), xiv. This definition forms the basis of that adopted in John Scott and Gordon Marshall, eds., *A Dictionary of Sociology*, 3rd rev. ed. (New York: Oxford University Press, 2009), s.v. "Secularization, Secularization thesis," 587. See also Bryan R. Wilson, ed., *The Social Dimensions of Sectarianism: Sects and New Religious Movements in Contemporary Society* (Oxford: Clarendon, 1990), 122.

43. McLeod, *The Religious Crisis of the 1960s*, 6. For surveys of the literature and the current status of secularization theory, see David Martin, "Secularisation: Master Narrative or Several Stories?" in John Stenhouse and Brett Knowles, eds., *Christianity in the Post Secular West* (Hindmarsh, Australia: ATF Press, 2007), 3–26; and Dominic Erdozain,

"Review-Article: 'Cause Is Not Quite What It Used to Be': The Return of Secularisation," *English Historical Review* 77, no. 525 (March 2012): 377–400.

44. David Martin, "Secularisation: Master Narrative or Several Stories?" 9.

45. Harvey Cox, *Fire from Heaven: The Rise of Pentecostal Spirituality and the Reshaping of Religion in the Twenty-First Century* (Reading, MA: Addison-Wesley, 1995), xv.

46. William M. Johnston, "The Spirituality Revolution and the Process of Reconfessionalisation in the West Today," in John Stenhouse and Brett Knowles, assisted by Antony Wood, eds., *The Future of Christianity: Historical, Sociological, Political and Theological Perspectives from New Zealand*, ATF Series 11 (Adelaide: ATF Press, 2004), 143–161.

47. Erdozain, "Cause Is Not Quite What It Used to Be," 398, 400.

48. For an illuminating comparison of two academic conferences on secularization, held twenty-six years apart, see the four papers in "Secularisation of Religion in New Zealand," 1976 (held at the Department of University Extension, Victoria University of Wellington), all of which take the process of secularization for granted; and the twenty-five papers from the 2002 "Future of Christianity in the West" Conference at the University of Otago, published in Stenhouse and Knowles, *The Future of Christianity*, and idem, *Christianity in the Post Secular West*, the majority of which question the secularization process to some extent.

49. Erich Kolig, "Coming through the Backdoor? Secularisation in New Zealand and Māori Religiosity," in Stenhouse and Knowles, eds., *The Future of Christianity*, 183–204.

50. Bruce Knox, "Christian Allegiance is Declining, Yet Theological Education Is Booming," in Stenhouse and Knowles, eds., *The Future of Christianity*, 73–87.

51. Ibid., 86.

52. Kevin Ward, "Rugby and Church: Worlds in Conflict?" *Reality* 33 (October/November 2002): 26–30, cited in idem., "No Longer Believing," in Stenhouse and Knowles, eds., *The Future of Christianity*, 63–64; and in idem., "Will We Find Church in a Future New Zealand?" in Stenhouse and Knowles, eds., *Christianity in the Post Secular West*, 213.

53. Ward, "Will We Find Church in a Future New Zealand?" 216.

54. Jürgen Habermas, for example, categorized this challenge as a "legitimation crisis," taking the revised Marxist view that "in the final analysis, [the] *class structure* is the source of the legitimation deficit." Jürgen

Habermas, *Legitimation Crisis*, trans. Thomas McCarthy (Boston: Beacon Press, 1975), 73, emphasis as cited.

55. Brett Knowles, "Vision of the Disinherited? The Growth of the Pentecostal Movement in the 1960s, with particular reference to the New Life Churches of New Zealand," in Bryan Gilling, ed., *"Be Ye Separate": Fundamentalism and the New Zealand Experience*, Waikato Studies in Religion 3 (Hamilton: University of Waikato and Colcom Press, 1992), 128–129.

56. Erdozain, "Cause Is Not Quite What It Used to Be," 400.

57. Principal Judith Forbes, comment to author, Dunedin, October 27, 2013. Used with permission.

58. Also known as "Servants to Asia's Urban Poor," http://servantsasia.org/ (accessed October 27, 2013).

59. See The Cohousing Association of the United States, "Cohousing: What Is cohousing?" http://www.cohousing.org/what_is_cohousing (accessed October 27, 2013).

60. Dan Hutchinson, "Housing Plan for School Site," *The Star* (October 3, 2013): 1.

61. Donald E. Miller, "Pentecostalism and Social Transformation," in Harold D. Hunter and Cecil M. Robeck Jr., eds., *The Azusa Street Revival and Its Legacy* (Cleveland, TN: Pathway Press, 2006), 335.

CHAPTER 19
ROMAN CATHOLIC CHARISMATIC RENEWAL IN ASIA: IMPLICATIONS AND OPPORTUNITIES

1. The statistics are taken from the vice president of ICCRS, Cyril John's paper, "Lay Movements and New Communities in the Life and Mission of the Church in Asia: Experiences from the Catholic Charismatic Renewal," which he presented at the Congress of Asian Catholic Laity, which met from August 31 to September 5, 2010 in Seoul, South Korea.

2. Ibid.

3. Stanley M. Burgess, "Charismatic Movements," in Scott W. Sunquist, David Wu Chu Sing, and John Chew Hiang Chea, eds., *A Dictionary of Asian Christianity* (Grand Rapids, MI: Eerdmans, 2001), 132–134.

4. The following discussion on El Shaddai in this essay is taken from Katharine L. Wiegele, *Investing in Miracles: El Shaddai and the Transformation of Popular Catholicism in the Philippines* (Honolulu: University of Hawai'i Press, 2005).

5. Ibid., 4.

6. As pointed out by the late Filipino liturgical theologian Anscar J. Chu-
pungco in his chapter, "Shaping the Filipino Order of Mass," in Anscar J.
Chupungco, *Worship: Beyond Inculturation* (Washington, DC: Pastoral
Press, 1994), 129–156.

7. Edmund Bishop succinctly described the genius of the Roman Rite as
"essentially soberness and sense" in his classic 1899 essay, "The Genius
of the Roman Rite," reprinted in Edmund Bishop, *Liturgica Historica:
Papers on the Liturgy and Religious Life of the Western Church* (Oxford:
Clarendon Press, 1918), 1–19. Bishop further observed that the Roman
Rite is marked by "simplicity, practicality, a great sobriety and self-con-
trol, gravity and dignity" (12).

8. For a full description and analysis of a typical El Shaddai *gawain*, see
Wiegele, *Investing in Miracles,* 147–150.

9. Ibid., 145–147.

10. Ibid., 153.

11. Ibid., 150.

12. Stanley M. Burgess, "Pentecostalism in India: An Overview," *Asian
Journal of Pentecostal Studies* 4, no. 1 (2001): 85–98.

13. Ibid., 94–95.

14. For discussion of the Khristbhakta movement, see Ciril J. Kuttiyanikkal,
*Khrist Bhakta Movement: A Model for an Indian Church? Incultura-
tion in the Area of Community Building* (Berlin: Lit Verlag, 2014), Jerome
G. Sylvester, "The Khristbhakta Movement: A New Paradigm of Faith
in Christ Jesus," *Vidyajyoti Journal of Theological Reflection* 27 (2013):
345–359 (Part I); 443–456 (Part II); and Herbert Hoefer, "Jesus, My
Master: 'Jesu Bhakta' Hindu Christian Theology," *International Journal
of Frontier Missions* 19, no. 3 (2002): 39–42. Sylvester's two-part essay in
Vidyajyoti is a précis of his "Hermeneutics of Khrist Bhakta Movement:
A Subaltern Reading of the Religio-Cultural Phenomenon in Varanasi"
(PhD thesis, University of Madras, 2010).

15. Sylvester, "The Khristbhakta Movement, I," 345.

16. Ibid., 348.

17. Ibid., 345–348.

18. Sylvester, "The Khristbhakta Movement, II," 448, 452, 453.

19. Ibid., 450.

20. Ibid., 448.

21. On the challenges posed by the subaltern classes, see Gayatri Chakra-vorty Spivak, "Can the Subaltern Speak?" in Cary Nelson and Lawrence Grossberg, eds., *Marxism and the Interpretation of Culture*, (Urbana, IL: University of Illinois Press, 1988), 271–313.

22. On the challenges of hybridized identities, see Homi K. Bhabha, "Signs Taken for Wonder," in Homi K. Bhabha, *The Location of Culture* (New York: Routledge, 1994), 102–122.

23. See, in particular, the excellent analysis of this paradigm shift in Wesley Granberg-Michaelson, *From Times Square to Timbuktu: The Post-Christian West Meets the Non-Western Church* (Grand Rapids, MI: Eerdmans, 2013); Jehu Hanciles, *Beyond Christendom: Globalization, African Migration, and the Transformation of the West* (Maryknoll, NY: Orbis Books, 2008); Philip Jenkins, *The Next Christendom: The Coming of Global Christianity*, revised and expanded edition (New York: Oxford University Press, 2007); and Andrew Walls, *The Cross-Cultural Process in Christian History: Studies in the Transmission and Appropriation of Faith* (Maryknoll, NY: Orbis Books, 2002).

24. Sylvester, "The Khristbhakta Movement, I," 348–349.

25. Joseph A. Komonchak, "Catholicity and the Redemption of History," in F. Chica, et al., eds., *Ecclesia Tertia Millennii Advenientis* (Casale Monferrato: Piemme, 1997), 602.

26. Ibid.

27. Ibid., 603. For a further discussion on how catholicity is understood during different epochs in the history of Christianity, see Yves Congar, *L'Eglise: Une, sainte, catholique et apostolique* [The Church: One, Holy, Catholic, and Apostolic] (Paris: Cerf, 1970), and Avery Dulles, *The Catholicity of the Church* (Oxford: Clarendon Press, 1985). Theological reflections on the different aspects of the church's catholicity include Michael A. Fahey, "The Catholicity of the Church in the New Testament and in the Early Patristic Period," *The Jurist* 52 (1992): 44–70; Joseph A. Komonchak, "The Local Church and the Church Catholic: The Contemporary Theological Problematic," *The Jurist* 52 (1992): 416–447; Jean-Marie Tillard, "The Local Church Within Catholicity," *The Jurist* 52 (1992): 448–454; and Wolfgang Beinert, "Catholicity as Property of the Church," *The Jurist* 52 (1992): 455–483.

28. *Lumen Gentium* 13, in Walter M. Abbott, ed., *The Documents of Vatican II* (New York: America Press, 1966), 31, emphasis added.

CHAPTER 20

UNLEASHING THE DRAGON: EXPLORATION OF THE POSSIBLE IMPACT
OF CHINESE CONFUCIAN CULTURE ON PENTECOSTAL HERMENEUTICS

1. Grabbe provides the following definition: "The prophet is a mediator who claims to receive messages directly from a divinity, by various means, and communicates these messages to recipients." See Lester L. Grabbe, *Priests, Prophets, Diviners, Sage: A Socio-historic Study of Religious Specialists in Ancient Israel* (Harrisonberg, PA: Trinity Press International, 1995), 83.

2. While the location of this passage is in Joel 3:1–5 in the Hebrew Masoretic Text, its location in the English/Chinese versions is used as this most commonly used by contemporary Pentecostals.

3. While there are many definitions and approaches to understanding culture, a simple definition is posited by Herskovitz as "essentially a construct that describes the total body of belief, behaviours, knowledge, sanctions, values and goals that mark the way of life of a people"; cited in Neil Ormerod and Shane Clifton, *Globalization and the Mission of the Church* (Maryknoll, NY: Orbis Books, 2010), 124.

4. J. Lee, "A Tilt Towards China? Australia Reconsiders Its American Ties," *World Affairs* (Nov/Dec 2012): 65.

5. For further exploration of this concept, see Joseph Nye, *Soft Power: The Means to Success in World Politics* (New York: Public Affairs, 2004).

6. Corinna Delkeskamp-Hayes, "Renewing Ritual Cultures: Paternal Authority, Filial Piety, and the Ethos of Self-Submission in Christianity and Confuciansim," in David Solomon, Ruiping Fan, and Ping-cheung Lo, eds., *Ritual and the Moral Life*, Philosophical Studies in Contemporary China 21 (Dordrecht: Springer Science+Business Media, 2012), 240.

7. Boagang He, "The Dilemmas of Chinas Political Science in the Context of the Rise of China," *Journal of Chinese Political Science* 16 (2011): 272.

8. He (ibid., 273) gives the example of the adoption of the Western calendar in China that exists alongside the Chinese lunar calendar, which continues to be preserved and valued. Within China, these two systems not only coexist, but there is a translation mechanism between them.

9. Ormerod and Clifton, *Globalization and the Mission of the Church*, 125.

10. Ibid., 127.

11. Ironically, Pentecostalism itself developed as a restorationist movement, based on the ideal of the New Testament church.

12. See Larry R. McQueen, *Joel and the Spirit: The Cry of a Prophetic Hermeneutic*, JPT Supplement Series 8 (Sheffield: Sheffield Academic Press, 1995), and Kenneth Archer, *A Pentecostal Hermeneutic for the Twenty-First Century: Spirit, Scripture, and Community* (London and New York: T & T Clark International, 2004).

13. The beginnings of Pentecostalism in North America are thus generally traced to two significant events: the first in Topeka, Kansas, when Agnes Ozman on January 1, 1901, first spoke in tongues (*glossolalia*). The second event occurred five years later in a Bonnie Brae Street prayer meeting, and then relocated to a disused African American Methodist Episcopal church on Azusa Street, Los Angeles. While it is acknowledged that Pentecostalism in its various global expressions do not all originate directly from the Azusa Street Revival (such as the development of Pentecostalism in Australia and even the development of the Church of God [Cleveland, TN]), the Azusa Street Revival generally functions in contemporary Pentecostalism as a symbol of early Pentecostalism.

14. Elizabeth Achtemeier, *Minor Prophets I*, NIBC (Peabody, MA: Hendrickson, 1996), 115.

15. McQueen, *Joel and the Spirit*, 39.

16. Achtemeier, *Minor Prophets I*, 148.

17. McQueen, *Joel and the Spirit*, 26.

18. Ibid., 39.

19. Ibid., 40.

20. Ibid.

21. Achtemeier, *Minor Prophets I*, 148.

22. McQueen, *Joel and the Spirit*, 41. McQueen emphasises the meaning of *basar* as humanity in their weakness or infirmity.

23. Ibid., 41.

24. Achtemeier, *Minor Prophets I*, 149

25. Ibid. It is noted that Achtemeier specifically refers to this as God's prevenient grace.

26. Ibid., 150.

27. Baogang He, "Four Models of the Relationship between Confucianism and Democracy," *Journal of Chinese Philosophy* 37, no. 1 (March 2010): 26.

28. Ibid., 21.

29. McQueen, *Joel and the Spirit*, 93.

30. Ibid., 103.

31. Ibid., 13.

32. Achtemeier, *Minor Prophets I*, 149.

33. Raymond Bryan Dillard, "Joel," in Thomas Edward McComiskey, ed., *The Minor Prophets: An Exegetical and Expository Commentary* (Grand Rapids, MI: Baker Books, 1992), 295.

34. Ibid.

35. McQueen, *Joel and the Spirit*, 15.

36. See Roger Stronstrad, *The Prophethood of All Believers: A Study in Luke's Charismatic Theology* (1999; reprint, Cleveland, TN: CPT Press, 2010).

37. McQueen, *Joel and the Spirit*, 93.

38. Dillard, "Joel," 295.

39. George Lakoff and Mark Johnson, *Metaphors We Live By* (Chicago: University of Chicago Press, 1980), 117.

40. Y. Nie and R. Chen, "Water Metaphors and Metonymies in Chinese: A Semantic Network," *Pragmatics and Cognition* 16, no. 3 (2008): 492.

41. Ibid., 502.

42. Ibid., 504.

CHAPTER 21
PENTECOSTALISM AT THE CROSSROADS

1. Augustin Poulain, *The Graces of Interior Prayer* (1910; reprint, Malden, MA: Kessinger Publishing 1996).

2. *Didache*, 10, 11.

3. Grant Wacker, *Heaven Below: Early Pentecostals and American Culture* (Cambridge, MA: Harvard University Press, 2001).

4. Dominic Erdozain, "Emerging Church: A Victorian Prequel," in Philip Harrold and D. H. Williams, eds., *The Great Tradition: A Great Labor* (Eugene, OR: Cascade Books, 2011), 92–114.

5. William K. Kay, "Modernity and the Arrival of Pentecostalism in Britain," *PentecoStudies* 10, no. 1 (2011): 50–71.

6. Bernice Martin, "From Pre- to Postmodernity in Latin America," in Paul Heelas, ed., *Religion, Modernity and Postmodernity* (Oxford: Blackwell, 1998), 102–46.

7. Ibid., 110.

8. Ibid., 126–130.

9. Ibid., 107.

10. Ibid., 130.

11. Ibid., 130–32.

12. Ibid., 137.

13. Donald E. Miller and Tetsunao Yamamori, *Global Pentecostalism: The New Face of Christian Social Engagement* (Los Angeles: University of California Press, 2007), 175–177.

14. Andrew Walker, "Thoroughly Modern: Sociological Reflections on the Charismatic Movement," in John Wolffe, ed., *Global Religious Movements in Regional Context* (Aldershot, UK: Ashgate, 2002), 197–223.

15. Ibid., 211.

16. Ibid., 198–199.

17. Ibid., 204.

18. Ibid., 206–208.

19. Ibid., 212–213.

20. Ibid., 216–217.

21. Ibid., 219.

22. Ibid., 220.

23. This is even more apparent in an earlier work coauthored with Tom Smail, Andrew Walker, and Nigel Wright, *Charismatic Renewal: The Search for a Theology* (London: SPCK, 1995).

24. Tom Smail, "The Cross and the Spirit: Towards a Theology of Renewal," in *Charismatic Renewal*, 55–58.

25. Peter Hocken, "The Meaning and Purpose of Baptism in the Spirit," *Pneuma* 7, no. 2 (Fall 1985): 125–133.

26. Simon Chan, *Pentecostal Ecclesiology: An Essay on the Development of Doctrine* (Blandford Forum, UK: Deo Publishing, 2011), 102–106.

27. For a history and critique, see Edgar R. Lee, ed., *He Gave Apostles: Apostolic Ministry in the 21st Century* (Springfield, MO: Assemblies of God Theological Seminary, 2005).

28. Wonsuk Ma, "Asian (Classical) Pentecostal Theology in Context," in Allan Anderson and Edmond Tang, eds., *Asian and Pentecostal: The Charismatic Face of Christianity in Asia* (Oxford: Regnum 2005), 65–66.

29. Martin Lindhardt, "More Than Just Money: The Faith Gospel and Occult Economies in Contemporary Tanzania," *Nova Religio* 13, no. 1 (2009): 41–67.

30. Smail, "The Cross and the Spirit," 58–61.

31. Nigel Wright, "The Theology and Methodology of 'Signs and Wonders'," in *Charismatic Renewal*, 71–85, at 74. See also Ricardo Barbosa de Sousa, "Spiritual Warfare and Job's Dilemma," in. A. Scott Moreau, et al., eds., *Deliver Us from Evil: An Uneasy Frontier in Christian Mission* (Monrovia, CA: MARC, 2002), 28–36.

32. Wright, "Theology and Methodology," 74.

33. Ibid.

34. Martin, "From Pre- to Postmodernity," 134.

35. See Smail, Walker, and Wright, "'Revelation Knowledge' and Knowledge of Revelation: The Faith Movement and the Question of Heresy," in *Charismatic Renewal*, 133–145.

36. One may recall the widespread use of *Scripture in Songs*, two volumes (Auckland, NZ: Scripture in Songs, 1979, 1981).

37. Tom Smail, "In Spirit and in Truth: Reflections on Charismatic Worship," in *Charismatic Renewal*, 109.

38. Ibid., 112.

39. Martyn Percy, *Words, Wonders and Power: Understanding Contemporary Christian Fundamentalism and Revivalism* (London: SPCK, 1996).

40. Lester Ruth, "*Lex Amandi, Lex Orandi*: The Trinity in the Most-Used Contemporary Christian Worship Songs," in Bryan D. Spinks, ed., *The Place of Christ in Liturgical Prayer: Trinity, Christology, and Liturgical Theology* (Collegeville, MN: Liturgical Press, 2008), 342–359.

41. Daniel H. Williams, "The Cultural Medium and the Christian Message: What Kind of Christians Do Contemporary Service Produce?" *Christianity Today* 55, no. 6 (June 1, 2011): 46–49.

42. Kay, "Modernity," 65.

43. Tan-Chow May Ling, *Pentecostal Theology for the Twenty-First Century: Engaging with Multi-Faith Singapore* (Aldershot, UK: Ashgate, 2007), 77.

44. Daniel P. S. Goh, "Chinese Religion and the Challenge of Modernity in Malaysia and Singapore: Syncretism, Hybridisation and Transfiguration," *Asian Journal of Social Science* 37 (2009): 129-37.

45. Mark R. Mullins, "What about the Ancestors? Some Japanese Christian Responses to Protestant Individualism," *Studies in World Christianity* 4, no. 1 (1998): 41–64.

46. Cf. Goh, "Chinese Religions," 133–134.

47. Os Guinness, *Dining with the Devil: The Megachurch Movement Flirts with Modernity* (Grand Rapids: Baker, 1993), 35–39.

48. Chuck Lowe, *Territorial Spirits and World Evangelisation?* (Sevenoaks, UK: OMF International, 1998), 149–151.

49. Tan-Chow, *Pentecostal Theology*, chapter 4.

50. Smail, "The Cross and the Spirit," 50-51.

51. *Lumen Gentium*, §12.

52. John Meyendorff, *Living Tradition* (Crestwood, NY: St. Vladimir Seminary Press, 1978).

53. See Chan, *Pentecostal Ecclesiology*, 50–73.

54. Marcellino D'Ambrosio, "Ressourcement Theology, Aggiornamento, and the Hermeneutics of Tradition," *Communio* 18 (Winter 1991): 530–555.

Index

CONNECT WITH US!

CHARISMA HOUSE

(Spiritual Growth)

Facebook.com/CharismaHouse

@CharismaHouse

Instagram.com/CharismaHouse

SILOAM

(Health)

Pinterest.com/CharismaHouse

REALMS

(Fiction)

Facebook.com/RealmsFiction